Programming for the Java™ Virtual Machine

Programming for the Java™ Virtual Machine

Joshua Engel

ADDISON-WESLEY

An imprint of Addison Wesley Longman, Inc.

Reading, Massachusetts • Harlow, England • Menlo Park, California
Berkeley, California • Don Mills, Ontario • Sydney
Bonn • Amsterdam • Tokyo • Mexico City

The publisher offers discounts on this book when ordered in quantity for special sales. For more information, please contact:

Corporate, Government, and Special Sales Group
Addison Wesley Longman, Inc.
One Jacob Way
Reading, Massachusetts 01867

Library of Congress Cataloging-in-Publication Data
Engel, Joshua, 1970-
    Programming for the Java virtual machine / Joshua Engel.
        p.   cm.
        q.
    Includes bibliographical references.
    ISBN 0-201-30972-6 (alk. paper)
    1. Java (Computer program language)   2. Java virtual machine.
    I. Title.
    QA76.73.J38E543   1999
    005.6—dc21   99-22853
                                                         CIP

Text printed on recycled and acid-free paper.

ISBN   0201309726

2 3 4 5 6 7   MA   02 01 00 99

2nd Printing   December 1999

To Chris, who helped me think
And to Jennifer, my love

Contents

Preface

Every time you compile a Java program to produce a `class` file, you've written a program for the Java virtual machine. This book is designed to take you to the next level: writing Java virtual machine (JVM) programs directly, without the aid of a Java compiler. A number of people would want to do this:

- Advanced Java programmers
- Security experts
- Language designers and compiler writers

Advanced Java programmers want to know how the JVM works, in detail. Learning the details of the JVM will help improve your understanding of what a Java program does. Some messages from the JVM will be clearer after you understand how the JVM looks at your program. This understanding can also help you improve the performance of your programs.

Another reason for advanced Java programmers to learn JVM programming is that it will help you understand how JVM code moves. One of the most important uses of Java is to download applets from the Internet (or other sources). The JVM uses a class called `ClassLoader` to incorporate code from the Internet into the JVM. The `ClassLoader` has many other uses. The Java Foundation Classes use subclasses of `ClassLoader` to load new Look and Feel classes. Some databases use other subclasses of `ClassLoader` to incorporate queries written in Java directly into the database.

Security experts already know that the Java language is designed with security features in mind. Java promises to allow users to download applets from the Internet without fear. However, these promises seem empty until you know precisely how the JVM keeps the promises Java makes. This book discusses in detail how the JVM verification algorithm works. Knowing the verification algorithm will give you greater confidence in the security of the JVM.

This book will give you the tools you need to build your own secure systems on top of the JVM, by explaining both what promises the JVM makes (and how it keeps them) and what promises it *doesn't* make.

Language designers want to design new languages for the Java virtual machine. Although the Java language is excellent, perhaps the best general-purpose programming language ever created, there are still times when a different language does the job better. Sometimes these are general-purpose languages built into an application (like WordBasic in Microsoft Word or Emacs Lisp). Others are tiny, special-purpose languages (like SQL, regular expressions, or filters in PhotoShop).

This book describes compilers for two languages, Scheme and Prolog, which are very different from Java. These compilers generate JVM code and use a subclass of ClassLoader to load it into the system. By compiling into JVM code, these non-Java languages gain some of the "Write Once, Run Anywhere" properties of Java without losing the power of the original language. These compilers can be used as a starting point for compiling other languages. Other languages already implemented for the JVM include Tcl, ML, Eiffel, Python, and Ada.

As more and more programs are written in Java, there is an increasing need to implement new languages. By implementing these languages using the JVM, you can get the portability and performance of the JVM.

Prerequisites

This book assumes that you have a good basic knowledge of Java. Many of the ideas in the book are explained in terms of Java; at the same time, the book tries to explain Java in terms of the JVM. Hopefully, this will reinforce your understanding of both the Java language and the Java virtual machine.

If you're new to Java, let me recommend *The Java Programming Language*, by Ken Arnold and James Gosling. It's an excellent introduction to the language written in part by the originator of Java himself, James Gosling.

Many sections have exercises. The exercises don't introduce new material, but they do reinforce the existing lessons. Most of the exercises ask you to write small pieces of code. For some exercises, answers are provided at the back of the book. If you're using this book for a class and you've been assigned the exercises as a homework problem, then turning in the answers at the back of the book is cheating! Fortunately, real JVM programmers are trustworthy.

Books

This book has been designed to stand on its own. You should be able to read it without owning any other books on Java. However, there are two books which you may find very useful.

One is *The Java Virtual Machine Specification* (*JVMS*), by Frank Yellin and Tim Lindholm. It is the "truth" of the Java virtual machine. All JVM implementers, including Sun itself, are expected to adhere to the definition of the Java virtual machine contained in the *JVMS*. Wherever your JVM implementation disagrees with the *JVMS*, it is always the *JVMS* that is correct. I recommend that you have a copy on hand if you want to do a lot of JVM programming, because it is the final word on any JVM-oriented question.

Another book I recommend is *The Java Language Specification*, by James Gosling, Bill Joy, and Guy Steele. This is a large, thick tome that contains the absolute truth about the Java language. It does an excellent job of specifying all the details of what a Java program means. It is meticulously precise, but it can still be a lot of fun to read because it throws in many funny examples and quotes. Even just browsing the index can be a treat. (Look up the index entry for *prime numbers* to see what I mean.)

Both of these books are available over the Internet at `http://java.sun.com/docs`. Paper copies are available at any bookstore.

While you're on the Internet, let me recommend one other source of information. The newsgroup `comp.lang.java.machine` is dedicated to discussing how the Java virtual machine works, how it is implemented, and so forth. I'm a frequent reader and contributor, and there are many other experts willing to share their copious knowledge.

Acknowledgments

I would like to thank Stefan Gower for giving me the original idea of implementing a Scheme compiler for the Java virtual machine. Christopher Cook, William Andersen, Brian Peterson, and Paul Brinkley were indispensable, allowing me to explain JVM concepts to them until I finally found a lucid explanation.

Marina Lang at Addison Wesley Longman was instrumental in guiding me through the process of getting a book written. Thanks also to the many reviewers she found who helped me turn drafts into something readable.

Finally, I would like to thank the regular posters to `comp.lang.java.machine`, the newsgroup for the JVM. They provided answers to a lot of questions and brought up questions I had not previously considered.

## CHAPTER 1

Introduction to the Java Virtual Machine

THINK about the CPU in your computer. No matter what make or model of CPU you own, it serves the same basic functions as any other CPU: it performs arithmetic calculations, controls access to memory, manages the flow of control of programs, and provides a way for programs to use hardware attached to the system.

Even though all CPUs perform essentially the same job, programs designed for one CPU do not work on another. The developers of Java had a simple idea: design an abstraction of a CPU, and implement it for a variety of computers. Once this virtual computer is implemented on a particular system, all programs written for the virtual computer will run on that system. This allows programmers to write a program once, then run it anywhere. This virtual computer is called the Java virtual machine (JVM).

Because the JVM isn't biased toward any particular CPU, it can provide a more abstract view of memory. Instead of providing direct access to the bits-and-bytes level of memory, the JVM treats memory as a collection of objects. This is a paradigm called *object-oriented programming*, and it offers a number of advantages.

One advantage is that it allows better control over which programs are allowed to access which parts of memory. This affords the JVM control over access to the hardware of the system. The JVM developers created a set of rules all programs must play by. As long as all programs play by the rules, it is possible to provide assurances to program users that the programs are not trying to damage the system.

These rules are made concrete in an algorithm called *verification*, which detects which programs follow the rules and which don't. A key goal of verification is to detect invalid programs even before they run. Only programs that are approved by the verification algorithm run. This prevents malicious or mistaken software from doing unpleasant things: it never gets a chance to run.

These and other features make the Java virtual machine one of the most interesting aspects of the very popular Java programming language. Throughout this book we will examine how to write programs for the Java virtual machine and explain how it fulfills some of its remarkable promises.

1.1   Java Virtual Machine and Java

If you know Java, then you already have a pretty good understanding of some of the most important concepts in the Java virtual machine. That's because the JVM was intended, first and foremost, as a platform for running Java programs. You already have some idea of what a class is, what methods are, what an `int` is, and so on.

A Java program is a collection of class definitions written in the Java language. A Java compiler translates the Java programs into a format the JVM implementation understands. This translation process is called *compilation*.

This compiled form of the Java program is a collection of bytes, represented in a form called the `class` file format. These bytes may be kept in a file, in memory, on a web server, in a database, or anywhere else you can store a collection of bytes.

The `class` file contains instructions. When a JVM implementation reads and executes these instructions, the effect is what the original Java program called for. In programming language terms, we say that the `class` file has the same *semantics* as the original Java program.

The JVM is free to perform the actions specified by the instructions in any way it chooses, as long as it continues to obey the semantics of the instructions. A JVM implementation can choose from several implementation techniques. It can interpret the instructions or translate them into native machine code. The layout of memory is up to the JVM implementation. Different implementation techniques have their advantages and disadvantages, but no matter what, the results must conform to *The Java Virtual Machine Specification*, the official reference for JVM implementations.

Although the Java virtual machine was originally designed for the Java language, it is theoretically possible to design a translator from any programming language into the Java virtual machine's world. In practice, some languages are very difficult to implement efficiently, but some very interesting languages translate quite well. We'll discuss how some languages besides Java can be translated for the Java virtual machine in chapter 11.

1.2   What Is the Java Virtual Machine?

The official arbiter of what constitutes a JVM is *The Java Virtual Machine Specification,* by Tim Lindholm and Frank Yellin. The *Specification* defines three things:

- A set of instructions and a definition of the meanings of those instructions. These instructions are called *bytecodes.*
- A binary format called the `class` *file format,* which is used to convey bytecodes and related class infrastructure in a platform-independent manner.
- An algorithm for identifying programs that cannot compromise the integrity of the JVM. This algorithm is called *verification.*

1.2.1   Instruction Set

The executable programs running in the JVM are expressed in terms of instructions called *bytecodes,* resembling the machine code of most computer architectures. The JVM instruction set is designed around a stack-based architecture with special object-oriented instructions.

The instructions are stored in the `class` file in a binary format that is readily readable by a computer but unintelligible to human beings. Throughout this book we use a language called Oolong.[1] The format of an Oolong program is nearly equivalent to a `class` file, but words and numbers are used in place of the binary values.

Here is a segment of Oolong code to compute 2 + 3:

```
bipush 2          ; Push the number 2
bipush 3          ; Push the number 3
iadd              ; Add them together
```

Initially, the operand stack is empty:

----

[1] Oolong is based on Jasmin, by Jon Meyer.

Each `bipush` instruction pushes its argument onto the operand stack. After the first two instructions, the operand stack looks like this:

The `iadd` instruction expects to find two numbers on the operand stack. It pops these numbers off, replacing them by their sum:

This is the result we were looking for.

One thing that distinguishes the JVM instruction set from the instruction sets of most CPUs is the way the JVM works with memory. Most computers view memory as a vast array of bytes. If you want to build an object, you allocate a collection of contiguous bytes. Different locations within this collection of bytes are the different parts of the object's state. To call a function, you jump to the location in memory where that function is located.

The JVM doesn't permit byte-level access to memory. Instead, it has instructions for allocating objects, invoking methods, and retrieving and modifying fields in those objects. For example, this code gets an object from a field, then calls a method on that object, passing a string as a parameter:

```
getstatic java/lang/System/out Ljava/io/PrintStream;
ldc "Hello, world"
invokevirtual java/io/PrintStream/println
   (Ljava/lang/String;)V
```

The first instruction retrieves the value of the out field from the class `java/lang/System`.[2] The value of this field is an object that must be of the class `java/io/PrintStream` (or a subclass).

---

[2] The JVM uses slashes (/) where the Java language uses periods (.). Throughout this book, we use slashes when talking about JVM concepts and periods when talking about Java concepts.

The second instruction pushes the constant string `Hello, world` onto the stack. The string is another object of the class `java/lang/String`. The stack now looks like this:

```
┌──────────────┐
│ Hello, world │
├──────────────┤
│     out      │
└──────────────┘
```

The final instruction invokes a method. The name of the method is `println`; its definition can be found in the class `java/io/PrintStream`. It expects an argument of type `java.lang.String` on the stack, and it returns nothing. It also expects an object of `class java/io/Printstream` to be on the stack below the arguments; this is the target of the method invocation. This calls the method, which prints

```
Hello, world
```

The method call removes both the argument and the target of the method invocation. The stack is now empty.

1.2.2 `class` File Format

The Java Virtual Machine Specification defines a binary format, called the `class` file, which represents a class as a stream of bytes. The Java platform has methods for converting `class` files into classes in the JVM.

The term "`class` file" is slightly misleading. Data in `class` file format does not have to be stored in a file. They can be stored in a database, across the network, as part of a Java archive file (JAR), or in a variety of other ways.

The key to using `class` files is the class `ClassLoader`, which is part of the Java platform. Many different subclasses of `ClassLoaders` are available, which load from databases, across the network, from JAR files, and so on. Java-supporting web browsers have a subclass of `ClassLoader` that can load `class` files over the Internet.

If you store your information in some nonstandard format (such as compressed) or in a nonstandard place (such as in a database), you can write your own subclass of `ClassLoader`. We'll discuss how to do this in chapter 8.

1.2.3 Verification

In order to ensure that certain parts of the machine are kept safe from tampering, the JVM has a verification algorithm to check every class. The purpose of verification is to ensure that programs follow a set of rules that are designed to protect the security of the JVM.

Programs can try to subvert the security of the JVM in a variety of ways. For example, they might try overflowing the stack, hoping to corrupt memory they are not allowed to access. They might try to cast an object inappropriately, hoping to obtain pointers to forbidden memory. The verification algorithm ensures that this does not happen by tracing through the code to check that objects are always used according to their proper types.

The verification algorithm is discussed in detail in chapter 6.

1.3   Java Platform

The Java virtual machine is great for performing fundamental computational tasks, like arithmetic and method invocation, but it lacks features for doing important computer-oriented things like displaying graphics, communicating over a network, and so on. It's also shy on helpful tools like hash tables, string manipulations, and so forth.

The Java platform includes the JVM and a collection of important classes. These classes begin with the package name "java." The package java.applet provides an interface to a web browser. The package java.io provides input and output capabilities. There are many others.

PersonalJava is a subset of the Java platform. It's designed for personal devices smaller than a home computer but bigger than the computer embedded in a toaster, such as hand-held computers and television set-top boxes. It includes the java.awt classes for displaying graphics, but some features may be disabled (like scroll bars). It also lacks the database connectivity features found in java.sql and the cryptography in java.security.

Even smaller than the PersonalJava platform is EmbeddedJava, which is designed to work in low-memory, low-computing-power environments like air conditioners, elevator controllers, and toasters.

The JVM cannot function independent of the Java platform. Throughout this book we will assume a tiny environment containing only some of the classes in java.lang:

- ◆ java.lang.Object, which is the base class of the entire Java class hierarchy
- ◆ java.lang.ClassLoader, which introduces new classes into the system
- ◆ java.lang.String, which represents strings of text
- ◆ java.lang.Class, which represents classes

Others are discussed as appropriate. This ultraminimal environment is found in all environments; all examples should run on any platform. Sometimes the examples include

references to classes in more complicated platforms, like java.awt.W
the example more flavor and to make it more realistic. In these cases
can easily substitute another, less interesting class.

1.4 Organization of the Java Virtual Machine

The JVM is divided into four conceptual data spaces:

- *Class area*, where the code and constants are kept
- *Java stack*, which keeps track of which methods have been called and the data associated with each method invocation
- *Heap*, where objects are kept
- *Native method stacks*, for supporting native methods

1.4.1 Class Area

The class area stores the classes that are loaded into the system. Method implementations are kept in a space called the *method area*, and constants are kept in a space called the *constant pool*. The class definitions also serve as templates for objects. Objects are stored in the heap (see section 1.4.3).

A class loader (see chapter 8) introduces new classes into the class area. When a class is no longer used, it may be garbage collected.

Classes have several properties:

- Superclass
- List of interfaces (possibly empty)
- List of fields
- List of methods and implementations, stored in the method area
- List of constants, stored in the constant pool

All properties of classes are immutable. That is, there's no way to change any property of a class once it has been brought into the system. This makes the machine more stable, since you know that a method will have the same code each time it's invoked, and each object of a particular class has the same fields as every other object of that class.[3]

---

[3] If a class is no longer used, then it may be unloaded and reloaded at a later time. The new definition may be different. However, this does not cause inconsistencies between objects, because the original definition of the class would not be unloaded if instances of it still existed.

ieties: static and nonstatic. For nonstatic fields, there is
object. For static fields, there is a single copy of the

picture of a class area. It depicts two classes: Game-
Each has fields and methods. Each field and method
f properties. The descriptor tells which type of values
parameters and return type of a method. The constant
n the figure. For more about the constant pool, see

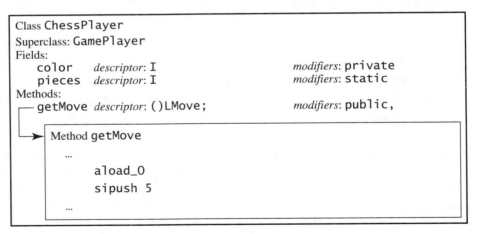

FIGURE 1.1: *Class area*

For methods that don't have the `abstract` property, there is a method implementation. Method implementations are defined in terms of instructions, which are discussed in chapter 2.

1.4.2   Java Stack

Each time a method is invoked, a new data space called a *stack frame* is created. Collectively, the stack frames are called the *Java stack*. The stack frame on top of the stack is called the *active stack frame*.

Each stack frame has an operand stack, an array of local variables, and a pointer to the currently executing instruction. This instruction pointer is called the *program counter* (PC). The program counter points into the method area. It points to the current instruction. Ordinarily, the program counter moves from one instruction to the subsequent instruction, but some instructions (like `goto`) cause the program counter to move to some other place within the method.

The top frame of the Java stack shows the current place of execution. It is called the *active frame*. Only the operand stack and local variable array in the active stack frame can be used. When a method is invoked, a new Java stack frame is created and that becomes the top of the Java stack. The program counter is saved as part of the old Java stack frame. The new Java stack frame has its own program counter, which points to the beginning of the called method.

When the newly called method returns, the active stack frame disappears and the stack frame below it becomes the active frame again. The program counter is set to the instruction after the method call, and the method continues.

Figure 1.2 shows a Java stack that has two stack frames. The first entry on the stack is at the bottom. It shows a call to the method `main` in the class `GamePlayer`. The program counter points to the instruction nine bytes from the beginning of the method.

Above that is the active stack frame. The active stack frame is a method called `getPlayerMove` in the class `ChessPlayer`, currently at instruction 17. It has two items on its operand stack and three slots in its local variable array. Two of those slots are uninitialized. Slot 0 contains a reference to an object in the heap. The references are represented by arrows that point to the objects. The heap is discussed in more detail in section 1.4.3.

1.4.3   Heap

Objects are stored in the heap. Each object is associated with a class in the class area. Each object also has a number of slots for storing fields; there is one slot for

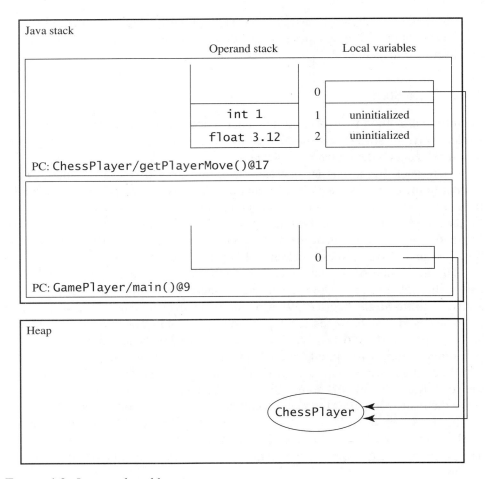

FIGURE 1.2: *Java stack and heap*

each nonstatic field in the class, one for each nonstatic field in the superclass, and so on. An example is shown in Figure 1.3. This heap contains a chess player named Pooky. A real heap has thousands or millions of objects in it.

The chess player is an object of class `ChessPlayer`. The `name` field is a reference to an object whose class is `java/lang/String`. This string contains a field called `data`, which points to an array of characters. (`[C` is the descriptor for an array of characters. See section 2.5 for more about descriptors.) This array is five characters long, containing the letters `P`, `o`, `o`, `k`, and `y`.

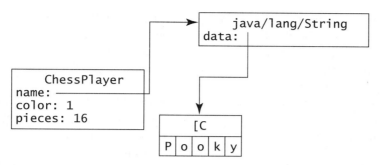

FIGURE 1.3: *Heap*

Another field of ChessPlayer is color, which is an int. This doesn't point to another object. Instead, it just holds the number 1.

1.4.4 Native Method Stacks

Native methods are used like other JVM methods, except that instead of being implemented using JVM instructions, they are implemented in some other language. They allow the programmer to handle situations that cannot be handled completely in Java, such as interfacing to platform-dependent features or integrating legacy code written in other languages.

When native methods are compiled into machine codes, they usually use a stack to keep track of their state. The JVM provides a native method stack that the native methods can use. They are often called "C stacks," because the most common way to implement native methods is to write them in C and compile them into native code.

Native methods do not exist on all JVM implementations, and different implementations have different standards for them, so they are not always portable. A common standard, the Java Native Interface (JNI), is often but not always available. This book focuses on JVM issues, so native methods are largely ignored. For more information about implementing native methods, consult the JNI documentation and the documentation for your particular JVM implementation.

1.4.5 Example

This example shows more detail of the Hello, world code shown earlier in relation to the Java stack, method area, and heap.

Figure 1.4 shows the state of the system after executing `getstatic` and `ldc`. There is one frame on the Java stack. The top of the stack points to the `Hello, world` string, and the next stack slot points to the object in `System.out`. There is one local variable, which points to the argument array. The program counter points to the `invokevirtual` instruction.

Figure 1.5 shows what happens when the `invokevirtual` instruction is executed. The operands to the instruction are popped off the operand stack. A new Java stack frame is created. The old stack frame is now inactive. It cannot be changed again until it becomes the active stack frame, which happens only when the newly called method terminates. (In the diagram, the reference lines from the old stack frame are dotted to make them easier to follow.)

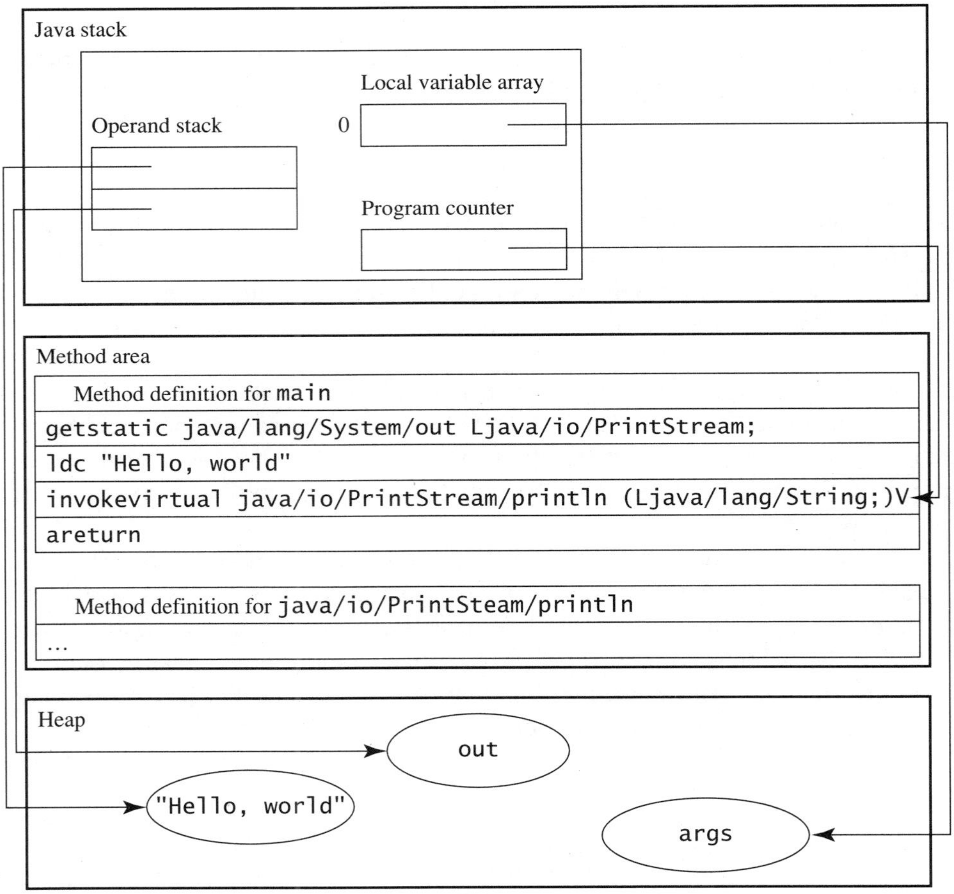

FIGURE 1.4: *Before executing* `invokevirtual`

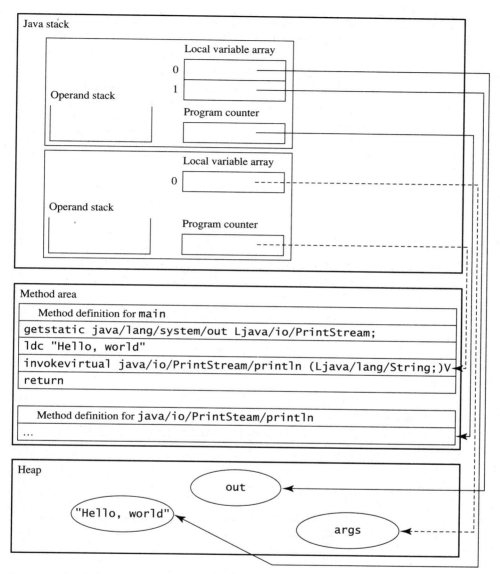

FIGURE 1.5: *While executing* `invokevirtual`

The new stack frame points to the first instruction of the `println` method. Notice that the first two entries in the local variable array are initialized to the parameters of the method call. Additional local variables may be present, depending on how the method is implemented. These are uninitialized. The new operand stack is empty.

The JVM now executes the instructions in `println` until `println` returns. Figure 1.6 shows what happens after the call to `println` returns. The new stack frame has been removed, so the previous stack frame is now the active stack frame. The parameters to the method have been removed from the operand stack, so the stack is now empty. The program counter has been moved to the next instruction. The JVM will continue with that instruction. Notice that two of the objects no longer have lines pointing to them. The storage for these objects may be reclaimed by the JVM and used for new objects. This is called *garbage collection,* and it is discussed in section 1.5.

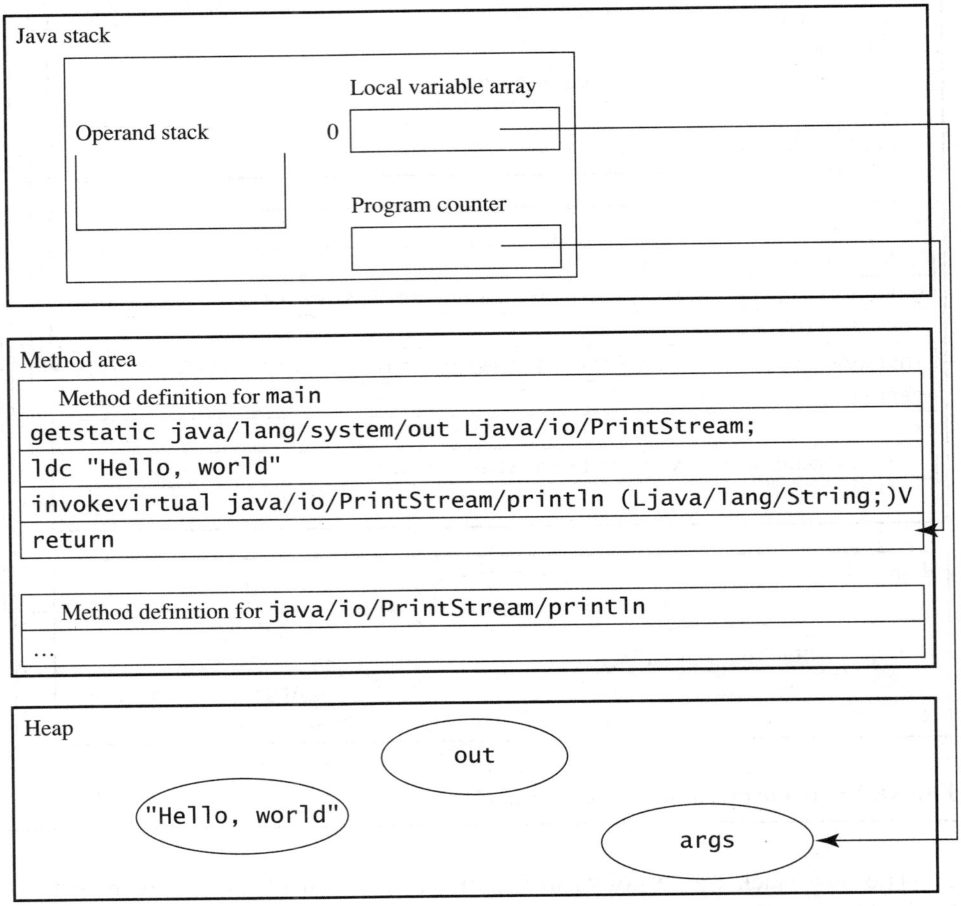

FIGURE 1.6: *After executing `invokevirtual`*

1.5   Garbage Collection

Each object consumes some memory, of which there is a limited amount. Eventually, the memory allocated to these objects must be reclaimed when they aren't used any more. The Java virtual machine reclaims these objects automatically through a process called *garbage collection*.

An object is ready to be garbage collected when it is no longer "alive." The rules for determining if an object is alive follow.

- ◆ If there's a reference to the object on the stack, then it's alive.
- ◆ If there's a reference to the object in a local variable, on the stack, or in a `static` field, then it's alive.
- ◆ If a field of an alive object contains a reference to the object, then it's alive.
- ◆ The JVM may internally keep references to certain objects, for example, to support native methods. These objects are alive.

Any object that isn't alive is dead. As an example, suppose that you have two classes, A and B, like this:

```
class A
{
    B b;                    // A field pointing to an object
                            // of type B
}
class B
{
    A a;                    // A field pointing to an object
                            // of type A
}
```

Suppose you have this code:

```
A foo = new A();           // Create an object of class A
                           // called foo
foo.b = new B();           // Create an object of class B
                           // and put a reference to it
                           // in the b field of foo
```

The code creates two objects, one of class A and one of class B (we'll call these A and B). There is a reference to A in the local variable foo (which is stored in local variable array slot 0) and a reference to B in the b field of A. The a field of B points to `null`, which is no object at all. Memory now looks like Figure 1.7. In this figure, both A and B are alive. A is alive because it is referenced by the local variable 0. B is alive because it is referenced in a field of A.

Suppose we break the link like this:

```
foo.b = null;
```

This sets the b field to point to no object at all. Now memory looks like Figure 1.8. Now B doesn't meet any of the four conditions for aliveness; there are no arrows pointing to it at all. This means that B is now dead, and it can be garbage collected. A is still alive, so it must not be garbage collected.

One thing can be a little confusing about the third rule: only a reference from a live object counts, not a reference from a dead one. Suppose there are objects like Figure 1.9. Even though these objects point to each other, neither is alive because one isn't alive. An object is dead unless it can prove that it's alive. Since the only claim that each has on life is the other one, they're both dead.

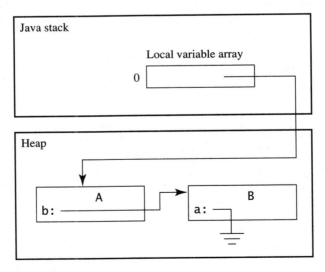

FIGURE 1.7: *Two live objects*

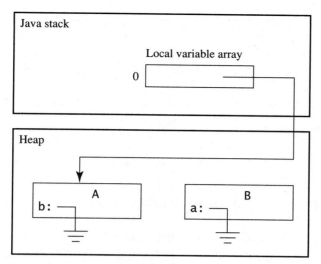

FIGURE 1.8: *The object on the right is dead*

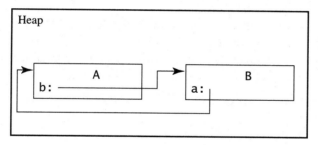

FIGURE 1.9: *These objects are both dead*

1.5.1 Finalization

In some cases, it is helpful to know when an object is no longer used so that you can do some final cleaning up. For example, if you write a class where each instance represents a connection to a database, a database connection object that is no longer used can inform the database that the connection is no longer necessary.

To handle this, provide a method called `finalize` in your class. This method is called when the garbage collector notices that the object is dead. The `finalize` method is defined in the class `java.lang.Object` to do nothing. You may override this method to do any last-minute chores your object should do before it is garbage collected.

To close the database connection, you might provide this method:

```
public void finalize()
{
    this.close();              // Close the connection
}
```

When this object becomes dead, the `finalize` method will be called and it will close the connection.

Note that you can't be sure *when* the connection will be closed, because the garbage collector may take some time before it notices that the object is dead. In fact, the garbage collector may never notice that the object is dead, or finalization may never occur for other reasons. Therefore, anybody using the connection should explicitly close the connection, not depend on `finalize`. The `finalize` method can be used as a backup, but in that case there is still the possibility that the connection will never be closed.

One trick you can play is to "resurrect" your object. The `finalize` method was called because there was no way to reach the object, but in the body of the `finalize` method there is a way to reach the object: it's available through `this`.

You can store the value of `this` into a field, like this:

```
static Vector resurrected_objects = new Vector();
void finalize()
{
    resurrected_objects.addElement(this);
}
```

This resurrects the object because now there is a way to get to it: it is stored in `resurrected_objects`, which maintains a reference to the object. The garbage collector will notice this, and the object is not reclaimed. The body of `finalize` may resurrect other objects that were presumed dead, or it may eliminate the last link to an object so that it is now dead. The garbage collector has to be very smart to correctly handle all these cases. You can be sure that an object will never be garbage collected until there is absolutely no way to resurrect it.

At some point in the future, the object may become dead again. The object will be garbage collected, but `finalize` will not run again. If you depend on `finalize` to clean things up, you must be very careful if you choose to resurrect the object during finalization: you get only one shot at it.

1.5.2   Timing of Garbage Collection

You shouldn't design your system to depend on finalization or garbage collection to run at any particular time or in any particular order. In fact, there is no guarantee that finalization will ever occur. Therefore, you should never write your programs to depend on finalization for correctness.

The garbage collector may run when you get low on memory. It may also run when the system is otherwise idle and the JVM decides to use the free time to tidy itself up. It may also run at the user's explicit command by calling the `gc` method in the class `java.lang.System`.

The garbage collector may be run automatically by the system at any time. The system can also undertake garbage collection at the explicit request of a program. Even if you knew when it was going to run, you couldn't be sure that it would collect all dead objects. Some garbage collectors take a quick-and-dirty look at the system to collect obviously dead objects and delay collection of objects that have been around for a long time until it has time to do a thorough examination of the state of memory.

1.6   JVM Implementations

One of the design goals of the virtual machine is that it can be emulated by a program on a real machine. This enables almost any actual computer to serve as a Java virtual machine by using a JVM emulator. A JVM implementation is a program for your system. Unlike Java virtual machine programs, which will run on any implementation, the JVM implementation depends on the specifics of your system.

Many different JVM implementations are available for a variety of platforms. One of the most popular is the Java Development Kit (JDK), from Sun Microsystems, which runs on both Solaris and Windows platforms (both NT and 95/98), covering over 90% of the computers in the world. It's free and available from `http://java.sun.com`. Because it comes from Sun, the inventor of Java, the JDK virtual machine is the standard against which all other implementations are measured. The full package contains a debugger, a Java compiler, and documentation, as well as an implementation of the Java virtual machine.

In the JDK, the JVM implementation is a program called `java`. It takes as an argument the name of the class to execute; the subsequent parameters become arguments to the JVM program. For example,

```
java Hello
```

finds a class named `Hello` and executes it. It begins in a method called `main`, which takes an array of strings as its argument. These strings are initialized to the rest of the words on the command line.

Other JVM implementations are available. Popular ones are made by Microsoft, Symantec, and Asymetrix. Most popular operating systems, including Solaris, Windows, and Macintosh, already incorporate JVM implementations. Kaffe is a free JVM implementation, available at www.kaffe.org.

Another common place to find Java virtual machines is as a part of a web browser. Both Netscape Navigator and Microsoft's Internet Explorer contain a Java virtual machine. It is accessed by loading an HTML page containing the APPLET tag, like this:

```
<APPLET CODE="HelloApplet.class" WIDTH=100 HEIGHT=200>
```

The CODE parameter names a file in the class file format. The browser's virtual machine interprets that class file, creates an instance of the class found inside, and calls its init method.

Yet another place to find Java virtual machines is as part of the system itself. Embedded systems, supporting the EmbeddedJava platform and the Java virtual machine, are becoming more common. These systems sometimes use existing processors, or Sun's picoJava processor, which runs JVM bytecodes as its native machine language. Embedded JVM systems include smart cards, which incorporate a JVM into a device as small as a credit card.

1.7   Versions of the Virtual Machine

The format of the class file, the meaning of the instructions, and the verification algorithm are defined in *The Java Virtual Machine Specification*. They have not changed significantly since Java was first released.

Over time the Java platform changes. New APIs are introduced. Occasionally, parts of old APIs are *deprecated*, meaning that they are replaced by something better and the old ones should no longer be used. Eventually, some deprecated features go away entirely.

Sun Microsystems is the steward of the Java platform. Sun is a publicly available specification (PAS) submitter for the International Standards Organization (ISO). Sun referees the process of changing the Java platform specification in accordance with a plan approved by the ISO.

The reference implementation of the Java platform is the Java Development Kit, a free set of software from Sun. Different platform releases get different numbers. The original Java platform was version 1.0. Later, substantial changes were made to the Java platform, signified by the release of JDK 1.1. This incorporated a new way of handling graphics and some minor changes to the Java language, along with a host of new APIs and extensions to existing ones.

The Java 2 platform is the latest platform as of this writing. It includes a new set of tools for building user interfaces, performance improvements, and enhancements to existing features. Although APIs have changed over time, the Java 2 platform represents the first changes to the JVM itself. These changes are quite minor: a change in version numbering and some new rules for floating point.

In a few cases changes in the platform come under the scope of this book. Most notably, the way classes are loaded with the `ClassLoader` class was altered slightly between JDK 1.0 and 1.1. We will discuss both versions.

Although new releases of the Java platform rarely affect the underlying JVM, this does not always mean that you can use your existing JVM implementations with the new features. Some of the new features require code to be written specifically for the platform hosting the computer to properly interact with the hardware on the platform. For example, the JDK 1.1 reflection methods, which allow programs to determine which methods and fields are available, require special support from the JVM implementation.

The special support comes in the form of *native methods*. A native method is called just like any other method in the JVM, but it is implemented using non-Java languages like C or C++. This allows it access to the internals of the JVM implementation and to devices and features that are specific to the particular hardware or operating system. These native instructions are different for each platform, just like ordinary programs before Java became available.

When the Java platform changes to require new native methods, the JVM implementation must usually be replaced. The core functionality, which loads and executes instructions, usually does not change, but new libraries are added.

Some platform changes do not require the addition of new native methods. The Java foundation classes, which are a collection of user-interface tools, and the JavaBeans classes, which enable visual program-building tools, were written entirely in Java and could be made to work even on JVM implementations built before the new APIs were invented.

When the original Java specification was released, many users obtained an implementation of the JVM with their web browser. Version 3 of both Netscape Navigator and Internet Explorer contain a JVM with the JDK 1.0 platform. Newer versions of these browsers support later versions of Java, but Navigator 3 and Explorer 3 are still widely in use.

1.8   Future of the Java Virtual Machine

The Java virtual machine is becoming ubiquitous. Originally it was found primarily in web browsers to support animated web pages. Now it is found inside databases, personal portable computers, smart cards, and cellular phones. Most popular operating systems come with an implementation of the JVM; if they don't, they will soon.

Because there are so many JVMs in place, the native part of the Java platform will gradually settle so that you don't have to replace your JVM implementation. Platform changes will still occur as new functionality is added, but this will increasingly come in the form of new Java class libraries. You can deliver these with your software to any JVM, which will make the Java slogan "Write Once, Run Anywhere" more true than ever.

As the JVM becomes more common, new languages besides Java will be required. There are many reasons for creating new languages. Sometimes things that are hard in one language are easy in another. If you write Perl, then you know that it's better than Java for processing streams of text; it's great for writing CGI scripts. Eiffel is great for large projects where you need to enforce contracts between programmers. Other languages encourage other features: parallel processing (Occam), symbol manipulation (Lisp), algebra (Maple and Mathematica).

Rather than pile all these features into Java, these and other languages may be implemented for the existing Java virtual machine. This allows programmers the best of both worlds: the ubiquity of the JVM and the features of a favorite language.

Another thing that will happen to JVMs is that they will get faster. The first JVM implementations worked as an interpreter, reading each instruction and calling an appropriate function to perform the operation. Newer JVMs work by first translating an entire method into native code, then executing the native code. This imposes a small burden at the beginning, but this burden is quickly lifted by the elimination of the need to translate each instruction one at a time.

The translation into native code will provide other benefits. Modern processors are extremely good at taking maximum advantage of their available power. For example, if one instruction adds the variables a and b and the next instruction multiplies the variables c and d, then why not execute both simultaneously? They use different parts of the CPU and different parts of memory. This lets you do the work in half the time. Designing your translator to take advantage of this requires careful study and planning, but the potential performance improvements are huge.

Similarly, targeting your compilation to a particular processor (like the 80486) means that you may miss out on optimizations made by other processors (like the Pentium). If you compiled just for the Pentium, then your program may not run on an 80486. You could build and ship two different versions, which will make your marketing department increasingly cranky. Expect future JVM implementations to do a good job at targeting native code generation to precisely the processor on which it is running for another performance boost.

These changes help bring Java closer to the performance of C or C++. Performance improves further when the JVM runtime system is able to make optimizations impossible in C and C++. In these lower-level languages, where memory is just a huge set of bytes, it is sometimes difficult to recognize when one pointer "shadows" another—that is, when the two pointers point to the same place. This can make it hard to optimize.

A piece of code might appear to write into a memory location that is never read, which means that you can eliminate the calculation. If there's a shadow pointer in some other section of code, then you may not make this optimization. In the JVM it's easier than in C to detect shadowing, which will allow this optimization to be made more often. This is only one example; the abstract nature of the JVM allows for much better translations than the bits-and-bytes thinking of C and C++.

Finally, who said that the translation from JVM bytecodes into native code has to happen only once? Often, optimizations are made based on guesses of what is going to happen. You have a limited number of fast registers; once you have used them up, other values must be placed in slower memory. You want to place the most-used values in registers, but sometimes it's hard to tell. The JVM can take its best guess, just like a C compiler, but the JVM has the option of watching what's going on and then changing the code if it guessed wrong, which a C compiler can never do. JVM implementations will be blazingly fast, probably sooner than you expect.

CHAPTER 2

Oolong

THIS chapter introduces Oolong, an assembly language for the Java virtual machine. The JVM uses a binary format called `class` files for communicating programs. Because it is difficult to edit and visualize `class` files, the Oolong language was created. It is nearly equivalent to the `class` file format but easier to read and write. The Oolong language takes care of certain bits-and-bytes-level details while allowing almost complete control of the `class` file.

To actually execute an Oolong program, it must be assembled into a `class` file. An Oolong assembler is provided with this book; Appendix B describes how to use it. It is a program called `Oolong`. This program is written in Java, so it should run on any JVM implementation you have.

You can edit Oolong source with any text editor. By convention, Oolong source file names end in `.j`.

This chapter provides a quick introduction to the overall structure of Oolong. The next chapters describe the details of writing methods, which are the executable parts of an Oolong class.

2.1 Hello, World

Let's look at an Oolong program in action. This is the source to the "Hello, world" program written in Oolong, as it would appear in an Oolong source file `hello.j`:

```
.class public hello
.super java/lang/Object

.method public static main([Ljava/lang/String;)V
.limit stack 2
.limit locals 1
    getstatic java/lang/System/out Ljava/io/PrintStream;
    ldc "Hello, world"
    invokevirtual java/io/PrintStream/println
      (Ljava/lang/String;)V
    return
.end method
.end class
```

2.1.1   .class and .super Directives

Lines that begin with periods (.) are called *directives*. The first directive is .class, which tells the Oolong assembler the name of the class being compiled. In the example, the name of the class being declared is hello. If the .class directive is missing, then the name of the class is assumed to be the same as the name of the source file, minus the .j extension.

The .class directive may also contain a set of modifiers that control access to the class. This class is declared public, meaning that it may be accessed from any other class in the JVM. This is identical to declaring a class public in Java.

The rest of the file up to the next .end class is considered part of the same class. The .end class directive is optional. If you don't include it, then the rest of the file is all part of the same class. You may have more than one class definition per file, as long as you end each class definition with an .end class directive.

The next line after the .class directive contains a .super directive. The .super directive tells Oolong the name of the superclass of this class. This example declares the superclass to be java/lang/Object, which is the default. The .super directive works like the extends clause in a Java program.

The name java/lang/Object names the same class as java.lang.Object does in Java. The JVM uses slashes (/) instead of periods (.) to separate parts of class names. If you were to look inside a class file created by compiling a Java program, you would see that all the periods in class names had been converted to slashes. Because Oolong is closer to the JVM class file format than Java, we use slashes instead of periods.

The .class and .super directives in this example are equivalent to the Java

```
public class hello extends java.lang.Object
```

In Oolong, you must use the full name of the class. In Java, this line is equivalent to

```
public class hello extends Object
```

because Java assumes that by `Object` you mean the particular `Object` found in the package `java.lang`. The `class` file does not make this assumption, so you must write out the full name of every class. That can get tiring, but it ensures that the class file is not ambiguous. This saves the JVM time trying to figure out which class you mean, and it ensures that you get the same result each time, even if new classes are added to the system.

2.1.2 `main` Method

The `.method` directive marks the beginning of a new method. Every line after that is a part of the method until the `.end method` directive. The `.method` directive here is

```
.method public static main([Ljava/lang/String;)V
```

The `.method` directive names the method being created. In this case, the method is named `main`.

Before the method name is a list of *access keywords,* which control how the class can be used. This method is marked `public`, meaning that it can be used by anybody, and `static`, meaning that it isn't attached to any particular instance of the class. Unlike Java, the access keywords may come in any order.

Also unlike Java, the return type of the method does not appear at the end of the list of keywords. Instead, the arguments and return types are written together in the *descriptor* following the method name. The descriptor is a way of expressing a type as letters and symbols. A method descriptor contains the types of the arguments between parentheses, followed by the return type.

Most types are represented by a single character: `V` for `void`, `I` for `int`, and so on. A left bracket (`[`) means an array of whatever type follows. `L` means an object of the type named by everything up to the next semicolon. Thus, `Ljava/lang/String;` is the type written as `java.lang.String` in Java, and `[Ljava/lang/String;` is an array of `java/lang/String`. The complete list can be found in section 2.5.

The descriptor of `main` is `([Ljava/lang/String;)V`. This says that `main` takes an array of strings, and returns a `void`.

The `.limit` directives tell how much space to allocate for the execution of this method: `.limit stack` puts an upper limit on how many slots on the operand stack the program will use; `.limit locals` specifies the number of local variable slots that will be used. The Oolong assembler will guess if the directive isn't given.

2.1.3   Instructions

The remaining lines up to `.end method` represent JVM instructions. The Oolong assembler translates the instructions into bytecodes. The first word of each instruction is called a *mnemonic*. Each mnemonic corresponds to an *opcode* in the `class` file, which is a single byte representing an instruction. It's called a mnemonic because it's supposed to be easier to remember than the actual opcode for the instruction. The mnemonic may be followed by several *arguments*. The allowable arguments depend on the mnemonic. They provide more detail about how the instruction should operate.

Let's look at what the instructions mean, one by one. The first instruction is

```
getstatic java/lang/System/out Ljava/io/PrintStream;
```

This instruction tells the JVM to get the value of the field `out` from the class `java/lang/System`. This is a static field, meaning that it is a property of the class as a whole instead of any individual object. The value of the object obtained from this operation is expected to be a `java/io/PrintStream` object. A reference to this object is placed on the stack.

The second instruction is

```
ldc "Hello, world"
```

This causes the JVM to create a `java/lang/String` object with the value `Hello, world`. This object is placed on the stack above the `out` object. The stack now looks like this:

"Hello, world"
java/lang/System/out

The next instruction is

```
invokevirtual java/io/PrintStream/println(Ljava/lang/String;)V
```

The `invokevirtual` instruction is used to invoke a method on an object. The arguments to the instruction name the method to be called (`println`), the class in which the method is to be found (`java/io/PrintStream`), and the descriptor of the method (`(Ljava/lang/String;)V`).

The JVM checks that the arguments that actually appear on the stack correspond to those expected by the method. The target of the invocation should be a java/io/PrintStream; that's the out object loaded by the first instruction. The argument should be a String; that's the Hello, world string loaded by the second instruction. The method is called, which removes both elements from the stack. The method does its job, then returns nothing (void), which means that the stack is empty.

The final instruction is

```
return
```

This instruction terminates the method and causes control to return to whoever called the method.

Exercise 2.1

Enter, compile, and run hello.j on your system.   ▲

Exercise 2.2

Try changing parts of hello.j and see what errors you get.   ▲

2.2 Structure of an Oolong Program

Now that we've looked over a particular Oolong program, let's look at Oolong programs in general.

One important part of an Oolong program is a comment. Comments always begin with a semicolon (;) and end at the end of the line. There are no directives or other funny stuff hidden inside the comment; you may put anything you like in them. They are completely ignored, and they don't have any effect on the generated .class file. For example,

```
; This is a comment
```

Throughout this book, we use the convention of a double semicolon to introduce a comment that documents omitted code. For example,

```
; This is a comment describing the main method
.method main([Ljava/lang/String;)V
    ;; Code is omitted
.end method
```

The first comment is used to actually document the method; you can think of it as a comment that would actually be included if you were really writing this program.

The second comment indicates that there should be code there, but for the purposes of making the book readable we have chosen to omit it. It is used in the book where actual code would distract from the point of the example. Double semicolon comments have no particular meaning to the Oolong assembler and are ignored just like any other comment.

2.3   Defining the Class

The beginning of an Oolong source file gives information about the class as a whole, including its name, superclass, and interfaces.

The .class directive names the class

```
.class public final foo/Bar
```

The class name is a collection of words separated by forward slashes (/). Everything up to the last slash is called the *package;* everything after it is the class name. Throughout the virtual machine, only the fully qualified name (both the package and class name) is used.

The Java import statement lets you refer to classes just by the class name. However, the JVM doesn't permit this, since it can lead to ambiguities. When a Java compiler turns the Java source into JVM bytecodes, it must figure out the fully qualified name before it builds the class file.

The .class directive may also list some properties of the class. The keywords in Table 2.1 may be used.

TABLE 2.1: .class *directive keywords*

Keyword	Meaning
public	This class may be referenced from anywhere. If it's not given, only other classes with the same package name may refer to it.
final	This class may not be subclassed; that is, no class may use it as a superclass.
super	In the method bodies for this class, the invokespecial instruction has a special meaning when it's used on methods of superclasses. See section 4.5.5 for more information.
interface	This class is used as an interface. It may not be instantiated.
abstract	Programs are not allowed to create instances of this class. This keyword must be given if any of the methods are marked abstract.
strictfp	All methods in this class use strictly conforming floating-point arithmetic. If this keyword is not present, implementations may use extra precision. (Ignored on pre-Java 2 platform JVMs.)

2.4   Superclasses

Another directive in the header is the `.super` directive which is used to indicate the superclass of the class. Every class must have a superclass; if no `.super` directive is given, `java/lang/Object` is assumed. The class `java/lang/Object` is special, because it doesn't have a superclass.

If you have

```
.class Bicycle
.super Vehicle
```

then we say that `Vehicle` is a *superclass* of `Bicycle`, and `Bicycle` is a *subclass* of `Vehicle`.

An instance of class *inherits* all the fields and all the methods of the superclass. The idea is that you can use an instance of a subclass anywhere you can use an instance of the superclass. This behavior is discussed in more detail in section 4.2.2.

2.5   Declaring Fields

To add a field to a class, use the `.field` directive. Every field has a name and a type. The type determines what kinds of values may be stored in that field. For example:

```
.field age I                      ; Name: age Type: int
.field weight F                   ; Name: weight Type: float
.field name Ljava/lang/String;    ; Name: name Type: String
.field friends [LPerson;          ; Name: friends Type: Person array
```

The last part of a `.field` directive is called the *field descriptor*. A descriptor is a written name for a type. Most of the descriptors are single letters, like `I` for `int` and `F` for `float`. Some are less obvious, like `Z` for `boolean` or `J` for `long`. Table 2.2 summarizes the field descriptors. The last entry in the table (`void`) isn't a valid field type. We encounter this type later when we work with methods.

If the value of a field is a reference to an object of type *classname*, then the descriptor is `Lclassname;`. In this case, the semicolon (`;`) is used to mark the end of the descriptor, not to begin a comment. For example,

```
.field out Ljava/io/PrintStream;  ; a PrintStream
.field me LI;                     ; A class named I, not an int
```

TABLE 2.2: *Type descriptors*

Type	Descriptor
array of *type*	[*type*
byte	B
boolean	Z
char	C
double	D
float	F
int	I
long	J
reference to *classname*	L*classname*;
short	S
void	V

In an array descriptor, the number of dimensions is signified by the number of left brackets ([) at the beginning. Following the left brackets is the element type of the array:

```
.field scores [I                        ; Array of ints
.field nicknames [Ljava/lang/String;    ; Array of Strings
.field matrix [[F                        ; Array of array of
                                         ; floats
```

You may have two different fields with the same name but different types:

```
.field grade C       ; Grade on last assignment, as a char
.field grade F       ; Slope of the road, as a float
```

Fields may be protected so that they may be accessed only from code within certain classes. This is done by adding keywords to the .field directive. These keywords are familiar to Java programmers, though unlike Java they may appear in any order.

The general form of the .field directive is

```
.field modifier₁ modifier₂ … name type = value
```

The modifiers are shown in Table 2.3. If none of the public, private, or protected keywords is given, then the field is given *package* access. It may be accessed from any class with the same package name but not from classes with different packages.

TABLE 2.3: *.field directive keywords*

Keyword	Meaning
public	Anyone may access this field.
private	This field may be accessed only by this class.
protected	This field may be accessed within subclasses and anywhere in the package.
static	There is only one instance of this field for the entire class, instead of one in each object.
final	This field's value may not be changed once it has been assigned.
volatile	This field's value should not be cached; it may change unexpectedly.
transient	This field is used only for temporary purposes, and the value should not be saved.

The `protected` keyword is a little misleading. A field that is `protected` is actually a little less protected than one with package access. It may be accessed from any subclass, as well as from any class within the package. Consider the declarations

```
.class public language/Greeting
.field protected introduction Ljava/lang/String;
.end class

.class deadLanguages/OldEnglish
.super language/Greeting
.end class

.class language/Translator
.super java/lang/Object
.end class

.class language/linguistics/Greeting
.super java/lang/Object
.end class
```

The `protected` field `language/Greeting/introduction` may be accessed from any method in `deadLanguages/OldEnglish`, since it has `language/Greeting` as a superclass. It may also be accessed from `language/Translator`, since it's in the same package as `language/Greeting`. However, it may not be accessed from `language/linguistics/Greeting`, since it is in a different package from `language/Greeting`.

The last part of the .field directive, = value, is optional. It can be used only with static fields. If it's present, the value must be a constant of the same type as the field. When the object is created, the field is initialized to that value instead of the default value for the field (0 for the numeric fields, null for reference fields). For example:

```
; A public String field initialized to "Hello"
.field public static introduction Ljava/lang/String; = "Hello"

; An int field with default access initialized to 999
.field static numberOfCheeseburgers I = 999

; A protected PrintStream field initialized to null
.field protected static out Ljava/io/PrintStream;

; This initializer is ignored, because the field isn't static
.field public columbusDiscoversAmerica = 1492
```

The initial value is limited to the numeric types (int, float, long, or double) or a String. Java permits you to initialize fields to objects—

```
public Bicycle my_wheels = new MountainBike();
```

—but in the JVM the initialization has to be a separate step from the declaration. If the field is not static, or if it is static but initialized to some other type of object besides String, then you should put code in the initializing method to initialize the field. See section 4.2 for more about initialization.

Exercise 2.3

Write a class Refrigerator, which stores the current temperature, the number of eggs, the current amount of milk, and a list of leftover pizzas (of class Pizza). ▲

Exercise 2.4

Write a class BinaryTree, that has left and right links that are both binary trees and a data field that stores an Object. ▲

2.6   Declaring Methods

A method declaration is similar to a field declaration. Here is an example of a method declaration that computes the sum of two floats:

```
.method public computeSum (FF)F
.limit locals 3
.limit stack 2
fload_1                        ; Push the first argument
fload_2                        ; Push the second argument
fadd                           ; Add them together
freturn                        ; Return the result
```

The `.method` directive is structurally identical to the `.field` directive. It begins with a list of modifiers, followed by the name and the descriptor. The descriptor is a little different for methods. It's written as

$$(type_1 type_2...) type_{return}$$

where the list of $type_i$ is the types of the arguments and $type_{return}$ is the type of the return. Each of these types is one of the types in Table 2.2 for fields. There aren't any spaces between the arguments. Some examples are shown in Table 2.4.

Methods may have modifiers, just like fields. The available modifiers are different for methods. A summary of the method modifier keywords is given in Table 2.5. The `.method` declaration continues until a `.end method` directive is found. In between `.method` and `.end method` are the instructions that make up the method. There are about 200 different instructions to do different things in the JVM. The instructions are the subject of the next few chapters.

In the `computeSum` example, the `fload_1` and `fload_2` instructions push values from local variables onto the stack. The `fadd` instruction adds the two `float` values on top of the operand stack, replacing them with the sum. The `freturn` returns the top of the stack.

Two special directives apply within method bodies: `.limit stack` and `.limit locals`. These tell the JVM how much space it should allocate for the method when it is executed: `.limit stack` limits the total height of the stack at any point, and `.limit locals` limits the size of the local variable array. Each may be as high as 65,536, but few programs require anywhere near that much space.

TABLE 2.4: *Some method descriptors*

Java method declaration	Descriptor
`void main(String argv[])`	`(Ljava/lang/String;)V`
`int read(byte[] data, int offset, int len)`	`([BII)I`
`String toString()`	`()Ljava/lang/String;`
`void println()`	`()V`

TABLE 2.5: *.method directive keywords*

Keyword	Meaning
public	This method is available to all other classes.
private	This method may be accessed only from within this class.
protected	This method may be accessed from any class in the same package or any class that is a subclass of this class.
static	This method is a class method.
final	This method may not be overridden in subclasses.
synchronized	The JVM will obtain a lock on this object before invoking the method. If this method is static, then the JVM will obtain a lock on the Class object corresponding to this class.
native	This method is implemented in native code; no implementation is provided.
abstract	This method has no implementation.
strictfp	This method uses strict floating-point semantics. If not given, the implementation may use additional precision. (Ignored on pre-Java 2 platform JVMs.)

The number in the directive is the number of slots to reserve. A slot is big enough to hold an int, float, or reference value. It takes two slots to hold a long or double.

If the .limit directives aren't given, the Oolong assembler takes its best guess. The assembler errs on the side of caution rather than efficiency.

These limits aren't just suggestions. The JVM implementation will enforce them. If you try to use more stack space or more local variables than you requested, the virtual machine will refuse to execute the method. It can tell even without executing the code how many variables are used, since all of the instructions that affect the local variable array have the number of the slot incorporated into the instruction as an argument. (That is, the number of slots that are used in each instruction is fixed in the instruction itself, not computed when the program is run.) Thus, if the program contains the instruction

```
lload 7
```

it knows that at least nine variables are used (variables 0 through 7 plus one more, since the lload instruction affects both variables 7 and 8).

Measuring the maximum height of the stack just from looking at the code is a little harder, but it can be done. The enforcement is the job of the verification algorithm. See chapter 6 for more information about the verification algorithm.

You can have multiple methods with the same name as long as they have different descriptors:

```
;; A method to print a float value
.method println(F)V

;; A method to print a String value
.method println(Ljava/lang/String;)V

;; A method to print a long value
.method println(J)V
```

This is called *method overloading*. In Oolong, when a method is called you must specify the entire descriptor, including the return type. This means that you can have two methods that differ only in the return type:

```
.method computeResult ()I     ; Return the result as an int

.method computeResult ()D     ; Return the result as a double
```

However, you won't be able to use the resulting class from Java programs, so the practice is discouraged.

In Java, two methods may not differ only in their return types. If you have two methods with the same name and identical arguments and different returns, it's an error. That's necessary because in Java methods are specified only by name. The Java compiler must infer which overloaded method is intended by looking at the types of the arguments. It isn't possible to infer using the return type, because it isn't always obvious from context. From this code—

```
float f = (float) computeResult();     // Which method?
```

—it is impossible to determine which version of `computeResult` is intended. Rather than creating some arcane rules, the Java designers simply ruled this illegal Java, even though it is legal for the JVM.

Exercise 2.5

The following represent method declarations in Java. What would the corresponding Oolong .method directives be?

```
void printTable(OutputStream out, String entries[][])
protected synchronized Integer addInts(Integer i, Integer j)
static native void shutdown()
```

▲

Exercise 2.6

Modify the example `computeSum` on page 35 to add three arguments instead of two.   ▲

Exercise 2.7

In the `computeSum` example, the method does not take advantage of variable 0, which is used to store the object on which the method was invoked (`this`). The method `computeSum` would be more efficient as a `static` method. Rewrite the method as a `static` method. Remember that the variable numbers must change.   ▲

2.7   Interfaces

An *interface* is a way to specify which methods a class supports without specifying implementations of those methods. Think of an interface as a list of requirements. It doesn't specify how things should be done, but it specifies what must be done. It forms a contract: any class that implements an interface agrees to abide by the terms of the contract.

Interfaces are introduced to the JVM using the same `class` file format used for classes. To create an interface using Oolong, suppose you wish to create an interface `Amiable`, which says that anything which is amiable must be able to smile and be able to shake hands with somebody else who is amiable. The Oolong definition is

```
.interface Amiable
.method public abstract smile ()V
; No implementation; there is no code here
.end method

.method public abstract shakeHands(LAmiable;)V
; No implementation; there is no code here
.end method
```

The methods are all marked with the `abstract` keyword, because no implementations are provided. This is a requirement in the JVM specification.

Interfaces are used with the `.implements` directive. If a class *implements* an interface, then it should provide implementations (that is, non-`abstract` methods) for all the methods in the interface. If any method that is declared in the interface isn't defined in the class, then that class itself must be declared `abstract` to prevent it from being instantiated.

Here is some code that defines a friendly person. A friendly person is a `Person` who implements the `Amiable` interface.

```
.class FriendlyPerson
.super Person
.implements Amiable

; Implementation of the smile method
.method public smile ()V
    ;; Implementation of smile omitted
.end method

.method public shakeHands (LAmiable;)V
    ;; Implementation of shakeHands omitted
.end method
```

Unlike the `.super` directive, there may be more than one `.implements` directive in a class. There can be at most one `.super` directive. If there isn't one, the Oolong assembler assumes that the superclass is `java/lang/Object`.

The reason you have exactly one superclass but any number of interfaces has to do with difficulties with multiple inheritance. Multiple inheritance can be hard, because it's easy for names of methods to conflict between the various superclasses. If you inherit two method definitions from two different superclasses, it becomes hard to tell which method implementation you should use. This isn't a problem with interfaces, because there is only one definition of each method; it doesn't inherit any implementations.

You have to have one superclass because that ensures that everything can be treated identically as an `Object`. For example, the `Vector` class in `java.util` can be used to store any object, because each object has `Object` as a superclass somewhere in its inheritance tree.

Interfaces may also implement other interfaces:

```
.interface Clever
.method public abstract solvePuzzles()V
.end method
.end class

.interface JavaProgrammer
.implements Amiable
.implements Clever
```

```
.method public abstract writeJavaPrograms()V
.end method
.end class
```

A JavaProgrammer is able to do all the methods in Amiable, all the methods in Clever, and the method writeJavaPrograms. This means that a Java programmer must be able to smile, shake hands, and be able to solve puzzles as well as write Jave programs to be considered a real Java programmer by the JVM.

In this case the directive .implements is a little misleading, because an interface doesn't really implement anything. The JavaProgrammer interface doesn't specify how to implement the methods in Amiable; it just specifies that they must be implemented by any class implementing JavaProgrammer. If an interface implements other interfaces, then it inherits the requirement to implement all of the methods in all interfaces.

The .interface directive is equivalent to using the .class directive with the interface keyword. For example,

```
.interface public java/util/Enumerator
```

is equivalent to

```
.class interface abstract public java/util/Enumerator
```

Exercise 2.8

Suppose you have an interface MarathonRunner:

```
.interface MarathonRunner
; Run some number of miles
.method public abstract run(F)V
.end method
```

Write a class that represents a person who is both a MarathonRunner and a JavaProgrammer. ▲

## CHAPTER 3

Writing Methods

WHEN you write a program, you perform two basic tasks: you define your data structures, then define the operations to perform on the data. In the Java virtual machine, the fundamental unit of operation is the *instruction,* which causes the JVM to perform a simple operation such as adding two numbers or retrieving a value from the heap. Each instruction by itself performs only a tiny piece of an overall task.

Instructions are collected into a unit called a *method*. The instructions in a method work together to perform a task such as multiplying matrices or drawing a three-dimensional figure on the screen. Methods may have just a few instructions or several thousand. A method has the ability to repeat parts of its code and skip over other parts. Many methods use other methods to assist in their task.

As we saw in chapter 2, methods are grouped together into classes, which define the data structures and the methods performed on them. A program is a collection of tasks taken together. Each program performs a complex task for the user, such as word processing or scanning through astronomical data looking for new quasars.

This chapter and the next few discuss the process of writing methods. This is partly a matter of learning which operations are provided by the JVM. You will also learn how these instructions fit together to perform useful computational tasks.

We start with basic instructions to manipulate the JVM's data storage areas and to perform arithmetic. We proceed by learning to use JVM objects. Finally, we discuss how JVM methods can control their own flow of execution to perform some tasks repeatedly and others not at all.

3.1   Some Definitions

An Oolong *method body* is a list of instructions. Each instruction is of the form

```
mnemonic argument₁ argument₂ …
```

The *mnemonic* says what you want to do: push a variable, add integers, call a method, and so on.

The *arguments* to an instruction affect the way the instruction works. They answer questions like "Which variable should be pushed?" and "Which method should be called?" The arguments to an instruction are the same each time an instruction is performed. For example, the instruction

```
aload 99    ; Push the local variable 99 onto the stack
```

has a single argument: the number 99. When this instruction is executed, the JVM copies the contents of index 99 of the local variable array onto the stack. The contents of that local variable may be different each time the instruction is executed (which is why it's called a *variable*), but it will always be local variable 99 that is loaded.

The *operands* to an instruction come from the operand stack. Unlike arguments, the operands may be different each time. An example is the instruction

```
iadd        ; Add the two integers on top of the stack
```

This instruction takes the top two items of the stack, which should both be int values. These values are the operands to the iadd instruction. If the two previous instructions push the values 2 and 3 onto the stack, then iadd will pop them both and push 5.

The next time this instruction is encountered, the operands may be different. If the top of the stack is now 3 and 4, then the result of the iadd is 7.

The point here is to define the terms *argument* and *operand,* which will be used quite heavily in the next few chapters. *Argument* always refers to additional information after the mnemonic, which never changes as the program runs. *Operand* refers to the elements on the operand stack; these change as the program runs.

3.2   Types

The JVM supports five basic data types:

- ◆ int (32-bit signed integer)
- ◆ long (64-bit signed integer)
- ◆ float (32-bit floating-point number)
- ◆ double (64-bit double precision floating-point number)
- ◆ reference

These data types are discussed in detail in the next few sections.

3.2.1   Numeric Types

The first four types are identical to the Java basic types of the same name. They are called *numeric types*. A member of this type is interpreted as a number. This number is an integer if it's a `long` or an `int`, or it is an approximation of a real number if it's a `double` or a `float`. The `long` and `double` values have larger ranges but require more memory. The `int` and `float` entries have smaller ranges and require a single entry on the stack or in the local variable array. The `long` and `double` have wider ranges, and these require two entries each.

When doing arithmetic or working with the operand stack and local variables, the Java types `boolean`, `byte`, `short`, and `char` are treated in JVM code as `int`s. The only difference between these types and `int` is the range of acceptable values.

A `boolean` is an `int` that can be only 0 (`false`) or 1 (`true`). A `byte` can range from −128 to 127, and a `short` goes from −32,768 to 32,767. The only unsigned type is `char`, which can be from 0 to 65,535. All these ranges are subsets of the `int` range, which is −2,147,483,648 to 2,147,483,647.

The JVM defines the arithmetic, local variable, stack, and comparison operations only on type `int`. There is no special support for comparing `boolean`s, `byte`s, `short`s, or `char`s. Instead, they are operated on exactly as if they were `int`s.

The JVM provides some special support for these types. There are special types for arrays of `short`s, `char`s, and `byte`s. This allows the JVM implementation to represent groups of these restricted `int`s in a smaller space. For example, to store 1,000 `int`s in an array, almost four kilobytes of memory might be required. An array of 1,000 `byte`s can be stored in less than 1K. The details vary from implementation to implementation of the JVM, depending on the goals of the implementor and the platform supporting the implementation.

The JVM also provides some special support for these types as arguments to methods and in fields. We discuss this in detail in section 2.6.

3.2.2   Object Types

A `reference` is a reference to a Java object of any class. As a Java programmer, you are already familiar with `reference`s. When you declare a field like this—

    Foo x;

—you have really said that you want to create a field that holds a `reference`. Furthermore, you have specified what sort of object it must be: it must be either an instance of `Foo` or one of the subclasses of `Foo`. The exact type of the object cannot be determined until the program is run.

A `reference` takes a single slot on the stack, but it means much more than that. A `reference` points to an object somewhere on the heap. You can make a copy of the `reference` without duplicating the object itself. Unlike a numeric type, an object has properties that are independent of the reference to the object.

A reference to an object is not the same thing as the object itself. When you make a copy of a reference, you are not creating a new object. Instead, you have two references to the same object. This distinction may seem pointless, but it's actually very important. When you have two references to an object, changing the underlying object affects the values you get from both references.

If you are a C programmer, you might think of `reference` types as being somewhat like pointers. This is true in a sense, but JVM `references` are very different from C pointers. For one thing, you can perform arithmetic on C pointers. You can go looking around in memory using pointers. This is not true of JVM `references`; once they point to an object, they always point to the same object. The operations available on `references` look only at the object that the `reference` points to, not at the memory around it.

Also, `references` point only to objects, not to local variables, stack entries, or fields within objects. This makes it easier to ensure that the data within each method is not altered by other methods you call. "Stray pointers," which point to memory that you didn't expect them to point to, are impossible in the JVM.

A `null` is a particular `reference` that refers to no object; you can store it any place you'd use a `reference`. However, if you try to access any of its fields or call any methods on it, an exception will be thrown.

In the JVM, `String`s are objects, so they're represented on the stack as `references` to objects of type `java/lang/String`. The Java language provides special syntax that makes `String`s easier to handle, but they are still objects, not values. From the JVM's point of view, there is no difference between `String`s and other objects.

3.2.3   Type `returnAddress`

There is a sixth type, `returnAddress`, which we tend to ignore in the following discussions. It is relevant only to the `jsr` and `ret` instructions, which are discussed in section 5.5. The use of `returnAddress` is quite restricted, so most of the time you can safely forget about it.

3.3   Mnemonic Naming Conventions

The Oolong mnemonics come from *The Java Virtual Machine Specification*. The *Specification* follows a naming convention for some of its mnemonics: the first

TABLE **3.1**: *Mnemonic type letters*

Letter	Type
a	reference
b	byte or boolean
c	char
d	double
f	float
i	int
l	long
s	short

letter of the mnemonic often tells you what type the mnemonic operates on. For example, `iconst_1` loads an `int` 1 onto the stack, while `lconst_1` loads a `long` 1 onto the stack. The letter `i` indicates an `int`, and the letter `l` indicates a `long`. Table 3.1 summarizes the mnemonic naming conventions.

Do not be misled by the naming convention into believing in mnemonics that do not exist. Each mnemonic corresponds to a number between 0 and 256 in the `class` file. This number is called an *opcode*. Just because there's an opcode for the mnemonic `iand` to compute the bitwise and of two `int`s, it doesn't mean that there's an opcode for the mnemonic `dand` to compute the bitwise and of two `double`s. The complete list of mnemonics can be found in appendix A.

3.4   Testing Code Examples

Code examples appear throughout this chapter. Unfortunately, we haven't really discussed how to do output, so it will be a little tricky to actually try out any of these code examples. Output involves some mucking about with method calls and sometimes with creating new objects and other such complicated things that are better left for a later chapter.

The good news is that you can use Java to assemble a test harness for these code samples. You can wrap the test code up in a small, easy-to-write class, then use Java to perform the input and output. For example, here is some code to answer the question, "What do you get if you multiply 6 by 9?"

```
bipush 6      ; Push 6
bipush 9      ; Push 9
imul          ; Result is 54
```

By itself, this code is not executable, because it's not part of a method. To make it executable, build a class:

```
.class Test                    ; Create a class Test
.method static run()I          ; Add a static method to the class
   ; This is the code example:
   bipush 6                    ; Push 6
   bipush 9                    ; Push 9
   imul                        ; Result is 54

   ireturn                     ; Return the result
.end method
```

The ireturn instruction is added to the end so that it returns the result. This is a complete class with a method you can call. You can run the Oolong assembler on this file, and it will produce the file Test.class containing the class Test. (See appendix B for more about using the Oolong assembler.)

If you want to see if the code sample actually does what the book claims that it does, you can write a Java class to test it:

```
class RunTest
{
    public static void main(String a[])
    {
        System.out.println("The result is: " + Test.run());
    }
}
```

The RunTest class works just like any other Java class; its meaning should be readily apparent. If you run this class through a Java compiler and execute it, the system should print

```
The result is: 54
```

A similar test harness can be assembled for other types besides int. Use freturn for floats, lreturn for longs, and dreturn for doubles. You must also change the return type in the type descriptor for run. Use F for floats, D for doubles, and J for longs. This last is not entirely intuitive—just memorize it.

For example, to rewrite the test to use doubles instead of ints:

```
.class Test
.method static run()D
ldc2_w 6.0D            ; Push the number 6 as a double
ldc2_w 9.0D            ; Push the number 9 as a double
```

```
    dmul              ; Multiply to get 54.0
    dreturn
    .end method
```

Here, the descriptor of the method is run()D instead of run()I, because the return type is a double rather than an int. For the same reason, the last instruction is dreturn instead of ireturn.

3.5   Returns

When a method is finished executing, it must return control to its caller. The caller is often expecting a value from the called method. For this purpose, the JVM has six return instructions, as summarized in Table 3.2. After one of the xreturn statements has been executed, control transfers to the instruction immediately after whatever invoke instruction began the method. The calling method sees this as though the invoke instruction were like any other instruction that had just completed, and it moves on to the next instruction after the invoke. Whatever value was on the stack when the xreturn instruction was executed is now on the top of the stack in the method returned to. (If the instruction was a return instruction, then there is no value.) The arguments to the method are removed.

The value returned by the xreturn statement must agree with the type of the method. If the return type is V for void, then only return can be used. If the return type is I for int, only ireturn can be used. If the return type is a reference, then the areturn opcode must be used, and you must be able to cast the returned value to the type specified in the method descriptor. (See section 4.6 for more about casting.)

TABLE 3.2: *Return instructions*

Mnemonic	Stack	Effect
areturn	*reference*	Control returns to caller with *reference* on the stack.
ireturn	*int*	Control returns to caller with *int* on the stack.
freturn	*float*	Control returns to caller with *float* on the stack.
dreturn	*double*	Control returns to caller with *double* on the stack.
lreturn	*long*	Control returns to caller with *long* on the stack.
return		Control returns to caller.

3.6   Constants

Constants are particular numbers and strings referred to by your program. The JVM supports constants of type int, float, long, double, and String. This section shows how to load constants onto the stack in Oolong.

3.6.1   General Constants

The ldc and ldc2_w instructions (for "load constant") are used to push a constant value onto the stack. These constants are specified in Oolong the same way they are in Java. The ldc instruction is used for int, float, and String constants, and ldc2_w is used with long and double constants.

Here are some examples of loading constants:

```
ldc "Hello, world"        ; Push a String onto the stack
ldc 1.0                   ; Push a float onto the stack
ldc2_w 2.7182818284D      ; Push a double onto the stack
ldc2_w 1234567890L        ; Push a long onto the stack
ldc 2                     ; Push an int onto the stack
```

The values loaded with ldc2_w each take up two entries on the stack; that's what the 2 stands for. The others take up one. If you were to execute all the instructions in this example one after the other, they would take up seven stack slots.

The _w part of ldc2_w stands for "wide." When the Oolong assembler builds the class file, it uses two bytes to form a reference to a long or double value in the constant pool. The constant pool contains the actual long or double value that is loaded onto the stack. The ldc2_w instruction takes up more space in the class file than the ldc instruction, which uses only one byte to form its constant pool reference. The constant pool stores all of the constants used with ldc, as well as other useful things for the class. This is explained in chapter 9.

There is also a ldc_w instruction, which is identical to ldc except that it also uses two bytes instead of one for specifying the index into the constant pool. Oolong converts between ldc and ldc_w as necessary, depending on where the constant value ends up in the constant pool.

3.6.2   Small Constants and null

Some numbers come up a lot. Small numbers are more likely to be mentioned than large numbers; 0 and 1 come up a lot, but 7,349,934 probably isn't mentioned explicitly in any program anywhere.

The JVM is optimized for working with small constants by providing instructions specifically for loading them. This eliminates the need for adding extra entries for the constant pool. Because of this, `ldc` and `ldc2_w` are actually fairly uncommon instructions, though you could use them anywhere you would use the specialized instructions.

For the most common numbers there are the `xconst_n` instructions, where *x* represents the type, and *n* is the value to push. For example,

```
fconst_1        ; Equivalent to ldc 1.0
iconst_m1       ; Equivalent to ldc -1
lconst_0        ; Equivalent to ldc 0L
```

The full set of constant-pushing instructions is found in Table 3.3.

For small integers outside this range you can use `bipush` (for values between −128 and 127) and `sipush` (for values between −32,768 and 32,767). These take the values as an argument, instead of requiring a constant pool entry. In bytecodes,

TABLE 3.3: *Constant-loading instructions*

Mnemonic	Argument	Effect
aconst_null		Push a `reference` to `null` onto the stack.
iconst_m1		Push an `int` −1 onto the stack.
iconst_0		Push an `int` 0 onto the stack.
iconst_1		Push an `int` 1 onto the stack.
iconst_2		Push an `int` 2 onto the stack.
iconst_3		Push an `int` 3 onto the stack.
iconst_4		Push an `int` 4 onto the stack.
iconst_5		Push an `int` 5 onto the stack.
lconst_0		Push a `long` 0 onto the stack.
lconst_1		Push a `long` 1 onto the stack.
fconst_0		Push a `float` 0 onto the stack.
fconst_1		Push a `float` 1 onto the stack.
fconst_2		Push a `float` 2 onto the stack.
dconst_0		Push a `double` 0 onto the stack.
dconst_1		Push a `double` 1 onto the stack.
bipush	*n*	Push *n* onto the stack, $-128 \leq n \leq 127$.
sipush	*n*	Push *n* onto the stack, $-32{,}768 \leq n \leq 32{,}767$.

bipush takes a one-byte argument, and sipush takes a two-byte argument. These instructions all have the effect of pushing the int 5 onto the stack:

```
iconst_5              ; Requires 1 byte
ldc 5                 ; Requires 2 bytes and a constant pool entry
bipush 5              ; Requires 2 bytes
sipush 5              ; Requires 3 bytes
```

In addition to the commonly used numbers, there is one reference value that is used frequently: null. Use the aconst_null instruction to push a null onto the stack.

Exercise 3.1

Replace each of the following instructions with the shortest equivalent:

```
sipush 9
bipush 4
ldc 1.0
ldc -901
ldc 123456
```

▲

Exercise 3.2

How many stack slots are consumed by the instructions in exercise 3.1?   ▲

3.7   Local Variables

Every method has a pool of up to 65,536 local variables. Very few methods use this many; most use fewer than 100. The actual number is given by the .limit locals directive immediately after the .method directive:

```
.method public foo ()V
.limit locals 5               ; No more than 5 locals may be used
```

If you omit the .limit locals directive, the Oolong assembler will guess that it should reserve enough space for the highest-numbered local variable in your method. You can use the .limit locals directive if you think you know better than the Oolong assembler.

Local variables are similar to, but not quite the same as, the local variables in Java programs. Oolong local variables don't have names. Variables are referenced by number, starting at 0. As with stack entries, long and double values take up two consecutive local variables. You refer to it by the lower number. You can have a long in variable 1, in which case you may not use variable 2 because it's already spoken for by the long in 1.

There's no requirement for aligning long and double values. You can have a double value in variables 1 and 2 and another one in 4 and 5.

The instructions that deal with local variables are called *load* and *store* instructions. These load values from the local variable onto the stack and store values from the top of the stack into a local variable. "Load" and "store" are familiar to most programmers as "push" and "pop." They are used like this:

```
aload 0      ; Push the reference in local 0 onto the stack

iload 5      ; Push the int in local 5

lstore 3     ; Store the long on top of the stack
             ; into locals 3 and 4
```

For efficiency reasons, there are special instructions to load and store local variables 0, 1, 2, and 3. You might imagine that local variable 0 is used much more frequently than local variable 245. For example,

```
fload_3
```

has exactly the same effect as

```
fload 3
```

except that the former requires slightly less space in the resulting class file. Depending on the JVM implementation you use, it might even be a little more efficient.

Unlike Java, variables are dynamically typed, not statically typed. You can store any of the five stack types (int, float, double, long, reference) in any variable. This means that you can use slot 3 to store an int early in the method, then use it again later to store a float or half a double. The verification algorithm even approves of this behavior.

A local variable can hold values of different types at different times. The following example stores a String, an int, and a double in the same local variable, one after the other:

```
ldc "A String"      ; Put a string onto the stack
astore_0            ; Store a string into variable 0
sipush 12345        ; Put an int onto the stack
istore_0            ; Store an int into the same variable
ldc 2.718281828D    ; Put a double on the stack
dstore_0            ; Store the double into variables 0 and 1
```

When you load from a local variable, you must use the load instruction that corresponds to the type of the value that is stored in the field. This code is illegal:

```
iconst_3                ; Load the constant 3 onto the stack
istore_2                ; Store it in variable 2
aload_2                 ; FOUL! Must use an iload instead
```

Also, you must use a `store` instruction appropriate to the value on top of the stack.

```
ldc "Hello"             ; Push a reference onto the stack
fstore 3                ; FOUL! You must use an astore instead
```

The JVM verification algorithm checks for illegal operations before the code is permitted to run. It errs on the side of caution: if it can't prove that the right instruction is used in every case, it rejects the class. The verification algorithm is discussed in detail in chapter 6.

Another thing to know about local variables is that `double` and `long` values take up two local variables, not one. For example,

```
ldc "Hello, world"   ; Push a String
astore_2             ; Store it in variable 2
ldc 3.14159D         ; Push a double-precision value
dstore_1             ; Store it in both variables 1 and 2
```

The former contents of variable 2 are wiped out, so if you now try

```
aload_2                 ; FOUL!
```

the JVM will find that variable 2 no longer holds a reference and the verification algorithm will reject the program.

Tables 3.4 and 3.5 summarize the `load` and `store` instructions.

3.7.1   Initializing Variables

All variables must be explicitly initialized before they are used. JVM fields are initialized to default values (0 for numeric types, `null` for reference types). Local variables are not initialized. Programs must store into a local variable before reading from it. Otherwise, the program will be rejected by the verification algorithm.

Initialization means that you have to do a store before you do any loading. To initialize variable 7 to an `int` 3, use these instructions:

```
.method static public someMethod()V
; All variables are currently uninitialized
iconst_3
```

TABLE 3.4: *Load instructions*

Mnemonic	Argument	Effect
iload	*n*	Push the int in local variable *n* onto the stack.
lload	*n*	Push the long in local variables *n* and *n* + 1 onto the stack.
fload	*n*	Push the float in local variable *n* onto the stack.
dload	*n*	Push the double in local variables *n* and *n* + 1 onto the stack.
aload	*n*	Push the reference in local variable *n* onto the stack.
iload_0		Push the int in local variable 0 onto the stack.
iload_1		Push the int in local variable 1 onto the stack.
iload_2		Push the int in local variable 2 onto the stack.
iload_3		Push the int in local variable 3 onto the stack.
lload_0		Push the long in local variables 0 and 1 onto the stack.
lload_1		Push the long in local variables 1 and 2 onto the stack.
lload_2		Push the long in local variables 2 and 3 onto the stack.
lload_3		Push the long in local variables 3 and 4 onto the stack.
fload_0		Push the float in local variable 0 onto the stack.
fload_1		Push the float in local variable 1 onto the stack.
fload_2		Push the float in local variable 2 onto the stack.
fload_3		Push the float in local variable 3 onto the stack.
dload_0		Push the double in local variables 0 and 1 onto the stack.
dload_1		Push the double in local variables 1 and 2 onto the stack.
dload_2		Push the double in local variables 2 and 3 onto the stack.
dload_3		Push the double in local variables 3 and 4 onto the stack.
aload_0		Push the reference in local variable 0 onto the stack.
aload_1		Push the reference in local variable 1 onto the stack.
aload_2		Push the reference in local variable 2 onto the stack.
aload_3		Push the reference in local variable 3 onto the stack.

```
    istore 7                    ; Variable 7 is now initialized to 3
    ;; The rest of the method
    .end method
```

This code is illegal:

```
    .method static public someIllegalMethod()V
    iload_0                     ; FOUL! Variable 0 is uninitialized
    ;; The rest of the method doesn't matter
    .end method
```

TABLE 3.5: *Store instructions*

Mnemonic	Argument	Effect
istore	*n*	Store an int in local variable *n*.
lstore	*n*	Store a long in local variables *n* and *n* + 1.
fstore	*n*	Store a float in local variable *n*.
dstore	*n*	Store a double in local variables *n* and *n* + 1.
astore	*n*	Store a reference in local variable *n*.
istore_0		Store an int in local variable 0.
istore_1		Store an int in local variable 1.
istore_2		Store an int in local variable 2.
istore_3		Store an int in local variable 3.
lstore_0		Store a long in local variables 0 and 1.
lstore_1		Store a long in local variables 1 and 2.
lstore_2		Store a long in local variables 2 and 3.
lstore_3		Store a long in local variables 3 and 4.
fstore_0		Store a float in local variable 0.
fstore_1		Store a float in local variable 1.
fstore_2		Store a float in local variable 2.
fstore_3		Store a float in local variable 3.
dstore_0		Store a double in local variables 0 and 1.
dstore_1		Store a double in local variables 1 and 2.
dstore_2		Store a double in local variables 2 and 3.
dstore_3		Store a double in local variables 3 and 4.
astore_0		Store a reference in local variable 0.
astore_1		Store a reference in local variable 1.
astore_2		Store a reference in local variable 2.
astore_3		Store a reference in local variable 3.

The JVM verification algorithm is capable of detecting whether or not all variables are initialized before allowing your code to run. If your code is running, you can be sure that there are no variables used before initialization. This feat is actually rather remarkable, since in general it's impossible to predict how a program will run just from looking at it. Read chapter 6 to find out how its done.

3.7.2   Local Variables as Method Arguments

Some local variables are initialized for you automatically by the JVM. These local variables are used as method arguments. For example, consider this method:

```
.class DemoClass
.method static lotsOfArguments(IJF[[Ljava/lang/String;)D
```

This corresponds to the Java method declaration

```
static double lotsOfArguments
    (int a, long b, float c, String[][] d)
```

Local variable 0 is assigned to the first argument, local variable 1 to the second, and so on. In this case, five local variable slots are required, corresponding to the Java variables a, b, c, and d. Five slots are required for four variables because variable b requires two slots because it is a long.

If you call the method like this (from Java),

```
DemoClass.lotsOfArguments(9, 1066L, 99.44, new String[5][10])
```

then variable 0 contains the int 9, variables 1 and 2 have the long 1066, variable 3 has the float 99.44, and variable 4 contains a reference to an array of Strings. If the method is not static, there is an additional argument. That argument is variable 0, and it corresponds to this in Java. For example,

```
.class MyClass
.method doSomeMath(IFF)F
```

Four local variable slots are initialized in this method. Local variable 1 is an int, and variables 2 and 3 are floats. Variable 0 is a reference to an instance of the class MyClass, and it's guaranteed not to be null. Suppose you invoke the method like this (from Java):

```
MyClass obj = new MyClass();
float return = obj.doSomeMath(100, 14.0, 3.14);
```

In the body of the method, variable 0 will be a reference to obj. Variable 1 will be 100, 2 will be 14.0, and 3 will be 3.14. Any other variables will be uninitialized.

The return of the method is *not* allocated a particular variable. Even though the method returns a float, there is no variable corresponding to that float. Unlike the arguments, the return value is not assigned a slot. Instead, the returned value comes from the operand stack.

3.8   Math

Numerical operations fall into two categories:

- ◆ Arithmetic operations: addition, subtraction, multiplication, quotient, and remainder
- ◆ Bitwise operations: shifts and boolean operations (OR, XOR, NOT, AND, etc.)

3.8.1   Arithmetic Operations

Arithmetic operations are the four operations you learned in elementary school: addition, subtraction, multiplication, and division. Actually, division is really two different operations: quotient and remainder. There is also an additional operation, negation, which is really just multiplication by –1. This is provided because most computers have hardware that can perform negation more quickly than going through the steps of multiplication. Each of these six operations is defined on each of the four basic numerical types: `int`, `long`, `float`, and `double`. That's a total of 24 operations, summarized in Table 3.6.

Each of these instructions takes no arguments. The operands are found on the stack. All of them except the negation take two operands; negation takes only one. The operands are popped off the stack and the result is pushed on in their place. When order matters, as in subtraction, the top of the operand stack is subtracted from the next element; division is similar. For example, to calculate –(100000 – 99*(22222/3+7)):

```
                          ; Stack:
    ldc 1000000           ; 100000
    bipush 99             ; 100000      99
    sipush 22222          ; 100000      99      22222
    iconst_3              ; 100000      99      22222     3
    idiv                  ; 100000      99      7407
    bipush 7              ; 100000      99      7407      7
    iadd                  ; 100000      99      7414
    imul                  ; 100000      733986
    isub                  ; -633986
    ineg                  ; 633986
```

Notice that the type of the result is always the same as the type of the operands. If you want to subtract a `float` from a `long` or another such unnatural act, you will

TABLE 3.6: *Arithmetic operations*

Mnemonic	Stack	Result
iadd	int i1, int i2	i1+i2
ladd	long l1, long l2	l1+l2
fadd	float f1, float f2	f1+f2
dadd	double d1, double d2	d1+d2
isub	int i1, int i2	i1−i2
lsub	long l1, long l2	l1−l2
fsub	float f1, float f2	f1−f2
dsub	double d1, double d2	d1−d2
imul	int i1, int i2	i1×i2
lmul	long l1, long l2	l1×l2
fmul	float f1, float f2	f1×f2
dmul	double d1, double d2	d1×d2
idiv	int i1, int i2	i1÷i2
ldiv	long l1, long l2	l1÷l2
fdiv	float f1, float f2	f1÷f2
ddiv	double d1, double d2	d1÷d2
irem	int i1, int i2	remainder of i1÷i2
lrem	long l1, long l2	remainder of l1÷l2
frem	float f1, float f2	remainder of f1÷f2
drem	double d1, double d2	remainder of d1÷d2
ineg	int i1	−i1
lneg	long l1	−l1
fneg	float f1	−f1
dneg	double d1	−d1

In the Stack column, the bottom of the stack is to the left.

need to convert one or the other so that both are the same type. The operations to do this are discussed in section 3.9.

Exercise 3.3

Write Oolong code to calculate ax^2+bx+c, where a, b, c, and x are int arguments to the method. Try it out with a=1, b=−2, c=−35, and x=7. What is the maximum stack height?   ▲

Exercise 3.4

Rewrite your answer to exercise 3.3 to use `doubles` instead of `ints`. How does the maximum stack height change?   ▲

Exercise 3.5

Rewrite your answer to exercise 3.3 using the formula `((ax+b)x)+c`. Compare your answers. Is there a reason to do it this way?   ▲

3.8.2   Nonnumbers and Infinity

The JVM `double` and `float` values can take on three values that aren't numbers in the usual sense: NaN (Not a Number), $+\infty$, and $-\infty$ (positive and negative infinity). Infinity is the result of dividing by zero. NaN is the result of dividing zero by zero or dividing infinity by infinity. Some examples:

```
fconst_0
fconst_0
fdiv                    ; Yields NaN
ldc 3.14159             ; Push Pi
fadd                    ; Yields NaN

ldc 2.71828             ; Push e
fconst_0                ; Push zero
fdiv                    ; Yields infinity
ldc 42.0                ; Push some other number
fadd                    ; infinity + anything = infinity
dup                     ; Put two infinities on the stack
sub                     ; infinity - infinity = NaN
```

The standard Java libraries keep NaN, positive infinity, and negative infinity values in `Float.NaN`, `Float.POSITIVE_INFINITY` and `Float.NEGATIVE_INFINITY`. The `double` equivalents are found in the class `Double`.

3.8.3   Bitwise Operations

You can think of `ints` and `longs` as strings of bits (32 bits for an `int`, and 64 for a `long`.) Sometimes you want to work directly with the bits. For example, if you have 50 `booleans` to keep track of, you can use the bits of a `long` to represent

TABLE 3.7: *Bitwise instructions*

Mnemonic	Stack	Result
ishl	int i1, int s	i1 << s
lshl	long l1, int s	l1 << s
ishr	int i1, int s	i1 >> s
lshr	long l1, int s	l1 >> s
iushr	int i1, int s	i1 >>> s
lushr	long l1, int s	l1 >>> s
iand	int i1, int i2	i1 & i2
land	long l1, long l2	l1 & l2
ior	int i1, int i2	i1 | i2
lor	long l1, long l2	l1 | l2
ixor	int i1, int i2	i1 ^ i2
lxor	long l1, long l2	l1 ^ l2

them with a single unit. This may be more efficient than keeping around 50 separate boolean values in an array.

Bitwise operations are used for performing boolean operations on the bits of ints and longs. They don't apply to floats or doubles, for which the internal representation is more complicated. There are six basic operations: and, or, xor, shift left, shift right, and arithmetic shift. The twelve bitwise instructions are summarized in Table 3.7. Most programmers are already familiar with bitwise operations, so we won't go into them in too much depth here. The only one that may require a bit of explanation is the arithmetic right shift.

The bits of a number are like the digits of your odometer. If 000001 is 1 and 000000 is 0, then 999999 can be treated like −1, 999998 as −2. Every number from 500000 to 999999 is treated as though you subtracted 1,000,000 from it. Every number from 000000 to 499999 is treated as itself. Using just zeroes and ones, −1 and −2 are represented in an int as

```
1111 1111 1111 1111 1111 1111 1111 1111
1111 1111 1111 1111 1111 1111 1111 1110
```

That's 32 ones for −1, and 31 ones followed by a zero for −2. If the leftmost bit is 1, then the number is interpreted as negative. (Numbers are grouped into sets of four for easier reading.)

Suppose you want to shift this number to the right one step. What do you put in the leftmost place? Should it be 0, 1, or something else? The JVM answers this question two different ways. The standard right shift, ishr, repeats the leftmost bit. This preserves the sign of the number. So –1 >> 1 and –2 >> 1 are, respectively,

```
1111 1111 1111 1111 1111 1111 1111 1111
1111 1111 1111 1111 1111 1111 1111 1111
```

That's –1 in both cases. The standard right shift by 1 is just like division by 2, rounding down. To shift by 2 is like dividing by 4; shifting by 3 is like dividing by 8. You get the idea.

The unsigned shift, iushr, always puts a 0 in the leftmost place instead of copying the leftmost bit. For example, –2 >> 1 is:

```
0111 1111 1111 1111 1111 1111 1111 1111
```

or 2,147,483,647. This is the largest positive number you can get in the JVM with ints.

A common use for iushr is to cycle through the bits of a number. You look at the rightmost bit, then do an unsigned shift to make the next-to-rightmost number the new rightmost number. Meanwhile, zeroes are shifted in at the left. When all the bits are 0, you're done.

Here's an example of some bit twiddling on ints. Bit twiddling on long values is similar, but there are twice as many bits involved.

```
                          ; Stack
iconst_m1                 ; 0xFFFFFFFF
ldc 0x12345678            ; 0xFFFFFFFF 0x12345678
ldc 0x87654321            ; 0xFFFFFFFF 0x12345678    0x87654321
iand                      ; 0xFFFFFFFF 0x02244220
ldc 0xFFFFCCCC            ; 0xFFFFFFFF 0x02244220    0xFFFFCCCC
ior                       ; 0XFFFFFFFF 0xFFFFCEEC
ixor                      ; 0x00003113
bipush 16                 ; 0x00003113 16
ishl                      ; 0x31130000
iconst_2                  ; 0x31130000 2
ishl                      ; 0xC44C0000
iconst_2                  ; 0xC44C0000 4
ishr                      ; 0xF1130000
```

Exercise 3.6

Write a method that computes the number of 1 bits in the binary representation of int. For example, the result should be 1 for 1, 2, 4, 8, 16, . . . It should be 2 for 3,

5, 9, 17, . . . For the number 99, the result should be 4. Hint: This can be done without a loop by repeating the same code 32 times. ▲

Exercise 3.7

There's another kind of shift called a *barrel shift*. When you barrel shift to the right, you take the rightmost bit and move it all the way to the left. For example, the barrel shift right of

```
0000 0001 0010 0011 0100 0101 0110 0111
```

is

```
1000 0000 1001 0001 1010 0010 1011 0011
```

Barrel shift is not explicitly supported by the JVM. Implement a method that does a barrel shift right by 1. Implement another method that does a barrel shift left by 1. ▲

Exercise 3.8

Bitwise operations are often used to represent sets. Build a collection of methods that uses an `int` as a set. Implement the following operations:

```
boolean test(int set, int x)          // Return 1 if bit x is set
int set(int set, int x, boolean v)  // Set the x-th bit to v
```
▲

3.8.4 Floating-Point Arithmetic and `strictfp`

The biggest change for the Java 2 platform to the JVM itself is the introduction of the `strictfp` bit in methods and classes. Certain computer architectures use wider floating-point representations than the original JVM specification calls for. Technically, using them would be in error: the additional bits of precision mean that floating-point arithmetic would be slightly different on different JVM implementations. In practice, however, the differences are rarely noticeable, and the performance boost of using native floating-point instructions is far more important than extremely accurate reproducibility of results. The compromise introduced in the Java 2 platform is to introduce the `strictfp` keyword.

When a method is marked `strictfp`, all floating-point operations within it are done exactly as the original JVM specification required. If `strictfp` is not present, the JVM may use its discretion for implementing floating-point arithmetic. You may also mark the class `strictfp`, which is equivalent to marking each method. Strictness applies to both `float` and `double` computations; `int` and `long` operations are not affected.

You may *not* use strictfp to get extra floating-point precision. At various points, the JVM implementation is still required to round numbers off to the standard precision. The rules for when this happens are somewhat arcane and of interest mostly to JVM implementers. As a JVM programmer, these rules mean that you must not assume any more bits of precision than are guaranteed by the JVM specification.

Programs produced with compilers prior to the Java 2 platform do not have the strictfp bit set. All pre-Java 2 implementations always do strict arithmetic. However, a program compiled with a Java 1.0 or Java 1.1 compiler may not yield precisely the same results on a Java 2 platform JVM.

Some applications require that you get the same results every time you run the program. For example, scientific experiments are often sensitive to small differences between strict and nonstrict floating-point arithmetic. If you require the same results no matter what JVM you run on, you should use the strictfp keyword and you should not use any methods that are not marked strictfp. In particular, the java.lang.Math libraries are not written with strictfp, so you should be very careful.

Using strictfp may slow a program down somewhat, since the JVM implementation may have to emulate strict floating-point arithmetic, which is slower than using the native floating-point instructions. By defaulting to nonstrict arithmetic, the JVM favors performance over exactness, but the strictfp keyword allows you to regain exactness.

3.9   Type Conversions

Since most of the arithmetic operations require two arguments of the same type, you will sometimes have to convert numbers of one kind into numbers of another. In Java, a conversion is written with syntax identical to a cast. For example,

```
String o = (String) x;      // This is a cast
int i = (int) 7.9;          // This is a conversion
```

Casts and conversions are actually very different operations. Casting alters the way you are allowed to treat an object without altering the object itself. Conversions have a real effect on the value on the top of the stack. Some conversions may lose information (for example, there's no int that is exactly equivalent to the float 2.71828), but the JVM does its best. See section 4.6 for more about casting.

The internal representation of the float 2 is different from that of the int 2. Although floats have a larger range and can store numbers with a nonintegral component, with large integer values they have to approximate. Take this Java program:

```
int i = 2147483647;
float f = i;
int i2 = (int) f;

System.out.println("i = " + i);
System.out.println("f = " + f);
System.out.println("i2 = " + i2);
```

The result is

```
i = 2147483647
f = 2.14748365E9
i2 = -2147483648
```

By taking i and converting it to a float, a little information was lost; the difference is about one part in a billion. When you convert back, that difference is enough to cause the value to tick over into negative territory, with the leftmost bit set. This is an extreme case, but it gives you the idea that converting between ints and floats is more than just a matter of what you call the number.

Conversions can affect the height of the stack. The f2d instruction converts a float to a double, which increases the stack height by 1. Converting it back reduces the stack size by 1.

You can convert any numerical type to any other numerical type with a single instruction that converts the top of the stack into some other element. The naming convention for these instructions is *x2y*, where *x* is the mnemonic for the type you're converting from and *y* is the type you're converting to. Table 3.8 summarizes these conversions.

3.9.1 Conversion Example

Following is an example of conversions:

```
ldc 1234567890123456789L  ; Push a very long number
l2d                       ; As a double: 1.23456789012345677e+18
d2l                       ; Back to long: 1234567890123456768
                          ; Some bits were lost on the right
l2i                       ; As an int: 2112454912
                          ; Lots of bits were lost on the left
i2f                       ; As a float: 2.11245e+9
f2l                       ; Back to long: 2112454912
```

TABLE 3.8: *Numeric conversions*

Mnemonic	Stack	Result
i2b	int	int; see section 3.9.2
i2c	int	int; see section 3.9.2
i2s	int	int; see section 3.9.2
i2d	int	double
i2l	int	long
i2f	int	float
f2d	float	double
f2l	float	long
f2i	float	int
l2d	long	double
l2f	long	float
l2i	long	int
d2l	double	long
d2f	double	float
d2i	double	int

3.9.2   Widening and Narrowing

Conversion from a number with a smaller range of magnitude (like int to long or long to float) is called *widening*. Conversely, conversion where there is the possibility of losing information about the magnitude of the number (like long to int or double to long) is called *narrowing.*

Narrowing operations may lose information about how big the number is. For example, converting the float 3.4028235e38 to long yields –9223372036854775808, a very different number. However, narrowing is not necessarily accompanied by the loss of information. For example, there is an exact representation of the double 1.0 in int: the int 1. Nor is widening necessarily without information loss. For example, converting the int 2147483647 to float produces 2.14748365e9, or 2,147,483,650. The difference is usually small, but it may be significant.

The goal of widening conversions is to produce no change in the magnitude of the number while preserving as much of the precision as possible. With narrowing conversions, some information may be lost, but the nearest representation is found whenever possible.

3.10 Stack Manipulations

The instructions pop and pop2 remove the top slot of the stack. The pop instruction removes a single slot value (int, float, or reference) from the stack. The pop2 instruction removes two slots from the stack, which can be either a double-slot value (long or double) or two one-slot values.

The pop instructions are most often used to pop off the results of method calls where you were more interested in the side effect of a method call than in what the method returns:

```
aload_0             ; Push a FileInputStream
ldc2_w          ; Skip up to 128 bytes, leaving the actual
                    ; number skipped on the stack
invokevirtual java/io/FileInputStream/skip (L)L
pop2                ; But I don't care about the result
```

The swap instruction swaps the top two slots on the stack, independent of their types:

```
                    ; The stack:
ldc "A String"   ; "A String"
iconst_3         ; "A String"      3
swap             ; 3               "A String"
```

The swap instruction can be used only on ints, floats, and references. If either of the top two entries is a double or a long, this operation is meaningless (since it will try to break up a two-slot type), and the verification algorithm will reject the program.

Another set of stack-manipulating instructions is the dup instructions. The most basic of these, dup, just duplicates the value on top of the stack:

```
                    ; The stack:
ldc 2.71728      ; 2.71828
dup              ; 2.71828 2.71828
```

More complicated is dup_x1, which creates a duplicate of the word on top of the stack and places the duplicate on the stack below the top two slots:

```
ldc "O"          ; "O"
ldc "S"          ; "O"      "S"
dup_x1           ; "S"      "O"        "S"
```

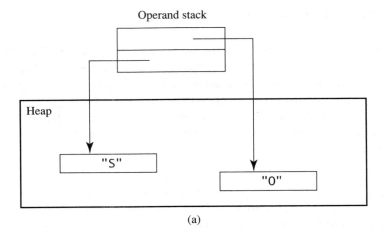

(a)

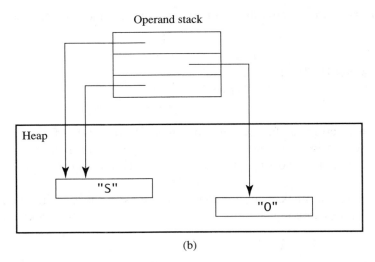

(b)

FIGURE 3.1: *(a) Before dup_x1 (b) After dup_x1*

When a `reference` is duplicated, you get two references to the same object, not two different objects. At the end of this sequence, the operand stack and heap look like Figure 3.1. There's also `dup_x2`, which puts the copy below the top three slots:

```
                    ; The stack:
ldc 3.14159         ; 3.14159
bipush 2            ; 3.14159    2
```

```
dup_x1          ; 2      3.14159    2
aconst_null     ; 2      3.14159    2         null
dup_x2          ; 2      null       3.14159  2   null
```

These instructions can work interchangeably on floats, ints, and references. To duplicate two-slot values (long and double), there are the dup2, dup2_x1, and dup2_x2 instructions. These work just like the corresponding dup instructions, but they duplicate the top two slots of the stack instead of the top one:

```
                          ; The stack:
ldc "Pi"                  ; "Pi"
ldc2_w 3.1415926368979    ; "Pi"             3.1415926368979
dup2_x1                   ; 3.1415926368979 "Pi" 3.1415926368979
```

Table 3.9 summarizes these instructions. (The top of the stack is towards the right.)

Recall that long and double values take up two positions on the stack. You are not allowed to use the pop and pop2 instructions to try to split up a long or double value. For example, it is illegal to use a pop instruction when a double-slot value is on top of the stack:

```
ldc 2345789L      ; Push a long value
pop               ; ILLEGAL! Attempt to remove
                  ; half of the value
```

Similarly, it is illegal to use pop2 like this:

```
lconst_1      ; Push a long value
bipush 6      ; Push an int
pop2          ; ILLEGAL!
```

TABLE 3.9: *Pop instructions*

Mnemonic	Stack	Result
pop	*word*	empty
pop2	*word$_1$ word$_2$*	empty
swap	*word$_1$ word$_2$*	*word$_2$ word$_1$*
dup	*word$_1$*	*word$_1$ word$_1$*
dup_x1	*word$_1$ word$_2$*	*word$_2$ word$_1$ word$_2$*
dup_x2	*word$_1$ word$_2$ word$_3$*	*word$_3$ word$_1$ word$_2$ word$_3$*
dup2	*word$_1$ word$_2$*	*word$_1$ word$_2$ word$_1$ word$_2$*
dup2_x1	*word$_1$ word$_2$ word$_3$*	*word$_2$ word$_3$ word$_1$ word$_2$ word$_3$*
dup2_x2	*word$_1$ word$_2$ word$_3$ word$_4$*	*word$_3$ word$_4$ word$_1$ word$_2$ word$_3$ word$_4$*

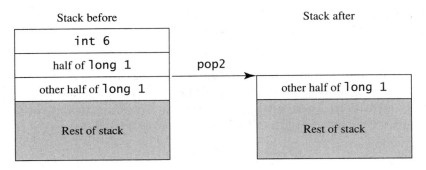

FIGURE 3.2: *Illegal pop2 instruction*

This illegality is illustrated in Figure 3.2. Before the pop2, the top two slots are the int 6 and half of the long 1. Removing them would leave half the long on the stack, an invalid state.

It is your responsibility to make sure you use the right kind of instruction in the right place. If you use the wrong kind of pop instruction, the JVM will detect it during verification and refuse to load the class.

Exercise 3.9

What should the .limit stack directive be for this code fragment? What about the .limit locals? How high is the stack at the end?

```
aload_3
iload 9
swap
dup
astore_2
sipush 99
bipush 101
imul
imul
```

▲

3.11   Arrays of Numbers

To create an array of a numeric type, the newarray instruction is used. Its argument is the Java type of the array you want (boolean, float, int, char, double, long, byte, or short). The length of the array is found on the stack. For example, to create an array of 99 booleans,

```
bipush 99
newarray boolean      ; Allocate an array of 99 booleans
astore_0              ; Store it in local variable 0
```

The result of a newarray instruction is a reference. We'll talk a lot more about how to work with references in chapter 4. For the moment, suffice it to say that you use aload and astore instructions to move them between the stack and the local variable array, just as you use iload and istore for ints. You can't use arithmetical operations on them, but you can swap them around and pop them off the stack as if they were ints or floats.

Unlike other parts of the virtual machine, the newarray instruction does distinguish between char, short, byte, boolean, and int types. This permits the JVM implementation to use a more efficient internal representation of the array.

Since boolean arrays are different from int arrays, special instructions are necessary to get information into and out of these arrays. These instructions are written as xaload, where x is the mnemonic for the type of the array (as shown in Table 3.1).

```
aload_0               ; Push the reference to the
                      ; array onto the stack
bipush 7
baload                ; Push the array[7] onto the stack
```

To set an array element in an array of ints, use the iastore instruction. First you push the array reference itself onto the stack, followed by an int that represents which element of the array you wish to set. Then push the value you wish to assign. The iastore instruction stores the value in the top slot to the array element. For example, to set array[7] to 0,

```
aload_0      ; Push the array reference
bipush 7     ; Push the array index
iconst_0     ; Push the value we wish to set
baload       ; Set array[7] to 0
```

Similarly, use fastore to set elements of float arrays, bastore for arrays of byte or boolean, aastore for arrays of references, etc. Table 3.10 summarizes the array operations.

To take best advantage of arrays, we must discuss control constructs. These allow you to repeat the same section of code for each element of an array, instead of having to write specific code for each element. Control constructs are important, so all of chapter 5 is devoted to them.

TABLE 3.10: *Array instructions*

Mnemonic	Arguments	Stack	Result
newarray	*type*	*n*	An array of *type* of length *n*
anewarray	*class*	*n*	An array of *class* of length *n*
multianewarray	*type dim*	$n_1 \ldots n_{dim}$	An array of *type* with dimensions $n_1 \times \ldots \times n_{dim}$
aaload		array of reference, *n*	Element *n* of the array
aastore		array of reference, *n*, *reference*	Stores *reference* into element *n* of the array
baload		array of byte or boolean, *n*	Element *n* of the array
bastore		array of byte or boolean, *n*, *int*	Stores *int* into element *n* of the array
caload		array of char, *n*	Element *n* of the array
castore		array of char, *n*, *int*	Stores *int-value* into element *n* of the array
daload		array of double, *n*	Element *n* of the array
dastore		array of double, *n*, *double*	Stores *double* into element *n* of the array
faload		array of float, *n*	Element *n* of the array
fastore		array of float, *n*, *float*	Stores *float* into element *n* of the array
iaload		array of int, *n*	Element *n* of the array
iastore		array of int, *n*, *int*	Stores *int* into element *n* of the array
laload		array of long, *n*	Element *n* of the array
lastore		array of long, *n*, *long*	Stores *long* into element *n* of the array
saload		array of short, *n*	Element *n* of the array
sastore		array of short, *n*, *int*	Stores *int* into element *n* of the array

3.12   Just Biding Your Time

If you've got time to kill, there's always the nop instruction. It takes no arguments, and it doesn't do anything at all:

```
nop                  ; Do nothing
```

It is useful as a spacefiller during the code-generation process when writing byte-codes directly rather than using Oolong. Because the operation doesn't do any-thing, you can reserve space in the `class` file you are building with a number of nops. Later, you can go back and replace the nops with operations that actually do something. If you don't replace them, then the correctness of your program is not affected, because the nops do nothing.

Of course, this works only when you are assembling `class` files. Once the class has been loaded into memory, it cannot be changed.

## CHAPTER 4

Classes and Objects

JAVA is an object-oriented programming language. To execute a Java program on the Java virtual machine, the JVM provides support for a number of basic object-oriented programming constructs. In this chapter we will explore that part of the JVM instruction set that facilitates an object-oriented programming style.

4.1   What Is an Object?

An object is an entity with four properties:

- ◆ It has an identity. An object is not the same object as any other object.
- ◆ It has a class. Each object is a member of exactly one class.
- ◆ It may have fields. A field is a slot for storing values. All objects of the same class have the same fields. When you alter the fields of an object, it does not affect any other object.
- ◆ It may have methods invoked on it. All objects of the same class have the same set of methods to invoke on them.

You can think of a class as a template for objects. When an object is created using the class as a template, we say that the object is an *instance* of the class. The object has a slot to store the value of each nonstatic field in the class. (Static fields and methods are independent of objects; they are discussed in section 4.10.) Each instance of a class shares the same fields, though the fields may hold different values. If you know the class of an object, then you can be sure that the object has all of the fields in that class.

The class also defines what methods may be invoked on the object. When one of these methods is invoked, the class of the object determines exactly which set of code is executed. There are actually four different kinds of invocation in the JVM, each with different rules about how to select which code is executed when a method is called.

The class definition determines how fields and methods may be accessed. This protection allows the programmer to limit the amount of code that has access to these objects, making programs easier to understand and debug, as well as offering a foundation on which secure systems can be built.

In addition to the four properties described here, each object has a fifth property called a *monitor*. The monitor is like a lock on the object: only one thread may have possession of the monitor at a time. Monitors are discussed in section 16.3.

4.1.1   Objects and References

Objects are represented by `references`. Think of a `reference` as a rope attached to the object. It's not the object itself, but you can use it to get to the object. Each `reference` takes up one slot on the stack or local variable array, just like an `int` or `float`.

When drawing pictures of the JVM memory space, we use numbers to represent values of the numeric types. To represent references, we use an arrow pointing into the *heap*. The heap is where objects are stored. For example, let's say that there is an object of type `Wallaby` (a kind of smallish kangaroo) in variable 0, the `int` 7 in variable 1, and the `float 2.99792458e8` in variable 2. The JVM memory looks like Figure 4.1. Variable 0 contains a reference to our object, represented by the arrow into the space labeled "Heap." This object has the class `Wallaby`. The object points back to the definition of `Wallaby` in the space labeled "Class definitions." The class definition says that any `Wallaby` must have two fields: an age and a color. It also has any fields `Wallaby` inherits from its superclass `Marsupial`. Because a `Marsupial` has a name, the `Wallaby` must also have a name.

In keeping with the definition of `Wallaby`, the object has three fields: `name`, `age`, and `color`. The `age` is one of the numeric types, so it shows the numerical value 17. The other two fields are object types. They contain `references` to other objects in the heap.

The `name` field of the `Wallaby` contains a `reference` to an object that is a `java/lang/String`, which has been abbreviated as `String`. A `String` is an object just like any other. The fields of a `String` are private, so you can't really see them. To avoid making the diagram even more cluttered, we have omitted the details of class `String`. We will just use the text of the `String` to represent the `String`. However, you must remember that it's really an object.

The `color` field holds a `reference` to an object of class `Color`. That object has a `name` as well, though this `name` is unrelated to the `name` of a `Marsupial`. The name of this color is the `String "gray"`.

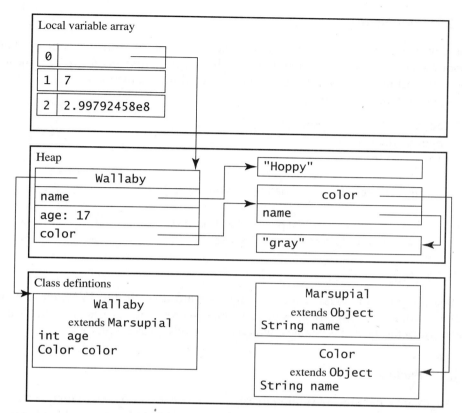

FIGURE 4.1: *JVM memory layout*

There is a special `reference` called `null`. Fields that contain references are initialized to `null`, which is a member of every class, but it represents no object at all. You can use it wherever you'd use a `reference`, but don't try to look at its fields or call a method on it. It's represented in a diagram like this:

For example, a newly created `Wallaby` object looks like this before it is initialized:

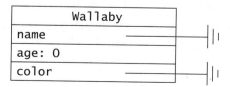

4.1.2   Class Names

The Java language allows you to abbreviate class names with the `package` and `import` statements. The JVM requires that all classes be *fully qualified*. This means that you must include the full package name each time you mention the class.

Consider this Java program.

```
package COM.yourcompany;
import java.io.*;
class Hello
{
    public static void main(String a[])
    {
        PrintStream output = System.out;
        output.println("Hello, world");
    }
}
```

In this program, the class names in Table 4.1 are used. In the JVM, classes are named with a string of letters, numbers, underscores, and slashes (/). This is different from the Java class names, which use periods (.) as separators.

4.1.3   Packages

Packages are a naming convention to assure that classes always have unique names, even if they come from different groups of developers who have never heard of each other. Packages are also used for determining access permissions between classes; classes that are in the same package have more privileges on each other than classes in different packages. A package is a collection of classes with the same names up to the last slash (/). For example, the package of `java/lang/String` is `java/lang`. An example of how packages work is given in Table 4.2.

In Java, the `import` statement allows you to use class names without the package names. Thus, the Java name `String` is really just shorthand for `java/lang/`

TABLE 4.1: *Fully qualified class name examples*

Java name	JVM name
Hello	COM/yourcompany/Hello
OutputStream	java/io/OutputStream
System	java/lang/System

TABLE 4.2: *Package examples*

Class name 1	Class name 2	Same package?
COM/company/Foo	COM/company/Bar	Yes
COM/company/Grape/Soda	COM/company/Cola/Soda	No
EDU/school/Cherry/Soda	EDU/school/Cherry/Cola/Soda	No
java/lang/String	String	No
Oyster	Clam	Maybe

String. This abbreviation isn't permitted in the JVM; fully qualified package names are required. This absolves the virtual machine of having to deal with ambiguously named classes. In general, the classes you create should be named after the organization you work for. The established convention for this is to use your Internet domain name, written in reverse:

COM/sun	Sun Microsystems
EDU/umd/cs	Computer Science Department, University of Maryland
GOV/nasa	U.S. National Aeronautics and Space Administration

If the package name is omitted, then the class is considered to be part of an "unnamed" package. Your system may have more than one unnamed package. When determining access to fields and methods, two classes in unnamed packages may or may not be treated as being included in the same package; it's up to the JVM implementation to decide.

Many examples in this book use the default unnamed package to make the examples easier to read. It's safe in the context of the book, because it's sitting on a page, not interacting with other classes. The executable code that comes with this book uses the domain-derived package name COM/sootNsmoke and subpackages beneath that. Any code you intend somebody else to use should incorporate a package name that is specific to you.

4.2   Creating Objects

Objects are created with the new instruction:

```
new ClassName
```

or

```
new java/lang/Integer
```

The class must not be marked `abstract`, and you must have permission to access it. If it's marked `public`, then you have permission. You also have permission if it isn't marked `public` but the class containing the `new` instruction is in the same package as the class being instantiated. When the `new` instruction is finished, there is a brand new uninitialized instance of the class on top of the stack.

You can't use the object until it has been initialized. To initialize the object, you must invoke one of the object's constructors. The constructor is always named `<init>`, and it always returns `void`. For example, there are two constructors for `java/lang/Integer`. Their descriptors are

```
<init> (I)V
<init> (Ljava/lang/String;)V
```

The first of these initializes the `Integer` from an `int`; the other uses a `String`.

The call to the constructor wipes the `reference` to the object being constructed off the stack. Therefore, there's almost always a `dup` between the `new` instruction and the constructor invocation.

Constructors are invoked with `invokespecial`. In order to use `invokespecial`, the stack must contain the object you are initializing, followed by any arguments to the constructor. (We'll talk more about methods and arguments in section 4.5.) For example, to construct an `Integer` using the constructor that takes an `int`,

```
new java/lang/Integer      ; Create the integer
dup                        ; Make a copy of the reference to it
bipush 27                  ; Push an argument
                           ; Call the constructor
invokespecial java/lang/Integer/<init> (I)V
```

4.3   Constructors

Constructors in the Java virtual machine are methods named `<init>`. This is different from the Java language, which names constructors after the class being constructed. Each constructor must call the constructor of its base class somewhere in the method. Alternatively, you may call another constructor in the same class. A Java compiler enforces this rule by making you do a call to `super` or `this` as the very first thing in the constructor.

To call the base class constructor, you use the `invokespecial` instruction, just as you did to call the constructor. Here's an example of a constructor.

```
.class MyClass
.super MySuperClass
```

```
; A constructor taking no arguments
.method <init>()V
aload_0                              ; Push this
invokespecial MySuperClass/<init>()V ; Call a superclass
                                     ; constructor on this

return                               ; Return to the caller
.end method
```

MySuperClass must call its superclass constructor, and so on up to java/lang/Object.

The requirement that all classes must call a superclass constructor ensures that nobody can use a class without making proper initializations. This is crucial to the security of the JVM. Some methods depend on the class having been initialized before they can work safely.

4.4   Using Fields

To get the value of a field from an object, use the getfield instruction. Static fields are handled differently; they're discussed in section 4.10. The getfield instruction expects to find the object from which to get the field on top of the operand stack. The arguments to the getfield instruction are the class, name, and descriptor of the field. It is necessary to include the descriptor so that the verification algorithm can check the class without having to load other class files to determine the type of the field.

We'll use this class, as defined in Java, for our examples.

```
class Greeting
{
    String intro = "Hello";
}
```

You can get the value of the field with

```
.method static useGreeting(LGreeting;)V
aload_0                     ; Push the greeting in variable 0
                            ; Now fetch the field
getfield Greeting/intro Ljava/lang/String;
; Now the String Hello is on top of the stack
```

The getfield instruction takes the Greeting object which is on top of the stack, and pushes onto the stack the value of its intro field. Diagrammed, memory looks like Figure 4.2 before the getfield instruction, like Figure 4.3 afterwards.

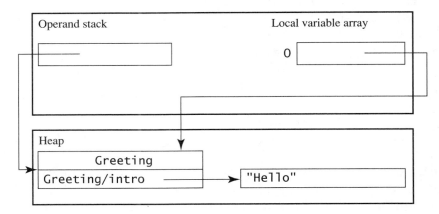

FIGURE 4.2: *Before getfield*

In Figure 4.2, the top of the stack contains a reference to a Greeting object, which has a field that points to the String labeled "Hello". Local variable 0 points to the same Greeting object. The stack and the local variable array contain identical copies of the same reference. Since they are the same, they point to the same object.

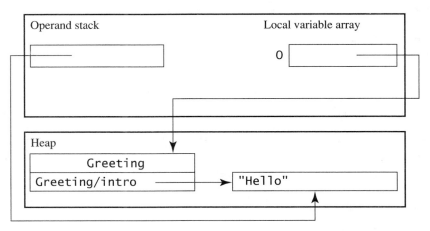

FIGURE 4.3: *After getfield*

When `getfield` is executed, the top of the stack is removed, and it is replaced with a `reference` to the "Hello" object. The local variable array is unchanged; only the stack has been altered.

The `reference` in the `intro` field of the `Greeting` object is the same as the one on top of the stack. The object itself has not been altered.

4.4.1 Types and `getfield`

The `getfield` instruction requires the type of the field that it is getting, as well as the name. This is true even if the field contains one of the numeric types. Suppose that you have a class `Point`:

```
class Point
{
    float x, y;
}
```

To add the value of the x and y fields, you would use `getfield` like this:

```
; This method takes a Point and returns the sum of its x and y
; coordinates
.method static xySum(LPoint;)F
aload_0                 ; Push the Point
getfield Point/x F      ; Get its x coordinate (must be a float)
aload_0                 ; Push the Point again
getfield Point/y F      ; Get its y coordinate (must be a float)
fadd                    ; Add them together
freturn                 ; Return the result
.end method
```

The JVM uses the type information in the arguments as part of the verification process. The x and y fields are required to be `float`s. As long as they are, it is safe to use the `fadd` instruction to add them together. This means that you can check the validity of the method without having to look at the `Point` class itself.

The JVM must ensure that there are x and y fields in the `Point` class when it gets around to loading the class. Then it can check that the fields have the correct type.

4.4.2   Inheriting Fields

When one class has another class as a superclass, it inherits all of the nonstatic fields of that class. Consider an extension to the Greeting class to handle greetings in Russian:

```
class RussianGreeting extends Greeting
{
    String intro = "Zdravstvuite";
}
```

An instance of RussianGreeting has two fields, both named intro. An instance of RussianGreeting looks like Figure 4.4. The full names of the fields are different. In Java, the English-language intro is *hidden* behind the Russian-language version. In Oolong, they are both equally accessible:

```
.method static internationalGreetings(LRussianGreeting;)V
aload_0                 ; There is a RussianGreeting in register 0
                        ; Push "Zdravstvuite":
getfield RussianGreeting/introduction Ljava/lang/String;
aload_0                 ; Reload the same object
                        ; Push "Hello":
getfield Greeting/introduction Ljava/lang/String;
;; Rest of the method omitted
.end method
```

At the end of the code shown, there will be two objects on the stack. The bottom of the stack will contain a reference to the String "Zdravstvuite", and above it will be a reference to the String "Hello".

4.4.3   Changing Field Values

To get the value of a field, use getfield, which takes an object on the stack and leaves in its place the value of the field. The counterpart of getfield for changing

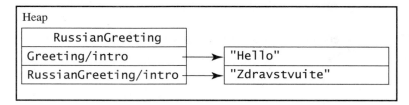

FIGURE 4.4: *An instance of RussianGreeting*

the value of a field is the `putfield` instruction, which uses the same arguments as `getfield` but expects both the object and the field value on the stack before it starts. For example, to change the value of the `intro` field,

```
.method static makeAustralian(LGreeting;)V
aload_0            ; Push the Greeting
ldc "G'Day"        ; Set up a new intro and store it
putfield Greeting/intro Ljava/lang/String;
return
.end method
```

This changes the value of the `Greeting/intro` field, whether the object is an ordinary `Greeting` or a `RussianGreeting`. If the argument is a `RussianGreeting`, its `RussianGreeting/intro` field is unchanged. Thus, this Java code:

```
Greeting g = new RussianGreeting();
makeAustralian(g);
System.out.println(g.intro);
System.out.println(((RussianGreeting) g).intro);
```

prints

```
G'Day
Zdravstvuite
```

Exercise 4.1

Write an Oolong declaration for the class `Dinosaur`, which has a name and a field indicating whether or not it is carnivorous. Include a constructor that initializes both fields. ▲

Exercise 4.2

Write Oolong code that creates a Velociraptor, which is a carnivorous dinosaur. Don't forget to initialize it. ▲

Exercise 4.3

Write an Oolong declaration for `CarnivorousDinosaur`, which is a subclass of `Dinosaur` that is carnivorous. Be sure to include a constructor to give the name. How would you create a Velociraptor using this class? ▲

4.5   Invoking Methods on Objects

The usual way to invoke a method on an object is to use an `invokevirtual` instruction. When `invokevirtual` is executed, a new stack frame is created, with a new operand stack and a new local variable array. The stack is empty, and the slots in the local variable array are uninitialized.

Execution continues with the first instruction of the invoked method. The new stack and variable pool are the only ones which can be accessed until the method returns or throws an exception. For example, consider this class.

```
.class RightTriangle
.method sumOfSquares(FF)F
; Variable 0 contains the RightTriangle object
; Variable 1 contains the first argument (a)
; Variable 2 contains the second argument (b)
fload_1           ; Compute a^2, leaving
dup               ;    the result on the stack
fmul
fload_2           ; Compute b^2
dup
fmul
fadd              ; Add the squares together
freturn           ; Return the result
.end method
```

This method takes two float values and returns the sum of their squares. In order to call this method, there must be three things on the stack, corresponding to the three initialized variables. The first thing must be a RightTriangle object, and the other two must be floats. The first is called the *receiver* of the method invocation; the other two are *arguments* to the method call.

This code fragment calls the sumOfSquares method:

```
; Assume that there's a RightTriangle object in variable 0 now
aload_0           ; Push a RightTriangle object onto the stack
                  ; as the receiver
ldc 3.0           ; Push 3.0 and 4.0 as arguments
ldc 4.0
invokevirtual RightTriangle/sumOfSquares (FF)F
; The result 25.0 is left on the stack
```

At the moment the invokevirtual is executed, the new stack frame is created, and the program counter points to the first instruction of the sumOfSquares method (the fload_1).

The stack is empty. Local variable 0 contains the RightTriangle object itself. Local variables 1 and 2 contain the operands of the invokevirtual instruction; in this case, the float values 3.0 and 4.0.

The method continues executing the instructions of the `sumOfSquares` method until it reaches the `freturn` statement. At that point, the new stack frame is removed, and the original stack frame is now on top. The operand of the `freturn` instruction, the `float` 25.0, is pushed onto the stack.

Methods that are `static` are invoked differently, using the `invokestatic` instruction. Unlike non-static methods, the `static` methods don't use a receiver. They only have arguments. For example, here's another method in `RightTriangle` that uses both non-static and static method calls:

```
.method hypotenuse(FF)F
; Variable 0 contains a RightTriangle object (this)
; Variable 1 contains a float (a)
; Variable 2 contains another float (b)
aload_0                                    ; Push this
fload_1                                    ; Push a
fload_2                                    ; Push b
invokevirtual RightTriangle/sumOfSquares(FF)F ; Compute a^2+b^2
f2d                                        ; Convert to
                                           ;    double
invokestatic java/lang/Math/sqrt(D)D       ; Compute square
                                           ;    root
d2f                                        ; Back to float
freturn
.end method
```

After invoking the `sumOfSquares` method just as in the earlier example, the method goes on to call the `sqrt` routine in the `Math` class, one of the standard Java platform classes. The `sqrt` method is `static`, which means that no receiver is used. It expects the stack to contain a `double`. The method takes the number and returns its square root as a `double`.

Because we were using `float` values, we have to convert the `float` result to a `double` before calling the method, then convert the result back to a `float` before returning it. These conversions are necessary to make the type of what's on the stack match the descriptor of `sqrt` and to match the return type of the `hypotenuse`.

Exercise 4.4

Modify the class `RightTriangle` to have two fields a and b. Modify `hypotenuse` to use the fields a and b instead of arguments.   ▲

4.5.1   Virtual Invocation

When you use `invokevirtual`, the method definition that's named in the arguments is not necessarily the one that's invoked. Instead, the JVM uses a procedure *virtual dispatch*[1] to select the method to call based on the method name, the method descriptor, and the type of the receiver at runtime.

In virtual dispatch, the JVM looks in the class of the receiver to find a method implementation with the exact name and type given. If it exists, that's the method that's invoked. If not, it looks in the superclass of that class and so on until the method is found.

To illustrate, suppose that you have two classes like these:

```
.class Hello
.method greet()V
getstatic java/lang/System/out Ljava/io/PrintStream;
ldc "Hello, world"
invokevirtual java/io/PrintStream/println (Ljava/lang/String;)V
.end method
.end class

.class Hola
.super Hello
.method greet()V
getstatic java/lang/System/out Ljava/io/PrintStream;
ldc "Hola, mundo"
invokevirtual java/io/PrintStream/println (Ljava/lang/String;)V
.end method
.end class
```

If you had an `Hola` object on top of the stack and executed

```
invokevirtual Hello/greet ()V
```

the program would print

```
Hola, mundo
```

The class name given as an argument to `invokevirtual` is not completely ignored. When the code is loaded, the JVM verification algorithm checks to see that the class named in the argument actually exists and that it has a method with the appropriate name and descriptor. It also examines the code to ensure that

---

[1] "Virtual dispatch" is unrelated to "virtual machine"; the word "virtual" is overused. The "virtual" in `invokevirtual` refers to virtual dispatch.

receiver of the method invocation is going to be an instance of that class or some subclass of that class. By enforcing these requirements, the verification algorithm makes sure that there is always an appropriate method implementation to match the name and descriptor.

4.5.2   Method Inheritance and Overriding

A Java compiler uses the invokevirtual instruction for most non-static methods. (For more about static methods, see section 4.10). You probably already have a pretty good idea how virtual method invocation works. Let's see how the JVM treats it.

Method inheritance is different from field inheritance. As we said in section 4.4.2, when a subclass declares a field with the same name and descriptor as one of its superclasses, all instances of the subclass actually have two different fields. This doesn't confuse the JVM because the two fields are really named differently, since the full name of the field incorporates the class name as well.

With methods, when a subclass has a method with the same name and descriptor as a superclass, then the subclass ends up with only a single implementation of each method. The technical term for this is that the subclass *overrides* the method implementation in the superclass.

Figure 4.5 is a diagram of the memory in the JVM, showing an instance of the class Hola on top of the stack. If you go to invoke the method greet with descriptor ()V, the JVM will discover that the object is of class Hola. It begins its search in the class Hola, which does have an implementation of the method. This is the method that prints the string "Hola, mundo" and then returns.

If you wanted to invoke the method toString() instead, using the descriptor ()Ljava/lang/String;, the method search would begin in Hola, but there is no matching method there. So the JVM tries Hello because that's the superclass of Hola, but there's no method there either. Finally it looks in java/lang/Object. There had better be a method there, because that's the last resort. Fortunately, there is a matching method implementation there, and that implementation is used.

If you don't like the idea of the JVM searching for a method implementation, another way to think of the class implementation space in the JVM is shown in Figure 4.6. There are a lot of arrows running around in this diagram, but here's what's going on: each class begins with a list of the methods of the superclass. The arrows point to the same place as the methods in the superclass do. This way, all methods are inherited from the superclass. The list is sometimes called a *vtable*. At the end of the list, you throw in any methods that are new to the subclass. This gives you the new methods. For any methods that are overridden, you replace the arrow to point to the new method implementation. This overrides the method implementation.

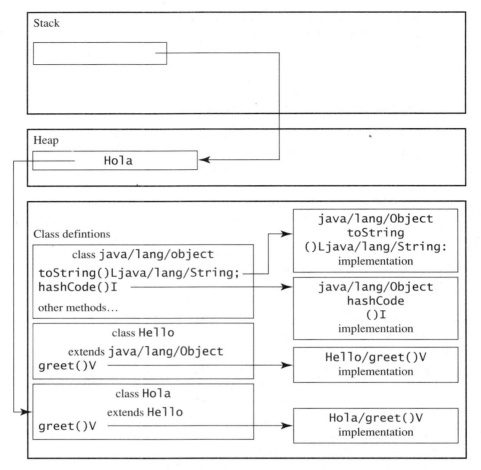

FIGURE 4.5: *Memory layout of class definitions*

Whenever you want to call a method, you go straight to the class definition for the receiver object and look up the name and descriptor. This gives you the exact method implementation to use, without having to look at any of the super-classes.

Suppose we added a new class that is a subclass of Hola:

```
.class AlternateHola
.super Hola
.method hashCode()I
;; A new implementation of hashCode
```

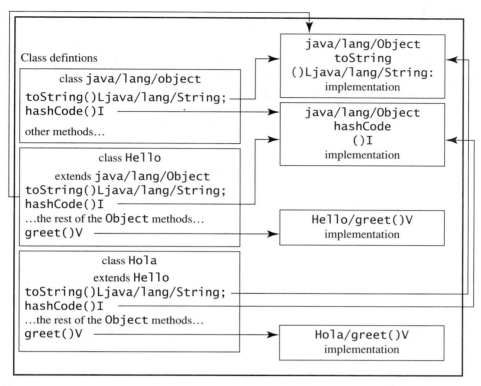

FIGURE 4.6: *Overriding greet()V*

```
.end method
.end class
```

The vtable for this class would contain exactly the same elements as for Hola, except that the arrow from hashCode would point to the new implementation. The classes Hello and Hola would be unchanged. This is one of the key features of the JVM: you can do whatever you like in subclasses without having to make any changes to the implementations of the superclasses.

An advantage of looking at classes this way is that you know that the greet method will always appear in the same place on the list, whether it's an Hola or a Hello or even an AlternateHola. This means that the JVM can call the method without having to do any name comparisons at all. This advantage is purely internal to the JVM, because it's up to the JVM to organize its memory in a way that best suits it. You can continue to arrange the methods in your class in any order at all, without affecting the correctness of your class.

4.5.3   Overloading and Method Matching

When the JVM goes searching for the method implementation in superclasses, it is looking only at the superclasses of the receiver object. It does not consider the superclasses or subclasses of the arguments. It looks only at an exact match of the method descriptor. You may even have two or more methods with the same name but different descriptors.

For example, suppose you have the following class definition:

```
.class Printer
.method print(Ljava/lang/Object;)V
getstatic java/lang/System/out Ljava/io/PrintStream;
ldc "Inside Printer/print(Ljava/lang/Object;)V"
invokevirtual java/io/PrintStream/println(Ljava/lang/String;)V
return
.end method

.method print(Ljava/lang/String;)V
getstatic java/lang/System/out Ljava/io/PrintStream;
ldc "Inside Printer/print(Ljava/lang/String;)V"
invokevirtual java/io/PrintStream/println(Ljava/lang/String;)V
return
.end method
```

Suppose you have a `Hello` object that you want to print using a `Printer` object. You can't say:

```
invokevirtual Printer/print(LHello;)V                    ; FOUL!
```

because there isn't any method implementation for `print` that takes a `Hello` object. Instead, you must write

```
invokevirtual Printer/print(Ljava/lang/Object;)V     ; OK
```

This can be the cause of some confusion. You might create a special subclass of `Printer` that can print `Hello` objects:

```
.class HelloPrinter
.super Printer
.method print(LHello;)V
getstatic java/lang/System/out Ljava/io/PrintStream;
ldc "Inside HelloPrinter/print(LHello;)V"
```

```
invokevirtual java/io/PrintStream/println(Ljava/lang/String;)V
return
.end method
```

Suppose you have a HelloPrinter in local variable 0 and a Hello in variable 1. What do you think you get from

```
aload_0                 ; Push the HelloPrinter
aload_1                 ; Push the Hello
invokevirtual Printer/print(Ljava/lang/Object;)V
```

The answer is that it prints

```
Inside Printer/print(Ljava/lang/Object;)V
```

It did not find the special subclass implementation of print that we defined for Hello objects, because it was looking only within Printer (and the superclasses of Printer) for a method named print that takes an Object and returns void. In order to use the new method implementation, we'd have to write

```
aload_0                 ; Push the HelloPrinter
aload_1                 ; Push the Hello
invokevirtual HelloPrinter/print(LHello;)V
```

This code assumes that variable 0 contains a reference to a HelloPrinter object. That would be true if the instruction immediately previous to this code was a getfield whose type descriptor was LHelloPrinter;, followed by an astore_0.

If the verifier cannot prove that variable 0 contains a HelloPrinter, then the code is rejected. Section 9.5 describes a technique for tracing through the code and observing the effect each instruction has on the stack and the local variable array. The verification algorithm looks only at the types of objects, not their actual values, which is why you can verify the program without actually running it.

The Java compiler actually has to do a fair bit of work to figure out the appropriate arguments for the invokevirtual instruction. It must look at all the arguments and find out which of the available implementations best fits them all. How to do this is described in chapter 10.

4.5.4   Invoking a Method Directly

The `invokespecial` instruction can be used to bypass the virtual dispatch mechanism used by `invokevirtual`. Suppose you have an `Hola` object in local variable 0:

```
aload_0                 ; Push an Hola object
invokespecial Hello/greet ()V
aload_0                 ; Push it again
invokevirtual Hello/greet ()V
```

The output reads

```
Hello, world
Hola, mundo
```

In the first case the JVM invokes `Hello/greet` directly, without involving the virtual dispatch mechanism. The method implementation invoked is precisely the one you asked for. In the second case the virtual dispatch mechanism is involved, so it uses the implementation of `Hola/greet` instead.

This is something you can't usually do in Java. The Java compiler almost always uses `invokevirtual`. One exception to this rule is when you use the `super` keyword within the subclass:

```
/** This method is part of Hola */
void greetInEnglish()
{
    super.greet();          // Call greet in Hello
}
```

When this method is compiled, it produces code equivalent to this in Oolong:

```
.method greetInEnglish()V
aload_0
invokespecial Hello/greet ()V
return
.end method
```

The `invokespecial` instruction is used here to bypass the virtual dispatch mechanism, ensuring that the correct method implementation is called. If the code used `invokevirtual`, it would print the greeting in Spanish instead of English, since the virtual dispatch mechanism would be used.

The `invokespecial` instruction is also used by Java compilers to implement calls to `private` methods. Since `private` methods can be invoked only by the class itself, they are not inherited by subclasses. This means that there's no reason to go through the trouble of dispatching the invocation virtually. Consider this class:

```
class Bonjour extends Hello
{
    private void saluent()
    {
        System.out.println("Bonjour, le monde");
    }

    void greet()
    {
        saluent();
    }
}
```

Within the greet method, only this saluent method can be called. It isn't possible to override saluent in a subclass of Bonjour, because private methods aren't inherited the way public, protected, and package-access methods are. The private methods are truly private to the class that defines them, and they are seen nowhere else.

Because the Java compiler can tell exactly which method implementation will be used, it can use invokespecial to call it. The greet method compiles into code equivalent to the following code in Oolong:

```
.method greet()V
aload_0
invokespecial Bonjour/saluent()V
return
.end method
```

4.5.5 invokespecial and super

Actually, the above description of invokespecial is a little too simplistic. In order to increase the robustness of Java programs whose base classes change, the meaning of invokespecial is a little different when invoked on an object whose class is marked super.

Here, super refers to the super keyword in the .class directive. In this code

```
.class super Cheddar
.super Cheese
```

the class Cheddar is marked super. A Java compiler automatically marks all classes as super, so the behavior discussed in this section applies to all classes compiled from Java.

When `invokespecial` is used to invoke a method in a superclass of the current class and the receiver is an instance of a class which is `super`, then invocation actually occurs using a variant of the virtual dispatch mechanism. The JVM starts looking for the implementation of the method in the superclass of the current class.

Take a look at these three Oolong class definitions:

```
.class super Bicycle
.method tuneUp ()V
getstatic java/lang/System/out Ljava/io/PrintStream;
ldc "Tune up a bicycle"
invokevirtual java/io/PrintStream/println(Ljava/lang/String;)V
return
.end method
.end class


.class super MountainBike
.super Bicycle

; This method did not exist when DownhillMountainBike was written
.method tuneUp ()V
aload_0
invokespecial Bicycle/tuneUp()V
getstatic java/lang/System/out Ljava/io/PrintStream;
ldc "Tune up mountain bike features"
invokevirtual java/io/PrintStream/println(Ljava/lang/String;)V
return
.end method
.end class


.class super DownhillMountainBike
.super MountainBike
.method tuneUp ()V
aload_0
invokespecial Bicycle/tuneUp()V
getstatic java/lang/System/out Ljava/io/PrintStream;
ldc "Tune up downhill mountain bike features"
invokevirtual java/io/PrintStream/println(Ljava/lang/String;)V
return
.end method
.end class
```

In each class, the `tuneUp` method begins with the generic `Bicycle` tune-up, then follows it up with special features for the specific kind of `Bicycle`.

When these classes were originally written, there was no `tuneUp` method in `MountainBike`, so the `DownhillMountainBike` tries to call the `Bicycle` implementation of `tuneUp` directly, missing out on the `MountainBike` `tuneUp`. The JVM recognizes that this sort of thing happens, so it doesn't actually invoke the `Bicycle` implementation of `tuneUp`, even though that's the method named in `invokespecial`. Instead, it does the equivalent of a virtual dispatch, starting from `MountainBike`, the immediate superclass of `DownhillMountainBike`. It finds an implementation of `tuneUp` with the appropriate parameters in `MountainBike`, so it calls that method, which proceeds to do a generic `Bicycle` tune-up before proceeding with its own tune-up.

Exercise 4.5

Using the results of exercise 4.1, add a field `color` to `Dinosaur`. The field stores a `String`, which is the name of the color. Add two methods called `setColor`. One takes a `String` and sets the `color` field to that string. The other takes a `java.awt.Color` and sets the `color` field to the result of calling `toString` on the argument. ▲

Exercise 4.6

Given that there is a `Dinosaur` object in variable 0, set its color to `java.awt.Color.green` (a `static` field). Then set its color to the `String` "green". ▲

4.6   Casting

Sometimes you know more about an object than the JVM can prove. For example, suppose you have a `Library` class that has a hash table to map a person's name (as a `String`) to the `Address` where they live:

```
.class Library
; This field maps a String to an Address
.field static addressMap Ljava/util/Hashtable;
```

The `get` method of `Hashtable` takes an `Object` and returns an `Object`. Here's how to get the address of a person, assuming that the name is in local variable 1:

```
; Take the person's name and use it to get their Address from
; the addressMap
getstatic Library/addressMap Ljava/util/Hashtable;
```

```
aload_1                          ; Push the name from variable 1
invokevirtual java/util/Hashtable/get
            (Ljava/lang/Object;)Ljava/lang/Object;
```

Since a `String` is an `Object`, it's perfectly legal to call the method like this. Now the top of the stack contains an `Address`, but the JVM doesn't know that. It knows only that the top of the stack contains an `Object`, since that is what the `get` method says it returns. If the next thing you try is to send an overdue notice to that address, something bad happens:

```
invokestatic Library/sendOverdueNotice (LAddress;)V ; ILLEGAL!
```

The problem is that the JVM can't prove that the `Object` returned by `get` is really an `Address`. You know it, since your program uses the `addressMap` so that it only has `Strings` as the keys and `Addresses` as the values. The JVM sees this as an attempt by the program to use an object in an illegal way that could potentially cause the machine to do something destructive, and it will refuse to load the class.

To get around this, the `checkcast` instruction checks to see if the object really has the type you expect it to have:

```
checkcast Address
; Now you know that the top of the stack is an Address
invokestatic Library/sendOverdueNotice(LAddress;)V   ; OK
```

Unlike most instructions, `checkcast` doesn't pop its operand off the stack; it just checks it. If the test succeeds, then it is as though nothing at all has happened. The class of the object has not changed. However, the verification algorithm will no longer complain that you're trying to send an incorrect argument to the method.

The `checkcast` instruction does not do anything to the `reference` on top of the stack. Both the object and the `reference` to it are unchanged. All that has changed is the JVM's perception of the class of the object that the `reference` refers to. If this perception turns out to be wrong at runtime, the JVM will throw an exception.

Suppose, however, that you accidentally did put something into the `addressMap` that wasn't an `Address`. The `Hashtable` class has no way to check this, since it is designed to handle any `Object`. In this case, the `checkcast` instruction will cause a `ClassCastException` to be thrown when the program reaches the `checkcast` instruction. For more about exceptions, see section 5.6.

The program cannot reach the `invokestatic` with an object of the wrong type. If a `checkcast` fails, then the flow of execution goes to an error handler instead of to the `invokestatic` instruction. If the `checkcast` is not present, then the JVM proves that the object on top of the stack must have the appropriate class;

otherwise, it rejects the class. Under no circumstances does the JVM invoke a method with an argument of the wrong type.

4.7   Casting, Fields, Methods, and Java

This example code may clarify some of the relationship between fields and methods. Consider these two classes in Java:

```java
class Greeting
{
    String intro = "Hello";

    String target()
    {
        return "world";
    }
}


class FrenchGreeting extends Greeting
{
    String intro = "Bonjour";

    String target()
    {
        return "le monde";
    }
}
```

What do you think happens if you run the following program?

```java
public static void main(String argv[])
{
    Greeting english = new Greeting();
    Greeting french = new FrenchGreeting();

    System.out.println(english.intro + ", " + english.target());
    System.out.println(french.intro + ", " + french.target());
    System.out.println(((FrenchGreeting) french).intro + ", " +
                    ((FrenchGreeting) french).target());
}
```

The answer is

```
Hello, world
Hello, le monde
Bonjour, le monde
```

This result is somewhat surprising, especially the multilingual second line.

The first line of output makes perfect sense. Both parts are in English, which is what you'd expect, since you're using the english object. The second line is a surprise, since it combines an English introduction with a French target, even though the object in both cases is the same object. Now the third line seems pretty surprising as well. The reference is the same one used on the second line, but now you get a different word from the same field of the same object. The only thing changed there is a cast, which does not affect the type of the underlying object.

This example demonstrates the difference between the virtual dispatch mechanism and the way fields are accessed. Remember that a class inherits *all* non-static fields from its parent. In the case of FrenchGreeting, this means that the object has two different fields named intro: one in English and one in French.

Figure 4.7 shows what the memory space looks like during the invocation of main. Variable 1 is english, and variable 2 is french. The Oolong equivalent of english.intro is

```
aload_1                                     ; Get english
getfield Greeting/intro Ljava/lang/String; ; Get the intro field
```

The translation of french.intro is

```
aload_2                                     ; Get french
getfield Greeting/intro Ljava/lang/String; ; Get the intro field
```

As we said in section 4.4, the target field is chosen based on both the class name and the field name. The Java compiler uses Greeting here because that's the declared type of the french variable. If you force the Java compiler to think of the french variable as a FrenchGreeting with

```
((FrenchGreeting) french).intro
```

then the Java compiler generates this code instead:

```
aload_2                                     ; Get french
checkcast FrenchGreeting                    ; Check type
getfield French/intro Ljava/lang/String;    ; Get the intro field
```

This code explains why you got different results for the first part (the intro) of lines 2 and 3. However, it doesn't explain why you got the same results for the

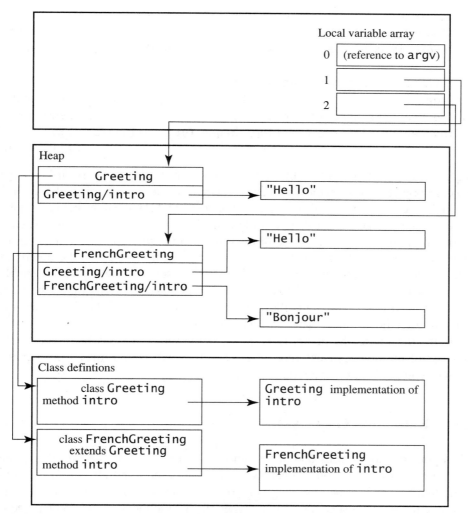

FIGURE 4.7: *Memory layout of* Greeting *and* FrenchGreeting *objects*

second part (the target). The reason is the virtual dispatch mechanism. Here is a translation of the three calls to target():

```
; english.target()
aload_1                                              ; Get english
invokevirtual Greeting/target ()Ljava/lang/String; ; Call target
```

```
; french.target()
aload_2                                          ; Get french
invokevirtual Greeting/target ()Ljava/lang/String; ; Call target


; ((FrenchGreeting) french).target()
aload_2                                          ; Get french
checkcast FrenchGreeting                         ; Check type
invokevirtual FrenchGreeting/target ()Ljava/lang/String;
                                                 ; Call target
```

The generated code is a little different in each case. In the first case, it loads the english object from variable 1 and calls `target`, using the `Greeting` class.

In the second case, it uses the same method name and class, but the method implementation that is actually called is different. That's because the `invokevirtual` instruction looks at the actual type of the object, not at the type given in the arguments, to determine which method to invoke. See section 4.5.1 for the details of virtual invocation. Referring to Figure 4.7, you can see that the object in variable 2 contains a reference to an object of class `FrenchGreeting`. Looking up the `target` method in this class yields the `FrenchGreeting` implementation of `target`, which returns the string `le monde` instead of `world`.

In the third case, the object is the same as the second case, which means that the class of the object is also the same. Therefore, when you invoke the `target` method, you get `le monde` again.

4.8   Returning Objects

When your method returns one of the numeric types, it's pretty easy to determine whether a return instruction is legal. If the method descriptor ends with an I, indicating that an `int` is to be returned, then you must use the `ireturn` instruction, and the top of the stack must contain an `int` when the instruction executes. With objects, things are slightly tougher. The top of the stack must not only be a `reference`, but the object that it points to must be compatible with the return type of the method.

Suppose your method begins

```
; A method that returns a MountainBike
.method public myRide ()LMountainBike;
```

Because this method returns a `reference`, you must use an `areturn` instruction. This code is clearly illegal in this method:

```
iconst_1
ireturn                ; Invalid: an int can't be a MountainBike
```

The JVM verification algorithm checks that the object that is returned is an instance either of the class `Bicycle` or of some subclass of it. For example, this code is legal, because a `DownhillMountainBike` is a kind of `MountainBike`:

```
new DownhillMountainBike      ; Create a DownhillMountainBike
dup
invokevirtual DownhillMountainBike/<init>()V
areturn                       ; Return the DownhillMountainBike
```

The `null` reference is special. It behaves as though it's an instance of every class, even though it's really an instance of no class at all. Therefore, this code is legal:

```
aconst_null
areturn            ; This is OK, since a null could be a Bicycle
```

4.9   Interfaces

An *interface* is a specification of what a class should do without actually telling how it should do it. An interface is defined much like a class, except that there aren't any fields. The methods must be `public` and `abstract`, and they can't be `static` or `native`. Because the methods are `abstract`, they have no method bodies.

Here is an example of an interface:

```
; Used to list objects
.interface Enumerator

; Get the next element
.method public abstract getNext ()Ljava/lang/Object;
.end method

; See if there is another object
.method public abstract anyMore ()Z
.end method

.end class
```

This specifies what methods an `Enumerator` must have, but it doesn't specify how to implement them. A class using the `.implements` directive claims that it implements the required methods. For example, this class implements an `Enumerator` for a linked list. (The `LinkedList` class has `value` and `next` fields.)

```
.class LinkedListEnum
.implements Enumerator
.field private list LLinkedList;

; Initialize the enumerator with the list
.method public <init>(LLinkedList;)V
aload_0
invokespecial java/lang/Object/<init>()V        ; Superclass init
aload_0
aload_1
putfield LinkedListEnum-list LLinkedList;        ; Save list
return
.end method

.method public getNext ()Ljava/lang/Object;
aload_0                                          ; Get the current value
getfield LinkedListEnum/list LLinkedList;
getfield LinkedList/value Ljava/lang/Object;
                                                 ; Leave it on the stack
aload_0                                   ; Store the tail of the list
aload_0                                   ; in list
getfield LinkedListEnum/list LLinkedList;
getfield LinkedList/next LLinkedList;
putfield LinkedListEnum/list LLinkedList;

areturn                                   ; Return the value
.end method

.method public anyMore ()Z
aload_0                                   ; Get the list
getfield LinkedList/list LLinkedList;
ifnull false                              ; Go to false label on null
iconst_1
ireturn                                   ; Return 1 if not null
false:
iconst_0                                  ; Return 0 if null
ireturn
.end method
```

You may have additional methods, but you must implement all the methods declared in the interface. In this example, we have added a constructor. You can even use more than one .implements directive, in which case you must implement all of the methods in all of the interfaces that the class implements.

An object of type LinkedListEnum can be treated as an Enumerator, as if Enumerator were the superclass of LinkedListEnum. For example,

```
.class Business
.field currentInventory LLinkedList;
.method public inventory ()LEnumerator;
new LinkedListEnum              ; Create a LinkedListEnum
dup

aload_0
getfield Business/currentInventory
    LLinkedList;                          ; Load the current
                                          ;     inventory list
invokespecial LinkedListEnum/<init>
    (LLinkedList;)V                       ; Initialize
                                          ;     the LinkedListEnum
                                          ; with the LinkedList
areturn                                   ; Return the
                                          ;     LinkedListEnum
.end method
```

The return instruction is legal, because the actual return type (LinkedListEnum) implements the interface given in the method descriptor (Enumerator).

If you call inventory on a Business, you can enumerate over its inventory using the anyMore and getNext methods (in Java):

```
Business business;
// Get a Business from somewhere
Enumerator e = business.inventory();
while(e.anyMore())
{
    System.out.println(e.getNext());
}
```

You don't have to say anything about LinkedListEnum. You only have to know that e contains an Enumerator, and you can call any of the methods defined there.

Since Business returns an Enumerator instead of a LinkedList, you can change the implementation of Business to use an ArrayEnum instead:

```
.class ArrayEnum
.implements Enumerator
```

```
.field private elements [Ljava/lang/Object;
.field current I

.method public getNext()Ljava/lang/Object;
;; Return elements[current], and increment current
.end method

.method public anyMore()Ljava/lang/Object;
;; Return false if current < the length of elements
.end method
```

The implementor of Business can change the implementation of inventory without altering any of the classes that use it, since the implementation of Enumerator was kept separate from the interface definition.

Invoking methods through interfaces is slightly different from invoking methods using invokevirtual or invokespecial. A third instruction, invokeinterface, is required. To call anyMore, use code like this:

```
; Assume there's a Business in local variable 0
aload_0                                      ; Get the
                                             ; Business
invokevirtual Business/inventory LEnumerator;   ; Get its
                                             ; inventory
invokeinterface Enumerator/anyMore ()Z 1     ; Call anyMore
```

The last argument to the invokeinterface instruction is the number of stack words used as parameters to the method call, including the receiver itself.[2] In this example, the only parameter is the Enumerator object itself, so the value is 1. For the interface:

```
.interface Searchable
.method find(Ljava/lang/String;)Ljava/lang/Object;
.end method
```

A call to find looks like this:

```
; Assume there's a Searchable object in register 1
aload_1            ; Get the object
ldc "potato chips"   ; We want an element named "potato chips"
invokeinterface Searchable/find
            (Ljava/lang/String;)Ljava/lang/Object; 2
```

---

[2] This number should not be necessary, since it can be derived from the method descriptor. However, it is included in the Oolong language because it is part of the underlying JVM bytecodes.

The number of words to pop is 2: one for the object, and one for its argument. As usual, if an argument is a `long` or `double`, it counts as two slots instead of one.

4.10 Static Fields and Methods

Fields and methods marked `static` are different from those not so marked. Static fields belong to the class as a whole, rather than having a slot in each object. Since a class may be loaded into the JVM only once, there is exactly one copy of a `static` field in the entire virtual machine. This makes `static` fields convenient for storing "absolute truths" of the system, like constants. They're also handy for storing a piece of system state shared by every object, such as a counter.

Static methods are the counterpart of `static` fields. They're invoked not on any particular object; they're just invoked. For that reason, local variable 0 is not reserved for the `this` object, as it is in other method invocations. Instead, the arguments start at 0.

To invoke a static method, use the `invokestatic` instruction. It's used exactly like `invokespecial` or `invokevirtual`, except that only the arguments appear on the stack. Because there is no object to use for computing virtual dispatch, the exact method named in the `invokestatic` instruction is invoked.

Similarly, `getstatic` and `putstatic` are used on static fields instead of `getfield` and `putfield`. For example,

```
.class Counter
.field static private nextValue I = 0
.method static getNext ()I
.limit stack 3
getstatic Counter/nextValue I ; Push the value
dup                           ; Copy it
iconst_1
iadd                          ; Add 1 to the copy, which yields
                              ; the next value
putstatic Counter/nextValue I ; Store the incremented copy
ireturn                       ; Return the original value
.end method
```

Although `static` fields and methods are accessed without respect to a particular object, they're still considered part of the class for purposes of figuring out which methods are permitted to access which fields and methods. The definition of `private` states that a field or method may be accessed from any method in the same class, even a `static` one.

For example, consider this part of an implementation of class `Complex`, for complex numbers. It uses a static method `add`, which adds two `Complex` numbers to produce a new `Complex`. Because it is part of the class, it is allowed to access the private `real` and `imaginary` fields, which are not accessible from outside the class.

```
.class Complex
.field private real F          ; Each complex number has a real
.field private imaginary F     ; and imaginary component

; The add method, though static, has access to the private state
; of its arguments
.method public static add(LComplex;LComplex;)LComplex;
.limit stack 5
.limit locals 3
new Complex                    ; Create a new complex number
dup
aload_0                        ; Get the real value of the first arg
getfield Complex/real F
aload_1                        ; Get the real value of the second arg
getfield Complex/real F
fadd                           ; Add them
aload_0                        ; Do the same for the imaginary parts
getfield Complex/imaginary F
aload_1
getfield Complex/imaginary F
fadd                           ; Initialize the object
invokespecial Complex/<init>(FF)V
areturn                        ; And return it
.end method
```

4.11   Class Initialization

There is a special static method called `<clinit>` that is used to initialize the class as a whole. It's often used to initialize static fields. The `<clinit>` method takes no arguments and returns nothing. It is called by the JVM when the class is loaded; there's no need for you to call it. For example,

```
; This class represents all the possible kinds of ice cream
.class IceCream

; These are the possible kinds of ice cream:
.field final public static vanilla LIceCream;
```

```
.field final public static chocolate LIceCream;
.field final public static strawberry LIceCream;

; A private constructor: only I can create IceCream objects
.method private <init>()V
aload_0
invokespecial java/lang/Object/<init> ()V  ; Call the superclass
                                            ; constructor
return
.end method

; The class constructor
.method static <clinit> ()V
.limit stack 2
new IceCream                            ; Create an IceCream
dup
invokespecial IceCream/<init> ()V
putstatic IceCream/vanilla LIceCream;   ; Store it in vanilla
new IceCream                            ; Create another IceCream
dup
invokespecial IceCream/<init> ()V
putstatic IceCream/chocolate LIceCream; ; Store it in chocolate
new IceCream                            ; Yet another IceCream
dup
invokespecial IceCream/<init> ()V
putstatic IceCream/strawberry LIceCream;; Store it in Strawberry
return
.end method
```

The fields vanilla, chocolate, and strawberry hold the instances of the class IceCream. The fields are set when the class is loaded by the <clinit> method.

Because the constructor is private, nobody can create new flavors without modifying the IceCream class. This is sometimes better than using int values to represent flavors. If you have an IceCream object, you can be sure that it is of one of the three recognized flavors, no others.

4.12 Arrays

The JVM has a set of instructions for allocating and using arrays. An array has two features: a type and a length. The type is fixed in the program, and the length is found on the operand stack. This arrangement makes it possible to type-check the program statically, but array bounds must be checked at run time.

4.12.1 Arrays of Reference

The anewarray instruction is used to create arrays of references. Like newarray (discussed in section 3.11), anewarray takes as an argument the type of elements you want in the array. To create an array of Strings five elements long:

```
iconst_5
anewarray java/lang/String
```

Note that the argument is the name of the class (java/lang/String) and not a type (Ljava/lang/String;).

This instruction creates a new object, which is an array of Strings. The type descriptor of the class of this object is [Ljava/lang/String;. The instruction leaves a reference to the new object on the operand stack.

The array object contains five slots, numbered from 0 to 4. All of them are initialized to null. The memory of the JVM looks like the diagram in Figure 4.8. To use this array, use aaload and aastore instructions. These instructions are just like ordinary load and store instructions, except that they require an additional operand: the number of the array element to retrieve. For example, to store Hello into slot 0 and World into slot 1, use these instructions (also see Figure 4.9):

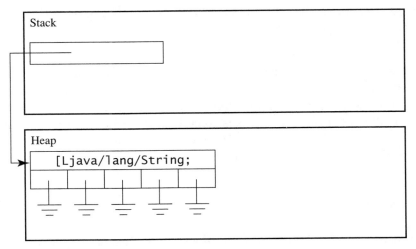

FIGURE 4.8: *New array of 5 Strings, all null*

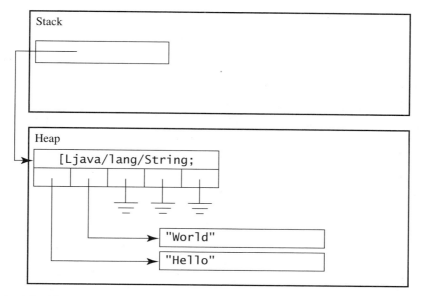

FIGURE 4.9: *After setting array slots 0 and 1*

```
dup                      ; Dup the array reference
ldc "Hello"              ; Store hello
iconst_0                 ; Into slot 0
aastore

; The array reference is still on the stack
dup
ldc "World"              ; Store hello
iconst_0                 ; Into slot 0
aastore
```

To get elements out of the array, you use aaload. To get the reference to "World" on the stack, use

```
iconst_1                 ; Push int 1
aaload                   ; Load array slot 1
```

Now the memory picture looks like the diagram in Figure 4.10. The top of the stack has been replaced with a reference to the World string.

You can think of an array as being a little like an object whose fields have numbers instead of names. Whenever you store into an array, you must meet the

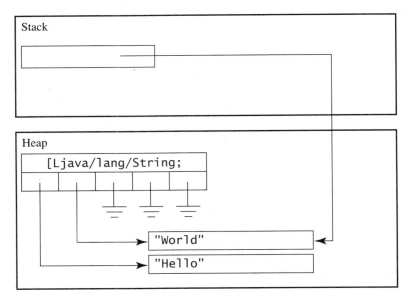

FIGURE 4.10: *After loading array slot 1*

same requirement as if you were storing into the field: the object you are storing must have the same class as the array element type or some subclass of that class. Similarly, when you retrieve a value from that array, it will have the appropriate type.

4.12.2 Multidimensional Arrays

Both `newarray` and `anewarray` create one-dimensional arrays. If you want an array of arrays, a third array-creation instruction is needed: `multianewarray`. To the JVM a·multidimensional array is really an array of arrays. The `multianewarray` instruction creates an object that is an array of arrays, and it may initialize some of those arrays.

Unlike `newarray` and `anewarray`, `multianewarray` takes a type name instead of a class name. It also takes a second argument: the number of dimensions to allocate (let's call it n). The JVM takes n `int` operands off the stack and uses them to determine how large an array to allocate.

To allocate a 3×5 array of `int`s, use

```
iconst_3
iconst_5
multianewarray [[I 2
```

This sequence of code allocates an array of three elements, each of which is a `reference` to an array of `ints`. Each of these subarrays is five elements long. In memory, it looks like the diagram in Figure 4.11.

There are no special instructions for getting values into and out of multidimensional arrays; you must handle each dimension individually. For example, to store the number 144 into the fifth column of the third row, you would say

```
; The object on top of the stack is [[I
iconst_2
aaload              ; Get the third element, which is
                    ; an array of ints ([I)
iconst_4            ; Store in the fifth element of
                    ; the subarray
ldc 144             ; Push the value to store
iastore             ; Store it in the fifth element
```

This code first loads the third element of the array. This is an array of `ints`. Then the code stores the value into the fifth element of that subarray. (All indexes are reduced by one in the code, because array indexes start at 0, so that the first element is element 0.)

It might seem that providing the number of dimensions to `multianewarray` is redundant, since it should be the same as the number of brackets at the beginning of the type. Actually, the number of dimensions may be less than the number of brackets, in which case you get an array of the same type with elements initialized

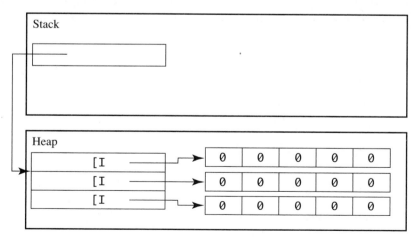

FIGURE 4.11: *An array int[3][5]*

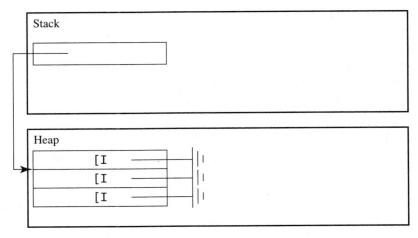

FIGURE 4.12: *An array int[3][]*

to null instead of to another array. Allocating an array of the same type as before, but with fewer dimensions initialized, you get

```
iconst_3
multianewarray [[I 1
```

The result of executing this code is shown in Figure 4.12. The object that was created is still an array-of-arrays-of-ints. However, only the first dimension has been initialized. You must always initialize at least one dimension of the array.

The only array-allocation instruction you really need is multianewarray since you can allocate a one-dimensional array of Strings of length 100 like this—

```
bipush 100
multianewarray [Ljava/lang/String; 1
```

—which has the same effect as

```
bipush 100
anewarray java/lang/String
```

4.12.3 Length of Arrays

In Java, to get the length of an array, you say

```
args.length
```

where `args` is a `reference` to an array object. Although the Java syntax for getting the length of an array looks as if you're getting the `length` field from the array object, that's not really what's happening. You must use the `arraylength` instruction on the array. To find out the length of the `args` array:

```
aload_0              ; Push the array reference
arraylength          ; Leaves the length of the array on the stack
```

This leaves the length of the array on the stack.

CHAPTER 5

Control Instructions

A program needs to be able to repeat code and skip over sections of the code. High-level languages like Java provide constructs such as for, if, and while for *structured programming*. Control structures like for, if, and while make it easy to see where control of a program goes, because programs can enter each loop only at the beginning and leave at the end. The idea behind structured programming is that larger units of code are divisible into smaller units, which are themselves composed of yet smaller units.

The JVM does not support structured programming directly. The only unit of code is the instruction. In place of structured programming constructs, the JVM provides instructions to jump directly from one place in the method to another. Most of these instructions transfer control to another location if some condition is met; otherwise, the program continues at the next instruction. In Oolong, the locations are written as identifiers called *labels*. The process of transferring control from one instruction to another is called *branching*.

Labels are written as an identifier followed by a colon (:). In bytecodes, the label is transformed into an offset (either positive or negative) between the beginning of the if instruction and the beginning of the destination instruction. The offset must point to the beginning of an instruction. If it points to the middle of an instruction, the virtual machine assumes that the program is corrupted or otherwise suspicious, and will refuse to load the class.

5.1 Comparing Integers

The next example is a method that takes an int. If it's greater than 20, the method returns the string "i > 20"; otherwise, it returns the string "i <= 20".

```
.method static compareTo20(I)Ljava/lang/String;
    ;load_0            ; Push variable i from slot 0
    bipush 20          ; Push the number 20
```

```
    if_icmpgt greater       ; Go to the code at label "greater"
                            ; if i > 20
    ; Execution continues here if the i <= 20
    ldc "i <= 20"
    areturn

greater:                    ; This is the "greater" label
    ; Execution continues here if i > 20
    ldc "i > 20"
    areturn
.end method
```

The goto instruction does a transfer no matter what. They're most often used to write loops like the following one, which loops until variable 0 reaches 21:

```
loop:                       ; Begin the loop
    iload_0                 ; Push variable i (in slot 0)
    bipush 20               ; Push 20
    if_icmpgt break         ; Break the loop if i>20
    iinc 0 1                ; Increment i by 1
    goto loop               ; And go back to the beginning of the loop
break:                      ; Go here after looping
```

The if instructions break down into three groups. The first group is used to compare ints to other ints. The mnemonics for these instructions are if_icmpgt, if_icmplt, if_icmpge, if_icmple, if_icmpeq, or if_icmpne. The last two letters of these instructions stand for "greater than," "less than," "greater than or equal to," "less than or equal to," "equal to," and "not equal to," respectively.

For example, if you wanted to loop until i was equal to 20 instead of greater than 20:

```
loop:                       ; Begin the loop
    iload_0                 ; Push variable i
    bipush 20               ; Push 20
    if_icmpeq break         ; Break the loop if i == 20
    iinc 0 1                ; Increment i by 1
    goto loop               ; And go back to the beginning of the loop
break:                      ; Go here after looping
```

The second group of branch instructions is like the first, except that instead of taking two ints and comparing them, they take one int and compare it to zero. The mnemonics for the instructions begin with `if` and end with the same suffix used for the first set. For example,

```
iconst_m1                   ; Push -1
ifle less_than_zero         ; Goes to less_than_zero
                            ; since -1 <= 0
bipush 42                   ; Push 42
bipush 26                   ; Push 26
isub                        ; Subtract 26 from 42, leaving 16
ifeq same_as_zero           ; Goes to the next instruction, since
                            ; 16 != 0
```

The compare-to-zero instructions are frequently used with boolean values, where 0 means `false` and 1 means `true`. For example,

```
aload_1                 ; Push a Double object
invokevirtual java/lang/Double/isInfinite ()Z
                        ; returns 1 if the number is infinite,
                        ; and 0 otherwise
ifne infinity           ; Go to infinity if the number is infinite
```

Branches may jump only within a single method. You're not allowed to branch to code outside a method. For example, this is illegal:

```
.method doSomething()V
loop:
;; Loop code goes here
goto loop
.end method

.method bigBranch()V
goto loop               ; Illegal!
return
.end method

.method someOtherMethod
```

If you try this, the Oolong assembler will report that the `loop` label is not found.

Labels have a lifespan only within the method. Because of this, you can use the same label several times in a single class:

```
.method methodOne()V
loop:
```

```
;; Loop code goes here
goto loop
.end method

.method methodTwo()V
loop:
;; More loop code goes here
goto loop
.end method
```

Exercise 5.1

Write a method that takes a char and returns `true` (1) if it is upper case, `false` (0) otherwise.   ▲

Exercise 5.2

The `main` method of a program takes an array of `Strings` that represent the arguments to the program. Write a `main` that prints out all the arguments to the program.   ▲

Exercise 5.3

Write a method that takes two arguments, a and b, and prints out all the numbers between a and b, inclusive. What happens if a>b? What can you do about it?   ▲

5.2   Comparing References

The third group of instructions is used to compare `references` to see if they are equal (`if_acmpeq`) or not equal (`if_acmpne`). Two `references` are equal only if they refer to the same object or if they are both `null`. For example,

```
aload_0
aload_0
if_acmpeq success          ; This test always goes to success,
                           ; since the same reference is loaded
                           ; twice

aload_1
dup
```

```
    if_acmpeq success          ; This test also goes to success,
                               ; since the duped value is equal
                               ; to the original

    new Cookie
    dup
    invokevirtual Cookie/<init> ()V  ; Make a cookie
    new Cookie
    dup
    invokevirtual Cookie/<init> ()V  ; Make another one
    if_acmpeq success          ; This comparison fails, since
                               ; it compares two different
                               ; Cookies

    new Cookie()
    dup
    invokevirtual Cookie/<init>()V   ; Make yet another cookie
    aconst_null                ; Put null on the stack
    if_acmpeq nullcookie       ; This test fails, because
                               ; no object is equal to null

                               ; Get the chocolate chip
                               ; cookie
    getstatic Cookie/chocolateChip LCookie;
    aconst_null
    if_acmpeq nocookie         ; If the chocolateChip Cookie is
                               ; null, go to nocookie
```

Since comparison to `null` is something JVM programs do frequently, there are two special instructions (`ifnull` and `ifnonnull`) that compare a single object to `null`. The last example can be rewritten

```
    getstatic Cookie/chocolateChip LCookie;
    ifnull nocookie            ; If the chocolateChip Cookie is
                               ; null, go to nocookie
```

Table 5.1 summarizes the branching instructions.

TABLE 5.1: *Branch instructions*

Mnemonic	Argument	Stack	Effect
goto	*label*		Control transfers to *label*.
if_acmpeq	*label*	*ref1 ref2*	If *ref1* references the same object as *ref2*, control branches to *label*.
if_acmpne	*label*	*ref1 ref2*	If *ref1* does not reference the same object as *ref2*, control branches to *label*.
ifnonnull	*label*	*ref1*	If *ref1* is not null, control branches to *label*.
ifnull	*label*	*ref2*	If *ref1* is null, control branches to *label*.
if_icmpeq	*label*	*int1 int2*	If *int1* == *int2*, control branches to *label*.
if_icmpne	*label*	*int1 int2*	If *int1* != *int2*, control branches to *label*.
if_icmplt	*label*	*int1 int2*	If *int1* < *int2*, control branches to *label*.
if_icmpge	*label*	*int1 int2*	If *int1* >= *int2*, control branches to *label*.
if_icmpgt	*label*	*int1 int2*	If *int1* >= *int2*, control branches to *label*.
if_icmple	*label*	*int1 int2*	If *int1* <= *int2*, control branches to *label*.
ifeq	*label*	*int1*	If *int1* == 0, control branches to *label*.
ifne	*label*	*int1*	If *int1* != 0, control branches to *label*.
iflt	*label*	*int1*	If *int1* < 0, control branches to *label*.
ifge	*label*	*int1*	If *int1* >= 0, control branches to *label*.
ifgt	*label*	*int1*	If *int1* > 0, control branches to *label*.
ifle	*label*	*int1*	If *int1* <= 0, control branches to *label*.

5.3   Other Comparisons

All control instructions test either ints or references. If you want to do a branch based on a comparison between two floats, longs, or doubles, you have to use a separate instruction to turn the non-int comparison into an int comparison. The instructions to do this are summarized in Table 5.2. These instructions leave 1, 0, or −1 on the stack if the first operand is greater than, equal to, or less than the second. This value is easily compared with zero as an int, using the ifeq, ifne, iflt, ifgt, ifle, or ifge instructions. For example, comparing double values:

```
getstatic java/lang/Math/PI D ; Get a good approximation of pi
ldc2_w 3.1416D              ; Get a worse approximation of pi
dcmpg                       ; Compare the two numbers
                            ; This leaves -1 on the stack,
                            ; since pi < 3.1416
iflt approxTooHigh          ; Goes to approxTooHigh, since
                            ; -1 < 0
```

TABLE 5.2: *Comparison operations*

Mnemonic	Stack	Effect
dcmpg	*double1 double2*	If *double1* == *double2*, leave 0 on the stack. If *double1* < *double1*, leave −1. If *double1* > *double1*, leave 1. If either is NaN, leave 1.
dcmpl	*double1 double2*	Same as dcmpg, except leave −1 if either is NaN.
fcmpg	*float1 float2*	If *float1* == *float2*, leave 0 on the stack. If *float1* < *float2*, leave −1. If *float1* > *float2*, leave 1. If either is NaN, leave 1.
fcmpl	*float1 float2*	Same as fcmpg, except leave −1 if either is NaN.
lcmp	*long1 long2*	If *long1* == *long2*, leave 0 on the stack. If *long1* < *long2*, leave −1. If *long1* > *long2*, leave 1.

Or for long values:

```
; Push the current time in milliseconds, a long value
invokestatic java/lang/System/currentTimeMillis()J
aload_0                   ; Push a Document
getfield Document/lastUpdatedTime J
                          ; Get the last time this
                          ; document was updated
lsub                      ; Figure out the difference
ldc 60000                 ; Was it more than 60 seconds ago?
lcmp                      ; Leaves 1 if more than 60 seconds
                          ; 0 if exactly 60 seconds, and
                          ; −1 if less than 60 seconds
ifle makeBackup           ; Make a backup if it was updated
                          ; <= 60 seconds ago
```

For the float and double comparisons, there are two almost identical operations for each: fcmpg/fcmpl and dcmpg/dcmpl. The difference is in the treatment of values that are NaN (not a number). Since NaN isn't really a number, it can't be compared to the other values. You choose the g variant or the l variant based on how you want your program to react if it encounters invalid numbers. If you want to see if a > b and you use dcmpg, then the test will succeed if either is NaN. If you use dcmpl, it will to fail.

5.4   Switches

Switches are a kind of specialized `if` instruction used for comparing `int` values. Where `if` instructions can branch only two ways, a switch can go to several different locations, depending on the value of its operand. The JVM has two instructions, `tableswitch` and `lookupswitch`, depending on whether the range of possible values is densely packed or sparse. Each provides a mapping between an `int` value and a label. It finds the label corresponding to the `int` operand and transfers to there.

For example, consider the `fcmpg` instruction. This instruction leaves −1, 0, or 1 on the stack. The `if` instructions can do only a two-way jump, but with the `lookupswitch` instruction you can directly handle each possible result:

```
; Assume a and b are floats on top of the stack
   fcmpg                        ; Compare the numbers
   lookupswitch
        -1:      less           ; Go to less if a<b
         0:      equal          ; Go to equal if a==b
         1:      greater        ; Go to greater if a>b
       default: fail            ; Not expecting this, but default
                                ; is required
less:                           ; Push "<" if a<b
   ldc "<"
   goto printItOut
equal:                          ; Push "==" if a==b
   ldc "=="
   goto printItOut
greater:                        ; Push ">" if a>b
   ldc ">"
   goto printItOut

fail:                           ; Something bad has happened. Control
                                ; should never get here.
```

The `default` case is required, and it has to come last. If the value on top of the stack matches any of the keys, then control transfers to the corresponding label. If it doesn't match any of them, control transfers to the label specified by `default`.

The `tableswitch` instruction is similar to `lookupswitch`, except that instead of having to specify pairs of keys and labels, you have to specify only a base value and a list of labels. The first label corresponds to the base, the second to base+1, and so on. The `lookupswitch` code can be written instead as

```
tableswitch -1
    less                    ; Go to less on -1
    equal                   ; Go to equal on 0
    greater                 ; Go to greater on 1
    default: fail           ; Fail otherwise
```

The `tableswitch` instruction is usually faster than `lookupswitch`. That's because it can be implemented in the JVM by using the value as an index into a table, which is very fast. For `lookupswitch`, it may have to compare the value to each of the keys. However, a `tableswitch` instruction might take up a lot of space if the only values you really wanted to check were −22, 197, and 2,000,163.

The virtual machine's implementation of `lookupswitch` might not be as slow as you'd expect, however. Finding the right match is a search problem, and the virtual machine implementor might use a binary search or hash table lookup to make the search much faster than comparing individual values.

Exercise 5.4

Rewrite your answer to exercise 5.1 using a `tableswitch`.   ▲

Exercise 5.5

Rewrite your answer to exercise 5.1 using a `lookupswitch`.   ▲

5.5   Subroutines

Another kind of special branch is the `jsr`, for jump subroutine. It's like a `goto` that remembers where it came from. Or you can think of it as a method invocation that doesn't create a new stack frame. For example,

```
state1:
jsr get_next_character   ; Go to the subroutine that leaves
                         ; the next char on top of the stack

lookupswitch             ; Jump to the next state
    65: state1           ; Go to state 1 if the value is 65
    66: state2           ; Go to state 2 if the value is 66
    default: state3      ; Otherwise, go to state 3

get_next_character:
; At this point, there's a returnAddress on top of the stack
astore_3                 ; Store it in variable 3
```

```
;; Do code to get the next character,
;; and leave it on top of the stack
ret 3                          ; Return to the location in variable 3
```

The jsr is used to take code that would otherwise have to be replicated in several places and put it in a single place. It's not quite as powerful as putting it into a separate method, since there's no explicit facilities for passing arguments. It is less expensive to use, however, since the machine doesn't have to create a whole new stack frame.

When jsr is executed, it branches to the location specified by the label, and it leaves a special kind of value on the stack called a returnAddress to represent the return address. It's your responsibility to remember this value by storing it in a local variable. The value is a kind of reference, so you use the aload and astore instructions to store its value. However, you can't call methods on it, store it in a field, or use it as an argument to a method. As with the other branches, the label must be inside the body of the same method as the jsr instruction.

At the end of a subroutine, you can return to the instruction after the jsr with a ret. A ret is different from a return, which is used to return from an invocation. The argument to ret is a number that represents a local variable. That variable should contain the return address that was on the stack at the beginning of the subroutine.

5.6   Exceptions

Exceptions are sort of super-goto which can transfer control not only within a method, but even terminate the current method to find its destination further up the Java stack. Exceptions are used to indicate that something has gone wrong with a program. Usually, an exception indicates that the problem is fairly severe and the operation being attempted should be aborted.

To indicate that a problem has occurred, the program *throws* an exception. When an exception is thrown, the JVM will try to find an *exception handler* that can handle the exception at the current location in the current method. This is called the *active exception handler*. If there is none, the JVM terminates the current method and checks again with the method that called the current method. It repeats this operation until it finds a handler. The handler should clean up the state of the system and correct the error, if possible.

An exception is thrown with the athrow instruction. The athrow instruction takes one operand from the top of the stack: an object that must be a subclass of java/lang/Throwable. Usually, when you create an exception class, it is a subclass of either java/lang/Exception or java/lang/Error, depending on the nature of the error.

This class declaration declares a SnackException, which indicates that some sort of problem has occurred while snacking:

```
.class SnackException
.super java/lang/Exception     ; Exception is a Throwable

; A constructor which takes a message string
.method <init> (Ljava/lang/String;)V
aload_0                        ; Initialize the superclass
aload_1
invokespecial java/lang/Exception/<init> (Ljava/lang/String;)V
return
.end method
```

A SnackException occurs when the program is having a snack and notices that it can't continue for some reason (for example, there's no more milk). To indicate that you're out of milk, use this code:

```
; I'm out of milk!
new SnackException          ; Create a SnackException
dup
ldc "Out of milk"           ; Initialize it with a message
invokespecial SnackException/<init> (Ljava/lang/String;)V
athrow                      ; Throw the exception
```

When an exception is thrown, control transfers to the most current *exception handler*. An exception handler is specified in Oolong with a .catch directive:

```
.catch class from begin-label to end-label using handler-label
```

Here, class is the type of exception to catch, and *begin-label* and *end-label* indicate the range of code within the method that is covered by the exception handler. This allows you to use different exception handlers for the same exception in different parts of the method. The *handler-label* designates which code will be called when the exception occurs.

When an exception occurs and the program is currently between *begin-label* and *end-label*, control transfers to *handler-label* as long as the exception object is an instance of the *class* or one of its subclasses. If a SnackException is thrown, it can be caught by an exception handler catching SnackExceptions, Exceptions, or Throwables but not by an exception handler catching Errors, because SnackException is not a subclass of Error. Similarly, an exception handler catching `SnackExceptions` does not catch `NullPointerExceptions`, because `NullPointerException` is not a subclass of `SnackException`.

For example,

```
.method nosh()V
.catch SnackException from begin to end using
      SnackExceptionHandler
begin:
; Do stuff which might cause a SnackException
getstatic Refrigerator/milkQuantity I  ; Do we have milk?
ifgt continue                          ; Drink if milk>0

; I'm out of milk!
new SnackException                 ; Create a SnackException
dup
ldc "Out of milk"                  ; Initialize it with a message
invokespecial SnackException/<init> (Ljava/lang/String;)V
athrow                             ; Throw the exception

continue:
; We do have milk, so we can drink some
end:

; The code here is not covered by the SnackException handler,
; because it is out of range.

return

SnackExceptionHandler:
;; Do something with the exception. Maybe notify the user
;; to go get some more milk.
return
.end method
```

An exception handler is active whenever the current instruction is between *begin-label* and *end-label*. "Between" means that the program counter is after *begin-label* and before *end-label*.

When an `athrow` instruction is executed, the JVM looks to see if there is an exception handler active in the current method that can handle the exception. If there is one, then control transfers to the handler.

The handler code begins with the thrown object on top of the stack. This is the object that was the operand to `athrow`. The following example shows what happens when you run out of cookies.

```
.catch SnackException from begin to end using handler
begin:
                                         ; Print a message
getstatic java/lang/System/out Ljava/io/PrintStream;
ldc "At begin"
invokevirtual java/io/PrintStream/println (Ljava/lang/String;)V

new SnackException                       ; Create a SnackException
dup
ldc "Out of cookies"
invokespecial SnackException/<init> (Ljava/lang/String;)V
athrow                                   ; Throw it

getstatic java/lang/System/out Ljava/io/PrintStream;
ldc "This code doesn't get executed due to the exception"
invokevirtual java/io/PrintStream/println (Ljava/lang/String;)V

end:
return

handler:
; The exception is now on top of the stack
invokevirtual java/lang/Throwable/getMessage
      ()Ljava/lang/String;
getstatic java/lang/System/out Ljava/io/PrintStream;
swap                                     ; Put out below the message
invokevirtual java/io/PrintStream/println (Ljava/lang/String;)V

return
```

When this code is executed, it prints

```
At begin
Out of cookies
```

The code after the `athrow` is never executed, because control went to the handler instead.

If there is no active exception handler that can handle the exception, then the current method is terminated and control passes back to the calling method right after the invocation. It's as if the method has returned, except that no value is returned, even if one was expected. The JVM continues looking for an exception handler from that point. This can continue indefinitely as long as no exception handler is found. If no exception handler is found anywhere, the exception is finally handled by the ThreadGroup, which usually prints out an error message like this one:

```
java.lang.NullPointerException
    at Program.bottomOfTheStack(Program.java:18)
    at Program.middleOfTheStack(Program.java:14)
    at Program.topOfTheStack(Program.java:10)
    at Program.main(Program.java:5)
```

Here's an example of how an exception can be thrown from one method invocation to another:

```
.class BedtimeRoutine
.method goToBed()V
.catch SnackException from begin to end using handler
    ; This call is not covered by the exception handler
    invokestatic BedtimeRoutine/putOnPajamas()V
    ; SnackException coverage begins here
begin:
    ; Invoke a function that might throw SnackException
    invokestatic BedtimeRoutine/haveMidnightSnack ()V
    ; SnackException coverage ends here
end:
    ; This call is not covered by the exception handler either
    invokestatic BedtimeRoutine/brushTeeth()V
    return                     ;Successful completion

handler:
    ;; Handle the exception that occured when trying to have
    ;; a snack
    return
.end method

.method static haveMidnightSnack()V
getstatic Refrigerator/milkQuantity I ; Do we have milk?
ifgt drink_milk                       ; Drink if got milk
```

```
; I'm out of milk!
new SnackException              ; Create a SnackException
dup
ldc "Out of milk"              ; Initialize it with a message
invokespecial SnackException/<init> (Ljava/lang/String)V
athrow                         ; Throw the exception

; Successfully got milk. Now drink it.
drink_milk:
getstatic java/lang/System/out Ljava/io/PrintStream;
ldc "Drinking milk"
invokevirtual java/io/PrintStream/println (Ljava/lang/String;)V
return
.end method
```

Suppose that program calls goToBed, which calls haveMidnightSnack. If there's milk, then everything is fine; you drink the milk, return to the goToBed method, and brush your teeth.

If you discover that you're out of milk in haveMidnightSnack, a SnackException is thrown. There's no handler for it in haveMidnightSnack, so the method is terminated and control returns to goToBed. This method does have a handler for a SnackException. What happens there is not specified, but you might skip the midnight snack and go straight to bed, or you might run down to the store to buy more milk.

5.6.1 Multiple Exception Handlers

When a particular instruction is covered by several exception handlers, the first applicable one within the frame is taken. For example,

```
.catch SnackException from begin2 to end2 using handler2
.catch java/lang/Exception from begin1 to end1 using handler1
begin1:
    invokestatic BedtimeRoutine/putOnPajamas()V
begin2:
    ; Invoke a function that might throw SnackException
    invokestatic BedtimeRoutine/haveMidnightSnack ()V
end2:
    ; This call is not covered by the exception handler either
    invokestatic BedtimeRoutine/brushTeeth()V
end1:
    return
```

```
handler2:
   ; The stack contains a SnackException; just return
   return

handler1:
   ; The stack contains a more general Exception; print an
   ; error message
   invokevirtual java/lang/Throwable/getMessage
      ()Ljava/lang/String;
   getstatic java/lang/System/out Ljava/io/PrintStream;
   swap                            ; Put out below the message
   invokevirtual java/io/PrintStream/println
      (Ljava/lang/String;)V
   return
```

There is an exception handler that covers the entire range from begin1 to end1. It handles the very general class java/lang/Exception, which covers exceptions like NullPointerException and ArrayIndexOutOfBoundsException, as well as SnackExceptions and most other application-defined Exceptions. These are handled by the code at handler1, which prints out the message associated with the exception. All exceptions inherit the method getMessage from java/lang/Throwable, which returns a detail message associated with the exception.

The code from begin2 to end2 is covered by two different exception handlers. If a SnackException occurs, then it is handled by the code at handler2. In this code, the snack exception isn't considered important, so the method just returns. If any other kind of Exception occurs, it is handled by the more general exception handler at handler1.

If a SnackException were to occur for some reason from brushTeeth or putOnPajamas, the handler at handler1 would handle the exception, since the other handler is not active while calling those two methods. Only the call to haveMidnightSnack is covered.

It is important to realize that the order of the .catch directives matters. If a SnackException occurs during haveMidnightSnack, the handler at handler2 is used because its .catch directive comes first—not because SnackException is more specific than Exception. Suppose you reversed the .catch directives:

```
.catch java/lang/Exception from begin1 to end1 using handler1
.catch SnackException from begin2 to end2 using handler2
```

In this case, the SnackException handler is totally hidden by the java/lang/Exception handler. The code at handler2 will never be called, because any SnackException thrown will be handled by the first exception handler.

As a general rule, write your code so that the more specific exception handlers come before the more general ones.

Exercise 5.6

Add two subclasses of SnackException called OutOfMilkException and OutOf-CookiesException. Give them constructors that have a default message. How would you modify the code to handle an OutOfMilkException differently from other SnackExceptions? ▲

Exercise 5.7

In Java, there can be several catches for a try:

```
try {
    foo();
}
catch(Exception e1) {
    System.out.println(e1.getMessage());
}
catch(NullPointerException e2) {
    System.out.println(e2.getMessage());
}
```

The Java compiler generates an error message for this code. Why do you think this is? ▲

5.6.2 .throws Directive

You can alert somebody using your method to what exceptions the method might throw with the .throws directive:

```
.method lateNightSnack()V
.throws OutofMilkException
.throws OutofCookiesException
```

The .throws directives are optional. They're used to support a Java language requirement that a method can throw only exceptions that are explicitly listed. The following Java method—

```
void eveningActivities()
{
    watchTV();
    lateNightSnack();
```

```
    goToBed();
}
```

—will evoke an error from the Java compiler stating that the OutOfCookiesException and OutOfMilkException exceptions must either be caught or listed in
the throws clause of the method declaration:

```
void eveningActivities() throws OutOfMilk, OutOfCookies
```

If you don't list the possible exceptions in a .throws clause, then the Java compiler won't know that your method might throw an exception, and somebody
using the eveningActivities method would be surprised if the method terminates abnormally. Writing .throws directives is more work for you, but it makes
life easier on the next programmer who uses the code.

5.6.3   Other Ways to Throw Exceptions

Besides athrow, exceptions can also be thrown by other untoward events happening in the virtual machine. For example, this code tries to divide 1 by 0:

```
iconst_1
iconst_0
idiv
```

It results in an ArithmeticException when you execute the program. Similarly,
attempting to call a method on null will cause an exception:

```
aload_null
invokevirtual java/lang/Object/toString ()Ljava/lang/String;
```

This will cause a NullPointerException.
    These machine-signaled exceptions can be caught with a .catch directive,
just like any other exception.

Exercise 5.8

Another kind of machine-generated exception is the java/lang/ArrayIndex-
OutOfBoundsException, which occurs when you try to use an element of an array
that does not exist. Use this fact to write a program that lists all its arguments
without using any if branches. (You may use a goto.)   ▲

5.7   A Gentler Way of Checking Type

The checkcast exception checks to see if an object has the appropriate type. If it
succeeds, it leaves the reference to the object on the stack. If it fails, it throws a
ClassCastException.

Sometimes you want to check the type of something without having it throw an exception if you guess wrong. In this case, use the `instanceof` instruction. It works much like `checkcast`, except that instead of throwing an exception in the case of failure, the JVM leaves a 1 or 0 on top of the stack indicating success or failure.

For example, suppose you have three classes, `Larry`, `Curly`, and `Moe`, each of which has `Stooge` as a superclass.

```
; Get a random stooge
invokevirtual Movies/getStooge()LStooge;
dup                          ; Copy the reference
instanceof Curly             ; Is it Curly?
ifeq notCurly                ; If the result is 0, go to notCurly
    ; Now we know that the top of the stack must be Curly
checkcast Curly              ; Let the machine know about that
    ;; Do whatever it is you want with Curly
return

notCurly:
    ;; Deal with Larry or Moe
return
```

If the stooge you get is a `Curly`, then the `instanceof` operator will leave 1 on the stack; otherwise, it will leave 0. The `ifeq` instruction goes to `notCurly` if the value on top of the stack is equal to 0. Otherwise, it will continue at the next instruction as usual.

Unlike `checkcast`, the `instanceof` instruction removes its operand from the stack, so you have to `dup` it if you want to use the `reference` that is being tested. The JVM doesn't use the information from the `instanceof` to change what it knows about the `dup`, so you still have to use `checkcast` if you want to use the object as an instance of the type.

Verification Process

THE verification algorithm is one of the most distinctive features of the Java virtual machine. Its purpose is to ensure that `class` files that are loaded into the machine follow certain rules. These rules guarantee that programs cannot gain access to fields and methods they are not allowed to access and that they can't otherwise trick the JVM into doing unsafe things.

The verification algorithm is applied to every class as it is loaded into the system, before instances are created or static properties used. This allows the JVM implementation to assume that the class has certain safety properties, which permit the implementation to make optimizations based on that assumption.

The verification algorithm makes it possible to safely download Java applets from the Internet. In a web browser, a class called the `SecurityManager` ensures that some JVM capabilities are available only to authorized programs, and the verification algorithm makes sure that the programs don't do anything that would enable them to circumvent the `SecurityManager`. We discuss the `SecurityManager` in more detail in chapter 15.

If you're writing in Java, a well-behaved Java compiler will generate only JVM classes that follow the rules. As a JVM programmer, you have the ability to bypass the restrictions of the Java language, which lets you write programs that are potentially dangerous. The verification algorithm ensures that even though you haven't had to pass your programs through a Java compiler, your programs still follow the rules.

The description of the verification algorithm in this chapter is not complete, but it does cover many of the most important points. For a complete list of the rules, read *The Java Virtual Machine Specification*. As you read this chapter, think to yourself of possible ways a program could try to do something unsafe, then prove to yourself using the requirements that the program can't pass the verification algorithm.

6.1　How the Verification Algorithm Works

Section 4.8 of *The Java Virtual Machine Specification* contains a large set of rules that programs must follow if they want to run in the machine. It is the job of the verification algorithm to prove that each and every one of these rules has been followed. These rules were designed to be verifiable by just examining each class, without resorting to running the class.

The verification algorithm works by asking a set of questions about the class file. These questions fall into five general categories.

1. Is it a structurally valid class file?
2. Are all constant references correct?
3. Are the instructions valid?
4. Will the stack and local variables always contain values of the appropriate types?
5. Do the classes used really exist, and do they have the necessary methods and fields?

These questions can be answered *statically,* that is, from looking at the bytecodes without executing the program. This enables the virtual machine to stop a badly behaving program before it starts. It also permits faster execution, because the virtual machine doesn't have to check some kinds of errors as the program runs. If the program has passed verification, then these errors cannot occur.

6.2　Is It a Structurally Valid class File?

There are some ways in which the verification algorithm can tell right away that it's not going to like a file. The first four bytes must contain the hex values CA, FE, BA, BE. This *magic number* lets the verification algorithm immediately reject files that have been garbled and files that were never intended to be thought of as class files (like Java source files, Java archive files, and all the other files hanging around in the system).

Following the magic number are the minor version and the major version. Each takes up two bytes and is interpreted as a 16-bit unsigned value. For JDK 1.0 and 1.1, the major version number is 45 (0x2d) and the minor version number is 3. The Java 2 platform also accepts major version 46 (0x23) and minor version 0, as well as minor versions greater than 3 for version 45.

The Java 2 platform is backward compatible. If your class files are not meant to be read on a JVM prior to Java 2, then they may be marked with version 46.

The Java 2 platform `javac` compiler supports this with the `-target` option; `-target 1.2` will produce a `class` file with version 46.0, and `-target 1.1` will produce a `class` file with version 45.3.

If all three numbers are acceptable, the verification algorithm scans the rest of the file to ensure that it has the correct format. Figure 6.1 depicts where the bytes belong in a properly formatted `class` file.

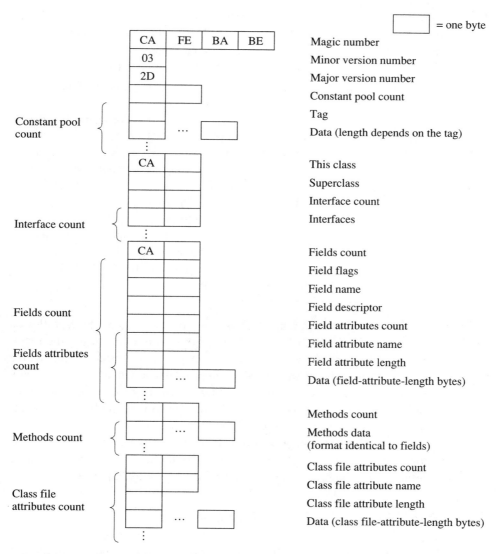

FIGURE 6.1: *Is the file properly formatted?*

TABLE 6.1: *Constant tags*

Tag	Type	Format	Interpretation
1	UTF8	4+*n* bytes	The first four bytes are an unsigned integer *n*; the remaining *n* bytes are the text of the constant.
2	*not defined*		
3	Integer	4 bytes	Signed integer
4	Float	4 bytes	IEEE 754 floating-point number
5	Long	8 bytes	Long signed integer
6	Double	8 bytes	IEEE 754 double-precision number
7	Class	2 bytes	Reference to a UTF8 constant that is the name of a class
8	String	2 bytes	Reference to a UTF8 constant that is the value of the String
9	Fieldref	4 bytes	The first two bytes are a reference to a Class; the second two point to a NameAndType.
10	Methodref	4 bytes	Same as Fieldref
11	InterfaceMethodref	4 bytes	Same as Fieldref
12	NameAndType	4 bytes	The first two bytes point to a UTF8 that is the name of the field or method; the second two point to a UTF8, which is its descriptor.

Most sections begin with a count, which is a two-byte unsigned integer, followed by that many instances of some pattern of bytes. For example, following the major version number is the count of the number of constants. Each constant begins with a tag describing what sort of constant it is, which in turn tells how many bytes make up the constant. The set of constant tags is defined by the virtual machine specification. If any constant tag is invalid, or if the file ends before the correct number of constants are found, then the file is rejected. The valid constant tags are given in Table 6.1.

Similar rules apply to the other sections. If the file ends before all of the parts are found, or if there are extra bytes at the end, then the file is rejected. For more about the details of the inner workings of the class file, see chapter 9.

6.3   Are All Constant References Correct?

After asking whether or not the file looks like a properly formatted class file, the verification algorithm knows where the constant pool is to be found and how many constants are in it. It also knows that all constant tags are valid. (If there was an invalid constant tag, it wouldn't know how many bytes that constant took up, and it would have rejected the file.) Now it can ask the question "Are the constants themselves correctly formed?" That is,

- Do `Class` and `String` constants have a reference to another constant that is a UTF8 constant?
- Do `Fieldref`, `Methodref`, and `InterfaceMethodref` constants have a class index that is a `Class` constant and a name-and-type index that is a `NameAndType` constant?
- Do `NameAndType` constants have a name index that points to a UTF8 and a type index that points to a UTF8?
- Does the `this` class index (found immediately after the constant pool) point to a `Class` constant?
- Does the `superclass` index (found right after the `this` class index) point to a `Class` constant?
- Do the name and descriptor fields of each field and each method entry point to a UTF8 constant?
- Are the type names referred to by `NameAndType` constants valid method or field descriptors?

Figure 6.2 depicts part of the constant pool for this class:

```
.class Foo
.super Bar
.implements Baz

.field field1 LFoo;
.method isEven (I)Z
;; …
.end method
```

In the figure, you can see how the `this` class and the `superclass` fields point to `Class` constants which point to the names `Foo` and `Bar`. There is one interface, which points to a `Class` constant that points to `Baz`. The field points to the name `field1` and the type `LFoo;` (since it is of type `Foo`). The method points to the name `isEven` and the type `(I)B` (since it takes an integer and returns a boolean). The order of the constants is irrelevant; constants may point to other constants both forward and backward.

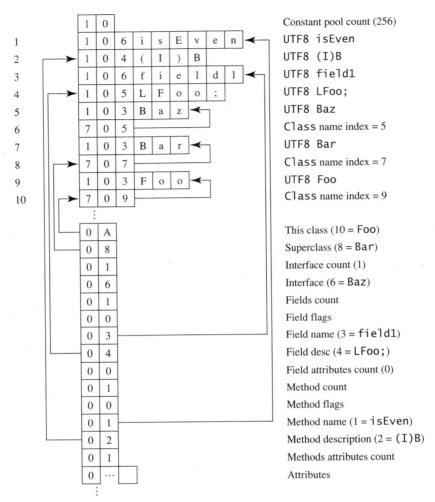

FIGURE 6.2: *Are all constant references correct?*

6.4   Are All the Instructions Valid?

Now that you know that the overall class structure is valid, you can look at the method bodies to see if the instructions within the method are correctly formed. Following are some of the questions to ask.

◆ Does each instruction begin with a recognized opcode?

◆ If the instruction takes a constant pool reference as an argument, does it point to an actual constant pool entry with the correct type?

- ◆ If the instruction uses a local variable, is the local variable range within the correct range?
- ◆ If the instruction is a branch, does it point to the beginning of an instruction?

These requirements ensure that the JVM never has to deal with an unidentified instruction or with improper arguments once it is running.

Because local variable numbers are always used as arguments to instructions, rather than as operands, the set of local variables that is used in the method is fixed. This makes it impossible to use an invalid local variable in a program that has been verified. Table 6.2 summarizes the argument requirements for instructions that require arguments. For example, take this Oolong program:

```
.method public static main([Ljava/lang/String;)V
getstatic java/lang/System/out Ljava/io/PrintStream;
ldc "Hello, world"
invokevirtual java/io/PrintStream/println(Ljava/lang/String;)V
return
.end method
```

TABLE 6.2: *Argument verification requirements for instructions*

Instructions	Bytes	Argument Requirements
ifeq ifne iflt ifge ifgt ifle if_icmpeq if_icmpne if_icmplt if_icmpge if_icmpgt if_icmple if_acmpeq if_acmpne goto jsr ifnull ifnonnull	2	The two bytes are taken as a 16-bit signed integer. When added to the location of the beginning of the instruction, this gives a new location. This location must be the beginning of an instruction, not the middle of an instruction.

Table continued on next page.

TABLE 6.2: *Argument verification requirements for instructions*   (continued)

Instructions	Bytes	Argument Requirements
goto_w jsr_w	4	Same as goto and jsr but use a 32-bit number.
iload lload fload dload aload istore lstore fstore dstore astore ret bipush sipush	1	Taken as a one-byte unsigned number, must be less than the local variable count.
iinc	2	First byte must be less than the size of the local variable array.
ldc	1	Must be a constant pool index of a String, Integer, or Float constant.
ldc_w	2	Must be a constant pool index of a String, Integer, or Float constant.
ldc2_w	2	Must be a constant pool index of a Long or Double constant.
new anewarray checkcast instanceof	2	Must be a constant pool index of a Class constant.
getstatic putstatic getfield putfield	2	Must be a constant pool index of a Fieldref constant.
invokevirtual invokespecial invokestatic	2	Must be a constant pool index of a Methodref constant.

TABLE 6.2: *Argument verification requirements for instructions*   (continued)

Instructions	Bytes	Argument Requirements
invokeinterface	4	First two must be a constant pool index of an InterfaceMethodref constant. Third byte must be the size of the arguments removed from the stack when the method is called. Last byte must be zero.
newarray	1	Must be between 4 and 11.
multianewarray	3	First two must be the constant pool index of a Class constant. Last byte must be less than or equal to the number of left brackets ([) at the beginning of the class name.
tableswitch	variable	Begins with 0–3 bytes of padding so that the next byte begins on a multiple of 4 from the beginning of the method. Followed by three four-byte numbers, default, high, and low. Must be followed by high–low+1 groups of four bytes, each of which must form a valid jump offset as for goto_w.
lookupswitch	variable	Begins with 0–3 byte pad, like tableswitch. Followed by two four-byte numbers, default and npairs. Must be followed by npairs pairs of match and offset. Offset must be a valid jump offset as for goto_w.
wide	variable	If the first byte is the opcode for a load or store instruction or ret, then there must be two bytes that must be less than the total size of the variable pool.
		If the first byte is the opcode for a iinc instruction, then the next two bytes must be a valid local variable index, followed by two more bytes.

Here are the relevant parts of the `class` file to verify this requirement:

							Constant pool	
08	00	18					`String`, value = 24	
07	00	19					`Class` name index = 25	
07	00	1A					`Class` name index = 26	
01	00	03	B	a	r		`Fieldref` 3, 6	
07	00	07					`Methodref` 3, 7	
0C	00	1C	00	1E			`NameAndType` 28, 30	
0C	00	1B	00	1F			`NameAndType` 27, 31	

$\vdots$

01	00	0C	H	e	l	l	o	⋯
01		13	j	a	v	a	/	⋯
01	00	10	j	a	v	a	/	⋯
01	00	07	p	r	i	n	t	⋯
01	00	03	o	u	t			

UTF8 `"Hello, world"`

UTF8 `"java/io/PrintStream"`

UTF8 `"java/lang/System"`

UTF8 `"println"`

UTF8 `"out"`

Method `main`

$\vdots$

B2	0	7
12	1	
B6	0	8
B1	4	

`getstatic` 4

`ldc` 1

`invokevirtual` 5

`return`

There are four instructions. The first is a `getstatic`, whose argument is the constant 4, which is a `Fieldref`. The second is a `ldc`, which has argument 1, a `String`. The third is `invokevirtual`, which has argument 5, a `Methodref`. Finally, the last `return` instruction requires no arguments. All are correct, so this class file would pass this stage of testing.

6.5   Will Each Instruction Always Find a Correctly Formed Stack and Local Variable Array?

What you'd really like is for the verification algorithm to prove that your program does what you meant it to do, but because the computer can't read your mind (yet), this isn't possible. Failing that, you'd like the verification algorithm to reject any programs that could do something illegal, like overflow the stack or apply the wrong type of instruction to a value, and accept all of those that won't. Unfortunately, this guarantee is also a little bit too strong to make. (See the sidebar "Decidability and Java Virtual Machine Verification.")

Decidability and Java Virtual Machine Verification

One of the most important theorems in computer science is the "Halting Problem," which states:

> It is not possible to determine in every case whether or not a program will halt.

There are many corollaries to this. You can never tell whether or not a particular instruction will be executed. You can never tell whether or not a particular variable will ever change. You can't predict the output of the program. These are called *undecidable* properties of a program, because you can't decide 100 percent of the time whether or not a given program has them.

The proof is very clever. If you claim to have a program that can tell whether or not a program will halt, then I will take your program and build another one. If your program says that the input program halts, mine won't, and if your program says it won't, mine will. Then I'll feed my program as input to itself. If my program halts, then it won't halt, and if it doesn't halt, then it will! This is clearly ludicrous, so I'm sure you can't build such a program.

So how can you possibly believe that the JVM verifier can predict whether or not a program will try to overflow the stack, or always find two `int`s on top of the stack whenever there's an `iadd` instruction to do, or any of the other possible ways that a program can fail?

The answer is: It doesn't have to.

Undecidability problems only apply to properties where you are trying to conclude whether *or not* a program has that property. I can easily write a program that checks that some programs halt. For example, if it has no loops in it, then it certainly halts. If it has a loop that terminates when a variable reaches a certain level, and there are only instructions that increase that variable, then the program will certainly halt. There are many other examples.

The verifier designers created a set of conditions which, if met, guarantee that the program won't overflow the stack, and `iadd` will always find appropriate operands, and so forth. These conditions can be checked very quickly. Usually, each instruction has to be checked only once or twice.

Plenty of programs which don't meet these conditions would be perfectly safe to execute, but they are rejected anyway. The verification algorithm identifies *only* safe programs, but it doesn't identify *all* safe ones. This means we're not dealing with an undecidable problem.

A person can recognize some programs that are safe, just like a person can recognize some programs that halt. But a person can't recognize all of the programs that are unsafe, just like a person can't recognize all programs that don't halt. So the verifier makes a compromise, identifying some of the programs that are safe, and rejecting all others.

The study of this fascinating topic is called *automata theory*. An excellent place to start is *Introduction to Automata Theory, Languages, and Computation,* by John Hopcroft and Jeffrey Ullman.

In the end, you have to settle for the somewhat weaker promise that it will reject any class that may do something illegal but it may also reject some safe classes. The verification algorithm asks these questions:

- Will the right elements always be on top of the stack?
- Each time an instruction at a particular location is executed, will the stack always be the same size?

The first requirement guarantees that each instruction will find the appropriate operands on the stack. The second requirement guarantees that the stack cannot overflow or underflow by adding or subtracting elements in a loop.

To test these conditions, the verification algorithm draws a picture of what types the stack and local variables will hold at the beginning of each instruction. In forthcoming sections, we shall go over some examples.

6.5.1   Example 1: Hello, World

The "Hello, world" program in Oolong looks like this:

```
.method static public main([Ljava/lang/String;)V
.limit stack 2
.limit locals 1
getstatic java/lang/System/out          ; Push the output stream
            Ljava/io/PrintStream;
ldc "Hello, world"                      ; Set the argument
invokevirtual java/io/PrintStream/println  ; Call the function
            (Ljava/lang/String;)V
return                                  ; Return
.end method
```

The verification algorithm can prove that this program is safe by drawing pictures to show what the stack must look like before each instruction:

Stack picture:

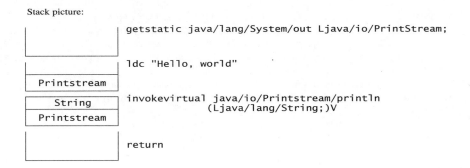

The diagram shows what the stack looks like before each instruction. You always start at the beginning of the method with an empty stack.

The `getstatic` instruction doesn't take anything off the stack, and it pushes a single value onto the stack. The type of that value is given by the last argument to the `getstatic` instruction. In this case, it's a `PrintStream`, so the resulting stack picture has just a `PrintStream` on it. The new stack picture is the input to the `ldc` instruction.

The `ldc` instruction doesn't take anything off the stack, either. It pushes one item, the type of which is determined by the type of the argument. In this case, the argument is a `String`. Now the stack has two elements on it, which is the limit for this method.

The next instruction is `invokevirtual`. It is expecting to find two operands on the stack: a `PrintStream` and a `String`, as described by the method descriptor. Since the return type is `V`, nothing is left on the stack. The stack is now empty.

Notice that the verification algorithm doesn't have to actually trace into the method to determine its effect on the stack picture. The verification algorithm can determine the method invocation's effect on the stack just by looking at the method descriptor.

When the system loads a class, it may delay loading classes that appear in field or method descriptors. The verification algorithm makes the temporary assumption that the other classes actually have all the fields and methods referenced in the code and that they have the appropriate descriptors.

Later, the system may be forced to load the other classes. This happens when an instance is created or when it is used as the superclass of some other class that is loaded or when a static field or method is used. When these classes are actually loaded, they are checked to make sure that they actually have all the methods and fields required by other classes already loaded. If not, the system throws an exception, which prevents that class from being used.

This delayed loading improves performance. If loading had to be done as soon as a class was loaded, the system would appear to hang until the classes were loaded. By delaying class loading, the system can spread out the load, which improves overall response times.

The last instruction in this example is a `return`. This instruction doesn't do anything to the stack; it just returns from the method. It is important to check that the method uses the right kind of return for the descriptor of the method. Since `main` returns `void` and `return` is the right kind of return for `void`, everything is good.

The stack does not have to be empty after returning from a method, but many programs do leave an empty stack. That's because JVM code is often arranged so that each unit of code expects an empty stack and leaves an empty stack, making it easy to combine units without risking violating stack constraints. Most Java compilers work this way. For more details, see chapter 10.

6.5.2   Example 2: gotos and ifs

Example 1 omitted some important details, like how to handle gotos, ifs, and local variables. We explain some of them with a slightly more complicated example: a loop that adds up an array of numbers.

```
.method public static addit ([I)V
.limit stack 2
.limit locals 3
; Variables:
; 0 is the array we're adding up (the parameter to the method)
; 1 is the running total
; 2 is a loop counter
    iconst_0               ; Initialize the total to 0
    istore_1
    iconst_0               ; Initialize the loop counter to 0
    istore_2

loop:
    aload_0                ; Compute the length of the array
    arraylength
    iload_2                ; Test if the loop counter is greater than
                           ; the length of the array
    if_icmpge end          ; If it is, go to the end of the method
                           ; Otherwise, do the body of the loop
body:
    aload_0                ; Push the array
    iload_2                ; Push the counter
    iaload                 ; Take the counter'th element of the array
    iload_1                ; Push the total
    iadd                   ; Add that number to the running total
    istore_1               ; Store the total back into variable 1
    iinc 2 1               ; Increment the counter
    goto loop              ; Repeat the loop
end:
return
```

This time there are local variables as well as a stack. A local variable picture looks a lot like the stack picture. The only difference is that instead of growing and shrinking like the stack, all the variables are allocated beforehand, though they may be uninitialized. Uninitialized variables are represented by an empty box.

As before, we start at the top of the method with an empty stack. There are three variables. The first is automatically initialized to the first parameter; the others are uninitialized. The first seven lines are straightforward: elements are loaded onto the stack, then stored into local variables. The code, annotated with stack and local variable pictures, looks like this:

Stack picture	Local variable picture 0 1 2		
	[I	✓	iconst_0
I	[I	✓	istore_1
	[I I	✓	iconst_0
I	[I I	✓	istore_2
	[I I I	✓ loop:	aload_0
[I	[I I I	✓	arraylength
I	[I I I	✓	iload_2
I I	[I I I	▶	if_icmpge end

▶ : instruction to check

✓ : already checked instructions

The if_icmpge instruction pops two elements off the stack. After executing it, the stack is empty. Control will go to either body (if the test fails) or end (if it succeeds). You have to annotate both instructions with the new stack picture:

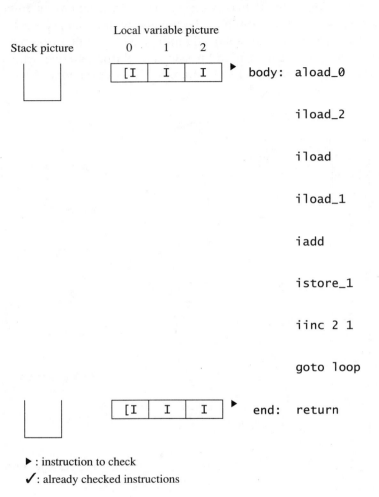

▶ : instruction to check
✓ : already checked instructions

You must check both paths, but it doesn't matter which one you choose to do first. In this example, we'll check the path through body first. We proceed as before until we hit the goto instruction. The picture now looks like this:

Local variable picture

Stack picture

	0	1	2			
	[I	I	I	✓	body:	aload_0
[I	[I	I	I	✓		iload_2
I [I	[I	I	I	✓		iload
I	[I	I	I	✓		iload_1
I I	[I	I	I	✓		iadd
I	[I	I	I	✓		istore_1
	[I	I	I	✓		iinc 2 1
	[I	I	I	▶		goto loop
	[I	I	I	▶	end:	return

▶ : instruction to check

✓ : already checked instructions

At this point, the goto before end says that control returns to loop. Since we've already been to loop, we need to make sure that the stack and local variable pictures currently at loop are identical with the picture after executing the goto. They are; the stack is empty both times, and the local variable pictures are identical. Any flow of control that made it to the goto could continue at loop and be sure that the stack and variables will always contain the proper types. Since we have already checked the instruction at loop, we don't need to check any further down that flow of control.

Actually, the stack pictures do not have to be identical. However, they must be compatible. See section 6.5.4 for an example.

We still need to go back to the other instruction we marked, at end. This instruction is a return. Since it's compatible with the return type of this method (void), there are no errors. The verification algorithm affirms that this is a valid method.

6.5.3   Example 3: Code That Doesn't Verify

Perhaps a better way to see what's happening is to look at a method that the verification algorithm rejects. Here's an example, a fragment of code that is intended to produce a stack containing the numbers 0 through 4.

```
; Loop 5 times. Each time, push local var 0 onto the stack
    iconst_5      ; Initialize variable 0 to 5
    istore 0
loop:
    iinc 0 -1     ; Decrement variable 0
    iload 0       ; Push it
    dup           ; Make a copy, leaving the number on the stack
    ifeq break    ; When we reach 0, break the loop
    goto loop     ; Otherwise, loop again


break:            ; More instructions
```

Here is an analysis of the code up to the goto.

Local variable picture

Stack picture   0

| | ✓ | | iconst_5 |

| I | ✓ | | istore_0 |

| I | ✓ | loop: | iinc 0 -1 |

| I | ✓ | | iload 0 |

| I | ✓ | | dup |

| I | ✓ | | ifeq break |

| I | ▶ | | goto loop |

| I | ▶ | break: | |

▶ : instruction to check
✓ : already checked instructions

We have annotated both the instruction at break and the goto with the picture that results after executing the ifeq: a single int on the stack.

The ifeq instruction branches to break if the top of the stack is 0; otherwise, it continues at the goto. The goto is supposed to go back to the instruction at loop, but there's a problem. The last time we looked at the instruction at loop, the stack was empty. This time, there's an int on the stack.

The verification algorithm will reject this method, because it can't be sure of a constant stack height. If it permitted this method to execute, the stack would grow by 1 each time. Eventually, the program might overflow the stack. Because you don't want that to happen, the verification algorithm rejects this code.

6.5.4   Example 4: Dealing with Subclasses

One more complication: it isn't necessary for two stack pictures to be identical when two different flows of control come to the same place. Here's a (somewhat contrived) example. The example depends on three classes:

```
abstract class Person {
    abstract void printName();
}

class Programmer {
    void printName() { /* Implementation goes here */ }
}

class Author {
    void printName() { /* Implementation goes here */ }
}
```

The code we wish to verify is

```
.method public static print(ZLProgrammer;LAuthor;)V
    iload_0                     ; Is the boolean false?
    ifeq false                  ; If not,
    true: aload_1               ; then push the programmer
    goto print
    false: aload_2              ; Otherwise, push the author
    print: invokevirtual Person/printName ()V
                                ; Call printName on the Person
                                ; This works whether it's an
                                ; Author or a Programmer,
                                ; since each is a Person
    done: return
.end method
```

This method takes three arguments: a `boolean` control, a `Programmer`, and an `Author`. If the control is `true` then it prints the name of the `Programmer`. Otherwise, it prints the name of the `Author`. The program arrives at `print` with either the `Programmer` or the `Author` on the stack. It is impossible to predict which will be there, but either way the value is certainly a `Person`.

After executing the `iload_0` on line 1, the program proceeds to either `true` or `false`, depending on the value. The two flows of control come together at `done`.

In the next diagram, we have traced through the entire flow of control in the case that the `ifeq` succeeds, and control goes to `false`. This means that the program arrives at `print` with an `Author` on top of the stack. The `invokevirtual` at `print` is legal, because `Author` is a subclass of `Person`. This leaves an empty stack picture at `done`, which is fine for a `return`. Since the method returns `void`, the `return` instruction is valid, and we're done checking this flow of control.

Returning to the mark at `true`, we begin with an empty stack. The `aload_1` pushes the `Programmer` onto the stack. The picture now looks like Figure 6.3. (The local variable picture is shown only once, because it does not change in this code.)

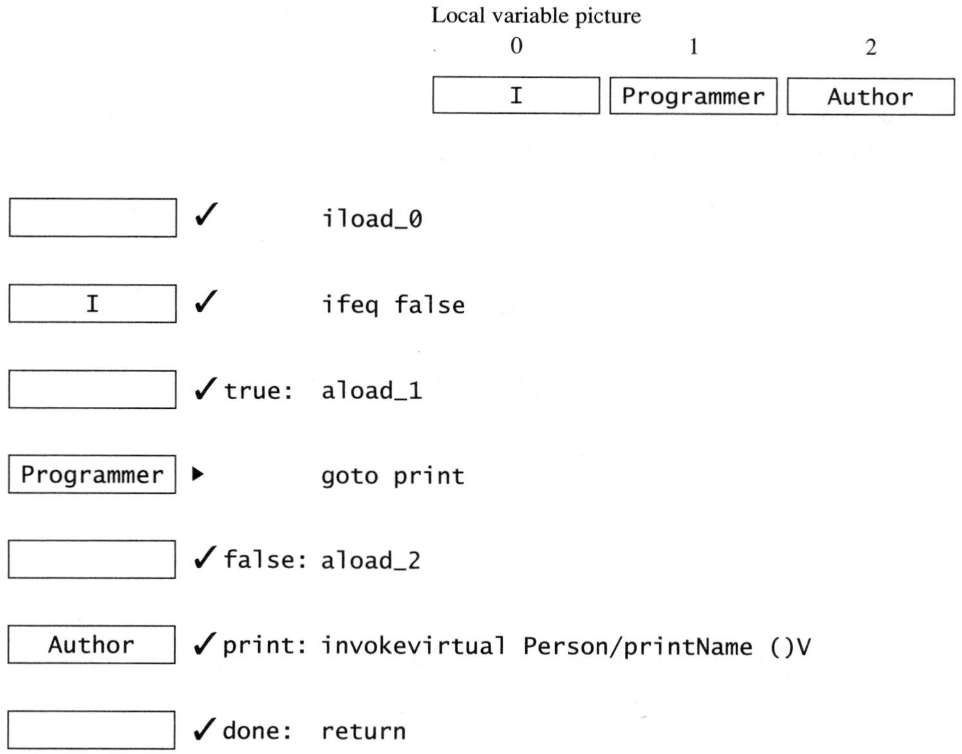

Local variable picture

0	1	2
I	Programmer	Author

	✓	`iload_0`
I	✓	`ifeq false`
	✓	`true:   aload_1`
Programmer	▶	`        goto print`
	✓	`false:  aload_2`
Author	✓	`print:  invokevirtual Person/printName ()V`
	✓	`done:   return`

FIGURE 6.3: *A possible conflict at print*

When we get to the mark in Figure 6.3, there is a slight hitch. We must go to `print`, but we've already visited `print` and the stack pictures are not identical: one has a `Programmer` and the other an `Author`.

The `print` problem is resolved by *unifying* the two stack pictures. You can only unify two stack pictures that are the same height; stacks of differing height violate the rules, and cause verification failure.

In Figure 6.3 at `print`, the stack height is 1 in both stack pictures. We unify the two stack pictures by taking each corresponding element and building a new picture that uses the most derived type that is super to both of them. We do that by listing the superclasses of each type in order and taking the lowest item that is the same on each list. This is what it looks like for `Programmer` and `Author`:

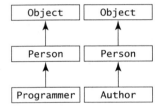

The most specific type common to both `Programmer` and `Author` is `Person`. Eventually, every class derives from `Object`, so you can always unify two reference types.

Now we have to redraw the stack picture, substituting `Person` for `Author` at `print`:

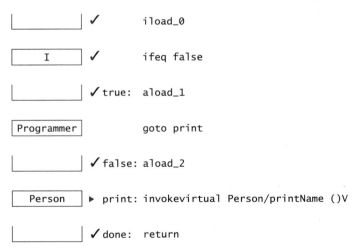

FIGURE 6.4: *After unifying the stack pictures at* print

Because the picture at print has changed, we need to leave a mark there and continue checking. The invokevirtual instruction here is still legal, because the stack contains a Person. The new stack picture is empty.

Control proceeds to done with an empty stack picture. Because we've already been to done, we need to unify the new stack picture with the old one. Since both pictures are empty, unification is trivial, and the unified picture is identical to the old one. This means that we don't need to check any further. Since there are no more marks and we haven't found any problems, the verification algorithm decides that this method is okay.

Everything said here about the stack picture also applies to the local variable picture. Local variable pictures are unified the same way: find the least common supertype of the classes and recheck if anything is different. If a variable slot is uninitialized in either local variable picture, then it will be uninitialized in the unified picture.

Note that you can't unify two non-reference types. You can't unify a float and an int or a float and a double. This code is illegal:

```
.method public static print(ZIF)V
iload_0          ; Is the boolean false?
ifeq false       ; If not,
iload_1          ; then push the int
goto done
false: fload_2   ; Otherwise, push the float
done:            ; ILLEGAL! Can't unify the stack pictures here
return
.end method
```

This example is identical to the last example, but it uses int and float in place of Programmer and Author. At done we would have to unify the stack containing a float with the stack containing an int. Because int and float are numeric types, not reference types, there is no unification between the two. The verification algorithm will reject this method.

Exercise 6.1

What is the most specific superclass shared by java.awt.Dialog and java.awt.Panel? ▲

6.5.5   Algorithm

This algorithm summarizes verification:

1. Initialize the stack picture for the first instruction to empty.

2. Initialize the local variable picture by labeling the local variables that correspond to method parameters with the types of the parameters. Label the rest *uninitialized*.

3. Mark the first instruction. Annotate it with the initial stack and local variable pictures.

4. Choose a marked instruction. If there aren't any, then you're done, and the method is okay.

5. Check that the top of the stack contains the proper number and types of arguments for this instruction. Ditto for the variable pool. For example, if it's an `iadd` instruction, then there must be two `int`s on top of the stack picture. If it's an `aload` instruction, there must be a `reference` in the named slot of the local variable picture. If it's an `invoke` instruction, the descriptor of the invoked method tells what should be on the stack. If the stack and local variable picture don't agree with the instruction, reject the method.

6. Build a new stack picture by taking the last stack picture, popping off the used operands, and pushing on whatever the instruction leaves. For example, an `iadd` leaves an `int`, and an `invoke` leaves whatever type is returned by the method. Do the same to make a new local variable picture. If the new stack is taller than the limit specified by the `.limit stack` directive, reject the method.

7. Figure out the set of follow-up instructions:

    ◆ For most instructions, the follow-up instruction is just the next instruction.

    ◆ For a `goto`, the follow-up instruction is the destination of the `goto`.

    ◆ For one of the `if` instructions, both the destination of the `if` and the next instruction are follow-up instructions.

    ◆ If the instruction is covered by an exception handler, then the exception handler is also in the set of follow-up instructions.

    ◆ For a `return` or `throw` instruction, there is no follow-up instruction.

8. For each follow-up instruction:

    ◆ Check whether the instruction is already annotated. If it isn't, annotate it with the new stack picture and local variable picture and mark the instruction. Go to the next step.

- ◆ If this instruction is already annotated, unify the new stack and local variable picture with the existing annotation. If you can't unify them, reject this method. If the merged stack picture is not identical to the original stack picture, then mark the follow-up instruction.
9. Go back to step 4.

While executing this algorithm, ask the following questions:

- ◆ Is each opcode valid?
- ◆ If the instruction refers to the constant pool, does the element referred to really exist? Is it of the proper type?
- ◆ Is the destination of a branch instruction (`goto`, `if`, and so on) always the beginning of an instruction? (Just pointing to a valid opcode isn't sufficient. For example, you can't point to the argument of a `bipush` instruction even if the value is a valid opcode.)
- ◆ If you've checked this instruction before, is the stack the same height it was last time?
- ◆ Is the height of the stack always less than the maximum permitted (as specified in the `max_stack` slot of the method)?
- ◆ Are all local variable references within the limit of local variables?
- ◆ Does the stack contain the right number of items, with the correct types, for each instruction?
- ◆ For a return instruction (`areturn`, `ireturn`, `lreturn`, `dreturn`, `freturn`, `return`), is the kind of the return compatible with the return type of the method?
- ◆ If the method is a constructor, does it call a superclass constructor or some other constructor in the class? (This is to make sure that every object is fully initialized. If an object were permitted to get away without calling its superclass constructor, then methods inherited from the superclass might run in an environment they weren't expecting.)
- ◆ Is a constructor called exactly once for each newly created object? (Calling a constructor twice is illegal.)
- ◆ Are the stack and constant pool free of uninitialized objects when a backward jump is executed? (This prevents you from trying to get away without initializing an object.)

If the answer to any of these questions is "no," then the method is invalid.

This algorithm is incomplete. For example, it does not describe what to do with `ret` and `jsr` instructions, or how to deal with exception handlers. For the complete algorithm, see *The Java Virtual Machine Specification,* section 4.9.

6.6   Do External References Check Out?

An external reference is an attempt to use a field or method of a class that isn't the class you're currently checking. Even if the class was defined in the same Java source file, it's still an external reference because it comes from a different `class` file.

Checking external references is a matter of loading all the classes referenced in the constant pool. These are loaded using the same class loader that used this class. (See chapter 8 for more on class loaders). When loading a class, you need to ask,

◆ Does the superclass list avoid looping?

To put it another way,

◆ Is there any way for a class to be a superclass of itself? If so, the class is invalid.

For example, the following is invalid:

```
.class Concept
.super Idea
.end class

.class Idea
.super Thought
.end class

.class Thought
.super Concept                    ; Whoops! Circularity.
.end class
```

Then, for each field or method accessed by the class you're checking, ask the following questions:

◆ Does the class have a field or method with the appropriate name and type?
◆ Does this class have permission to use it?

This way of checking external references gives JVM programmers tremendous flexibility to change classes without having to recompile all the classes that use them. You only have to check for the fields and methods that are actually used. You can add or delete fields and methods, without altering the correctness of classes that don't use them.

In addition, because they're checked by name and type, you can move methods around in the source file without affecting other classes that use this class. This helps solve the "fragile base class" problem familiar to C++ programmers, who know that even a seemingly negligible change such as changing the order of methods can require recompilation of every file in the project. It is a cause of many subtle and mysterious bugs in C++ projects.

Many JVM implementations, including Sun's Java Development Kit, don't actually test external references until they are needed. This can save a lot of time. You can start using the class immediately, without having to wait for all the related classes (and all the classes related to those classes, and so on) to load. It's quite possible that many of the references will never need to be checked because the field or method is never used.

6.7 Java Language and Verification Algorithm

The most common programming language for writing Java virtual machine programs is Java. One thing the language guarantees is that anything you can say in Java can be translated into virtual machine code that will pass the verification algorithm.

The verification rules state that the arithmetic instructions (`iadd, ddiv`, etc.) always take two values of the same type (two `ints`, two `doubles`, etc.). Say you have the following Java program fragment:

```
int i = 70;          // Call this variable 1
float j = 111.1;     // Call this variable 2
double k = i+j;      // Call this variable 3 (and 4)
```

A naïve (and invalid) translation into bytecodes would be

```
bipush 70       ; Initialize i (variable 1) to 70
istore_1
ldc 111.1       ; Initialize j (variable 2) to 111.1
fstore_1
iload_1         ; Push the integer 70
fload_2         ; Push the float 111.1
```

```
fadd                   ; Add two floats (This is an error!)
dstore_3               ; Store it in variables 3 and 4 (Another error!)
```

The verification algorithm rejects this, because it attempts to apply a `fadd` instruction when the top of the stack contains an `int` and a `float` instead of two `float`s. The attempt to store a `float` value with a `dstore` instruction is also invalid.

The Java language has a complex set of implicit and explicit type conversion rules, described in chapter 5 of *The Java Programming Language Specification*. One of those rules says that when you apply an arithmetic operator to a `float` and an `int`, you must first convert the `int` into a `float`. This is done automatically by the compiler. A proper Java compiler would instead generate

```
bipush 70              ; Initialize i (variable 1) to 70
istore_1
ldc 111.1              ; Initialize j (variable 2) to 111.1
fstore_1
iload_1                ; Push the integer 70
i2f                    ; Convert the integer to a float
fload_2                ; Push the float 111.1
fadd                   ; Now adding two floats is legal
f2d                    ; Convert the result to a double
dstore_3               ; Store it in variable 3
```

The verification algorithm has no problem with this code.

The verification rules also require that no matter how you get to a particular instruction, whether by falling through from the previous instruction or by use of a `goto` or one of the `if` instructions, the stack will always have the same structure. A Java compiler can make sure that this is true by following two rules of its own:

- Each Java statement translates so that it leaves nothing on the stack.
- You can branch only to the beginning of a statement.

To see how these two rules help the compiler enforce the JVM verification algorithm rules, consider the following code from a class called `Parser`:

```
if(isLegalToken)
    getNextToken();
else
    printErrorMessage("Invalid token");
```

with the following declarations

```
static int getNextToken();
static void printErrorMessage();
```

A Java compiler generates code like

```
line1: getstatic Parser/isLegalToken Z
line2: ifeq 16              ; if(isLegalToken)
                            ; getNextToken();
line3: invokestatic Parser/getNextToken ()I
line4: pop
line5: goto 18
line6: ldc "Invalid token"  ; else
                            ; printErrorMessage("Invalid
                                token");
line7: invokestatic Parser/printErrorMessage
       (Ljava/lang/String;)V
line8:                      ; The method continues here
```

The statement `getnextToken();` translates into `line3` and `line4`. The statement `printErrorMessage("Invalid Token")` translates into lines `line6` and `line7`.

The call to `getNextToken` leaves its result on the stack (an `int`). The instruction at `line4` pops that value off the stack, since the program doesn't use the value. The program pushes a message onto the stack on `line6`, but the call to `printErrorMessage` pops it off and leaves nothing in its place. In each case, the net effect is an empty stack.

Both branches of the `if` end up at `line8` with nothing on the stack. That means that the `if` statement as a whole also works as a statement. You could put this `if` statement inside another `if` or inside a `for` loop. Since its net effect on each statement on the stack is zero, you'll never violate the virtual machine's rules.

A Java compiler is free to generate any virtual machine code it wants to, as long as the resulting code does the same thing as the original Java program. By breaking these rules in carefully controlled ways a compiler can generate much faster code with the same thing, without compromising safety.

6.7.1 Fooling the Virtual Machine with a Java Compiler

There are a number of ways to fool a Java compiler into generating code that will fail to verify. One of the verification rules states that references to methods and fields in other classes must be able to be resolved. If you go back and alter those `class` files after the Java compiler has turned your Java source into a `class` file, then that `class` file will fail to verify when you load it.

At the time the Java compiler wrote the code, it followed its own rules. However, by changing some Java code without recompiling all of it, you can potentially make changes that cause the program as a whole to break. That's one of the reasons the verification algorithm is there. Besides catching malicious code, it can also catch mistakes when you accidentally change something, even if you haven't recompiled those things that need to be compiled.

6.7.2   Other Languages and the Verification Algorithm

Java isn't the only language that can be successfully translated into virtual machine code. In chapter 11 we'll see how various non-Java language constructs can be translated into verifiable machine code. In chapters 12 and 13 we'll look in detail at Scheme and Prolog and produce working compilers that generate verifiable code.

6.8   Other Safety Requirements

Despite all this careful checking, some kinds of safety requirements cannot be statically verified. These have to be checked when the instruction is executed. This does not decrease the security of the Java virtual machine; it only moves some of the checking from loadtime to runtime.

Some of the requirements checked when the program is run are:

◆ When invoking a method, or setting or getting a field, the receiver `reference` must not be `null` (checked by the `invokespecial`, `invokevirtual`, `invokeinterface`, `getfield`, and `putfield` instructions).

◆ When getting or setting a value in an array, the array `reference` must not be `null`. Also, the index must be nonnegative and less than the upper bound of the array (checked by the `iaload`, `iastore`, `aaload`, `aastore`, and other array instructions).

◆ When casting a `reference` to another type, the object specified by the reference must really have that type and must not be `null` (checked by the `checkcast` instruction).

◆ When storing into an array of objects, the element being stored must be compatible with the array type (checked by the `aastore` instruction).

When the instructions notice that the program has failed to meet one of these requirements, an exception is thrown. This prevents the instruction from executing invalidly.

The last requirement supports an oddity in the JVM type system when it comes to arrays. Programmers expect that an array of `Strings` is a subclass of an array of `Objects`. This is legal in Java, and the JVM equivalent is also legal:

```
Object[] array = new String[10];
Object o = array[0];
```

This matches the programmer's intuition that an array of `Strings` holds things that are `Objects`. However, `array` doesn't behave exactly like an `Object[]`: you can't store non-`String` objects into it:

```
array[1] = new Integer(9);
```

This causes the program to throw an `ArrayStoreException`. If it were allowed to succeed, then there would be an `Integer` in an array that should hold only `Strings`. In the JVM code, this exception is thrown by the `aastore` instruction.

6.9   Checking Verification

To see if a class will pass verification, you need an implementation of the verification algorithm. In early versions of the Java Development Kit, there was a `-verify` flag to `javap` that would print whether or not the class passes verification. Adding the `-verbose` flag would cause `javap` to print additional information on why verification failed.

Later versions of the JDK omit this option. Instead, you should use `java -verify` *classname*. If your class does not have a `main`, and the class passes verification properly, then `java` prints a message that `main` could not be found, which means that it accepted the class but could not run it. If the class does have a `main`, it will be run.

If the class fails verification, an error is printed. You may be able to get more information using the `-verbose` flag.

A word of caution: Commercial JVM implementations usually expect programs from Java compilers, which always produce verifiable code. Therefore, the error messages they emit when encountering a class that fails verification can be cryptic. Your best bet is to trace the code as described in this chapter, drawing stack pictures and checking that each instruction receives the correct arguments. Also ensure that local variable and local stack limits are set high enough. (Running `javap -verbose` will tell you these limits.)

If all else fails, try writing the equivalent of the class in Java, and then disassembling the resulting `class` file using the Gnoloo disassembler. The differences between the class you wrote by hand and the one produced by the Java compiler may be revealing.

## CHAPTER 7

Debugging

O NE of the biggest problems facing users of any new language is a lack of tools to support it, particularly debugging tools. The Java virtual machine provides a set of language-independent tools at the virtual machine level. Any new language you create for the JVM can take advantage of these tools. You can even use existing debuggers with new languages.

The Oolong assembler by default will not generate any debugging information, even if you provide the special debugging directives discussed in the next sections. To tell the Oolong assembler to include debugging information, use the -g flag on the Oolong assembler command line.

7.1   Debugging Directives in Oolong

A source-level debugger can execute JVM bytecodes and show you the corresponding parts of your original source program. The debugger tries to show you the source code line that generated the currently executing bytecodes. It also shows you the value of local variables, the structure of objects, and other data.

Even after your program is compiled, it is easy for the JVM to show you certain kinds of information. For example, the class file includes the names of classes and the names and types of fields. However, some kinds of information are not directly reflected in the bytecodes. In the JVM, local variables have only numbers, not names. The class file allows you to provide a mapping from the numbers to names. Also, it is impossible to tell which bytecodes came from which line of source code. The class file allows you to provide a mapping from bytecode address to the source line it came from.

These mappings were originally designed to support the Java language, but they can be adapted to support just about any language you might want to create. Almost all languages have the concepts of "line number" and "local variable."

Most Java debuggers are willing to show any file at all as the source, even if it's not Java.

The Oolong language has a way for you to fill in the mappings for the `class` file with the `.source`, `.line`, and `.var` directives. If you compile your program from some other language (like Prolog, Lisp, or Logo) into Oolong and then use an Oolong assembler to build the `class` file, you can use these directives to provide a link from the `class` file back to the original source program.

7.1.1   `.source` Directive and `.line` Directives

The `.source` directive names the file that contains the source of this class so that a debugger can show you the source code. This allows you to name the actual source of the file if the Oolong program is an intermediate from something else. If no `.source` directive is given, then Oolong uses the name of the file it's reading. For example, suppose you've written a file `EightQueens.P`, a Prolog program. A Prolog-to-Oolong compiler could translate it into the Oolong source `Eight-Queens.j`. To connect the `.j` file back to the original file, the file would start with

```
.class EightQueens
.source EightQueens.P
```

You should include only the actual file name, not the path to the file. It's up to the debugger to locate the source file `EightQueens.P` when it loads the `class` file.

The `.line` directive is used to map Oolong instructions to source code in the original file. The `.line` directives are interspersed with the Oolong instructions; each instruction after a `.line` directive is considered part of the same line, until the next `.line` directive comes along. For example, consider this Logo program in the file `DrawAngle.logo`:

```
forward 60
right 90
forward 20
```

Compiled into Oolong, it becomes

```
.class DrawAngle
.super LogoProgram
.source DrawAngle.logo

.method public run()V
.line 1                              ; forward 60
aload_0                              ; Push this
```

```
bipush 60                       ; Push 60
invokevirtual LogoProgram/forward(I)V ; Draw forward 60

.line 2                         ; right 90
aload_0
getfield LogoProgram/theta I    ; Push the angle
bipush 90                       ; Push 90 degrees
iadd                            ; Add 90 degrees to the angle
sipush 360                      ; Compute the remainder of
irem                            ; (theta+90)/360
aload_0                         ; Store it back into theta
swap
putfield LogoProgram/theta I

.line 3                         ; forward 20
aload_0
bipush 20
invokevirtual LogoProgram/forward(I)V

return
.end method
```

You can use the same line number more than once within a method. That's particularly useful for control structures like Java's for, where some control code occurs both before and after the enclosed code:

```
for(i = 0; i < 10; i++)
{
    // Do stuff
}
```

If the for loop appears on line 10 of the source file, then this becomes:

```
.line 10                ; Begin at the beginning
loop_begin:
    iload_1             ; Push i
    bipush 10           ; Push 10
    if_icmpge break     ; If greater than 10, break out of the loop

.line 12
    ;; Do stuff
```

```
.line 10                ; Now we're back doing stuff from line 1
    iinc 1 1            ; Increment i
    goto loop_begin     ; And go back to the beginning of the
                        ; program

.line 14                ; Now we're outside the loop
break:
```

7.1.2   .var Directive

Although fields of objects are referenced in bytecodes by name, local variables are referenced only by number. The .var directive is used to assign names to the variables. Naming variables is entirely optional. The names aren't used by the JVM itself; they're only used by the debugger.

The format of the .var directive is

```
.var number is name type [ from label1 to label2 ]
```

where number is the number of the local variable, name is the name that you want to give it, and type is the type that the variable holds. For example, in this Java program fragment,

```
public void main(String args[])
```

you might use the .var directive

```
.var 0 is args [Ljava/lang/String;
```

The from part of the .var directive is optional. A particular local variable slot may have different names at different parts of the program. The Oolong language uses label1 and label2 to indicate the range where a variable is given a particular name. The same variable may have different names or different types in different ranges. For example,

```
static void fahrenheitToCelsius(float fahrenheit)
{
    float celsius = (fahrenheit - 32) * 5 / 9;
    System.out.println(celsius);
}
```

You never need both fahrenheit and celsius at the same time, so they can both be stored in the same local variable. For part of the computation, that variable is named fahrenheit, and for the rest, it's named celsius. Translated into Oolong, this method is

```
.method static fahrenheitToCelsius (F)V
.limit stack 2
.var 0 is fahrenheit from begin to end_of_computation
.var 0 is celsius from end_of_computation to end
begin:
    fload_0                 ; Push fahrenheit in variable 0
    ldc 32.0                ; Subtract 32
    fsub
    ldc 5.0                 ; Multiply by 5
    fmul
    ldc 9.0                 ; Divide by 9
    fdiv
end_of_computation:
    fstore_0                ; Now variable 0 is celsius
    getstatic java/lang/System/out Ljava/io/PrintStream;
    fload_0                 ; Print variable 0
    invokevirtual java/io/PrintStream/println (F)V
    return
end:
.end method
```

It's also possible in Java for two different variables to have the same name in different parts of a method:

```
{
    int i;
    /* i is variable 1 */
}
{
    int j;
    int i;
    /* Here, j is variable 1 and i is variable 2 */
}
```

To let the debugger know which variable is named what, use this Oolong code:

```
.var 1 is i I from scope1begin to scope1end
.var 1 is j I from scope2begin to scope2end
.var 2 is j I from scope2begin to scope2end
scope1begin:
    ;; Here variable 1 is i, and variable 2 is unnamed
```

```
scope1end:
   ;; …
scope2begin:
   ;; Here, variable 1 is j, and variable 2 is i
scope2end:
```

7.2   Debugging Oolong Programs

The .source and .line directives are used primarily when you're using Oolong as an intermediate stage between a program in some other language and the class file. If you're writing Oolong by hand, the Oolong compiler's -n directive will cause .source and .line directives to be generated automatically. Line debugging information will be generated for each instruction, naming the source line of that instruction in the Oolong source file. The .var directive can be used as before to assign names to local variables.

If you provide debugging information, you can use existing debuggers to debug Oolong programs. For example, Figure 7.1 shows Symantec Café version 1.8 debugging an Oolong program.

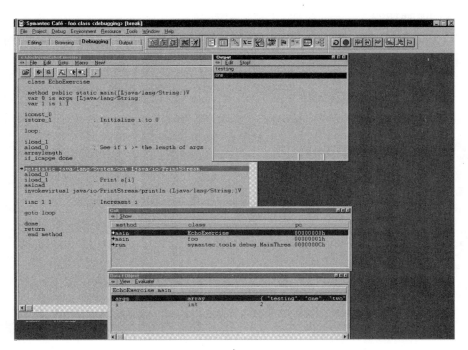

FIGURE 7.1: *Symantec Café debugging an Oolong program*

7.3 Runtime Tracing

The class java.lang.Runtime has two methods designed to help you debug things in the absence of a debugger. These methods are

```
public native void traceInstructions(boolean on);
public native void traceMethodCalls(boolean on);
```

The boolean on controls whether to turn tracing on or off. It's up to the JVM implementation to determine what, if anything, happens when you call these methods. Many implementations ignore these requests for performance reasons.

For machines that do something interesting, the output can be quite extensive. Here is a method that computes Fibonacci numbers:

```
.method static fib (I)I
iload_0.var 0 is i I
iconst_2
if_icmpgt recurse     ; If i > 2, recurse
iconst_1              ; If i <= 2, return 1
ireturn

recurse:
iload_0               ; Compute fib(i-1)
iconst_1
isub
invokestatic fib/fib(I)I

iload_0               ; Compute fib(i-2)
iconst_2
isub
invokestatic fib/fib(I)I

iadd                  ; Add them up and
ireturn               ; return the sum

.end method
```

This code runs a method trace using the method fib:

```
public static void main(String a[])
{
    Runtime.getRuntime().traceMethodCalls(true);
    System.out.println(fib(3));
}
```

Using the Java Development Kit's JVM implementation, this code prints:

```
# main [ 1] | > fib.fib(I)I (1) entered
# main [ 2] | | > fib.fib(I)I (1) entered
# main [ 2] | | < fib.fib(I)I returning
# main [ 2] | | > fib.fib(I)I (1) entered
# main [ 2] | | < fib.fib(I)I returning
# main [ 1] | < fib.fib(I)I returning
```

Here's a sample instruction trace, with traceInstructions set to true:

```
F600A8 1D1997F          iconst_3
F600A8 1D19980          invokestatic fib.fib(I)I
F600A8 1D19980          invokestatic_quick fib.fib(I)I (1)
Entering fib.fib
F600A8 1D199C0          iload_0 => 3
F600A8 1D199C1          iconst_2
F600A8 1D199C2          if_icmpgt goto 1D199C7 (taken)
F600A8 1D199C7          iload_0 => 3
F600A8 1D199C8          iconst_1
F600A8 1D199C9          isub => 2
F600A8 1D199CA          invokestatic fib.fib(I)I
F600A8 1D199CA          invokestatic_quick fib.fib(I)I (1)
Entering fib.fib
F600A8 1D199C0          iload_0 => 2
F600A8 1D199C1          iconst_2
F600A8 1D199C2          if_icmpgt goto 1D199C7 (not taken)
F600A8 1D199C5          iconst_1
F600A8 1D199C6          ireturn 1
Leaving fib.fib
F600A8 1D199CD          iload_0 => 3
F600A8 1D199CE          iconst_2
F600A8 1D199CF          isub => 1
F600A8 1D199D0          invokestatic fib.fib(I)I
F600A8 1D199D0          invokestatic_quick fib.fib(I)I (1)
Entering fib.fib
F600A8 1D199C0          iload_0 => 1
F600A8 1D199C1          iconst_2
F600A8 1D199C2          if_icmpgt goto 1D199C7 (not taken)
F600A8 1D199C5          iconst_1
F600A8 1D199C6          ireturn 1
```

```
Leaving fib.fib
F600A8 1D199D3              iadd => 2
F600A8 1D199D4              ireturn 2
Leaving fib.fib
F600A8 1D19983              istore_1 2 => r1
```

This instruction trace was produced using Sun's `java_g` virtual machine, available with the Java Development Kit.

## CHAPTER 8

Class Loaders

Unix systems have .so files. Windows systems have DLLs. As far as the JVM is concerned, all programs are dynamically linked. Each class is loaded one at a time, and new classes are loaded as needed. This provides uniform access to all features, without having to trouble the programmer about what is loaded dynamically and what isn't.

The heart of the JVM's ability to load class files dynamically is the class java.lang.ClassLoader. In this chapter, we discuss how the ClassLoader works and how you can build your own (and why you might want to). Though class loaders are intimately tied to class files, it is rarely necessary to write the class loader itself in Oolong. Throughout this chapter, we use the Java language to write new class loaders.

8.1   How Classes Are Loaded

Class loading takes place in two phases. In the first phase, called *loading,* the name of a class is used to find some chunk of bytes in the form of a class file (as described in chapter 9), and those bytes are introduced to the JVM as the implementation of the class. The ClassLoader also loads the superclass (which involves loading the superclass of the superclass, and so on). After loading, the virtual machine knows the name of the class, where it fits into the class hierarchy, and what fields and methods it has.

In the second phase, called *linking* or *resolution,* the class is verified to ensure that it is well formed and doesn't try to violate any of the virtual machine's security constraints. Then the static initializer <clinit> is invoked. Other classes may be loaded as a side effect of the verification process. After linking, the class is ready to use.

This two-stage process allows classes to reference one another without causing infinite loops when two classes reference each other. If class Student has a field of class Teacher, and class Teacher has a field of class Student, then you can load Student without loading Teacher, and vice versa. Whichever one you need first is linked, and all other classes it uses are loaded but not linked until you actually require them. This also helps improve performance by delaying class loading and linking until it's absolutely necessary. The linking procedure may take some time, and if it can be avoided in some cases, then a program will run that much faster.

8.1.1   Loading

A class loader is a subclass of the class java.lang.ClassLoader. The load phase starts in a method called loadClass. ClassLoader itself has a method called loadClass, but it's abstract, so it has no implementation. Subclasses of Class-Loader must provide an implementation. The descriptor of loadClass is

```
Class loadClass(String name, boolean resolve);
```

where name represents the name of the class that loadClass is to load. The name will be fully qualified (that is, it might be java.lang.Object, not Object), and it will contain periods (.), not slashes (/), to separate package components. The parameter resolve tells loadClass whether or not to proceed to the linking stage.

The class loader uses name to find a bunch of bytes that it wants to load as a class. These bytes can be anywhere: on disk, in an array in memory, in a database, over the network. They can be encrypted or in a nonstandard class file format. It is the responsibility of loadClass to convert them into a form that the virtual machine can understand.

Next the class loader has to inform the virtual machine that this particular set of bytes forms the class it's looking for. This is done with the defineClass method in ClassLoader. Since defineClass is protected, only subclasses of ClassLoader can introduce new classes into the system. Combined with the checkCreateClassLoader method of SecurityManager, which can be used to prevent new ClassLoaders from being created, this gives the system a degree of control over who can load new classes into the system.

The method defineClass takes the array of bytes and makes some superficial checks that the class file is properly formatted. Then defineClass calls load-Class to load (but not link) the superclass. The method loadClass loads the superclass, using defineClass to define it, and so on. Eventually it finds either java.lang.Object, which has no superclass, or defineClass finds that it has gone in a loop. If defineClass detects a loop, it throws a ClassCircularityError. This

prevents the class loader from succeeding, so the circular class de
loaded.

The method defineClass returns a Class object. At this r
loaded, but it is not ready for use. The virtual machine know'
class, the names of its superclasses, and the names and type
methods. It has not necessarily loaded any of the interface c'
they don't contribute to the set of methods that the class s
contribute to the methods it's supposed to support, and this is ꞏ
linking.

While loading superclasses, the process may eventually come to a class that
the class loader can't find but is instead expected to come from the system itself.
For example:

```
class CoolWidget extends java.awt.Panel
```

The class loader loading CoolWidget probably does not find a definition for
java.awt.Panel, since that's a standard system class. The class loader can ask
the system to load the class by calling findSystemClass, passing it the string
"java.awt.Panel". The method findSystemClass returns a Class object for
java.awt.Panel. This class has no class loader; if you call getClassLoader on
the Class object, the result will be null.

8.1.2 Linking

The class must be linked before it can be used. During linking, the class is verified
to make sure it meets certain criteria, and initialization takes place. Linkage happens in a method in ClassLoader called resolveClass. The method resolve-
Class is usually called at the end of loadClass when loadClass is asked to
resolve the class (that is, when the resolve argument is true). You don't have to
write resolveClass; it's defined in ClassLoader and marked final. Before a
class can be linked, its superclass must be linked, and so on.

The first thing resolveClass does is verification. Verification is such an
important topic that this book devotes a whole chapter (chapter 6) to the subject.
During verification, the JVM ensures that classes obey certain rules, among them

- All the methods required by the interfaces are implemented.
- The instructions use constant pool references correctly (that is, the constant
  actually exists, and it's of the correct type).
- The methods don't overflow the stack.
- The methods don't try to use an int as a reference.

Once the class is successfully verified, the class is initialized. Space is allocated for all of the static fields and the JVM assigns default values (either the standard default values of 0 for numbers and null for references or some other value if there is a ConstantValue attribute attached to the field).

Finally, the virtual machine invokes the <clinit> method of the class. In a Java program, <clinit> is where the Java compiler places all the code that appears outside any method. This includes field initializers and code marked static without a method name. When <clinit> terminates, the class is ready. (If <clinit> threw an uncaught exception, then the class is actually not ready; resolveClass throws an ExceptionInInitializerException, and the Class object can't be used.)

8.2   Loading Classes without a Class Loader

Some classes are loaded without a class loader. (You knew that there had to be at least one such class, since the first class loader couldn't load itself!) These classes are called *system classes*.

The virtual machine has a built-in way to load classes independent of the ClassLoader class. It varies from implementation to implementation, but one common way is to use an environment variable called CLASSPATH to contain a list of directories. When loading the class named *name*, the system looks for a file called *name*.class in each directory in the CLASSPATH, treating each period-separated part of the package name as a subdirectory. Once a file is found, the loading and linking proceeds the same way it does for a class loaded with a class loader.

Array classes are also loaded without a class loader. An array is an object and must have a class. However, there's no need to locate a definition for the class, since all the properties of an array class are known just from its name. The JVM constructs this class internally.

If you have a class named foo, then an array of these objects is called [foo. When the system sees a name like this, it internally creates a class definition for an array of foo. Of course, foo may be an array itself. This class extends java.lang.Object and defines no methods or fields of its own.

8.3   Making Your Own Class Loader

You can't create instances of the ClassLoader class, since it is abstract and does not implement the loadClass method. You can make your own class loader by creating a class that subclasses ClassLoader and implements loadClass.

Here's a template for writing class loaders using the Java 1.0 platform:

```
class TemplateClassLoader extends ClassLoader
{
    /** Provide a place to store the classes */
    Hashtable cache = new Hashtable();

    /** Override loadClass to load classes from some special
        place */
    protected Class loadClass(String name, boolean resolve)
        throws ClassNotFoundException
    {
        // First, look for it in the cache.
        Class c = (Class) cache.get(name);

        if(c == null)
        {
            // Second, look for it in the special place.
            // If you find it there, define those bytes to be the
            // class. If not, look for it as a system class.
            byte bytes[] = findClass(name);
            if(bytes == null)
                c = findSystemClass(name);
            else
                c = defineClass(bytes, 0, bytes.length);
        }
        if(resolve)
            resolveClass(c);
        return c;
    }

    /** Find the class with the given name. This is entirely up
     * to you. If you can't find one, return null.
     */
    protected byte[] findClass(String name)
    {
        return null;
    }
}
```

Under the Java 1.1 and later platforms, the call to `defineClass` is replaced with

```
c = defineClass(name, c, 0, c.length);
```

The first example is acceptable under Java 1.1 but deprecated (that is, it's considered bad style, and one day it may no longer be acceptable). If the `name` doesn't match the name of the class found in the bytes, then a `ClassFormatError` is thrown.

If the class is found neither in the cache nor wherever `findClass` looks for it, the class loader calls `findSystemClass` to see whether the system can locate a definition for the class. If `findSystemClass` doesn't find it, it throws a `ClassNot-FoundException`, since that was the last chance to find the class.

8.3.1   Caching Classes

It's important that a class loader return the same `Class` object each time it's given a particular name. If the same class were loaded more than once, it would be confusing to users who might find that two classes with identical names aren't identical. Class static constructors might be invoked multiple times, causing problems for classes that were designed to expect them to be called only once.

Under Java 1.0, it was the responsibility of the class loader to cache classes itself. This is usually done with a `Hashtable`, as shown in the template. However, this still leaves the possibility of confusion, since two different class loaders might each load a class into the system with the same name. Java 1.1 resolves this problem by handling the caching itself. It makes this cache available to the class loader developer through a method called `findLoadedClass`:

```
Class findLoadedClass(String name);
```

A call to `findLoadedClass` replaces the cache lookup. When `defineClass` is called, it maps the name of the class to the `Class` that is returned. After that, `findLoadedClass` always returns that `Class` whenever it's given the same name, no matter which class loader invokes it.

When implementing your class loader, you will have to decide whether to use the Java 1.0 interface or the 1.1 interface. The 1.0 interface is supported on virtual machines supporting Java 1.1 but not vice versa. However, using the 1.0 interface will have different results on a JVM 1.1 if the class loader tries to define a class more than once. On a JVM 1.0, it would actually load the classes multiple times, and the system would have two different classes with the same name. These classes wouldn't share `static` fields or use `private` fields or methods on the other. On 1.1 and later JVMs, however, `defineClass` throws an exception when it's asked to define the class a second time anywhere in the virtual machine, even if the bytes are identical.

8.3.2 Examples

Many web browsers have class loaders in them to load Java applets. An applet loader based on the TemplateClassLoader might look like this:

```
import java.net.URL;
class AppletLoader extends TemplateClassLoader
{
    /** Where the code should come from */
    private URL codebase;

    AppletLoader(URL codebase)
    {
        this.codebase = codebase;
    }

    public byte[] findClass(String name)
    {
        try {
            URL code_url = new URL(codebase, name + ".class");
            URLConnection connection =
                code_url.openConnection();
            connection.connect();
            int length = connection.getContentLength();
            byte[] bytes = new byte[length];
            connection.getInputStream().read(bytes);
            return bytes;
        }
        catch(IOException e) {
            // Something went wrong
            return null;
        }
    }
}
```

The findClass method uses the java.net.URL class to create a URL for the applet based on the code base. If the code base is http://appletsource.com/applets/page.html, then it will see the applet package/MyTestApplet at

http://appletsource.com/applets/package/MyTestApplet.class

It reads in the entire text of the applet and returns it as an array of bytes. Later, when MyTestApplet references the class package/GreenButton, the system uses the same class loader to load it.

This is only a trivial example; more sophisticated browsers have the ability to download a collection of related classes simultaneously by loading a file in Java Archive (JAR) format. A JAR file may contain many classes, and the class loader has to search the JAR file for the class it's looking for.

Another kind of class loader is exemplified by `ByteArrayClassloader`, which is used in conjunction with dynamic compilation. New classes are created while programs are running and given to the class loader for later use with the method `store`. This is the code for it:

```java
import java.util.*;
public class ByteArrayClassLoader extends TemplateClassLoader
{
    /** Used for storing dynamically created classes */
    private Hashtable dynamicCache = new Hashtable();

    public byte[] findClass(String name)
    {
        return (byte[]) dynamicCache.get(name);
    }

    /** Associate the name with the bytecodes in data in the hash
        table
     * dynamicCache, for use later.
     */
    public void store(String name, byte[] data)
    {
        dynamicCache.put(name, data);
    }
}
```

This class is used by a program that dynamically creates bytecodes. After it creates the bytecodes for a class, it calls `store` with those bytecodes and the name of the class.

Later, when the program wants to create an instance of the class, it calls `loadClass`, passing it the name of the class and `true` for `resolve`. If this is one of the classes stored with `store` and it hasn't been seen before, the class will get the class definition from `dynamicCache`.

8.4   Working with `Class` Objects

The result of loading a class with your own `ClassLoader` is an object of type `Class` that represents the class you just loaded. Once that class has been resolved, you can use it. But what can you use it *for?* There are no special JVM instructions for working with Class objects.

Class supports several methods that mimic certain instructions. You can create an instance of this class with newInstance. This creates a new instance of whatever Class represents, invokes the default constructor (the one that takes no arguments), and returns it to the calling code as an Object.

For example, suppose you've created a Logo-to-JVM compiler that turns Logo programs into bytecodes, then runs them. The class generated is a subclass of LogoProgram, which has a method called run to run the compiled Logo program. Here's how you might use such a compiler:

```
// Make a loader
ByteArrayClassLoader loader = new ByteArrayClassLoader();

// Compile a Logo program into the class Program1
byte[] bytecodes = LogoCompiler.compile(
    "Program1",
    "PenDown Forward :X Left 90 Forward :Y Left 90 Forward :X Left
        90");

// Cache the definition in the class loader
loader.store("Program1", bytecodes);

// Load it and resolve it
Class programOneClass = loader.loadClass("Program1", true);

// Create an instance of Program1
Object o = programOneClass.newInstance();
```

The reference returned from newInstance is an instance of class Program1. However, you can't use any of the Program1 methods on it since the Java program doesn't know what methods it has. All the Java program can be sure of is that it's an Object.

You know, however, that the LogoCompiler creates all objects as subclasses of LogoProgram. You can cast it to a LogoProgram, and use those methods. This involves a dynamic cast; if the object isn't really a LogoProgram, then a ClassCastException will be thrown. If LogoProgram has a method called run, then you can do this:

```
LogoProgram aProgramOneInstance = (LogoProgram) o;  // Dynamic
                                                     // cast

aProgramOneInstance.run();
```

8.5   Reflection

The Java 1.1 reflection API offers another way to access classes that are loaded with class loaders. You can examine the class to find out what fields and methods it has and even invoke the methods and read or assign the fields. Check out the getMethods and getFields methods in Class. These enable a program to call methods and use fields it did not know about when the program was compiled.

Reflection requires several new classes to represent fields and methods. The new classes are found in the package java.lang.reflect. Fields are represented by instances of class Field, methods by instances of Method.

The Logo program shown has two variables, X and Y. If the Logo compiler compiles these as fields in the Program1 class, they can be set like this:

```
Field x = programOneClass.getField("X");
Field y = programOneClass.getField("Y");
x.setInt(o, 90);                   // Set X to 90
y.setInt(o, 20);                   // Set Y to 20
```

Now the fields X and Y are set to 90 and 20, respectively, in the object.

Reflection also permits you to call constructors that take arguments. Reflection uses a special class called Constructor to represent constructors. If the compiler added a constructor Program1(int x, int y) to Program1, then a new Program1 can be created with

```
// The arguments array represents the types we want to pass as
// arguments
// Integer.TYPE is the type for the int type.
Class[] arg_types = { Integer.TYPE, Integer.TYPE };
Constructor programOneConstructor =
    programOneClass.getConstructor(arg_types);
Object[] arguments = { new Integer(1000), new Integer(12) };
Object newProg1 = programOneConstructor.newInstance(arguments);
```

This code will create a new object of type Program1, calling the constructor that takes two ints instead of the no-argument constructor. The method getConstructor returns the constructor taking the arguments given by the arguments array, in this case, two ints.

The method newInstance takes a list of the arguments to the constructor. It should have the same length as the argument array and the types should correspond to the constructor types. Since you can't put ints into an array of Objects, you have to wrap them up as Integers; the system is smart enough to unwrap them before it passes them to the constructor as an int.

Similar techniques can be used to call methods on the objects. Take this Logo program:

```
to square
params [x]
repeat 2 [forward :x left 90 forward :x left 90]
end
```

You can compile this into the class `Program2`, which has a method called `square` taking an `int` argument. This method can be compiled and invoked like this:

```
// Compile a Logo program into the class Program2
byte[] bytecodes = LogoCompiler.compile(
    "Program2",
    "to square " +
    "params [x] " +
    "repeat 2 [forward :x left 90 forward :x left 90]" +
    "end");

// Define it to the virtual machine
loader.store("Program2", bytecodes);

// Load it and resolve it
Class program2Class = loader.loadClass("Program2", true);

// Create an instance of Program2
Object program2object = program2Class.newInstance();

Class[] arg_types = { Integer.TYPE };
Method rectangle = program2class.getDeclaredMethod("square",
        arg_types);
Object[] square_size = { new Integer(99) };
rectangle.invoke(program2object, square_size);
```

These features were added to the Java API to support JavaBeans, a component architecture that makes much use of dynamically loaded classes. A JavaBeans builder is a visual application developer. A builder can read in the definition of a class using a class loader and use reflection to get the list of methods and fields. The list can be presented to the user, who can use the methods and fields to connect methods together to build new classes.

Exercise 8.1

Create your own class loader that reads the class definition from a file. Have it print a message whenever it starts to load a class, when it resolves it, and when it's done. Try it out on some classes, and observe the order in which it loads and resolves classes.   ▲

## CHAPTER 9

Inside a Java class File

Y OUR first Java program probably looked something like this:

```
public class hello
{
    public static void main(String argv[])
    {
        System.out.println("Hello, world");
    }
}
```

You ran it through the Java compiler

```
> javac hello.java
```

to create the file hello.class. Then you ran the program

```
> java hello
Hello, world
>
```

and exulted in having mastered another programming language.

The hello.class file contains a Java virtual machine bytecode class that produces the intended effect of hello.java. The file hello.class is called a class file. The class file format is described in chapter 4 of *The Java Virtual Machine Specification*. All JVM implementations are required to treat this file in the same way. This is the heart of the "Write Once, Run Anywhere" promise of Java.

The DumpClass program, provided with this book and detailed in appendix B.3, provides a byte-by-byte disassembly of a class file. This chapter examines the output of the DumpClass program on the hello.class file to explore the concepts of the class file in more depth.

9.1   class File Header

DumpClass prints three columns. The left column is an offset, in hex, into the file.
The middle column is the bytes at that location, also presented in hex. The right
column is the interpretation of the bytes.

The class file begins by identifying itself as a class file and providing some
version information:

```
000000 cafebabe        magic = ca fe ba be
000004 0003             minor version = 3
000006 002d             major version = 45
```

The first four bytes of any class file, taken as a 32-bit unsigned integer, are
3,405,691,582, or (in hex) CAFEBABE. This is the "magic number" that makes it
easy to quickly reject anything that is not a class file. Most of the numbers in the
class file are treated as unsigned integers, unless stated otherwise.

The next two bytes are the major and minor versions of the class file format.
The proper values are 45 for the major version and 3 for the minor version for
JVMs before platform 2. The Java 2 platform accepts versions from 45.3 to 46.0,
inclusive.

9.2   Constant Pool

The next part of the class file is called the constant pool. Its purpose is to contain
some constant values where they can be easily referenced elsewhere in the class
file. The constant pool for this file follows.

```
000008 0020             32 constants
00000a 08001f           1. String #31
00000d 07001d           2. Class name #29
000010 070018           3. Class name #24
000013 07000e           4. Class name #14
000016 070013           5. Class name #19
000019 090002000a       6. Fieldref class #2 name-and-type #10
00001e 0a00040009       7. Methodref class #4 name-and-type #9
000023 0a0003000b       8. Methodref class #3 name-and-type #11
000028 0c000c0017       9. NameAndType name #12 descriptor #23
00002d 0c0016001c       10. NameAndType name #22 descriptor #28
000032 0c001b001e       11. NameAndType name #27 descriptor #30
000037 010007           12. UTF length=7
```

```
00003a 7072 696e 746c 6e                        println
000041 01000d        13. UTF length=13
000044 436f 6e73 7461 6e74 5661 6c75 65         ConstantValue
000051 010013        14. UTF length=19
000054 6a61 7661 2f69 6f2f 5072 696e 7453 7472  java/io/PrintStr
000064 6561 6d                                  eam
000067 01000a        15. UTF length=10
00006a 4578 6365 7074 696f 6e73                 Exceptions
000074 01000a        16. UTF length=10
000077 6865 6c6c 6f2e 6a61 7661                 hello.java
000081 01000f        17. UTF length=15
000084 4c69 6e65 4e75 6d62 6572 5461 626c 65    LineNumberTable
000093 01000a        18. UTF length=10
000096 536f 7572 6365 4669 6c65                 SourceFile
0000a0 010005        19. UTF length=5
0000a3 6865 6c6c 6f                             hello
0000a8 01000e        20. UTF length=14
0000ab 4c6f 6361 6c56 6172 6961 626c 6573       LocalVariables
0000b9 010004        21. UTF length=4
0000bc 436f 6465                                Code
0000c0 010003        22. UTF length=3
0000c3 6f75 74                                  out
0000c6 010015        23. UTF length=21
0000c9 284c 6a61 7661 2f6c 616e 672f 5374 7269  (Ljava/lang/Stri
0000d9 6e67 3b29 56                             ng;)V
0000de 010010        24. UTF length=16
0000e1 6a61 7661 2f6c 616e 672f 4f62 6a65 6374  java/lang/Object
0000f1 010004        25. UTF length=4
0000f4 6d61 696e                                main
0000f8 010016        26. UTF length=22
0000fb 285b 4c6a 6176 612f 6c61 6e67 2f53 7472  ([Ljava/lang/Stri
00010b 696e 673b 2956                           ng;)V
000111 010006        27. UTF length=6
000114 3c69 6e69 743e                           <init>
00011a 010015        28. UTF length=21
00011d 4c6a 6176 612f 696f 2f50 7269 6e74 5374  Ljava/io/PrintSt
00012d 7265 616d 3b                             ream;
000132 010010        29. UTF length=16
000135 6a61 7661 2f6c 616e 672f 5379 7374 656d  java/lang/System
```

```
000145 010003          30. UTF length=3
000148 282956                                        ()V
00014b 01000c          31. UTF length=12
00014e 4865 6c6c 6f2c 2077 6f72 6c64                 Hello, world
```

The constant pool of the `class` file begins with a two-byte unsigned number that indicates how many constants are used in the class. There are 32 constants in this class. However, there are only 31 constant entries in the file: constant 0 is reserved for the virtual machine's own use. The first constant in the file is numbered 1, the last 31.

Each constant begins with a one-byte tag that tells what sort of constant is coming up. The tag defines the format of the bytes following it. There are 11 different tags, numbered from 1 to 12 (tag 2 is undefined); they are listed in Table 9.1.

TABLE 9.1: *Constant pool tag definitions*

Tag	Type	Format	Meaning
1	UTF8	2-byte unsigned integer Bytes	Length of the bytes Text
3	Integer	4-byte signed integer	`int` constant
4	Float	4-byte floating-point number	`float` constant
5	Long	8-byte signed long integer	`long` constant
6	Double	8-byte double-precision number	`double` constant
7	Class	2-byte UTF8 index	Names a class
8	String	2-byte UTF8 index	`String` constant
9	Fieldref	2-byte `Class` index	Class containing the field
		2-byte `NameAndType` index	Field name and type
10	Methodref	2-byte `Class` index	Class containing the method
		2-byte `NameAndType` index	Method name and type
11	Interface Methodref	2-byte `Class` index	Interface containing the method
		2-byte `NameAndType` index	Method name and type
12	NameAndType	2-byte UTF8 index 2-byte UTF8 index	Name of the field or method Type descriptor

Constant pool entries often reference other constants, using a two-byte unsigned integer as the index into the constant pool. The DumpClass output displays such references by prefixing the index number (in decimal) with a "#." Order is not significant, and both forward and backward references are permitted.

9.2.1 UTF8 Entries

The most common kind of constant is the UTF8 constant, represented by tag 1. UTF-8 stands for "UCS Transformation Format, 8 bits," which is a standard defined by the X/Open Company. It is a way of coding 16-bit Unicode strings so that they mimic 7-bit ASCII text. UTF8 constants are used to store arbitrary strings of information, and they are capable of storing arbitrary-length data. They're used by some of the other constants to hold variable-length information, like the values of strings and the names of methods.

A UTF8 constant starts with two bytes that represent the length of the data, which may be up to 64 kilobytes. For example, in constant 31, the first four bytes are 000c, meaning that there are 12 bytes of data.

The next 12 bytes are the actual data bytes. Each byte between 1 and 127 is interpreted as the ASCII value corresponding to that value. In this case, there are 12 bytes that are interpreted as the ASCII string "Hello, world."

Non-ASCII characters are represented using two or three bytes having values greater than 127. The specifics of the code are defined in *File System Safe UCS Transformation Format (FSS_UTF), X/Open* Preliminary Specification, X/Open Company Ltd., Document number P316. The UTF8 standard is also documented in ISO/IEC 10646, Annex P.

9.2.2 Constant Entries

The first constant in the constant pool is a String constant, identified by the tag byte 1. It's used to represent the value of string literals within the Java program. String constants are used in conjunction with ldc instructions and as field initializers.

The value of a String constant is two bytes, taken together as a 16-bit unsigned integer referring to a UTF8 constant. The UTF8 constant is the value of the String. In constant 1, the two bytes are 001f, which points to constant 31. In hello.class, constant 31 is a UTF8 with the value Hello, world.

Constants 3, 4, 5, and 6 represent the various kinds of numeric constants that can appear in Java programs. This file didn't contain any. Like String constants, these constants are used in conjunction with the ldc (push constant) instruction and with field initializers.

Integer and Long constants are written as two's complement signed integers, with 32 and 64 bits respectively, written from most significant byte to least significant byte. For example, suppose the program contained this line:

```
long distance_to_sun = 149669000000;   // Distance to sun in
                                       meters
```

The compiler generates a Long constant. The eight bytes of this constant are:

```
0000 0022 D8F7 B340
```

Float and Double constants are also 32- and 64-bit values, but they are interpreted as representing floating-point numbers according to the IEEE 754 floating-point format (Table 9.2).

The value is negative if the sign is 1, positive if the sign is 0. The exponent and mantissa are unsigned integers. For example, the line

```
double pi = 3.14159265358979323;
```

would cause the compiler to add a Double constant with the bytes:

```
4009 21FB 5444 2D18
```

The sign of this number is 0, since the leftmost bit is 0. The exponent is 400 in hex, or 1024 in decimal. The mantissa is 921FB54442D18, or 2,570,638,124,657,944 decimal. Plugging this into the formula for double, you get the value of pi.

The String, Integer, and Float constants are usually the first in the constant pool. This allows them to have low numbers, which means that the short form of the ldc instruction can be used. If there are more than 255 of these constants in the constant pool, those with numbers 256 or above have to be used in conjunction with the ldc_w instruction, which takes up more space in the bytecodes. (Double and Long constrants require the ldc2_w instruction.)

TABLE 9.2: *Format of floats and doubles*

	Float	Double
Sign	1 bit	1 bit
Exponent	8 bits	11 bits
Mantissa	23 bits	52 bits
Value	$(2^{23}+\text{Mantissa}) \times 2^{\text{Exponent}-150}$	$(2^{52}+\text{Mantissa}) \times 2^{\text{Exponent}-1075}$

9.2.3 Field, Method, and Class Entries

Constants with the tags 9, 10, or 11 have identical formats. They are used to refer to fields and methods in field and method instructions, such as getfield, putstatic, and invokevirtual.

Constant 7 is an example of the Methodref constant. A Methodref constant contains two values that point to two other constants. The first points to a Class constant, which names the class containing the method. The second points to a NameAndType constant, which gives the name of the method and the method descriptor.

Constant 7 points to constant 4 as the Class constant and constant 9 as the NameAndType constant. The Class constant in 4 contains a single piece of information: a reference to a UTF8 constant naming the class. In this case, that's the UTF8 constant 14: java/io/PrintStream.

The NameAndType constant 9 contains the name and the type descriptor, each of which is a reference to a UTF8 constant. The values in this case are println and (Ljava/lang/String;)V.

Putting all this together provides enough information to name the method to be called. Constant 7 could be used in the assembly of an instruction:

```
invokevirtual java/io/PrintStream/println (Ljava/lang/String;)V
```

In this instruction, the class is java/io/PrintStream, the method is println, and the descriptor is (Ljava/lang/String;)V.

InterfaceMethodref and Fieldref constants are identical to Methodref constants. For an InterfaceMethodref, the Class entry refers to an interface instead of a class. For a Fieldref, the NameAndType entry points to a field instead of a method.

9.3 Class Information

Following the constant pool is information about the class itself: its name, type, and access flags. For this class, the class information section is

```
00015b 0021        access_flags = 33
00015d 0005        this = #5
00015f 0003        super = #3
000161 0000        0 interfaces
```

The first two bytes are access flags for the class. They are interpreted as a bit vector, revealing some class-level information. The meaning of these bits, from right to left, is shown in Figure 9.1 and Table 9.3.

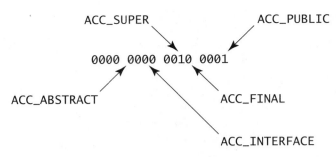

FIGURE 9.1: *Class access flags with value 33*

ACC_PUBLIC means that the class is public; that is, any other class in any package may reference it. The ACC_SUPER bit has a special meaning for classes containing the invokespecial instruction, as discussed in section 4.5.5. ACC_SUPER corresponds to the super keyword on the .class directive. All class files generated from Java programs should have this bit set.

The next two bytes are a reference into the constant pool that indicates the name of this class. It is expected to be a Class entry. A Class entry contains a reference to a UTF8 constant, in this case constant 19, hello. Similarly, the next two bytes name the superclass of this class. In this case the name of the superclass is java/lang/Object. If the value of these two bytes is 0, then there is no superclass. Only the class java.lang.Object is permitted to have no superclass; in any other class, it is an error. This ensures that Object is always the root of the class hierarchy.

TABLE 9.3: *Class access flags*

Bit	Name	Meaning
1	ACC_PUBLIC	The class is public
2-4		unused
5	ACC_FINAL	The class is final
6	ACC_SUPER	The class is super
7-9		unused
10	ACC_INTERFACE	The class is an interface
11		unused
12	ACC_ABSTRACT	The class is abstract

9.4 Fields and Methods

The next four bytes describe the number of fields and methods in the class:

```
000163 0000              0 fields
000165 0002              2 methods
```

This class has no fields and two methods. Fields and methods have identical formats. This class has no fields, so the next bytes form the definition of the first method.

```
                         Method 0:
000167 0009              access flags = 9
000169 001a              name = #26<main>
00016b 001b              descriptor = #27<([Ljava/lang/String;)V>
```

A field or method starts off with two bytes of access flags. The meaning of these bits, from right to left, is shown in Figure 9.2 and Table 9.4.

The `main` method is both `public` and `static`, so bits 1 and 4 are set. This yields the value 9, which is the value of the access flags field. Following the access flags are two two-byte constant pool references, giving the name of the field or method (`main`) and the type descriptor (`([Ljava/lang/String;)V`). The type descriptor says that this is a method that takes an array of `String`s and returns `void`.

After the general method or field information, the file contains a list of attributes. Field and method definitions have identical formats, giving the name, type, and access information, followed by a list of attributes. Fields and methods

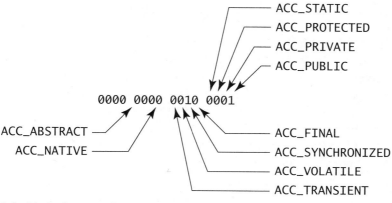

FIGURE 9.2: *Method access flags with value 9*

TABLE 9.4: *Method access flags*

Bit	Name	Meaning
1	ACC_PUBLIC	The field/method is public
2	ACC_PRIVATE	The field/method is private
3	ACC_PROTECTED	The field/method is protected
4	ACC_STATIC	The field/method is static
5	ACC_FINAL	The field/method is final
6	ACC_SYNCHRONIZED	The method is synchronized
7	ACC_VOLATILE	The field is volatile
8	ACC_TRANSIENT	The field is transient
9	ACC_NATIVE	The method is native
10		unused
11		unused
12	ACC_ABSTRACT	The method is abstract

have different kinds of attributes. Methods usually have a single attribute giving the implementation of the method. Most fields don't have any attributes at all. Only the ConstantValue attribute is defined for fields, which specifies the initial value of some fields. ConstantValue is discussed in section 9.6.1.

The attribute for this method begins

```
00016d 0001                 1 method attributes:
                            method attribute 0
00016f 0015                 name = #21<Code>
000171 00000025             length = 37
```

Every attribute begins with two pieces of information: a constant pool entry indicating the name of the attribute as a UTF8 constant and four bytes indicating the length of the attribute data. The data follow. In this case, the name of the attribute is Code, and the Code attribute takes up the next 37 bytes of the file.

The name of the attribute may be anything you can fit into a UTF8 constant. *The Java Virtual Machine Specification* defines the name and data structure of some attributes, such as the Code attribute shown here. A JVM implementation ignores any attributes it does not recognize.

The next 37 bytes form the value of the Code attribute. They begin with some information about the resources the method requires to run:

```
000175 0002                 max stack: 2
000177 0001                 max locals: 1
```

This information indicates the maximum height of the stack and the maximum number of local variables permitted in the method. These let the program know how much space to allocate when the method is run. Since these are 16-bit numbers, the stack is limited to 65,536 slots and 65,536 local variables. Fortunately, real programs never require this much space.

This information is checked during the verification process, and if the program attempts to use more stack space or more local variables than requested here, then the class will be rejected before it gets a chance to run. For more information on how this is determined, see chapter 6.

After the method information, the `class` file includes the actual code for the method.

```
000179 00000009        code length: 9
00017d b20006          0000 getstatic #6
000180 1201            0003 ldc #1
000182 b60007          0005 invokevirtual #7
000185 b1              0008 return
```

The first four bytes indicate that the code is nine bytes long. Since this is a four-byte number, the code may be up to four gigabytes long. However, other limitations limit practical code size to 64 kilobytes.

The next nine bytes are interpreted as Java virtual machine instructions, or bytecodes. The rightmost column of the `DumpClass` output gives the address of the code relative to the beginning of the code, followed by the instruction at that address.

An instruction consists of a single-byte opcode and a few bytes of arguments. The opcode determines how many bytes are used as arguments for the instruction. The next instruction begins immediately after the arguments for this instruction.

Some instructions have no arguments, like the `return` instruction at offset 185. Others, like the `getstatic` instruction at location 17d, use two bytes to represent a constant in the constant pool. The `getstatic` instruction at 17d points to constant 6, a `Fieldref` constant.

The `ldc` instruction at location 180 is a little unusual. Its argument is only one byte wide, but it's still interpreted as a constant reference. This constant must be an `Integer`, `Float`, or `String` constant.

There are two forms of the `ldc` instruction: `ldc` and `ldc_w`. The former requires one argument byte, which is interpreted as a reference to a constant between 0 and 255. The latter uses two bytes for its argument and may refer to any constant. In either case the constant pool entry must be a `Integer`, `Float`, `Double`, `Long`, or `String` entry.

The ldc instruction is provided because it requires less space in the class file. The constant entries are usually placed in the lowest values of the constant pool so that the ldc instruction can be used instead of ldc_w.

Rewriting all the constants in Oolong form, the code for the method is

```
getstatic java/lang/System/out Ljava/io/PrintStream;
ldc "Hello, world"
invokevirtual java/io/PrintStream/println (Ljava/lang/String;)V
return
```

This is the same code we've seen elsewhere in the book to write the Hello, world program in Oolong. The first instruction fetches the value of out, which is a PrintStream used for writing output to the console. The second instruction loads the constant "Hello, world", which is to be printed. The third instruction invokes the println method on out, passing it "Hello, world" as an argument. The final instruction terminates the method.

```
000186 0000              0 exception table entries:
```

Following the bytecodes is an exception table, which begins with a two-byte count of the number of exception table entries. These entries determine how exceptions are handled when they are raised during the execution of this method. This method doesn't catch any exceptions, so the length of the table is 0.

Following the exception handler table, the code attribute may have attributes of its own. The attributes follow the same format as before: name, length, and a collection of bytes. Code attributes are used to store information about the code itself, such as debugging information. The main method has one attribute, a LineNumberTable:

```
000188 0001              1 code attributes:
                         code attribute 0:
00018a 0011                name = #17<LineNumberTable>
00018c 0000000a            length = 10
                           Line number table:
000190 0002                length = 2
000192 0000                  start pc: 0
000194 0005                  line number: 5
000196 0008                  start pc: 8
000198 0003                  line number: 3
```

This line number table has two entries in it, as indicated by the 0x0002 at byte 0x0190. Each entry maps a location in the bytecodes (called the start pc) to a line in the file (called the line number). The start pc and the line number are each given as a two-byte number, which tends to limit Java source files to 65,536 lines and the bytecode to 65,536 bytes.

The first entry maps the beginning of the method (at location 0) to line 5 of the source, which is the line containing the `println`. The second entry is for the `return` instruction at location 8. Since there is no explicit `return` in the source code, the compiler maps the `return` instruction to the first line of the method, on source line 3.

Instructions that don't have explicit mappings are assumed to be on the same line as the previous instruction in the file. Since the instructions at 3 and 5 aren't explicitly mapped, they're all assumed to be part of the source line 5, since that's where 0 is mapped to. This is reasonable, since they're all part of the `println` statement on line 5.

That's all there is to the `main` method of this program. However, the `class` file indicated that there was another method. Besides, there are still some bytes left in the file. Any file that ends prematurely or that has junk bytes at the end is rejected by the verification algorithm.

```
                              Method 1:
00019a 0000                     access flags = 0
00019c 001c                     name = #28<<init>>
00019e 001f                     descriptor = #31<()V>
```

The method is named `<init>`; it's the constructor for the `hello` class. Since no constructor was given in the Java source, the Java compiler added this method automatically. This is what `Dumpclass` prints for `<init>`:

```
0001a0 0001               1 method attributes:
                          method attribute 0
0001a2 0015                 name = #21<Code>
0001a4 0000001d             length = 29
0001a8 0001                 max stack: 1
0001aa 0001                 max locals: 1
0001ac 00000005             code length: 5
0001b0 2a                   00000000 aload_0
0001b1 b70008               00000001 invokespecial #8
0001b4 b1                   00000004 return
0001b5 0000                 0 exception table entries:
0001b7 0001                 1 code attributes:
                            code attribute 0:
0001b9 0011                   name = #17<LineNumberTable>
0001bb 00000006               length = 6
                              Line number table:
0001bf 0001                   length = 1
```

```
0001c1 0000                          start pc: 0
0001c3 0001                          line number: 1
```

Like the `main` method, the `<init>` method has exactly one attribute: its `Code` attribute. It promises to push at most one thing at a time onto the stack and uses only one local variable.

The code for this method is equivalent to the Oolong:

```
aload_0
invokespecial java/lang/Object/<init> ()V
return
```

This code invokes the superclass constructor on the object, which is the argument in local variable 0. If this method were not provided, it would not be possible to create an instance of the `hello` object, since an object must be constructed before it can be used. The verification algorithm requires that each constructor call a superclass constructor to ensure that objects are always completely initialized.

Like the `main` method, `<init>` also has an attribute that contains a table of line numbers. It's a little odd that there can be a line number table for a method that doesn't have any source code, but the compiler adds it anyway for the benefit of debuggers. All the instructions are mapped to the beginning of the class on line 1.

9.5   Class Attributes

The `class` file ends with a list of attributes. These are formatted just like field or method attributes. As with other attributes, the `class` file can have any attributes it wants here, but only the `SourceFile` attribute is defined in *The Java Language Specification:*

```
0001c5 0001                  1 class file attributes
                             Attribute 0:
0001c7 0012                      name #18<SourceFile>
0001c9 00000002                  length = 2
0001cd 0010                      SourceFile #16<hello.java>
```

The `SourceFile` attribute is only two bytes long. Those two bytes are used to specify a UTF8 constant that names the file used as input to the compiler. This can be used by debuggers in conjunction with the `LineNumberTable` attributes to show the source line being executed.

The value of the attribute is the name of the source file without any path information. Therefore, `hello.java` is acceptable here, but `/home/josh/hello.java` would not be.

9.6   Other Attributes

Any attributes the JVM implementation isn't expecting may be ignored. The only attributes that are absolutely crucial for proper functioning of a JVM are the Code attribute, discussed earlier, and the ConstantValue attribute, which is used to initialize fields. This section discusses some of the attributes defined in *The Java Virtual Machine*.

Attributes are not reflected directly in an Oolong program. A ConstantValue attribute added to a field if the Oolong program has an initializer for the field. Use of the .throws directive causes an Exceptions attribute to be added to the method.

9.6.1   ConstantValue Attribute

The ConstantValue attribute is used to initialize static final fields. The ConstantValue class contains a reference to an Integer, Float, Long, Double, or String constant, which is the initial value of the field. The field is initialized to that value by the JVM. For example, suppose you have a class Human that defines the standard temperature of the human body as 98.6 degrees:

```
class Human
{
    public static final double standardTemperature = 98.6;
}
```

When this class is compiled, the definition of the standardTemperature field is

```
0000d2 0019                 access flags = 25
0000d4 0012                 name = #18<StandardTemperature>
0000d6 000b                 descriptor = #11<D>
0000d8 0001                 1 field/method attributes:
                            field/method attribute 0
0000da 000a                     name = #10<ConstantValue>
0000dc 00000002                 length = 2
0000e0 0004                     Constant value: #4
```

The field is named StandardTemperature, and it is a double. It has a ConstantValue attribute, which is defined by constant 4. The definition of constant 4 is

```
000015 064058a66666666666 4. Double 98.6
```

When this class is loaded, the value of the field is initialized to 98.6. No code is required to set the value of this field. This makes it easier to analyze the code for the purpose of making optimizations, because the field's value is always the same. The JVM can internally replace an instruction like

```
getstatic Human/standardTemperature D
```

with

```
ldc 98.6
```

which is usually faster.

The JVM implementation is required to understand this attribute, since failure to assign the value to the field would cause programs to execute incorrectly. All other attributes (besides Code) are useful to debuggers, Java compilers, optimizing JVMs, and other programs, but virtual machines may safely ignore them.

9.6.2   Exceptions Attribute

The Exceptions attribute is added to a method definition to name the exceptions that may be thrown by this method. It contains a list of the classes specified in the .throws directive of an Oolong program or the throws clause of a Java program.

For example, this fragment of a ClassLoader throws a ClassNotFound-Exception:

```
public Class loadClass(String name, boolean resolve)
    throws ClassNotFoundException
{
    // Load the class
}
```

Compiled into JVM code, it becomes

```
00068f 0001              access flags = 1
000691 007f              name = #127<loadClass>
000693 0055              descriptor = #85
000695 0002              2 field/method attributes:
                         field/method attribute 0
000697 005d                  name = #93<Code>
000699 000002de              length = 734
00069d 0005                  max stack: 5
00069f 0007                  max locals: 7
0006a1 000001f6              code length: 502

       .                         .
       .                         .
       .                         .

                     field/method attribute 1
```

```
00097b 0060              name = #96<Exceptions>
00097d 00000004          length = 4
000981 0001              Exception table length: 1
000983 0017              0. exception table entry: #23
```

There are two attributes for this method: the Code attribute, which contains the implementation of the method, and the Exceptions attribute. After the attribute header, the Exceptions attribute has two bytes giving the number of classes. In this case, there is just one. This is followed by a list of exceptions, each two bytes long, representing an address in the constant pool. Each constant must be a Class constant naming the exception class.

The relevant parts of the constant pool are

```
00004c 070078                      23. Class name #120

0004ca 010020                      120. UTF length=32
0004cd 6a61 7661 2f6c 616e 672f 436c 6173 734e    java/lang/ClassN
0004dd 6f74 466f 756e 6445 7863 6570 7469 6f6e    otFoundException
```

Java compilers use this information to enforce the rule that exceptions must either be explicitly caught or listed in the throws clause of the method. When a class references a method or field in another class, the compiler does not need the source code to enforce this rule. It can determine which exceptions are thrown based on the Exceptions attribute in the compiled class file. Even though the information is available, this rule is not enforced by the JVM.

9.6.3   InnerClasses Attribute

The InnerClasses attribute was introduced to the Java platform in version 1.1. The Java virtual machine provides no special support for nesting classes within classes; all classes are top-level classes. Classes that are defined within another class are given special names to avoid naming conflicts. For example, this implementation of a Stack class uses an inner class nameEnumerator:

```
public class Stack {
    // Push, pop, etc. methods go here

    class Enumerator implements java.util.Enumeration
    {
        // Definitions for hasMoreElements and nextElement go here
    }

    public java.util.Enumeration elements()
```

```
        {
            return new Enumerator();
        }
    }
```

When this code is compiled, two class files are produced: Stack and Stack$Enumerator. Stack$Enumerator contains the definition of Enumerator within the Stack class. Whenever either refers to Enumerator, it really means Stack$Enumerator.

An attribute is added to each class at the file level to point out that the two classes are related. This is called the InnerClasses attribute, and for Stack it looks like this:

```
000185 0010                  name = #16<InnerClasses>
000187 0000000a              length = 10
00018b 0001                  number of classes = 1
00018d 0002                      inner class: #2
00018f 0001                      outer class: #1
000191 000e                      inner name: #14
000193 0002                      flags: 2
```

The relevant constants are

```
00000a 070014                1. Class name #20
00000d 070015                2. Class name #21

000076 01000a                14. UTF length=10
000079 456e 756d 6572 6174 6f72            Enumerator

0000cf 010005                20. UTF length=5
0000d2 5374 6163 6b                        Stack
0000d7 010010                21. UTF length=16
0000da 5374 6163 6b24 456e 756d 6572 6174 6f72 Stack$Enumerator
```

The first four bytes of the attribute data name the inner class and the outer class: Stack and Stack$Enumerator. The next two bytes give the name of the inner class before it was mangled: Enumerator. By explicitly providing the name, it relieves the program from having to know any conventions about how the mangled name was created.

Finally, the flags tell what access is permitted to the class. These flags are the same as for top-level classes, as shown in section 9.3. The 2 indicates that this is a private class.

## CHAPTER 10

Compiling Java

THE Java virtual machine was originally designed to run programs written in Java. A Java compiler translates Java programs into `class` files, which can be executed on any JVM implementation. Although the JVM is equipped with sufficient instructions to handle any language, many instructions are particularly well suited to Java. In particular, it is always possible to compile any valid Java program into a JVM `class` file that will pass the verification algorithm's checks.

This chapter discusses how Java programs are converted into JVM programs. We look at Java programs from the point of view of a Java compiler (or a Java compiler writer). A complete definition of the Java language in terms of the JVM would stretch to hundreds of pages, so a lot of details must be omitted. The reader can fill in the details.

A simplified view of how a Java compiler sees a Java file appears in Figure 10.1. The input file contains a series of class declarations, which are made up of a series of field and method declarations. Method declarations in turn are made from statements, which are built from expressions. In the forthcoming sections, we look at a Java program from the inside out, starting at expressions and ending with completed `class` files. The translations are shown in terms of Oolong code. While Oolong is not exactly equivalent to bytecodes, it is extremely close and a lot more readable.

The code shown in this chapter is not necessarily identical to the code generated by any actual Java compiler. The code created by real Java compilers is generally more efficient but less straightforward than the code shown in this book. The `class` files produced by different Java compilers are different but equivalent from the point of view of the user.

One of the best ways to learn how the JVM works is to compile examples written in Java using a commercial Java compiler such as `javac` in the Java Development Kit. Then use the `Gnoloo` disassembler provided with this book to produce a readable version of the `class` files. You can also use `javap` with the `-c` option, which also produces a disassembly of the bytecodes; `javap` comes with the Java Development Kit.

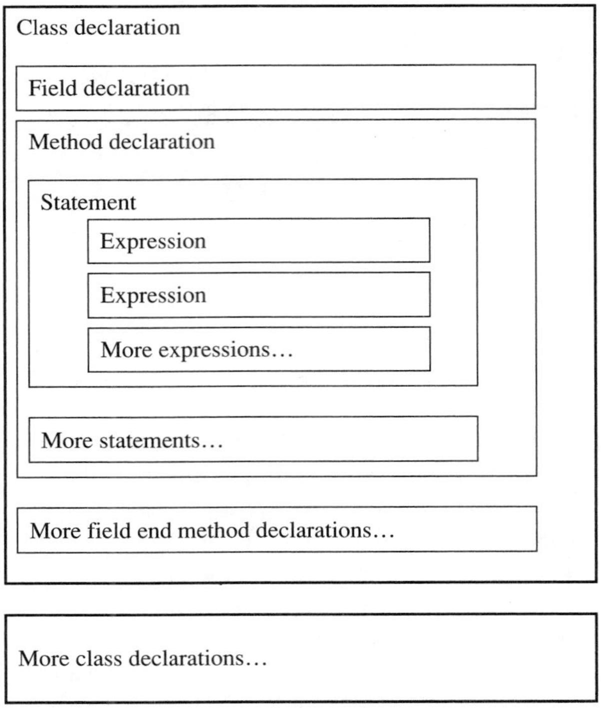

```
┌─────────────────────────────────────────────────────┐
│ Class declaration                                   │
│ ┌─────────────────────────────────────────────────┐ │
│ │ Field declaration                               │ │
│ └─────────────────────────────────────────────────┘ │
│ ┌─────────────────────────────────────────────────┐ │
│ │ Method declaration                              │ │
│ │ ┌─────────────────────────────────────────────┐ │ │
│ │ │ Statement                                   │ │ │
│ │ │ ┌─────────────────────────────────────────┐ │ │ │
│ │ │ │ Expression                              │ │ │ │
│ │ │ └─────────────────────────────────────────┘ │ │ │
│ │ │ ┌─────────────────────────────────────────┐ │ │ │
│ │ │ │ Expression                              │ │ │ │
│ │ │ └─────────────────────────────────────────┘ │ │ │
│ │ │ ┌─────────────────────────────────────────┐ │ │ │
│ │ │ │ More expressions…                       │ │ │ │
│ │ │ └─────────────────────────────────────────┘ │ │ │
│ │ └─────────────────────────────────────────────┘ │ │
│ │ ┌─────────────────────────────────────────────┐ │ │
│ │ │ More statements…                            │ │ │
│ │ └─────────────────────────────────────────────┘ │ │
│ └─────────────────────────────────────────────────┘ │
│ ┌─────────────────────────────────────────────────┐ │
│ │ More field end method declarations…             │ │
│ └─────────────────────────────────────────────────┘ │
└─────────────────────────────────────────────────────┘

┌─────────────────────────────────────────────────────┐
│ More class declarations…                            │
└─────────────────────────────────────────────────────┘
```

FIGURE 10.1: *Structure of a Java source file*

10.1   Expressions and Statements

An expression is a fragment of Java code that yields a value. Expressions include field references, method calls, arithmetic operations, and constants. Expressions may be built up from other expressions. Some examples of expressions are listed in Table 10.1.

A statement is a unit of code that does not yield a value. Instead, it affects program state by producing some sort of side effect. Statements can set field values, control the flow of execution, or terminate methods, among other things. Statements usually end with semicolons (;). Some kinds of statements are composed of expressions or other statements. Sometimes a statement is composed of nothing but an expression. For example,

```
System.out.println("Hello, world");
```

TABLE 10.1: *Examples of Java expressions*

Expression	Explanation
`"A String"`	Constant expression of type `String`
`2+2`	Arithmetic expression composed of two constants combined with the + operator
`x*x`	Arithmetic expression composed of two field-reference subexpressions combined with the * operator
`x*x+y*y`	Expression composed of two subexpressions, `x*x` and `y*y`, combined with the + operator
`Math.sqrt(x*x+y*y)`	Method-call expression with one subexpression, `x*x+y*y`
`(String)` `cache.get(key)`	Cast expression made from a method-call expression. The method-call expression has two subexpressions, `cache` and `key`, which are combined into a single method-call expression.

This statement consists of nothing but a method-call expression followed by a semicolon. The method-call expression has two subexpressions: `System.out` (a field-reference expression) and `"Hello, world"` (a constant `String` expression). The value of the expression is `void`, which means that it doesn't really yield a value when evaluated.

Following is another example of a statement:

```
i = i+1;
```

This statement is made up of the expression `i = i+1`. The value of that expression is the new value of `i`. By adding a semicolon (`;`) at the end, it becomes a statement.

You may put several statements together using braces (`{}`) to make a *block,* or compound statement. A compound statement doesn't have a semicolon at the end of it. The effect of a compound statement is the cumulative effect of all the statements within it executed sequentially. For example, this is a block with three statements:

```
{
    System.out.print(i + " ");
    int fact = factorial(i);
    System.out.println(fact);
}
```

Some kinds of statements, such as `if`, `for`, and `while`, include a substatement:

```
// Print "Hello, world" 10 times
for(int i = 0; i < 10; i++)
    System.out.println("Hello, world");
```

A `for` statement may use a compound statement as its substatement:

```
for(int i = 0; i < 10; i++)
{                           // Braces denote a compound statement
    System.out.println(i);
    int i = factorial(i);
    System.out.println(fact);
}
```

10.2   Expression Types

The Java type system is slightly different from the one in the JVM, but they are very similar, and the JVM type system is used to implement the Java type system.

Java has eight numeric types: `int`, `double`, `long`, `float`, `byte`, `boolean`, `short`, and `char`. These types designate entities from a fixed universe. These entities do not have to be created; they just exist.

The other kind of type is the object type. Classes are the types of objects. Each time an object is created, a new element is added to the set of elements of that class. The object is said to be an instance of that class. All of the instances of the class are in the set of that class.

Each class has a superclass, except for the special class `java.lang.Object`. All instances of that class are also instances of the superclass. The instances of the subclass form a subset of the instances of the superclass. Another way of saying this is that the subclass is a subtype of the superclass.

The term subtype refers to the type and all of the types within it. A type is always a subtype of itself. All the subtypes of a type, but not the type itself, are called the proper subtypes of that type.

Figure 10.2 shows a diagram of part of the Java type system. To make it fit more easily onto a page, package names have been omitted. All the classes depicted are part of the standard Java platform. Many others have been omitted.

10.2.1 Numeric Types

At the top of Figure 10.2 are the numeric types: `int`, `long`, and so forth. The relative sizes give a rough idea of how many values are in that type. The figure is not

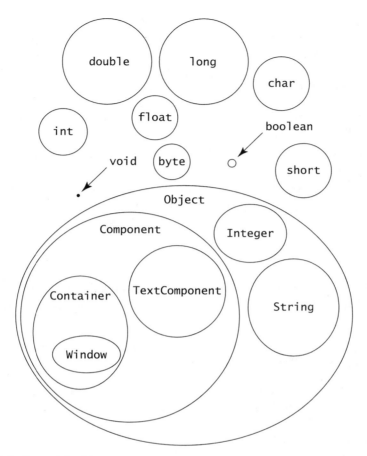

FIGURE 10.2: *Part of the Java type system*

drawn to scale: `long` is actually 4 billion times larger than `int`. The type `boolean` contains just two members: `true` and `false`. The special type `void` actually contains no members. It is used as a placeholder type for methods that don't return a value.

Notice that all the numeric types are disjoint. The `int`s are not a subset of the `long`s, and the `short`s, `byte`s, and `char`s are not a subset of the `int`s. This is different from the JVM itself, where `short`s, `int`s, `byte`s, `char`s, and `boolean`s are all represented the same way.

To convert from an `int` value 1 to a `short` value, a special conversion operation must be performed, which maps the elements from the set of `int`s onto the elements of the set of `short`s. This operation is called a *coercion*. Sometimes the

Java compiler performs the coercion automatically (see section 1.8.1), but it always happens when you want to use a value of one type as a value of another.

Similar conversions may be performed on almost any pair of numeric types. However, you can't convert a `boolean` to or from anything else. Since there are no elements in the set of `void`, no conversions are possible there, either.

10.2.2   Object Types

At the bottom of Figure 10.2 is the set of classes, with subclasses shown as smaller bubbles within other bubbles. Each bubble is entirely contained within exactly one other (except for `Object`, which occupies a privileged position at the top). The figure shows that a `Window` is a `Container`, which is a `Component`, which is an `Object`. A `String` is also an `Object`, but a `String` is not a `Component`, nor is a `Component` a `String`.

An interface is like a class, except that it may span multiple supertypes. All members of any class that implements the interface are included in the domain of the interface. From the point of view of an expression, an interface type is treated identically to a class type, except when it is used as the receiver of a method invocation.

10.2.3   Expression Result Types

When an expression is executed, it yields a result. Executing an expression is sometimes called evaluating the expression. Each result is an entity from somewhere in the type system; each result has a type. The type of the result actually produced when the expression is executed is called the *runtime type*.

The runtime type of an expression is not always the same each time an expression is executed. For example, consider this expression:

```
vector.elementAt(5)
```

where `vector` is an object of type `java.util.Vector`. The return type of the `elementAt` method in `Vector` is `Object`. This means that whatever is returned will fit somewhere in the domain of `Object`. The exact runtime type may be a `String` or a `Window` or any other kind of object, depending on what the program put into the `vector`.

It is impossible for a Java compiler to predict the exact runtime type of an expression. It may even be different each time the expression is evaluated. However, it is always possible for the compiler to deduce something about the runtime type. For example, in this case the compiler can deduce from the declared return type of the `elementAt` method that the returned value will be some sort of

`Object`. This doesn't tell you a lot about the result, but it does tell you that it isn't an `int` or a `long` or other numeric type.

The most specific thing the compiler can deduce about the type is called the *compile-time type* of the expression. The compiler uses rules like these to deduce the compile-time type of each expression:

- The compile-time type of adding two `int`s together is another `int`.
- The compile-time type of invoking a method is the return type of that method.
- The compile-time type of a constant value is the type of that constant.
- The compile-time type of reading a field is the type of that field.
- The compile-time type of reading a local variable is the declared type of that local variable.

And so on.

The rules guarantee that the runtime type of the result will either be the same as the compile-time type of the expression or some subtype of the compile-time type. The runtime type is said to conform to the compile-time type.

Since the numeric types don't have subtypes in Java, the runtime type of an expression that returns a numeric type is always exactly the same as the compile-time type. If the type is an object type, then the runtime type may be a subtype of the compile-time type.

10.2.4 Compile-Time Types and Type Restrictions

Types restrict what operations can be performed on values of that type. The compiler uses the compile-time type to deduce what sorts of operations will be legal on the runtime type. For example, look at these declarations:

```
class Point
{
    // Definition omitted
}
class Rectangle
{
    boolean contains(Point p)  { /* implementation omitted */ }
    void move(Point p)         { /* implementation omitted */ }
}
int a,b;
float f1, f2;
```

TABLE 10.2: *Examples of compile-time types*

Expression	Compile-time type
a + b	int
f1 * f2	float
r.contains(p)	boolean
o.toString()	java.lang.String
r.toString()	java.lang.String
o = r	java.lang.Object
r.move(p)	void

```
Point p;
Rectangle r;
Object o;
```

Some legal expressions are given in Table 10.2. The last one doesn't actually produce a value, since there are no members of the type void. The type void is used to make sure that every expression has a type. Since no operations apply to void values, the result of this expression can't be used as part of other expressions.

Illegal expressions are given in Table 10.3. In the last one, it may be that o is really a Rectangle, since Rectangles are included in the domain of Objects. If

TABLE 10.3: *Illegal expressions*

Expression	Illegal because...
p1 + p2	Points can't be added.
r * r	Rectangles can't be multiplied.
r = o	The object identified by o may not be a Rectangle.
r = 5	An int is not a Rectangle.
a.move(p1, p2)	There is no method called move in Rectangle that can take two Points.
r.contains(f1)	There is no method called contains in Rectangle that can take a float.
r.contains(p, p)	There is no method named contains in Rectangle that can take two Points.
o.contains(p)	There is no method in Object named contains that takes a Point.

this were the case, then the method call to `contains` would be legal, since there is a method called `contains` in `Rectangle` that takes a `Point` as its argument. However, the Java compiler can work only on the basis of what it can prove when it is compiling. Since the object in `o` might not be a `Rectangle`, the Java compiler flags the expression `o.contains(p)` as illegal.

10.2.5 Type Safety and Verifiability

The type rules discussed briefly here define which operations are legal and which are not. If a program does only legal things, then it is said to be *type-safe*. A Java program must be type-safe in order for the resulting bytecodes to be verifiable by the bytecode verification algorithm. If it is not type-safe, then the compiler will reject the program.

The reason that type-safe Java programs produce verifiable JVM bytecodes is that the type checking applied to JVM instructions is similar to the Java type deduction rules. The compile-time types used by the Java compiler to determine whether or not a program is safe is analogous to the rules applied by the JVM verification algorithm when verifying a program.

The key is that each expression produces a known compile-time type, and the code that is generated can be shown to always produce a value at runtime that conforms to that type. The various operations combine values of these types, producing results that are predictable, at least where type is concerned.

In forthcoming sections, as we discuss how various Java constructs translate into JVM code, you should check how the various constructs compile into code that produces values of a type that can be checked by the verification algorithm.

The discussion of Java types given here is extremely abbreviated. A full explanation of type safety can be found in chapter 13 of *The Java Language Specification*.

10.3 Compiling Statements and Expressions

A Java compiler generally follows three rules about the stack when compiling expressions and statements. These rules help guarantee that the code produced will be verifiable.

1. Each statement begins with an empty stack, and there is an empty stack when it ends.

2. Each expression has no effect on the stack except to place an additional element on top of the stack.

3. If a compound expression or statement is composed of subexpressions, the subexpressions are evaluated first, leaving the result of each on the stack. The subexpressions are used as operands to the compound expression or statement, which removes them from the stack.

The steps of evaluating a statement may cause the stack to grow temporarily, but at the end the stack will be empty. Evaluating an expression increases the height of the stack by exactly one, without affecting any of the elements on the stack beneath it.

If a statement uses subexpressions, then each subexpression increases the height of the stack by one, but each is removed before the statement is finished executing. For example, consider the statement

```
System.out.write(bytes, 0, bytes.length);
```

where `bytes` is an array of type `byte`. This statement contains four subexpressions, `System.out`, `bytes`, `0`, and `bytes.length`. In accordance with the third rule, the subexpressions are evaluated first. Suppose that `bytes` is contained in local variable 1. The subexpressions are translated into

```
getstatic java/lang/System/out Ljava/io/PrintStream ; System.out
aload_1                                               ; bytes
iconst_0                                              ; 0
aload_1                                               ; bytes
arraylength                                           ; .length
```

In compiling the expression `bytes.length`, the code first evaluates the subexpression `bytes` by loading variable 1 onto the stack. Then it applies the `arraylength` instruction to it, which pops the result of the subexpression `bytes` and pushes the value of `bytes.length`.

The four expressions have increased the height of the stack by four. To finish the statement, all four must be removed from the stack. The next instruction is a method call:

```
invokevirtual java/io/PrintStream/write ([BII)V
```

This instruction takes four values off the stack (a `PrintStream`, an array of `bytes`, and two `ints`), returning nothing. Thus, there is no net effect on the stack, even though the stack height was as high as four.

As the compiler compiles the code, it remembers the maximum height the stack can achieve during execution. The `class` file must specify the maximum allowable height of the stack for each method. This allows the JVM to allocate the smallest possible amount of memory when the method is invoked, improving execution time and memory efficiency. The JVM verification algorithm rejects any programs that attempt to use more stack space than the maximum stack height permits.

10.4   Local Variable Declarations

A local variable declaration looks a bit like a statement in that it ends with a semi-colon, but it generates no code. Instead, it causes the compiler to allocate a local variable slot (or two, in the case of `long` or `double` declarations). The declaration gives the compile-time type of all values read from that variable. Also, all values written to that variable must conform to compile-time type.

A compiler may use any of a variety of strategies to allocate local variables to slots in the resulting JVM code. Generally, the compiler tries to minimize the number of slots used, because that makes for better performance.

In Java, local variables are scoped, which means that a local variable defini-tion is restricted to the block in which they were declared. (Recall that a block is a set of statements enclosed in curly braces). Consider this method definition:

```
void foo(int a, long b)                     // Declares a and b
{
    String name = "Joshua";                 // Declares name
    boolean state = false;                  // Declares state
    while(state)
    {
        String output = "Hello, world";     // Declares output
        System.out.println(output);
        state = true;
    }
    if(name == null)
    {
        String msg = "No name";             // Declares msg
        int output = b-a;                   // Declares output
        System.out.println(output);
    }
}
```

Figure 10.3 is a diagram of the scopes and the local variables in each.

In this code there are three different scopes: the outermost scope is the whole body of the method. It contains two other scopes: the one inside the `while` and the one inside the `if`.

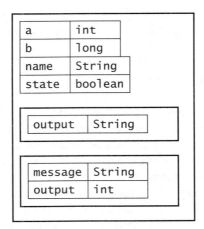

FIGURE 10.3: *Scopes of method* foo

Notice that you can have two different variables with the same name in different scopes. They can even have different types. Both the inner scopes contain an output; it is a String in one place and an int in the other.

For each scope, the compiler allocates the variables to local variable slots. When a scope terminates, later scopes may reuse those local variable slots. All the code within that scope uses those assignments. Each enclosed scope incorporates the assignments from the enclosing scope. For example, the compiler might allocate local variable slots as in Table 10.4.

This information does not need to be explicitly stated within an Oolong program. However, it can be provided for debugging purposes using the .var directive:

```
.var 0 is a I
.var 1 is b J
.var 3 is name Ljava/lang/String;
.var 4 is state Z
.var 5 is output Ljava/lang/String; from scope1begin to scope1end
.var 5 is message Ljava/lang/String; from scope2begin to
scope2end
.var 6 is output I from scope2begin to scope2end

scope1begin:
;; Code within the body of the while scope
scope1end:
```

TABLE 10.4: *Assigning variables to slots*

Variable	Slot
Outermost `scope`:	
a	0
b	1 and 2
name	3
state	4
Scope inside the `while`:	
output	5
Scope inside the `if`:	
msg	5
output	6

```
scope2begin:
;; Code within the body of the if scope
scope2end:
```

Scoping is also used to determine the compile-time types of variables. For example, there are two calls to `println`. Each takes a variable named `output`, but in the first case `output` is a `String` and in the second case `output` is an `int`. This is legal. In the first case the compiler generates code to call the method named `println`, which takes a `String`, and in the second case the compiler uses the method that takes an `int`. This is called overloading. For more about overloading, see section 10.9.5.

10.5   Fields and Variables

A Java program keeps track of state in three different ways:

- ◆ Local variables
- ◆ Object fields
- ◆ Static fields

Three different kinds of instructions are used. To read the state of local variables, the load instructions (`fload`, `aload`, `iload`, etc.) are used. For object fields, `getfield` is used. For static fields, `getstatic` is used. To change the state, corresponding `store` and `put` instructions are used.

To change the state of any of these variables, an assignment expression is used. An assignment expression is written using the = operator. On the right side of the = is an expression that gives the value of the assignment. The left side names some local variable, object field, or static field. Look at the following example.

```
class Employee
{
    /** The total payroll */
    static float payroll;

    /** The employee's name */
    String name;

    /** The employee's salary */
    float salary;

    /** Give the employee a raise. This involves raising the
     * employee's salary and increasing the total payroll
     */
    public void increase_salary(float raise_percentage)
    {
        float raise;
        raise = raise_percentage * salary;
        this.salary = this.salary + raise;
        Employee.payroll = Employee.payroll + raise;
    }
}
```

The increase_salary method uses all three kinds of state: raise and raise_percentage are local variables; salary is a field in the Employee object; payroll is a static field shared by all Employees.

Note that the left side of an assignment is not an expression. Rather, it designates the *target* of the assignment. In increase_salary, the code fragments raise, this.salary, and Employee.payroll are the targets of the assignments. The first names a local variable, the second a field, and the third a static field.

To compile these expressions, evaluate the equation on the right-hand side and then assign the results to the target. The instruction used for the assignment depends on the target. The increase_salary method translates to

```
.method increase_salary(F)V
.var 0 is this LEmployee;
.var 1 is raise_percentage F
.var 2 is raise F
```

```
; raise = raise_percentage * salary
fload_1                          ; Push raise_percentage
aload_0                          ; Push this
getfield Employee/salary F       ; Get this.salary
fmul                             ; Compute raise_percentage * salary
fstore_2                         ; Store the result in raise
```

The first four instructions in this method compute `raise_percentage * salary`. (For more about how to compile arithmetic operations, see section 10.8.) The `fstore_2` instruction stores the result of the expression into `raise`, which is represented by local variable 2.

The Java declaration of `raise` states that any value stored in it must be a `float`. This is the case, so the method is type-safe so far.

```
; this.salary = this.salary + raise
aload_0                          ; Push this as target of the assignment
aload_0                          ; Get this.salary
getfield Employee/salary F
fload_2                          ; Push raise
fadd                             ; Compute this.salary + raise
putfield Employee/salary F       ; Store into this.salary
```

An assignment to a field is of the form *expression.fieldname = expression*. The first expression results in the object that holds the target of the assignment. The result must be an object. The field name must be a field within that class of that object. In this case, the target expression is `this` and the field name is `salary`. The type of `this` is `Employee`, and `salary` is a nonstatic field within that class.

The code begins by evaluating `this` with the instruction `aload_0`. This will hold the target of the assignment. It is left on the stack until the assignment is performed.

Next comes the evaluation of the right-hand side: `this.salary + raise`. This compiles into code ending in `fadd`, which leaves the result of the computation on the stack. This is an expression, so it leaves exactly one value on the stack. The compile-time type of this expression is `float`.

Now the stack contains the target of the expression and the value to assign. The `putfield` instruction assigns the value to the field. As before, the type of the value must conform to the type of the target. In this case they are both `float`s, so the method is type-safe so far.

```
; Employee.payroll = Employee.payroll + raise
getstatic Employee/payroll F ; Get Employee.payroll
fload_2                          ; Push raise
fadd                             ; Compute Employee.payroll + raise
```

```
putstatic Employee/payroll F       ; Store into Employee.payroll
return                             ; Terminate the method
.end method
```

The final statement assigns to the static field `payroll`. Because a static field does not belong to any particular object, it isn't necessary to push an object onto the stack at the beginning of this assignment. After evaluating the expression `Employee.payroll + raise`, the `putstatic` instruction is used to store the value into the static field.

As before, the type of the value and the type of the field agree. Since that is the end of the method and all the statements are type-safe, the entire method is considered safe.

10.5.1 Abbreviations

The body of `increase_salary` might be rewritten as

```
raise = raise_percentage * salary;
salary = salary + raise;
payroll = payroll + raise;
```

This omits unnecessary parts of the expressions, like `this.` to indicate fields of the current object and `Employee.` to indicate static fields of the current class.

How does the compiler know to use `fload/fstore` with `raise`, `getfield/putfield` with `salary`, and `getstatic/putstatic` with `payroll`? It is necessary to deduce this from context during the compilation process.

When an identifier is used in an expression, the compiler looks for it in three places.

- ◆ First, it checks to see if there is a local variable by that name. If so, the name is treated as a local variable.

- ◆ Failing that, it checks to see if there is a nonstatic field with that name in the current class. If so, the target of the assignment or value of the expression is the field with that name in the object `this`. (This step applies only if the method being compiled is itself nonstatic, since static methods do not have a `this` variable.)

- ◆ Finally, it checks to see if there is a static field with that name in the current class. If so, that static field is used.

If nothing is found after the compiler has looked in all three places, the compiler gives up and signals an error.

10.5.2 Other Assignments

The Java language has several other assignment expressions, for example,

```
i++
```

which means the same thing as

```
i = i + 1
```

whether i is a local variable, an object field, or a static field.

Table 10.5 lists other assignment expressions. They work exactly as shown when x names a local variable or static field. When x is of the form *expression.field*, the meaning is slightly more complex. The expression to compute the object should be evaluated only once, not twice. This prevents any side effect from occurring more than once. Consider a method like this:

```
Employee print_employee()
{
    System.out.println(this);
    return this;
}
```

This method has the side effect of printing some information about the employee before returning the Employee itself. Suppose joe is an employee in this computation:

```
joe.print_employee().salary *= 1.15
```

TABLE 10.5: *Other assignment expressions*

Expression	Meaning
x++	x = x + 1
x--	x = x - 1
x += expression	x = x + expression
x -= expression	x = x - expression
x *= expression	x = x * expression
x /= expression	x = x / expression
x %= expression	x = x % expression
x &= expression	x = x & expression
x |= expression	x = x ^ expression
x ^= expression	x = x | expression

The intention is that `print_employee` prints some debugging information about joe, then returns joe so that he can receive a raise. The compiler must not be naive and treat this expression as though it were equivalent to

```
joe.print_employee().salary = joe.print_employee().salary * 1.15
```

The new salary is correct, but the console will print the information about joe twice, not once. A better translation is

```
Employee temporary = print_employee(joe);
temporary.salary = temporary.salary * 1.15
```

which has the intended effect, as long as `temporary` is some new variable name not used anywhere else in the method.

10.5.3 Assignments as Expressions

An assignment is actually an expression. The value of an expression is the value of the right-hand side. Consider this statement:

```
x = y = z = 0;
```

This statement is composed from three assignment expressions, grouped from the right:

```
x = (y = (z = 0));
```

To compile this code, the compiler starts with the rightmost expression. The right-hand side is the expression 0, a constant expression. It is assigned to z, which alters the state of z and has the result 0. The result is used in the next expression, which assigns the result to y and then again to z. This statement can be translated into Oolong using dup instructions before the assignment:

```
.var 1 is x I
.var 2 is y I
.var 3 is z I

iconst_0              ; Evaluate the right-most expression
dup                   ; Dup it
istore_3              ; Store one copy into z

; The original expression result remains on the stack, and we
; can assign it to y
dup                   ; Dup it again
istore_2              ; Store one copy in y
```

```
; We are in the same position as before, except now with x
dup                     ; Dup yet again
istore_1                ; Store one copy in x


; To turn the expression into a statement, we must remove the
; value on the stack to ensure that the stack is empty
pop
```

Usually, the final dup and pop are eliminated for efficiency reasons. Examples in previous sections are shown with the dup and pop eliminated for clarity.

10.5.4 Type-Checking in Assignments

In an assignment, the type of the expression on the right-hand side must conform to the type of the target on the left-hand side, independent of whether the target is a variable, a static field, or an object field. For example,

```
int x;

x = 0;
```

The expression 0 is of type int, which conforms to the type of x, which is also int.

When the type is an object type rather than a numeric type, the type checking must check that the compile-time type of the right-hand side is a subtype of the compile-time type of the left-hand side. This involves checking subtyping relationships if the two classes are not the same. This example shows some legal assignments:

```
class Employee
{
}

class Supervisor extends Employee
{
}

Object object;
Employee employee1, employee2;
Supervisor supervisor;

object = employee1;          // OK
employee2 = supervisor;      // OK
```

```
object = supervisor;              // OK
employee1 = employee2;            // OK
```

Since the type of the right-hand side is always a subtype of the type of the variable on the left-hand side, those assignments are legal. Reversing these assignments:

```
employee1 = object;         // ERROR!
supervisor = employee2;     // ERROR!
supervisor = object;        // ERROR!
employee2 = employee1;      // OK
```

The last case is okay because both have the same type. The other cases are errors since the Object is not necessarily an Employee, and an Employee is not necessarily a Supervisor.

Sometimes, the assignment can't work either way:

```
String greeting = "Hello, world";

employee1 = greeting;       // ERROR! Employee is not a String
greeting = employee1;       // ERROR! String is not an Employer
```

The compiler must check all assignments before generating compiled code. If any of the types do not conform, then the program must be rejected.

10.6   Creating New Objects

Suppose you have this class definition:

```
class Person
{
    String firstName;
    String lastName;

    Person(String first, String last)
    {
        firstName = first;
        lastName = last;
    }
}
```

To create a new Person object, you would use a Java expression like this one:

```
new Person("James", "Gosling")
```

To compile this expression, two steps are necessary. First, the object itself must be created. Second, the constructor must be called. The code translates as

```
new Person                  ; Create the uninitialized Person
dup                         ; Duplicate the reference
ldc "James"                 ; Push the first argument
ldc "Gosling"               ; Push the second argument
                            ; Call the constructor:
invokespecial Person/<init>
    (Ljava/lang/String;Ljava/lang/String;)V
```

The first line creates the object but does not initialize it. The second instruction duplicates the reference to that object. When the invokespecial instruction is performed, it uses one of the copies of that reference, leaving the other on the stack. The entire sequence of code leaves exactly one item on the stack, a reference to the created and initialized Person object. This is the intended result of the new expression, which yields the newly created object.

The constructor is always named <init>, no matter what the name of the class is. There can be more than one method named <init>. The compiler looks for one that matches the arguments given. This process is called *overloading,* and it's described in section 10.9.5.

10.7   Class Name Abbreviations

The Java language permits you to abbreviate class names by omitting the package name if the class has been imported. JVM instructions always require the fully qualified form of the class name. If a Java program uses an abbreviated class name, then the compiler has to find the class name in the list of imported classes.

Imported classes are listed at the beginning of the Java program, right after the package statement. Suppose the program being compiled starts like this:

```
package your.package;
import my.package.Person;
import java.util.Hashtable;
import java.io.*;
```

The * means that every class with that package name is imported. It's up to the compiler to find the definitions for those classes. The way the definitions are found varies from compiler to compiler. For many Java compilers, an environment variable called CLASSPATH is used. The CLASSPATH environment variable contains a list of directories. The Java compiler scans those directories looking for files ending in .class. These are treated as class files. If the package name of the class matches the import directive, then the class is imported.

Importing a class doesn't add any code to your program. The only effect is to allow you to abbreviate names in Java code.

Every program has two implicit import statements:

```
import java.lang.*;
import thisPackage.*;
```

where *thisPackage* is the package name specified on the package statement; in this case, it is your.package. This Java expression creates a new instance of the class Hashtable:

```
new Hashtable()
```

The compiler looks for every imported class named Hashtable. One such class is java.util.Hashtable, which was imported explicitly. The compiler checks all the other imported classes, looking for others named Hashtable. It checks for a your.package.Hashtable, a java.io.Hashtable, and a java.lang.Hashtable.

If none is found or if more than one is found, then the compiler doesn't know which class the programmer is referring to by the name Hashtable, and it should be treated as an error. If exactly one is found, then the compiler uses that as the full name of the class.

The code generated for this new expression is

```
new java/util/Hashtable
dup
invokespecial java/util/Hashtable/<init>()V
```

Note the shift from periods (.) to slashes (/) in the package separator. JVM programs always use slashes and Java programs always use periods.

10.8 Arithmetic Expressions

For arithmetic expressions in Java, the Java virtual machine instruction set has an instruction corresponding to the operator and the type of the arguments. Table 10.6 summarizes the choices. Although each binary operator requires two subexpressions, only one type is given in the table. That's because it's assumed

TABLE 10.6: *Selecting an arithmetic operator*

Operator	Type			
	int	long	float	double
+	iadd	ladd	fadd	dadd
−	isub	lsub	fsub	dsub
/	idiv	ldiv	fdiv	ddiv
*	imul	lmul	fmul	dmul
%	irem	lrem	frem	drem
unary −	ineg	lneg	fneg	dneg
&	iadd	land	−	−
|	ior	lor	−	−
^	ixor	lxor	−	−

that both subexpressions have the same type. If the expressions have different types, then one must be coerced to have the same type as the other.

10.8.1 Numeric Coercions

Coercion is the process of converting a value of one type into a value of a different type. Although the two values are completely different to the JVM, they mean something similar to the user. The number 1.0 (the floating-point number 1) is completely different from the number 1 (the integer 1); arithmetic instructions that apply to one of them do not apply to the other. However, it is clear that 1.0 and 1 are corresponding values in the different domains of numbers.

For example, consider this Java expression:

```
1.0 + 1
```

According to *The Java Language Specification,* the result should be the floating-point number 2.0. The naïve transformation into bytecodes is this:

```
fconst_1        ; Push 1.0
iconst_1        ; Push 1
fadd            ; ERROR! Can't add a float to an int
```

In order to make these two values have the same type, it is necessary to convert one of them to have the same type as the other. The primary goal is to preserve the magnitude of the number, and the secondary goal is to preserve the precision.

To accomplish this goal, the Java language specifies a hierarchy of numerical types:

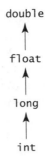

Because the floating-point types `double` and `float` are capable of representing both wide ranges of numbers and numbers with a fractional part, they are at the top of the hierarchy. The 64-bit types `double` and `long` appear above their 32-bit counterparts because the longer types are capable of holding more information. There are certain values of `long` that cannot be represented precisely with `float`s, especially very large numbers, but they can be represented with some loss of accuracy.

When an operator is applied to two numeric values, the one with the lower position in the hierarchy is converted so that it is "promoted" to the type of the other one. The conversion can be performed in a single instruction chosen according to Table 10.7.

Look again at the expression shown earlier:

```
1.0 + 1
```

To make this work, the `int` value must be promoted to match the `float`. From the table, the instruction to do this is `i2f`, which results in the code

```
fconst_1              ; Push the float 1
iconst_1              ; Push the int 1
```

TABLE 10.7: *Type conversion instructions*

To	From			
	int	long	float	double
int	–	i2l	i2f	i2d
long	l2i	–	l2f	l2d
float	f2i	f2l	–	f2d
double	d2i	d2l	d2f	–

```
i2f                             ; Now the stack has two floats
fadd                            ; This is now a valid instruction
```

Suppose you have these declarations:

```
long l;
float f;
int i;
double d;
```

Some other results are shown in Table 10.8. Note that the conversion depends only on the types of the operands. It is not necessary to look at which operand comes first. The operation being performed is also irrelevant.

The shorter int types char, byte, and short do not require any explicit conversion instructions to convert to ints. In the Java language, they are treated as distinct types; that is, char is not a subtype of int. In the JVM, however, they are treated as identical to ints. When an arithmetic operator is applied to these operators, they are automatically treated as full ints. Now suppose you have:

```
byte b1, b2;
short s1, s2;
char c1, c2;
```

Table 10.9 summarizes the expression types of various Java expressions. This makes sense from the point of view of a JVM bytecode programmer, since the JVM does not distinguish between int, byte, short, and char values. The JVM also treats booleans as identical to ints, but the Java language does not permit this:

```
int i = 1;                      // OK
boolean b = true;               // OK
```

TABLE 10.8: *Examples of numeric coercion*

Expression	Conversion	Result
l+f	Convert l to a float	float
f+l	Convert l to a float	float
d/f	Convert f to a double	double
d*f	Convert f to a double	double
i*f	Convert i to a float	float
i*i	None	int
l*i	Convert i to long	long

TABLE 10.9: *Operations resulting in ints*

Expression	Conversion	Result
c1+c2	None	int
b1*b2	None	int
s1/s2	None	int
c1-s2	None	int
b1/c2	None	int

```
int q = i+b        // ERROR! Can't add a boolean to an int
int r = b;         // ERROR! Can't assign a boolean to an int
```

You might expect that q would be assigned 2, since internally the value of b is represented by the int value 1, but this is not correct. The only operations that the Java language permits on boolean values are the boolean operators, which are discussed in section 10.11.

10.8.2   Casting Numeric Values

Only the upper half of Table 10.7 is used for promotions. The lower half contains demotions that convert doubles to floats or floats to ints and so on. These demotions are called *narrowing*.

The programmer may explicitly request a type coercion with a cast. For example,

```
(int) 1.0 + 1
```

The result of this operation is the int 2, not the float 2.0. The value 1.0 is converted to an int, so when the + operation is performed it sees two int values. The code generated is:

```
fconst_1           ; Push float 1.0
f2i                ; Convert it to an int 1
iconst_1           ; Push int 1
iadd               ; 1+1=2
```

The cast operation binds more tightly than the + operation. This expression is equivalent to

```
((int) 1.0) + 1
```

Parentheses can cause a different interpretation:

```
(int) (1.0 + 1)
```

In this case, there are two different conversions going on. An implicit conversion promotes 1 to a float, and then the two numbers are added together. Then the result of the addition is a float, which is then demoted to an int by the explicit cast. In Oolong, this is

```
fconst_1          ; Push float 1
iconst_1          ; Push int 1
i2f               ; Convert the int to a float
fadd              ; 1.0+1.0=2.0
f2i               ; Convert 2.0 to 2
```

The final result is the int 2. Although this simple case didn't show it, the order of operations is very important:

```
(int) (1.5*2)          yields 3
```

but

```
((int) 1.5)*2          yields 2
```

In the first case, the 2 is converted to a float, and the multiplication operation is carried out on the float values before the result is converted to an int. In the second case, 1.5 is rounded to 1 when it's converted to an int, and 1*2 == 2.

Neither result is wrong; the programmer is given the option of choosing which result is desired when the program is written. This underscores the necessity of getting the order of operations correct.

Explicit casts may perform either promotions or demotions. If no change is called for, then no code is generated. Some results of casts, assuming the earlier definitions, are listed in Table 10.10. A few additional operations apply to conversions to short, char, or byte. Respectively, these are i2s, i2c, and i2b. They are generated only as a result of a specific cast:

```
(byte) 4444          // Convert to 92
```

which compiles as

```
ldc 4444             // Push the int 4444
i2b                  // Convert to a byte
```

The number is truncated to the appropriate number of bits (16 for i2s and i2c, 8 for i2b). For i2b and i2s, the resulting number is sign-extended, which means that the leftmost bit of the result after truncation is copied into the bits left of the

TABLE 10.10: *Casting numeric types*

Expression	Result
(int) f	Demote f to an int.
(double) f	Promote f to a double.
(long) f	Demote f to a long.
(float) l	Promote l to a float.
(int) i	No change
(double) i+f	First i is converted to a float, then the final result is converted to a double.

truncation. This means that the char value is always positive, but the short and byte equivalents may be negative. Table 10.11 lists some examples of what happens when you cast an int to a smaller type.

10.8.3   ~ Operator

The ~ operator is not represented in Table 10.6. The ~ operator takes an int or a long and inverts each bit. There is no instruction for this operator. Java compilers take note of the fact that, for a single bit x, computing ~x is equivalent to computing x + −1, where + is the exclusive-or operator. To invert all the bits in the number at once, the Java compiler uses the lxor or ixor instruction with the value consisting of 64 or 32 1's. In the two's complement notation used in the Java virtual machine, an integer consisting of all 1's is equal to −1. For example,

~x

TABLE 10.11: *Converting between int types*

Expression	Result
(short) 65555	−1
(char) 65535	65535
(byte) 65535	−1
(short) 160	160
(char) 160	160
(byte) 160	−2

compiles to

```
iload_1          ; Push x
iconst_m1        ; Push -1 (1111...)
ixor             ; Compute ~x
```

If x is a long, ~x is

```
lload_1          ; Push x
ldc2_w -1L       ; Push -1 (1111...)
lxor             ; Compute ~x
```

10.9 Method Calls

Java method calls compile into invokevirtual, invokespecial, invokeinterface, and invokestatic instructions. A Java programmer might not realize that although essentially the same syntax is used on every method call, there are actually four different kinds of method calls.

10.9.1 Virtual Method Calls

Consider this expression:

```
System.out.println("Hello, world")
```

This is a virtual method call: it executes with respect to a particular object, called the receiver of the method invocation. The receiver is the result of the expression to the left of the method name. In this case, the receiver expression is System.out, which returns the value of the out field of the java.lang.System class. The receiver must be an object.

To compile a virtual method call, first the receiver expression is evaluated, followed by code to evaluate the arguments. These are all left on the stack, where they are used by an invokevirtual instruction.

```
; This instruction evaluates the expression System.out
getstatic java/lang/System/out Ljava/io/PrintStream;

; This instruction evaluates the expression "Hello, world"
ldc "Hello, world"

; This is the method invocation
invokevirtual java/io/PrintStream (Ljava/lang/String;)V
```

10.9.2 Static Method Calls

Here is an example of a static method call:

```
Math.max(10, 20)
```

The method max in the class java.lang.Math is marked static. This means that instead of having a receiver expression, you use the name of the class.

To compile this expression, use an invokestatic instruction. As with virtual method invocations, the code for the argument expressions is written immediately before the invokestatic. The difference is that there is no need to compile code for the receiver. The above example compiles to

```
bipush 10               ; Push the constant 10
bipush 20               ; Push the constant 20
invokestatic java/lang/Math/max(II)I
```

10.9.3 Example of Method Calls

This class uses both static and virtual method invocations:

```
class RightTriangle
{
    double a;                       // Two sides of a triangle
    double b;

    /** Print a debugging message */
    void debug(double i, double j)
    {
        // Print out the value of i and j; code omitted
    }

    /** Compute the hypotenuse of the triangle */
    double hypotenuse()
    {

        debug(a, b);
        return Math.sqrt(a*a + b*b);
    }
}
```

In the method hypotenuse, the call to debug is a virtual call with the receiver omitted. It is equivalent to

```
this.debug(a, b);
```

The receiver is this. There are two subexpressions, a and b. Using the search order described in section 10.5.1, the compiler finds that a and b are treated as fields of the current object. The statement compiles as

```
aload_0                              ; Push this for the method call

aload_0                              ; Push this.a
getfield RightTriangle/a D

aload_0                              ; Push this.b
getfield RightTriangle/b D

invokevirtual RightTriangle/debug(DD)V      ; Call the method
```

The call to Math.sqrt is a static call with a single argument. This argument is the result of evaluating the expression a*a+b*b. We have already seen how the compiler finds a and b; the compiler must also generate code to do the rest of the arithmetic. Because * has a higher priority than +, both multiplications are done before the addition. The statement

```
return Math.sqrt(a*a+b*b);
```

compiles as

```
aload_0                              ; Push a
getfield RightTriangle/a D
dup
dmul                                 ; Compute a*a

aload_0                              ; Push b
getfield RightTriangle/b D
dup
dmul                                 ; Compute b*b

dadd                                 ; Compute a*a+b*b

; Now there is a single argument on the stack: a*a+b*b. Use that
; as the argument to sqrt
invokestatic java/lang/Math/sqrt(D)D  ; Call sqrt
dreturn                              ; Return the result
```

10.9.4 Overriding

The rules of Java subtyping are defined so that any operation that can be applied to an instance of a class can also be applied to any instance of any subclass. For example, consider a class `Rectangle` and a class `Square` that extends it:

```
class Rectangle
{
    boolean contains(Point p)
    {
        // Return true if this rectangle contains p; false
           otherwise
    }

    boolean setLocation(int x, int y)
    {
        // Set the location of the rectangle to (x,y)
    }

    boolean setLocation(Point p)
    {
        // Set the location of the rectangle to p
    }
}

class Square extends Rectangle
{
    boolean contains(Point p)
    {
        // Return true if this square contains p; false otherwise
    }
}
```

Since `Square` is a subclass of `Rectangle`, any instance of `Square` is also an instance of `Rectangle`. This means that any method that can be applied to `Rectangles` can also be applied to `Squares`. By default, the implementation of the methods is the same for `Squares` as it is for `Rectangles`. We say that `Square` *inherits* the definitions of these methods from `Rectangle`.

If the `Square` class provides a definition of a method with the same name and the same arguments as one of the methods that it would inherit, then we say `Square` *overrides* that method. In the example, `Square` overrides the definition of `contains`, since there is an identical method declaration in the class `Rectangle`.

When the overridden method is invoked, the decision about which definition is executed is based on the runtime type of the object on which the method is invoked. For example, suppose r is a `Rectangle` and p is a `Point`; r may contain a `Square` or it may contain a plain old `Rectangle`. Consider:

```
r.contains(p);
```

At runtime, if r contains a non-`Square` `Rectangle`, then the `Rectangle` definition of `contains` will be used. If r contains a `Square`, then `Square`'s definition will be used. Which definition will be used can be determined only by running the program.

Because the determination of which method will be used depends on the receiver of the method invocation, only nonstatic methods can be overridden. However, static methods can give the appearance of inheritance. For example, consider this code:

```
class A
{
    static int compute() { /* Do something */ }
}

class B extends A
{
}
```

You can use the Java expression `B.compute()`, which actually invokes the method `compute` in class A. However, B does not really inherit the method. Instead, method implementation in the nearest superclass is used in the `invokestatic` instruction. When `B.compute()` is compiled, it produces the Oolong

```
invokestatic A/compute() I
```

You can see this effect if you actually add a method `compute` to B. If you don't recompile the expression `B.compute()`, it will still invoke the definition from A.

10.9.5 Overloading

If two methods have the same name but different arguments, the methods are said to be *overloaded*. They are effectively two different methods that happen to share the same name. This is similar to the way the + operator means one thing when applied to `int`s and another applied to `float`s.

In the class `java.awt.Rectangle` there are two methods named `setLocation`: one takes two `int` values as arguments, the other takes a `java.awt.Point`. These two methods are not required to return the same type, though they happen to in this case. They have the same name, which implies to the programmer that the two operations are somehow related, but the Java language considers them to be completely different.

Unlike overriding, which is handled by the definition of the `invokevirtual` instruction, overloading requires the compiler to disambiguate which method is to be called at compile time. It does this by specifying both the name and the type of the method in the `invokevirtual` instruction.

The determination is based on the compile-time definitions of the arguments. For example, given that `r` is a `Rectangle` and `p` is a `Point`, here are two calls to `setLocation`:

```
r.setLocation(10, 20)
r.setLocation(p)
```

Let's assign `r` to variable 1 and `p` to variable 0. The first call compiles as

```
aload_1                          ; Push r
bipush 10                        ; Push 10
bipush 20                        ; Push 20
                                 ; Call setLocation using two ints
invokevirtual java/awt/Rectangle/setLocation(II)V
```

In this case, the two arguments are both `int`s. This matches the definition of `setLocation`, which takes two `int`s. The second case requires a `Point`, so it compiles to

```
aload_1                          ; Push r
aload_2                          ; Push p
                                 ; Call setLocation using a Point
invokevirtual java/awt/Rectangle/setLocation(Ljava/awt/Point;)V
```

There are more complicated situations. Sometimes arguments with numeric types must be promoted to make one of the arguments match. Sometimes arguments with object types must be treated as members of superclasses. If more than one argument is involved, it may be ambiguous which arguments should be promoted to make a type match. For more details, see section 15.11 of *The Java Language Specification*.

Note that over*riding,* as in the case of `contains`, is different from over*loading,* as in the example with `setLocation`. Overriding is declaring a method with the same name and same arguments declared in a subclass. Overloading is declaring two methods with the same name but different arguments; these are really two different methods.

If two methods are overloaded, the determination of which one will be used is made at compile time, based on the compile-time types of the arguments. If one method overrides another, the determination of which will be used will be made at runtime, based not on the arguments but only on the class of the receiver of the invocation.

10.9.6 Interfaces

An interface specifies a set of methods that a class must support. One example of an interface is `java.util.Enumeration`, which is used to give a collection of elements one at a time. Here is the definition of `Enumeration`, which is found in the package `java.util`:

```
package java.util;
interface Enumeration
{
    boolean hasMoreElements();
    Object nextElement();
}
```

Interfaces may be used as the declared type of a variable or field, and they may be used as the type of a method argument or return. For example, the declaration of the method `elements` in `java.util.Vector` is:

```
Enumeration elements();
```

This means that `elements` returns only instances of classes that support the `Enumeration` interface. They may be of any class, as long as that class supports `Enumeration`.

The interface can also be used to declare variables and fields:

```
Enumeration e;
```

This declaration means that only instances of classes that support the `Enumeration` interface can be assigned to the variable `e`. For example, suppose `vector` is an instance of the class `java.util.Vector`:

```
e = vector.elements();
```

The methods of `Enumeration` can be invoked on `e`:

```
while(e.hasMoreElements())
    Object o = e.nextElement();
```

Here, the compile-time type of the receiver of the method invocations of has-MoreElements and nextElement is an interface instead of a class as was shown in previous sections. This is called *invoking through an interface,* and it's compiled a bit differently from virtual method invocation (section 10.9.1).

The generated code is similar to virtual invocations. First the receiver expression is evaluated, followed by the argument expressions. At the end, instead of an invokevirtual instruction, an invokeinterface instruction is used. Assuming that e is stored in variable 1, the call to e.hasMoreElements() compiles to

```
aload_1                            ; Push e
invokeinterface java/util/Enumeration/hasMoreElements ()Z 1
```

The invokeinterface instruction requires an additional argument, as described in section 4.9. That argument is the number of stack slots popped off the stack when the method is called. In this case, only a single slot is removed: the receiver of the instruction. If there were additional arguments to the method call, they would have to be included. As usual, longs and doubles count for two, all others count as one.

10.10 Expressions as Statements

Some expressions can be turned into statements by adding a semicolon to the end. To skip an element in an Enumeration, one might execute this statement:

```
e.nextElement();           // Throw away what's returned
```

This is a statement consisting of the expression e.nextElement(). The expression returns a value of type Object. The statement compiles to

```
.var 1 is e Ljava/util/Enumeration;
aload_1                                  ; Push e
invokeinterface java/util/Enumeration/nextElement
                ()Ljava/lang/Object; 1    ; Call the method,
                                          ; leaving the result
                                          ; on the stack
pop                                       ; Remove the result
```

The pop is necessary to ensure that the stack is empty after executing the expression.

It is actually pretty rare that a pop must be included explicitly. Usually, when a method returns a value, it is used as part of another statement or expression that needs the value. The code for the enclosing statement or expression has the responsibility for removing the result of the subexpression.

When the result of a method call is void, it isn't necessary to remove the value returned from the method. That's because the method does not really return a value. We have seen this code compiled many times before in this book:

```
System.out.println("Hello, world");
```

The println method returns void, so there is no pop included after the method call.

10.11 Ifs and Booleans

Java's type boolean has two values: true and false. Though booleans may be stored in variables, they are primarily used as the conditions for if, while, and for statements.

10.11.1 Boolean Values

Within JVM programs, the Java type boolean is represented by an int, with 1 representing true and 0 representing false. The expression true compiles to

```
iconst_1
```

and false to

```
iconst_0
```

Consider this statement:

```
debug = false;
```

The expression false is pushed onto the stack, then assigned to the boolean variable debug (in variable 1, for example):

```
iconst_0              ; Push false
istore_1              ; Store into debug
```

You can test boolean values with ifne, which will branch on true values, or ifeq, which will branch on false values. Remember that ifne and ifeq compare to zero, so you can read ifeq as "Branch if the top of the stack is equal to false" and ifne as "Branch if the top of the stack is equal to true." This is a simple if statement:

```
if(debug)
{
    // Print debugging information
}
```

This statement translates into

```
iload_1                  ; Get the value of debug
ifeq end_of_if           ; Skip debugging if debug is false
;; The compound statement to print debugging information goes here
end_of_if:               ; Continue here
```

If debug is `false`, then the `ifeq` test succeeds, and control continues at `end_of_if`. If debug is `true`, then the test fails, and control continues with the next instruction. The next instruction is the compiled code to print debugging information. After printing debugging information, control proceeds to `end_of_if`.

If the `if` statement includes an `else`, then there are two different substatements. One should be executed if the test succeeds, the other if the test fails. Both statements must be compiled. For example,

```
boolean weekend;

if(weekend)
    sleep_late();
else
    go_to_school();
```

Suppose we assign variable 1 to hold weekend. This code compiles as

```
iload_1                          ; Push the value of weekend
ifne true_case                   ; If it's not 0,
                                 ; then go to the true case

false_case:                      ; Do this on failure
    invokestatic Student/go_to_school()V
    goto end_of_if               ; Skip to the end of the if

true_case:                       ; Do this on success
    invokestatic Student/sleep_late()V

end_of_if:                       ; Continue here in either case
```

There are two cases here, represented by the code at `true_case` and `false_case`. The program should execute one or the other depending on the value of the boolean expression weekend. If weekend is true, then control skips over the `false_case` and goes to `true_case`. If weekend is false, control continues at the `false_case`.

At the end of the `false_case` code, a `goto` causes the program to skip to `end_of_if`. The program will also end up at `end_of_if` if it went to `true_case`. If the `goto` weren't there, the program would try to both `sleep_late` and `go_to_school`, which any student will tell you is impossible.

10.11.2 if Statements

The general form of an if statement is

```
if(test-expression)
    true-statement
else
    false-statement
```

The general pattern for compiling an if statement is

```
code to evaluate test-expression
branch to true_case if expression is true

    code to execute false-statement
    goto end_of_if

true_case:
    code to evalute true-statement

end_of_if:
```

We have already discussed how to compile the expression and the substatements. There are many different ways the branch can be compiled, depending on the form of *test-expression.* The next sections discuss this in more detail.

10.11.3 Comparisons

According to the Java language, expressions that involve comparison operators, such as <, >=, and ==, evaluate to boolean values:

```
float temperature = check_thermometer();
boolean freezing = temperature < 32.0;
```

This code assigns true to freezing if the temperature is below 32 degrees Fahrenheit, false otherwise. The code to compute the value of the expression temperature < 32.0 is

```
.var 1 is temperature F
fload_1             ; Push the temperature
ldc 32.0            ; Push 32 degrees
fcmpg1           ; Compare the two
iflt true_case      ; Go to the true case
iconst_0            ; Push false
goto end_of_if      ; Skip over the true case
```

```
true_case:            ; Go here if true
iconst_1              ; Push true
end_of_if:            ; The flow of control ends up here
                      ; Either 1 or 0 is now atop the stack
```

There are two paths through this code, depending on the value of `temperature`. Either way, the stack height will increase by 1 at the end of this code. The top of the stack will contain either `true` or `false`. Nothing else on the stack has changed. That's what you'd expect from code for an expression.

This may seem like a lot of jumping around for a relatively simple expression. Usually, boolean values are not represented explicitly. Instead, comparisons are usually done as part of an `if`, `while`, or `for` statement. Consider this code:

```
if(temperature < 32.0)
    predict_snow();
else
    predict_rain();
```

It's never necessary to actually compute the `boolean` value of the comparison. Instead, the compiler uses the result of the `fcmpg` instruction directly to branch to either `predict_rain` or `predict_snow`:

```
fload_1              ; Push the temperature
ldc 32.0             ; Push 32 degrees
fcmpg1               ; Compare the two

iflt true_case       ; Go to the true case if temp < 32
invokestatic Weatherman/predict_rain()V    ; Call for rain
goto end_of_if       ; Skip over the true case
true_case:
invokestatic Weatherman/predict_snow()V    ; Call for snow
end_of_if:           ; Continue here
```

The `fcmpg` instruction puts –1 on the stack if the temperature is less than 32, 0 if it's exactly equal to 32, or 1 if it's greater than 32. The test succeeds if the temperature is less than 32, which makes the result of `fcmpg` less than 0.

This technique works for `double` and `long` values as well, using `dcmpl` or `lcmp`, respectively. For example, with `long` values,

```
// Get the current time as the number of milliseconds from
// January 1, 1970.
long now = System.currentTimeMillis();
if(now >= 978307200000)
    System.out.println("Welcome to the 21st century");
```

This code compiles as

```
invokestatic java/lang/System/currentTimeMillis()J
ldc2_w 978307200000
lcmp                        ; Compare now to the first msec
                           ; of the 21st century
iflt end_of_if             ; If we're not there yet, skip
                           ; to the end of the if
getstatic java/lang/System/out Ljava/io/PrintStream;
ldc "Welcome to the 21st century"
invokevirtual println(Ljava/lang/String;)V
end_of_if:
```

The particular kind of branch instruction used depends on the comparison and whether or not there's an `else` case. The `ifne` mnemonic stands for "Skip if not equal," the opposite meaning of ==, and `ifle` stands for "Skip if less than or equal to," the opposite meaning of >. The `if` operator is chosen as the opposite of what the mnemonic suggests: `ifne` for ==, `ifle` for >, and so on. That's because the `if` is being used to skip over the code to be executed if the test succeeds. It's like a double negative making a positive: "Skip over this code if the opposite of the test is true" is the same as "Execute this code if the test is false."

10.11.4   Floating-Point Comparisons and NaN

In addition to affecting the type of `if` chosen, the operator also affects the instruction used for the comparison. If the comparison is a < b or a <= b, where a and b are both `doubles`, the dcmpg instruction is used; otherwise, the dcmpl instruction is used. Generally, dcmpg is used in conjunction with `ifgt` or `ifge`, and dcmpl is used in conjunction with `iflt` or `ifle`.

In ordinary cases, dcmpl and dcmpg are identical. The difference is seen when either a or b turns out to be not-a-number (NaN). NaNs are the result of an undefined calculation, such as 0/0. All comparisons to NaN should fail; that is, this program

```
double not_a_number = 0.0/0.0;    // Results in NaN
if(not_a_number < 0)
    System.out.println("0/0 < 0");
if(not_a_number > 0)
    System.out.println("0/0 > 0");
if(not_a_number == 0)
    System.out.println("0/0 == 0");
```

doesn't print anything, since NaN is not less than, greater than, or equal to 0. This is how the code compiles:

```
dconst_0                        ; Compute 0/0 (NaN)
dconst_0
ddiv
dstore_1                        ; Store NaN in 1 and 2

dload_1                         ; Push the NaN
dconst_0                        ; Compare it to 0 with dcmpg
dcmpg                           ; This leaves 1
ifge end_of_if1                 ; Skip, since 1 >= 0
;; Print the message 0/0 < 0
end_of_if1:

dload_1                         ; Push the NaN
dconst_0                        ; Push 0
dcmpl                           ; This time, the result is -1
ifle end_of_if2                 ; Skip again, since -1 <= 0
;; Print the message 0/0 > 0
end_of_if2:

dload_1                         ; Push the NaN
dconst_0                        ; Push 0
dcmpl                           ; This time, the result is -1
ifne end_of_if3                 ; Skip again, since -1 != 0
;; Print the message 0/0 == 0
end_of_if3:
```

In the first comparison, dcmpg leaves 1 on the stack if either operand is NaN. Since 1 >= 0, the ifge treats the comparison as success, so it skips over the code. This is another of those two-negatives-make-a-positive situations: the comparison succeeds, so it doesn't do the code inside the if statement.

Similarly, the second comparison uses dcmpl. Since dcmpl leaves −1 on the stack, the comparison succeeds, so the print code is not executed.

In the third case, where the comparison is ==, either dcmpl or dcmpg could be used; it is up to the discretion of the compiler writer. The results are the same no matter which instruction is chosen.

There is a similar distinction between fcmpl and fcmpg. There's only one form of lcmp, since there's no way for a long to be not-a-number. When a long value is divided by 0, an ArithmeticException is thrown instead of resulting in NaN.

10.11.5 Integer Comparisons

Compiling `int` and `reference` comparisons is different from compiling `double`, `float`, and `long` comparisons. In the interests of efficiency, the compare instruction and the branch instruction have been rolled into one. For example, suppose that `i` is an `int` in

```
if(i < 10)
{
    // Do something
}
```

This code compiles to

```
iload_1          ; Push i from variable 1
bipush 10        ; Push the constant 10
if_icmpge done   ; If i >= 10, skip the next code
;; Do something
done:            ; Control continues here
```

The `<` operator translates into a single `if_icmpge` instruction, which does both the comparison and the branch.

10.11.6 References and Object Equality

The Java `==` operator, when applied to two expressions that evaluate to objects, is `true` when the two `references` point to exactly the same object or if both are `null`, `false` otherwise. For example,

```
LinkedList head = new LinkedList();
LinkedList tail = head;
```

This code compiles to

```
new LinkedList        ; Create a new linked list
dup                   ; Initialize it
invokespecial LinkedList/<init>()V
astore_0              ; Store it in head (var 0)
aload_0               ; Retrieve the value
                      ; Now the same reference is found both
                      ; in var 1 and on the stack
astore_1              ; Now both var 0 and var 1 refer to
                      ; the same object
```

Variables 0 and 1 (`head` and `tail`, respectively) point to the same object; the references they contain are identical. The JVM variable pool and heap look like the diagram in Figure 10.4. Currently, `head == tail` is `true`, since they both point to the same object. However,

```
head.next == tail
```

is `false`, because the left side is `null` and the right side is non-`null`. References to `null` are equal only to themselves, which means that

```
head.next == tail.next
```

is `true`, not because `head == tail` but because both `head.next` and `tail.next` are both `null`.

Suppose you add a new element to the end linked list:

```
Object new_item = new LinkedList();
tail.next = new_item;
tail = new_item;
```

This code compiles as

```
aload_1                    ; Push tail
new LinkedList             ; Create the new link
```

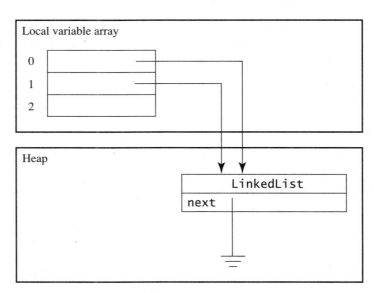

FIGURE 10.4: *After creating head and tail*

```
dup
invokespecial LinkedList/<init>()V
astore_2                            ; Put it in variable 3
                                    ; temporarily

aload_2                             ; Get it back
astore LinkedList/next LLinkedList; ; Store the new link in
                                    ; the next of the current
                                    ; tail
aload_2
astore_1                            ; Set tail to the new link
```

This code changes what `tail` in variable 1 points to. The JVM state is diagrammed in Figure 10.5. Now `head` and `tail` point to different objects. The `next` field of the original element is now set to the new element, instead of to `null`. For that reason,

```
head == tail
```

will result in `false`, because they point to different objects. However,

```
head.next == tail
```

will result in `true`, because both point to the same object (the new one).

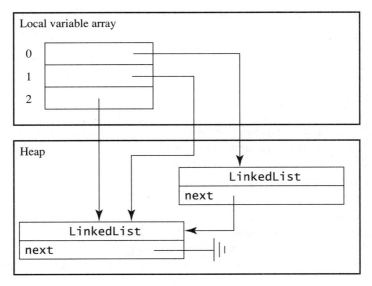

FIGURE 10.5: *After adding a new element*

Note that two objects created with new are always different objects, even if the values of the objects are the same. The code fragment

```
String s1 = new String("This is a String");
String s2 = new String("This is a String");
if(s1 == s2)
    System.out.println("The two Strings are identical");
else
    System.out.println("The two Strings are NOT identical");
```

will always print

```
The two Strings are NOT identical
```

This code compiles to

```
new java/lang/String              ; Build the first string
dup
ldc "This is a String"
invokespecial java/lang/String/<init> (Ljava/lang/String;)V
astore_1                          ; Store it in variable 1

new java/lang/String              ; Build the second string
dup
ldc "This is a String"
invokespecial java/lang/String/<init> (Ljava/lang/String;)V
astore_2                          ; Store it in variable 2

aload_1                           ; Compare them
aload_2
if_acmpne false_case:

getstatic java/lang/System/out Ljava/io/PrintStream;
ldc "The two Strings are identical"
invokevirtual java/io/PrintStream/println (Ljava/lang/String;)V
goto cont:

false_case:
getstatic java/lang/System/out Ljava/io/PrintStream;
ldc "The two Strings are NOT identical"
invokevirtual java/io/PrintStream/println (Ljava/lang/String;)V

cont:
```

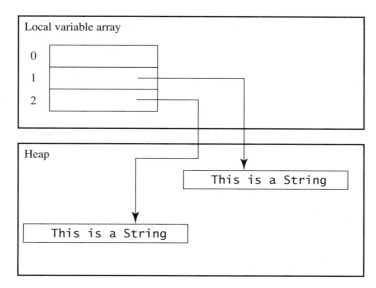

FIGURE 10.6: *Two different Strings*

After executing this code, memory looks like the diagram in Figure 10.6. The references can be compared only to see whether or not they are equal. Use if_acmpeq and if_acmpne with references exactly as you'd use if_icmpeq and if_icmpne on ints. It is meaningless to say that one reference is "less than" or "greater than" another. The Java language permits you to use == and != on references but not <, >, <=, or >=. The instructions if_acmplt, if_acmpgt, if_acmple, and if_acmpge do not exist.

If you want to compare two objects to see if their *contents* are equal, instead of being identical references, use the method equals. The implementor of the class provides this method, because only the person who wrote the class knows exactly what is meant by the two objects having equal contents.

The definition of equals in Object returns true only if the two references are identical. This method definition is inherited by all other classes unless it is overridden by the implementor. For example, the class String has a definition of equals that is true if the strings have identical sets of characters.

You can compare the two strings in the example code to see whether they have identical text with

```
aload_1              ; Push the first string
aload_2              ; Push the second string
invokevirtual java/lang/Object/equals(Ljava/lang/Object;)Z
```

This code will leave 1 on the stack if they are equal, 0 if they are not. In this case they are equal, since they have the same text, even though variable 1 and variable 2 point to different objects. You must be careful here: if variable 1 contains `null`, this code will throw a `NullPointerException`. You must check for this case separately.

10.11.7   Boolean Operators

Java's && and || operators work much like `if`s: the second operand is not evaluated if the first argument makes it unnecessary. Consider

```
class Demo
{
    static boolean a()
    {
        System.out.println("In a");
        return false;
    }
    static boolean b()
    {
        System.out.println("In b");
        return true;
    }

    public static void main(String args[])
    {
        System.out.println("a && b == " + (a() && b()));
    }
}
```

When this class is executed (that is, `main` is run), it prints

```
In a
a && b == false
```

`b()` is never called; if it had been, the message "In b" would have been printed. That's because a() returned `false`. It doesn't matter what b returns, since `false` && anything is `false`. This is called *shortcutting*. Shortcutting is required by the Java language; if the compiler had generated code that printed both In a and In b, the compiler would have been wrong.

The expression

```
a() && b()
```

compiles into JVM code as

```
invokestatic Demo/a ()Z    ; Evaluate a()
ifeq false_case            ; Shortcut over b() if a() fails
invokestatic Demo/b ()Z    ; Evaluate b()
ifeq false_case            ; Go to true_case only if both
true_case:                 ; a() and b() return true
    iconst_1               ; Push 1 if true
    goto end
false_case:
    iconst_0               ; Push 0 if false
end:                       ; The rest of the program
```

A similar form of shortcutting occurs with the || operator, except that the shortcut occurs if the first operand is true. The expression

```
a() || b()
```

compiles to

```
invokestatic boolean_demo/a ()Z      ; Evaluate a()
ifne true_case             ; Shortcut over b() if a() succeeds
invokestatic boolean_demo/b ()Z      ; Evaluate b()
ifne true_case             ; Go to false_case only if both
false_case:                ; return false
    iconst_0               ; Push 0 if false
    goto end               ; Skip the true case
true_case:
    iconst_1               ; Push 1 if true
end:                       ; The rest of the program
```

If || and && expressions are used inside an if statement, then the iconst_0 and iconst_1 instructions used above are replaced by the success and failure statements of the if statement.

10.12 Other Control Structures

Java has other ways to combine groups of statements besides if. One is the switch statement, implemented using the tableswitch and lookupswitch instructions described in section 5.4. Java also has looping constructs like for and while, discussed in the forthcoming sections.

10.12.1   Loops

The Java language has three looping constructs: for, while, and do/while:

```java
// Loop 100 times. Each time, the variable i takes on a
// different value from 0 to 99.
for(int i = 0; i < 100; i++)
    System.out.println("f(" + i + ") = " + f(i));


// Loop forever, printing out "Hello, world"
// an infinite number of times
while(true)
    System.out.println("Hello, world");


// Loop until the character c is EOF
char c;
do
{
    c = nextToken();        // Get the next token
    processToken(c);        // Process the token
}
while(c != EOF);
```

In each of these three statements, a substatement is *guarded* by an expression whose compile-time type is boolean. The statement is performed over and over again. Before the statement is executed, the guard is evaluated. If the expression is true, then the statement is executed. Otherwise, the loop is terminated, and control continues with the next statement after the loop.

In a while loop, the expression is evaluated before the statement has been executed even once, but the do/while loop executes the statement once before testing the loop for the first time. The do/while loop is used when the statement must be evaluated at least once.

A for loop is a lot like a while loop, with a little extra syntactic sugar. Many loops use a special variable called the *index variable*. The index variable is initialized before the loop, then incremented each time the statement is executed. This continues as long as the expression evaluates to true.

The for loop in the example can be rewritten as a while loop like this:

```java
{
    int i = 0;
    while(i < 10)
    {
```

```
            System.out.println("f(" + i + ") = " + f(i));
            i++;
        }
    }
```

The extra braces around the whole thing ensure that the variable declaration of i does not conflict with other definitions of i later in the same method. (See the discussion of scoping in section 10.4.) The variable i is local to the loop.

10.12.2   Compiling Control Constructs

Compiling a while statement is a lot like compiling an if statement, as discussed in section 10.11. If the test is true, the statement is executed, followed by a goto back to the test. If the test is false, control skips to the next statement. For example,

```
while((c = nextToken()) != EOF)
{
    processToken(c);
}
```

The expression (c = nextToken()) != EOF depends on the fact that the result of an assignment is the value assigned, as shown in section 10.5.3. This expression calls nextToken() and assigns the result to c. The value of the assignment expression as a whole is the same as the value assigned to c. The value is then compared against EOF. This comparison is used as the guard expression of the loop.

Compiling this code is similar to compiling an if. If the expression is true, then do a backwards goto to the beginning of the loop. If not, break out of the loop. The example statement compiles to

```
.var 1 is c I
loop:                                   ; Loop starts here
    invokestatic Lexer/nextToken()I     ; Get the next token
    dup                                 ; Dup it so that the value
                                        ; remains on the stack
                                        ; after assignment
    istore_1                            ; Assign it to c
    getstatic Lexer/EOF I               ; Get the EOF value
    if_icmpeq break_loop                ; Compare and break the loop
                                        ; if EOF is found
```

```
; This is the body of the loop:
iload_1                                      ; Push c
invokestatic Lexer/processToken(I)V      ; Process the token


    goto loop                 ; And loop again
break_loop:                   ; Next statement goes here
```

The do/while loop is similar to a while loop, except that the test is moved from the beginning of the loop to the end. Consider the same code written as a do/while loop instead of a while loop:

```
// Assume that c has some initial value
do
{
    processToken(c);
}
while((c = nextToken()) != EOF)
```

The meaning of this loop is the same as that of the while loop, except that processToken is called once before entering the loop. This is fine as long as c has some initial value.

The resulting bytecodes are similar to the while loop shown earlier, except that the code has been rearranged to ensure that the body is executed at least once:

```
.var 1 is c I
loop:                                        ; Loop starts here
   ; The body of the loop now goes here at the beginning
   iload_1                                   ; Push c
   invokestatic Lexer/processToken(I)V      ; Process the token

   ; Perform the test, and break the loop if the test fails
   invokestatic Lexer/nextToken()I          ; Get the next token
   dup                                       ; Dup it so that the
                                             ; value remains on
                                             ; the stack
   istore_1                                  ; Assign it to c
   getstatic Lexer/EOF I                     ; Get the EOF value

   if_icmpeq break_loop            ; Compare and break the loop
                                   ; if EOF is found
   goto loop                       ; Loop again if not EOF
break_loop:                        ; Next statement goes here
```

10.12.3   Compound Statements and Verification

Statements can be combined to make a block by concatenating the code for them together. Since each statement by itself has no effect on the stack, there is no effect from putting one after the other.

Consider this method, which takes an array of strings that represent numbers and computes the sum and product of all those numbers:

```
public static void main(String args[])
{
    int sum = 0;
    int product = 1;
    for(int i = 0; i < args.length; i++)
    {
        int n = Integer.parseInt(args[i]);
        sum += n;
        product *= n;
    }
    System.out.println("sum = " + sum);
    System.out.println("product = " + product);
}
```

The value `args` is found in variable 0, since it's the first (and only) argument to the static method. The assignment of variables to slots is

```
.var 0 is args [Ljava/lang/String;
.var 1 is sum I
.var 2 is product I
.var 3 is i I
.var 4 is n I
```

The loop body

```
int n = Integer.parseInt(args[i]);
sum += n;
product *= n;
```

compiles into

```
; int n = Integer.parseInt(args[i])
aload_0                 ; Push args
iload_3                 ; Push i
iaload                  ; Get a[i]
                        ; Compute parseInt(a[i])
```

```
invokestatic java/lang/Integer/parseInt (Ljava/lang/String;)I
istore 4                        ; Store the result in n
; The stack is now empty

; sum += n;
iload_1                         ; Push sum
iload 4                         ; Push n
iadd                            ; Compute sum+n
istore_1                        ; Store the result in sum
; The stack is now empty

; product *= n;
iload_2                         ; Push product
iload 4                         ; Push n
imul                            ; Compute product*n
istore_2                        ; Store the result in product
; The stack is now empty
```

The code for each statement has no effect on the stack, so when the statements are put together the net effect is zero. Together, they act like a single statement. This is important when you want to use the statement as the body of a loop construct.

The for statement can be compiled into

```
iconst_0                ; Inititalize i to 0
istore_3
    ; The stack is now empty
loop:                   ; The beginning of the for loop
    iload_3             ; See if i < args.length
    aload_0
    arraylength
    ifge break          ; If i >= args.length, break

    ;; Insert the code for the big substatement here
    ; The stack is now empty

    iinc 3 1            ; Increment i by 1
    goto loop           ; And loop again

break:
```

When the verification algorithm looks at this code, one thing it checks is whether or not the stack is always the same each time the code hits loop. Because the stack is empty each time, the verification algorithm approves this code.

10.13 Returns

A `return` statement in Java translates into one of the six instructions: `areturn`, `ireturn`, `freturn`, `dreturn`, `lreturn`, or `return`. The instruction chosen depends on the return type of the method.

The simplest case is where the return type of the method is `void`:

```
public static void main(String a[])
{
    System.out.println("Hello, world");
    return;
}
```

The `return` statement translates simply into a `return` instruction. No arguments are required. The full compilation of this method is

```
.method public static main([Ljava/lang/String;)V

; System.out.println("Hello, world");
getstatic java/lang/System/out Ljava/io/PrintStream;
ldc "Hello, world"
invokevirtual java/io/PrintStream(Ljava/lang/String;)V

; return;
return

.end method
```

At the end of a `void` method, if no `return` statement is given, the Java compiler assumes one. Thus, this code would compile the same way even if the `return` statement were omitted. This is possible only because there is no return value.

If the return type is not `void`, then the `return` statement must include an expression that evaluates to the value to return. The type of that expression must conform to the return type of the method. For example,

```
float five()
{
    return 5;
}
```

Because the declared return type of this method is `float`, the return type must be `freturn`. The expression 5 is an `int`, but it can be automatically promoted to a float. The return statement compiles into an evaluation of the expression, followed by a cast, followed by the appropriate returning instruction:

```
.method five()F
iconst_5                 ; Push the constant 5
i2f                      ; Automatic promotion to float
freturn                  ; Return that value
.end method
```

As with arithmetic expressions, only promotions are considered, not demotions. This is illegal:

```
int six()
{
    return 6.0;          // ILLEGAL! Can't automatically
                         // convert float to int
}
```

If the return type is an object type, then an areturn instruction is used. The compile-time type of the expression must be a subtype of the return type of the method. For example,

```
Object name()
{
    return "Murray";
}
```

returns a String where an Object is expected. This is legal, because a String is an Object. This method compiles as

```
.method name()Ljava/lang/String;
ldc "Murray"
areturn
.end method
```

The generated code is acceptable to the verification algorithm, because the stack contains a java/lang/String when the areturn instruction is executed. This meets the requirements for an areturn.

10.14 Field Declarations

Here are some examples of field declarations:

```
long number;
public int x;
protected volatile String name = "Nobody";
static private Employee[] employee_list;
```

The basic pattern is that it begins with a (possibly empty) string of modifiers (such as `private`, `public`, `static`, and so on). The modifiers are followed by the type of the field (such as `int`, `String`, or `Employee[]`). Next comes the name of the field. Finally, there may be an *initializer,* indicated by an = followed by an expression. As with other assignments, the compile-time type of the expression type must conform to the declared type of the field. The Java compiler imposes the restriction that a class may have only one field with a particular name, even if the fields have different types. The JVM does not have this restriction, but if you intend your JVM classes to be used with Java code, then you should observe the restriction anyway.

Compiling field declarations is just a matter of converting the type expression into the appropriate JVM equivalent:

```
.field y I
.field public x I
.field protected volatile name Ljava/lang/String;
.field static private employee_list [LEmployee;
```

The modifiers are left as they are. In the class file that results, they are used to turn on bits in the `FieldInfo` structure of the class file. The Java virtual machine interprets those bits to mean what the equivalent modifier keywords are supposed to mean in Java.

The initializers do not appear in the `.field` directive unless the field is both `static` and `final` and the initializer is one of the basic numeric types. They translate into code in the body of the constructor, as discussed in section 10.16.3.

10.15 Method Declarations

Here are two examples of method declarations:

```
public abstract void function();
public static int add(int a, int b)
{
    return a+b;
}
```

Syntactically, field and method declarations are very similar. There are a few differences between a method declaration and a field declaration:

- ◆ Different modifier keywords are used.
- ◆ Following the method name is a list of arguments enclosed in parentheses. The parentheses are required; they are the key distinguishing syntax between field and method declarations.
- ◆ Blocks of code are used instead of initializers. This block of code is required if the abstract keyword is not used.

To compile method declarations, the .method directive is used instead of .field. The method descriptor includes the argument types and the return type. Following the .method directive is a translation of the body of the method translated into bytecodes. The body may also contain .limit directives, which instruct the JVM how much memory to allocate for the method. The .method declaration is terminated with .end method.

The two example methods compile into

```
.method public abstract function()V
; No method body, since the method is abstract
.end method

.method public static add(II)I
.limit locals 2
.limit stack 2
iload_0
iload_1
iadd
ireturn
.end method
```

10.16 Constructors

Every Java class must have a constructor. The constructor is a method with the same name as the class and no return type. For example,

```
class MyClass extends SuperClass
{
    MyClass()
    {
        super();
```

```
        }
    }
```

Compiling the constructor is similar to compiling any other method except that name of the generated method is <init>. The return type of <init> is always void. The MyClass constructor compiles to

```
.method <init>()V
aload_0                                 ; Invoke the superclass
invokespecial SuperClass/<init> ()V     ; constructor
return                                  ; Return
.end method
```

The keyword super in Java is used to indicate a direct call to the constructor of the immediate superclass of the current class. This call must bypass the virtual invocation mechanism, since otherwise this definition of <init> would appear to override the SuperClass definition and the above call would recursively invoke the current method again. For this reason, the compiler uses invokespecial instead of invokevirtual to call the superclass constructor.

The syntax of the Java language requires that the call to the superclass constructor (or to some other constructor in the current class) must be the first step in the method. If the call is not provided explicitly, then the compiler adds a call to the constructor with no arguments. This is the Java language's way of ensuring that the superclass constructor is always called, one of the requirements for verification of an <init> method. Forcing the superclass constructor to be the first step in the method is actually somewhat more than the Java virtual machine requires, but it ensures that the superclass method is called.

Constructors in Java are always written without any return type. This is not a constructor:

```
void MyClass()
{
    // Code for the method
}
```

The Java compiler compiles this as

```
.method MyClass()V
;; Code goes here
.end method
```

Because a return type was specified, this compiles into a method named MyClass returning void instead of to a method named <init>. This is not a constructor.

10.16.1 Using Other Constructors in the Same Class

Instead of calling a superclass constructor, the code may call another constructor for the same class by using `this`:

```
class AnotherClass
{
    int value;
    /** A constructor that initializes value to the argument */
    AnotherClass(int i)
    {
        super();           // Call the superclass constructor
        value = i;
    }
    /** A different constructor that initializes value to 0 by
     * reusing the other constructor
     */
    AnotherClass()
    {
        this(0);           // Call the other constructor
    }
}
```

You could use this feature to get around the superclass-call requirement like this:

```
class UselessClass
{
    UselessClass(int i)
    {
        this();                        // Call the other constructor
    }
    UselessClass()
    {
        this(42);                      // Call the other constructor
    }
}
```

Nowhere in either constructor is there a call to a superclass constructor, yet this is a perfectly legal class. However, as the name implies, it is a useless class, since any attempt to use the constructor will cause the machine to call the two constructors in a mutually recursive fashion, with neither one ever returning. The JVM will rapidly run out of stack space and terminate the program.

10.16.2   Default Constructors

If no constructor is provided, then the Java compiler automatically adds a default one. Here is the smallest possible Java class:

```
class Small
{
}
```

The generated `class` file contains no fields, but it does contain a single method so that you can construct an instance of `Small`. In Oolong, this is written as

```
.method <init>()V
aload_0                                    ; Invoke the super's
invokespecial java/lang/Object/<init>()V   ; no-args constructor
return                                     ; Done
.end method
```

This works only when the superclass has a constructor that takes no arguments. (That constructor may itself have been generated automatically by the Java compiler.) If there is no zero argument constructor or if the constructor has access controls such that this class may not use it, then the Java compiler will report an error.

10.16.3   Field Initializers and the Constructor

Whether the constructor is automatically generated or explicitly written, the compiler adds code to perform field initializations. This code is generated after the call to the superclass constructor but before the rest of the method.

Consider this class declaration:

```
class Chemistry
{
    /** Avogadro's number */
    float avogadro = 6.022e23;

    Chemistry()
    {
        super();
        System.out.println("In Chemistry constructor");
    }
}
```

The code generated for the Chemistry constructor is

```
.method <init>()V
aload_0               ; Call the superclass constructor
invokespecial java/lang/Object/<init> ()V

aload_0               ; Initialize avogadro
ldc 6.022e23
putfield Chemistry/avogadro F

; Print the message
getstatic java/lang/System/out Ljava/io/PrintStream;
ldc "In Chemistry constructor"
invokevirtual java/io/PrintStream/println(Ljava/lang/String;)V
.end method
```

The code to initialize avogadro is inserted between the call to the superclass constructor and the call to print the message. All fields are initialized before the body of the constructor begins.

The same code would be generated if the explicit superclass constructor call were eliminated: the compiler would first generate the constructor call, then the field initializations, followed by the rest of the constructor method.

10.17 Conclusion

This has been a brief introduction to the concepts required for compiling Java into JVM bytecodes. For more information about the Java language, the best place to start is *The Java Language Specification,* by James Gosling, Bill Joy, and Guy Steele (Addison-Wesley, 1996). It is the definitive authority on exactly what a Java program means.

## CHAPTER 11

Compiling Other Languages

O<small>NE</small> of the best uses for Java virtual machine programming is translating languages other than Java into virtual machine code. Compiled programs run faster than interpreted ones, and compilers are often easier to write than interpreters. By taking advantage of the JVM's built-in debugging features, you can even use standard debuggers for your new language.

There are many different kinds of languages. Some are *complete* in the sense that they are powerful enough to write programs for any computation. In this sense, Java, C, Lisp, and Basic are all complete. Completeness in this sense refers to the ability of a language to compute mathematical functions, not to its ability to manipulate hardware (such as graphics) or whether hooks are provided to a particular operating system feature.

Each of these languages includes features not included in the others, which gives each language a different flavor. A language designer carefully chooses the features to include in a language to make it powerful enough to write concise programs but not so complicated that it is hard to learn or hard to implement.

The Java language designers chose a set of features appropriate to general-purpose programming:

- Class-based object-oriented design
- Single inheritance of implementation (through the `extends` clause)
- Multiple inheritance of abstract type (through the `implements` clause)
- Virtual dispatch of method calls (through ordinary method invocation)
- Nonvirtual dispatch of static calls (through static method invocation)
- Static type checking (since each field and variable has a declared type)

- Garbage collection mechanism to remove objects that are no longer used (provided by the JVM)
- Object locking (through `synchronized` methods and the `synchronized` statement)

Other languages have features not included in Java:

- Parametric polymorphism (C++ templates, Sather type parameters)
- Closures (Lisp lambda expressions)
- Multiple inheritance of implementation (C++, CLOS, or Eiffel multiple inheritance)
- Weak type checking (Lisp, C)
- Coroutines (Sather iterators, Scheme `call-with-current-continuation`)

It is possible to design a translator from any of these languages into JVM code. Sometimes the mapping from one language into JVM features is easy. For example, it is easy to see how the arithmetic instructions of the JVM instruction set can be used to implement numerical calculations of any language.

Other features, like pointer arithmetic in C++, are considerably harder—though not impossible—to implement using the JVM instructions.

A language does not have to be computationally complete to be useful. For example, regular expressions are widely used in search engines, although it is not possible to do general computation with them. Another example is SQL, the database query language, which is well suited to joining tables together but not for general-purpose calculations. The limited scope of these languages allows them to be better suited to a particular task than a general-purpose language like Java or C++.

This chapter suggests how some of these languages may be compiled into bytecodes and executed on any JVM implementation.

11.1   Java Version 1.1

The Java virtual machine was developed with the original Java language in mind. When Java 1.1 was introduced, some changes were made to the Java language itself. The JVM is flexible enough that the changes to the language do not require any change to the virtual machine. This section discusses how some of the new constructs are implemented without requiring any alterations to the JVM specification.

11.1.1 Class Literals

In order to get the Class object for a class named Foo in Java 1.0, you had to say

```
Class c;
try {
   c = Class.forName("Foo");
}
catch(ClassNotFoundException e) {
   // Not expecting an error
}
```

This is tedious to write. Java 1.1 allows you to substitute the more elegant

```
Class c = Foo.class;
```

The Java compiler adds a method called class$[1] to your class, which takes the name of a class as a String and returns the Class object for the class with that name. It caches the results in a field class$Foo, so it only has to find the class once.

The Java compiler translates the expression Foo.class into Oolong instructions as

```
                              ; First, check the cache
getstatic MyClass/class$Foo Ljava/lang/Class;
ifnonnull cont              ; Skip if found in the cache
ldc "Foo"                   ; Call class$ with "Foo"
invokestatic MyClass/class$
   (Ljava/lang/String;)Ljava/lang/Class;
                              ; Cache the result
putstatic MyClass/class$Foo Ljava/lang/Class;
cont:                       ; Load from the cache
getstatic MyClass/class$Foo Ljava/lang/Class;
```

The compiler adds the following declarations to the class:

```
.field static class$Foo Ljava/lang/Class;  ; The cache

.method static class$ (Ljava/lang/String;)Ljava/lang/Class;
.catch java/lang/ClassNotFoundException from begin to end using
   end
```

---

[1] The use of a $ in names should be restricted to automatically generated code, according to *The Java Language Specification*. Therefore, there should be no conflict between the compiler-generated names and your programs.

```
begin:
    aload_0                          ; Call Class.forName with the arg
    invokestatic java/lang/Class/forName
                     (Ljava/lang/String;)Ljava/lang/Class;
    areturn
end:                                 ; ClassNotFoundException handler
    astore_1                         ; Throw a NoClassDefFoundError
    new java/lang/NoClassDefFoundError
    dup                              ; Use the message string from the
    aload_1                          ; ClassNotFoundException
    invokevirtual java/lang/Throwable/getMessage
                     ()Ljava/lang/String;
    invokespecial java/lang/NoClassDefFoundError/<init>
                     (Ljava/lang/String;)V
    athrow

.end method
```

The generated code for the expression Foo.class is essentially equivalent to the code generated by a Java compiler for the longer statement required under Java 1.0. However, the new syntax is much more convenient.

The Java compiler marks class$ and class$Foo with a new attribute, Synthetic, in the class file. This signals other class file-using programs (debuggers, optimizers, compilers for other languages, and so on) that this field or method isn't part of the original source. Debuggers shouldn't display them, and optimizers may freely inline or rearrange them while still complying with the original intent of the programmer.

11.1.2   Inner Classes

The original specification of the Java language does not permit classes to contain other classes, the way C++ does. This can lead to problems in large packages, where small classes with common names like Enumerator or Adapter can proliferate, causing naming conflicts. This happens very frequently in programs that use the JavaBeans specification, which use many small classes which serve as callbacks for events.

One solution would be to force programmers to adopt a naming convention to keep these classes from conflicting, but this doesn't help when unrelated groups of programmers try to use their code together. A better way is to nest classes within other classes. Classes defined within other classes aren't visible from outside the class, so naming conflicts are prevented.

Here is an example of inner classes:

```
package data.structure;
class Stack {
    /** Enumerator for a Stack data structure */
    class Enumerator implements java.until.Enumeration {
        public boolean hasMoreElements() { /* implementation */ }
        public Object nextElement() { /* implementation */ }
    }
}

class Queue {
    /** Enumerator for a Queue data structure */
    class Enumerator implements java.util.Enumeration {
        public boolean hasMoreElements() { /* implementation */ }
        public Object nextElement() { /* implementation */ }
    }
}
```

Here we have two classes named Enumerator. One is contained within Stack, and the other belongs to Queue. The names do not conflict, since they appear within different classes.

To compile this code for the Java virtual machine, it is necessary to "flatten" this hierarchical class structure, since the JVM doesn't have a concept of "nested class." A Java compiler compiles the code into four classes: Stack, Stack$Enumerator, Queue, and Queue$Enumerator:

```
.class data/structure/Stack
    ;; Code using data/structure/Stack$Enumerator
.end class

.class data/structure/Stack$Enumerator
.implements java/util/Enumeration
    ;; Implementation of the Enumerator for the stack
.end class

.class data/structure/Queue
    ;; Code using data/structure/Queue$Enumerator
.end class
```

```
.class data/structure/Queue$Enumerator
.implements java/util/Enumeration
    ;; Implementation of the Enumerator for the queue
.end class
```

By prefixing the name of the inner class with the name of the outer class, the compiler prevents naming conflicts. In the code for Stack and Stack$Enumerator, any reference to Enumerator is replaced with Stack$Enumerator. Similarly, in Queue and Queue$Enumerator, any reference to Enumerator is replaced with Queue$Enumerator.

A similar technique can be used for classes without any names at all:

```
package data.structure;
import java.util.Enumeration;
class Heap {
    Enumeration elements() {
        return new Enumeration() {
            /* This is a class with no name
             * that implements Enumeration */
            int count = 0;
            public boolean hasMoreElements()
                { /* implementation */ }
            public Object nextElement()
                { /* implementation */ }
        }
    }
}
```

The value returned from elements is an instance of a class that has no name; this class implements Enumeration. The Java compiler chooses a name for the anonymous class, such as Heap$1. The digit 1 is a counter to distinguish between anonymous classes within the same class, and the name is prefixed with Heap$ to distinguish it from anonymous inner classes from other classes. The class Heap compiles to

```
.class data/structure/Heap
.method elements()Ljava/lang/Object;
new data/structure/Heap$1          ; Create an instance of the
                                   ; anonymous enumerator
dup
invokespecial data/structure/Heap$1/<init>()V
areturn
```

```
    .end method
    .end class

    .class data/structure/Heap$1
    .implements java/util/Enumeration
    .method hasMoreElements()Z
    ;; Implementation of hasMoreElements
    .end method

    .method nextElement()Ljava/lang/Object;
    ;; Implementation of nextElement
    .end method
    .end class
```

The Java compiler adds a class attribute, `InnerClasses`, which lists the inner classes associated with the class. A disassembler like `javac` uses this information to reconstruct the original class definition, even though the compiled version of the inner class is in a separate `class` file.

11.1.3 Variable Scoping with Inner Classes

Inner classes are allowed to use fields of the enclosing object. For example, here is the definition of `Stack`, with more of the details included:

```
class Stack {
    /** This stores the list of elements in the stack */
    Object[] elements;

    /** Pointer to the top of the stack */
    int top = 0;

    class Enumerator implements java.util.Enumeration {
        int count = top;

        public boolean hasMoreElements()
        {
            return count > 0;
        }
```

```
        public Object nextElement()
        {
            if(count == 0)
                throw new NoSuchElementException();
            else
            {
                count--;
                return elements[count];
            }
        }
    }
}
```

The inner class Enumerator within Stack uses the fields elements and top from Stack. These refer to the fields within the object that created the Enumerator.

To support these, the translation includes a reference to the enclosing object, called this$0. It is initialized in the constructor to the object responsible for the creation of the Enumerator. All references to top and elements come from this reference.

The compilation of Enumerator produces these definitions:

```
.class Stack$Enumerator
.implements java/util/Enumeration

.field this$0 LStack;          ; The enclosing object
.field count I                 ; The current count

.method <init>(LStack;)V
aload_0                        ; Call super constructor
invokespecial java/lang/Object/<init>()V
aload_0                        ; Store the enclosing object
aload_1                        ; in this$0
putfield data/structure/Stack$Enumerator/this$0/Stack/

aload_0                                    ; This is the body of the
aload_1                                     ; constructor:
getfield Stack/top I                        ; count = top;
putfield count I

return
.end method
```

In the body of nextElement, the expression elements[count] generates the code

```
aload_0
getfield this$0 LStack;                        ; Get enclosing
                                               ; object
getfield Stack/elements [Ljava/lang/Object; ; Get the elements
aload_0                                        ; Get count
getfield Stack$Enumerator/count I              ; Get
aaload                                          ; elements[count]
```

The ability of inner classes to remember the state in which they were generated is similar to the way closures are treated in Scheme. See chapter 12 for a detailed description of how to implement Scheme closures in the Java virtual machine.

11.2 Regular Expressions

Regular expressions can be thought of as programs whose job it is to see if a string of text fits a pattern. These programs are often executed by translating them into a *finite state machine*, a kind of virtual computer with a very limited instruction set and no memory. Here is an example of a regular expression that matches floating-point numbers in Java:

```
[0-9]*.([0-9]*)?([eE][-+]?[0-9]+)?[fFdD]?
```

Figure 11.1 shows how you interpret this expression. Here is how a regular expression matches the string of characters 3.14. The 3 matches [0-9]* in the first box. The period matches the beginning of the second box. The digits 1 and 4 match the rest of the second box. The third and fourth boxes are optional (indicated by the ? at the end). Similarly, a more exotic number like 6.022e+23d also matches the regular expression.

Something like 2BorNot2B does not match. Although the 2 matches with the first box, the letter B does not match with anything.

An easy way to find out whether or not a regular expression matches a string of input text is to use a finite state machine. Figure 11.2 shows a finite state machine for the example regular expression. Each circle represents a *state*. The labeled arrows between states are called *transitions*. The double circles are special states called *terminal states*.

To use a finite state machine, you start at the state labeled **start**. Then you look at the first character in the input. If you see an outbound arrow from **start** labeled with that character, then follow the arrow to the new state. Repeat with the

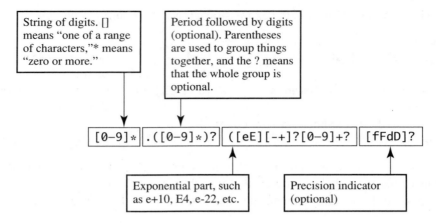

FIGURE 11.1: *Reading a regular expression*

next character, using the new state, until you reach the end of the input. If you end up in a terminal state, then the regular expression matches the input string. If the final state isn't a terminal state, or if you find yourself in a state where there is no

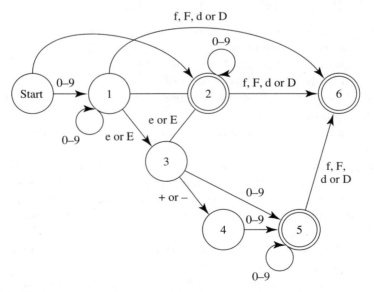

FIGURE 11.2: *Finite state machine recognizing floating-point numbers*

outbound arrow labeled with the next input character, then the regular expression does not match the input string.

To recognize the number `6.022e+23`, you would follow the diagram like this:

State	Next character	New state
Start	6	1
1	.	2
2	0	2
2	2	2
2	2	2
2	e	3
3	+	4
4	2	5
5	3	5

Since 5 is a terminal state, the number `6.022e+23` is a valid floating-point number. By contrast, `2.eD` is not:

State	Next character	New state
Start	2	1
1	.	2
2	e	3
3	D	none

Since there is no transition from state 3 labeled `D`, the string `2.eD` is not a valid floating-point number.

To write a program to match regular expressions to input strings, programs often incorporate virtual machines to simulate the finite state machines. As a JVM programmer, you've got a portable virtual machine always accessible, without having to create one of your own. This is the plan: each state is a location in the program. Transitions are gotos from one state to another. At each state, read the next character and do a goto to the next state based on the character.

Here is the code to match the finite state machine shown:

```
.method static matchFloatingPoint(Ljava/lang/String;)Z
.var 0 is string Ljava/lang/String;
                        ; String to match
.var 1 is index I       ; Current index
.var 2 is length I      ; Length of the string
iconst_m1
istore_1                ; Initialize index
```

```
aload_0
invokevirtual java/lang/String/length()I
istore_2                    ; Initialize length

start:
jsr next_char_non_accept
lookupswitch
'.': state2
'0': state1 '1': state1 '2': state1 '3': state1 '4': state1
'5': state1 '6': state1 '7': state1 '8': state1 '9': state1
default: fail

state1:
jsr next_char_non_accept
lookupswitch
'e': state3 'E': state3
'f': state7 'F': state7
'd': state7 'D': state7
'.': state2
'0': state1 '1': state1 '2': state1 '3': state1 '4': state1
'5': state1 '6': state1 '7': state1 '8': state1 '9': state1
default: fail

state2:
jsr next_char_accept
lookupswitch
'e': state3 'E': state3
'f': state6 'F': state6
'd': state6 'D': state6
'0': state2 '1': state2 '2': state2 '3': state2 '4': state2
'5': state2 '6': state2 '7': state2 '8': state2 '9': state2
default: fail

state3:
jsr next_char_non_accept
lookupswitch
'+': state3 '-': state4
'0': state5 '1': state5 '2': state5 '3': state5 '4': state5
'5': state5 '6': state5 '7': state5 '8': state5 '9': state5
default: fail

state4:
```

```
jsr next_char_non_accept
lookupswitch
'0': state5 '1': state5 '2': state5 '3': state5 '4': state5
'5': state5 '6': state5 '7': state5 '8': state5 '9': state5
default: fail

state5:
jsr next_char_non_accept
lookupswitch
'f': state6 'F': state6 'd': state6 'D': state6
'0': state5 '1': state5 '2': state5 '3': state5 '4': state5
'5': state5 '6': state5 '7': state5 '8': state5 '9': state5
default: fail

state6:
; No more input is expected, and a float has been recognized
goto succeed
```

The code at `next_char_accept` and `next_char_non_accept` are subroutines. Each retrieves the next character from the input and places it on the stack. If there is no next character, `next_char_accept` goes to `succeed`, and `next_char_non_accept` goes to `fail`. The subroutine `next_char_accept` is used in the terminal states, where the end of the input means that the input is acceptable. The subroutine `next_char_non_accept` is used in nonterminal states, where more input is expected. The code for these subroutines is

```
; Go to the next character, and fail if it's EOF
next_char_non_accept:
astore_3              ; Store the return address
iinc 1 1              ; Increment index
iload_1
iload_2
if_icmpge fail        ; If index is past the end, fail
aload_0               ; Push character
iload_1
invokevirtual java/lang/String/charAt (I)C
ret 3

; Go to the next character, and succeed if it's EOF
next_char_accept:
astore_3              ; Store the return address
iinc 1 1              ; Increment index
```

```
        iload_1
        iload_2
        if_icmpge succeed     ; If index is past the end, succeed
        aload_0               ; Push character
        iload_1
        invokevirtual java/lang/String/charAt (I)C
        ret 3


succeed:
    ; The input string matches the regular expression
    iconst_1
    ireturn               ; Return true


fail:
    ; The input string does not match the regular expression
    iconst_0
    ireturn               ; Return false
.end method
```

The method takes a `String` as its input and returns `true` if it is a valid floating-point number, `false` otherwise.

Each state begins with a call to a subroutine, either `next_char_accept` or `next_char_non_accept`. If the current state is a terminal state, then it calls `next_char_accept`; otherwise, it calls `next_char_non_accept`.

The difference between `next_char_accept` and `next_char_non_accept` is what happens when you run out of input. Subroutine `next_char_accept` is called from a terminal state, which means that the input is acceptable if there are no more characters, so the method returns `true`. Subroutine `next_char_non_accept` is called from a nonterminal state, which means that the input is not acceptable, and the method returns `false`.

Both subroutines read the next character in the input and leave it on the stack. This character drives the `lookupswitch` instruction, which uses it to determine which state to go to next. The code for the `lookupswitch` follows directly from the diagram in Figure 11.2. For each transition, there is an entry in the `look-upswitch` that sends the finite state machine to that state. If the character isn't recognized, then go to `fail`.

As long as there is more input, the method keeps jumping from location to location. When there is no more input, the method goes to either `succeed` or `fail`, depending on whether the last state was a terminal state or not. This action returns `true` or `false`, whether the input was acceptable or not.

11.3   Iterators

Iterators are a looping construct in the language Sather, a language developed at the International Computer Science Institute at Berkeley. Iterators are based on an idea in the language CLU. Iterators are designed to be safer than ordinary looping constructs, since creation, succession, and termination operations are defined where the iterator is defined, instead of depending on the code using the iterator to perform them.

11.3.1   Iterators in Sather

This example defines an iterator called fibonacci!, which yields Fibonacci numbers. In Sather, all iterators end with the character !.

```
fibonacci! : INT          -- Declare an iterator which returns
                          -- integer values
   a : INT := 1;          -- Initialize a and b
   b : INT := 2;
   yield a;               -- Return 1 the first time
   yield b;               -- Return 2 the second time
   loop                   -- Loop forever
       c : INT := a + b;  -- The next value is the sum
                          -- of the two previous values
       yield c;           -- Return that value
       a := b;            -- Copy the values backwards,
       b := c;            -- to set up the next iteration
   end;
end;
```

An iterator is used as a method is used in Java. A yield is similar to a Java return. A yield statement returns a value, and control returns to the calling procedure. However, when the calling procedure calls the iterator again, the iterator picks up at the same point that it left off, right after the yield.

For example, here's some code that prints out the first ten Fibonacci numbers:

```
loop                          -- Loop until quitting
   i : INT := range!(1, 10);  -- An iterator that yields values
                              -- from 1 to 10 before quitting
   f : INT := fibonacci!;     -- Get the next Fibonacci number
   #OUT + i + ' ' + f + '\n'; -- Print it out
end;
```

This code uses two iterators, `range!` and `fibonacci!`. The loop continues until one of them issues a `quit` command instead of yielding a value. The `fibonacci!` iterator never quits, so it's up to `range!` to terminate the loop.

The first time through the loop, `range!` yields the value 1, so `i` is set to 1. Next, it calls `fibonacci!`, which transfers control to the iterator. The iterator `fibonacci!` first sets the value of a to 1 and b to 2. The next thing it does is `yield` the value of a. This causes control to return to the caller, while the iterator is suspended. The value returned by the iterator call is 1, since that was the value of a when it was yielded. It is assigned to f. The expression #OUT + i + ' ' + f + ' \n' prints out the values of i and f, followed by a carriage return.

Next, the loop goes back to the beginning. This time, `range!` yields the value 2. Calling `fibonacci!` again, the iterator picks up where it left off after the line `yield a`. The next thing it does is yield the value of b, which is 2. This is printed out, and the outer loop continues.

The `range!` iterator yields 3 this time. Calling `fibonacci!` again, the iterator begins its own loop. It calculates c, which turns out to be 3, and yields that value. The iterator is suspended, right in the middle of the loop, while the outer loop continues with the yielded value 3.

The next time `fibonacci!` is called, it picks up right after `yield c`. The value of c is still 3. It copies b into a and c into b. Then it loops again, this time calculating c to be 5. It yields this value of c.

The iterator continues this way, with `fibonacci!` yielding 8, 13, 21, 34, 55, and 89. After it yields 89, the program loops back and calls `range!` again. This time, `range!` finds that it was going to yield 11, which is larger than its maximum range. Instead of yielding a value, it quits. This terminates the entire loop, so `fibonacci!` is not called again.

Iterators have many other uses. All arrays in Sather have an iterator called `elt!`, which yields successive elements of the array. This makes it easy to sum up all of the elements in an array:

```
a:ARRAY{INT} := | 43, 49649, 194 |;      -- Create an array of
                                         -- integers with 3
                                         -- elements
total:INT := 0;
loop
   total:= total + a.elt!;               -- Sum up the elements
end;
```

Each time `elt!` is called, it yields the next element of the array: first 43, then 49649, then 194. These are accumulated in `total`. After yielding 194, the `elt!` iterator quits, which terminates the enclosing loop.

The summation loop can be done even more succinctly with the `sum!` iterator from the Sather library:

```
loop
    total := sum!(a.elt!);
end;
```

Each time `sum!` is called, it yields the sum of all of the values that have been passed in so far. The loop continues until `elt!` quits. It is not necessary to write a different `sum!` iterator to deal with linked lists, trees, or other data structures, since the semantics of element access are separated from the semantics of computing a sum. The semantics of summation are encapsulated within `sum!`, and the semantics of working with array elements are encapsulated within `elt!`.

This encapsulation prevents many common bugs that occur when loops are used. There is no possibility of failing to initialize the total to 0 or of accessing an invalid array element. By comparison, this is the equivalent Java code:

```
int[] a = { 43, 49649, 194 };
int total = 0;
for(int i = 0; i < a.length; i++)
    total += a[i];
```

In this code, the `for` loop is responsible for knowing that the array begins at 0 and ends *one before* `a.length`. The loop is also responsible for knowing that computation of a sum involves adding numbers successively, starting with 0. If a were a `Vector` or some other data structure, then code would have to be written differently.

The Sather `sum!` iterator encapsulates all the semantics of summation, and the `elt!` iterator encapsulates all the semantics of enumerating all of the elements of a data structure. This makes code not only more concise but also more likely to be correct. You have to write `sum!` correctly only once, then put it in the library; it can be used many times.

11.3.2 Implementing Iterators

To implement iterators in the Java virtual machine, each iterator must be able to keep the state of its local variables, as well as its current position. One way to do this is to make each iterator its own class, using an instance of the iterator inside the loop. The class keeps track of the state of the iterator with an integer value, using the `tableswitch` statement to continue where it left off.

Here is one possible implementation of the `fibonacci!` iterator. To get the next value from the iterator, call the method `next`. The variables a, b, and c are implemented as fields of the object. Because they are fields instead of local variables, they persist from one invocation of next to the next. The variable state$ is used to keep track of the last place that the next method was before it returned. The initial value of state$ is 0. There are four possible states: one for the beginning of the iterator, and one for each yield.

```
.class fibonacci

.field private a I                      ; Variables local to the
.field private b I                      ; iterator
.field private c I
.field private state$ I                  ; Keeps the state

.method public next ()I
.throws QuitException
    aload_0
    getfield fibonacci/state$ I     ; Jump to the current state
    tableswitch 0                   ; Initally, the state is 0
        state0
        state1
        state2
        state3
        default: done

; Start here, since state$ is initialized to 0
state0:
    aload_0                             ; Initialize a and b
    iconst_1
    putfield fibonacci/a I

    aload_0
    iconst_2
    putfield fibonacci/b I

    aload_0
    getfield fibonacci/a I          ; Compute return value (a)

    aload_0
    iconst_1
    putfield fibonacci/state$ I     ; Change to state 1

    ireturn                         ; Yield a
```

```
    ; Pick up here when state$ is 1
state1:
    aload_0
    getfield fibonacci/b I          ; Compute return value (b)

    aload_0
    iconst_2
    putfield fibonacci/state$ I     ; Change to state 2

    ireturn                         ; Yield b

; Begin here when state$ is 2
state2:
loop:
    aload_0
    aload_0                         ; Compute c=a+b
    getfield fibonacci/a I
    aload_0
    getfield fibonacci/b I
    iadd
    putfield fibonacci/c I

    aload_0
    getfield fibonacci/c I          ; Get c to return

    aload_0                         ; Change to state 3
    iconst_3
    putfield fibonacci/state$ I

    ireturn                         ; Yield c

state3:
    aload_0                         ; Shuffle b->a and c->b
    aload_0
    getfield fibonacci/b I
    putfield fibonacci/a I

    aload_0
    aload_0
    getfield fibonacci/c I
    putfield fibonacci/b I
    goto loop                       ; Continue with the loop
```

```
done:                              ; Default case: quit by
    new QuitException              ; throwing an exception
    dup
    invokespecial QuitException/<init> ()V
    athrow

.end method

.method <init> ()V                 ; Basic constructor
    aload_0
    invokespecial java/lang/Object/<init> ()V
    return
.end method
```

Wherever the Sather code says to `yield` a value, the `next` method uses an `ireturn`. Before the return, the `state$` variable is set to the next state. This variable corresponds to a label in the code that picks up right after the `ireturn`.

The code begins with a `tableswitch`, which jumps to some place within the body of the code. The first time through, `state$` is 0, so the method starts at `state0`. It initializes a and b, then returns a. Before it returns, it sets `state$` to 1. This yields the value of a and prepares the class to resume the next time the iterator is called.

The next time it is called, the `tableswitch` causes the code to start at `state1`, which returns b and sets `state$` to 2.

The third call begins at `state2`, which corresponds to the beginning of the loop in the Sather program. The code computes c and returns the value. Before it returns, it sets the state to 3.

On all subsequent calls, the `tableswitch` causes the program to jump right into the middle of the loop at state 3, right after the `ireturn` which returned the value of c. It finishes the loop body, which updates a and b. Then it jumps back to the beginning of the loop, which computes and returns the next value of c.

All subsequent calls jump directly to `state3`, since the state never changes again. The default case at `done` never happens. Section 11.3.3 shows an iterator that does terminate.

An interesting thing to note is that this program doesn't correspond to any Java-language program, since you cannot write a `switch` that jumps directly into the middle of a loop. It is possible to write an equivalent method in Java, but the translation is less straightforward than this one.

11.3.3 Iterators with Arguments

The `range!` iterator is used to yield all numbers within a certain range. Unlike `fibonacci!`, the `range!` iterator requires arguments. In Sather, it is implemented as

```
    range!(min, max:INT) : INT is    -- Define the iterator range!
                                     -- It takes 2 arguments, min
                                     -- and max, which are both
                                     -- integers
        x : INT := min;              -- Initialize the loop variable
        loop                         -- Loop until quitting
            if x > max               -- Quit when x > max
                then quit
            end;
            yield x;                 -- Yield the next value
            x := x + 1;              -- Increment x
        end;
    end;
```

This iterator initializes a loop variable x, adding 1 to x after each yield, until it reaches the upper bound max. Since there is only one yield statement, there are only two states: the beginning of the iterator and after the yield. The Oolong translation is

```
.class range

.field x I
.field state$ I

.method public next (II)I
    aload_0                     ; Jump to the current state
    getfield range/state$ I
    tableswitch 0
        state0
        state1
        default: done

state0:
    aload_0                     ; Initialize x to min
    iload_1
    putfield range/x I

loop:
    aload_0
    getfield range/x I
    iload_2
    if_icmpgt done              ; Break the loop if x>max
```

```
        aload_0
        getfield range/x I          ; Get return value (x)

        aload_0
        iconst_1
        putfield range/state$ I     ; Change to state 1
        ireturn                     ; Yield x

state1:
        aload_0                     ; Increment x
        aload_0
        getfield range/x I
        iconst_1
        iadd
        putfield range/x I

        goto loop                   ; Loop again

done:
        new QuitException           ; Throw a QuitException when
        dup                         ; done
        invokespecial QuitException/<init> ()V
        athrow
.end method
```

In this iterator, min and max are local variables, which are initialized each time the iterator is called. We represent x as a field, since its state is persistent across invocations.

The loop first checks to see if the termination condition is met. If the test fails, then the iterator returns the latest value of x. On subsequent calls to this iterator, control begins at state1, right after the yield. This increments x and jumps back to the termination test. It continues to do this, yielding subsequent values of x, until the termination test succeeds.

When the termination test succeeds, then control passes to done. At done, the method throws a QuitException. This signals to the enclosing loop that it is time to stop calling the iterator.

11.3.4 Using Iterators

To use the iterators implemented here, it is necessary to create an instance of each iterator contained in the program, calling next each time a value is desired. This

Sather program uses the `fibonacci!` and `range!` iterators to print the first ten Fibonacci numbers.

```
loop                           -- Loop until quitting
    i : INT := range!(1, 10);  -- An iterator that yields values
                               -- from 1 to 10 before quitting
    f : INT := fibonacci!;     -- Get the next fibonacci number
    #OUT + i + ' ' + f + '\n'; -- Print it out
end;
```

This code can be implemented in Oolong as

```
.catch QuitException from loop to end using end
.var 1 is fibonacci Lfibonacci;
.var 2 is range Lrange;
.var 3 is i I
.var 4 is f I

    new fibonacci                      ; Create the iterators,
    dup                                ; storing them in
    invokespecial fibonacci/<init> ()V ; variables 1 and 2
    astore_1

    new range
    dup
    invokespecial range/<init> ()V
    astore_2

loop:                                  ; Beginning of the loop
    aload_2                            ; Call range! with 1, 10
    iconst_1
    bipush 10
    invokevirtual range/next (II)I
    istore_3                           ; Put that into i

    aload_1                            ; Call fibonacci!
    invokevirtual fibonacci/next ()I
    istore 4                           ; Store the result in f

;; Print out i and f (code omitted)

    goto loop                          ; Loop again
```

```
end:
    pop                          ; Remove the exception
    ;; Control continues here after the loop
```

The code begins by creating instances of the range and fibonacci iterator classes to represent the two iterators.

After initializing the iterators, the code goes into an infinite loop. It continues until an iterator terminates by throwing a QuitException. When the exception is thrown, it is caught out of the loop at end, and control continues there. The exception itself is unimportant, so it is removed from the stack.

In this code, the variables fibonacci, range, i, and f were represented by locals, since this code never yields. If there were a yield in the loop, some of the variables would have to be represented instead by fields, which would ensure their persistence across yields.

11.4   Parameterized Types

Parameterized types are found in a diverse set of languages, from Eiffel (one of the first object-oriented languages) and Haskell (a purely functional language without any side effects) to C++. In C++, parameterized types are called *templates*.

A parameterized type allows the programmer to write programs without specifying all the types that are used. A parameterized type is often used to define a collection of objects. For example, here is code for a binary tree, written in Eiffel:

```
class BINARY_TREE[T -> COMPARABLE]
feature
    left : BINARY_TREE[T]
    right : BINARY_TREE[T]
    value : T

    insert(node : T) is
        -- Insert the node into the tree
        -- This code can use < on node and value, since they
        -- are both COMPARABLEs
    end;
end
```

All the values in the binary tree described must be of type T, and each of the subtrees must also be binary trees that store T. Different trees may use a different type for T. T is called a *type variable*.

The notation T -> COMPARABLE means that T must be a descendant of the COMPARABLE class. This is called *constrained genericity*. The symbol < is a *feature* of all classes that are descendants of COMPARABLE. A feature is like a method in Java: it is called to produce a value. The symbol < is used to compare elements. All descendants of COMPARABLE support the < feature.

You can create a binary tree of some particular type by substituting that type for T. For example, to create a binary tree of real numbers, write

```
real_tree : BINARY_TREE[REAL]     -- Create a tree of reals
```

A programmer might add to the system a new class that supports the COMPARABLE features, such as this definition of a dictionary entry:

```
class DICTIONARY_ENTRY
    inherit COMPARABLE
feature
    -- provide definitions for the COMPARABLE features
end;
```

This code defines a class DICTIONARY_ENTRY that inherits the definitions from the class COMPARABLE. The Eiffel inherit clause is similar to the Java super clause in a class declaration, except that Eiffel permits multiple inheritance.

The programmer can use this definition to create a dictionary that is a binary tree of dictionary entries:

```
dictionary : BINARY_TREE[DICTIONARY_ENTRY]
```

If the programmer attempts to enter a DICTIONARY_ENTRY into real_tree or a REAL into the dictionary, then the compiler signals a type violation.

There are two basic ways to implement type parameters in the Java virtual machine. One is to create one generic class. The other is to create new classes for all possible values of the type parameters.

11.4.1 Implementing Parameterized Types with a Generic Class

The following code implements BINARY_TREE in bytecodes using a single generic class:

```
.class BINARY_TREE
.field left LBINARY_TREE;
.field right LBINARY_TREE;
.field value LCOMPARABLE;
```

```
.method insert(LCOMPARABLE;)V
;; Code for the method, making no assumptions about the argument
;; except that it is a COMPARABLE
.end method
```

Since the type of value is constrained to being a descendent of COMPARABLE, it may be treated as a COMPARABLE. If there were no constraint provided, you could substitute java/lang/Object for COMPARABLE, since java/lang/Object is the superclass of all classes.

To properly implement Eiffel programs this way we have to provide classes for basic types like REAL and INT. REAL and INT would implement the COMPARABLE interface, allowing the programmer to use the BINARY_TREE class to create trees of numerical values as well as objects.

One difficulty with implementing binary trees this way is that it does not force all elements of the binary tree to be of the same type. If you created an instance of this class, then you could insert either a REAL or a DICTIONARY_ENTRY into it. In fact, you could insert entries of both at different times.

This is not necessarily a problem. The class BINARY_TREE is not intended to be used from other JVM programs. It is created by the Eiffel compiler, and it should not be used except by other classes generated by the Eiffel compiler. Eiffel does compile-time checking to ensure that the programmer does not try to insert a DICTIONARY_ENTRY into a BINARY_TREE[REAL] or vice versa. The JVM does not need to further check that the types are compatible.

11.4.2 Implementing Parameterized Types as Templates

A different way of implementing parameterized types in the JVM is to create a new class for each instantiation of the parameter template that is used in the program. This is the approach C++ compilers use to implement templates.

For BINARY_TREE[REAL] and BINARY_TREE[DICTIONARY_ENTRY], two new classes are generated, one for binary trees of REALs and another for binary trees of DICTIONARY_ENTRYs. The names are mangled to ensure that they don't conflict with existing types. The definitions of these classes follow.

```
.class BINARY_TREE$REAL
.field left LBINARY_TREE$REAL;
.field right LBINARY_TREE$REAL;
.field value LREAL;
.method insert(LREAL;)V
;; Code for the insert method, specialized using
;; a REAL as the argument
.end method
```

```
.class BINARY_TREE$DICTIONARY_ENTRY
.field left LBINARY_TREE$DICTIONARY_ENTRY;
.field right LBINARY_TREE$DICTIONARY_ENTRY;
.field value DICTIONARY_ENTRY;
.method insert(LDICTIONARY_ENTRY;)V
;; Code for the insert method, specialized using a
;; DICTIONARY_ENTRY as the argument
.end method
```

One reason to use this technique of implementing parameterized types is that the JVM does additional type checking for you. Even if the Eiffel compiler were to permit you to generate JVM code that tried to insert a REAL into a BINARY_TREE[DICTIONARY_ENTRY], the JVM would catch it.

Another advantage is that the compiler can optimize the code to use unwrapped, native JVM implementations of the numeric types. Instead of wrapping the numbers in an object such as REAL, which implements the COMPARABLE interface, the class BINARY_TREE$REAL can use floats. The implementation could be specialized to use the single instruction fcmpg to compare floats, instead of looking in COMPARA-BLE for the method that corresponds to the < operator in Eiffel.

The problem with this technique is that it requires extensive analysis of the code at compile time to determine which classes may be used. If the programmer uses many different kinds of binary trees, many different classes will be created. Adding new classes or changing the implementation of BINARY_TREE may cause substantial recompilation.

11.5   Multiple Inheritance

Java is a single-inheritance language, like Ada 95 and Smalltalk. Each class (except for Object) is based on exactly one other class; the derived class extends the class it is based on. An instance of the derived class may be used in any place where an instance of the base class is called for. The derived class has all of the behaviors of the base class, and it may add a few of its own.

There are several reasons for a class to have only one superclass. One is a matter of performance. There are implementation techniques for the JVM that execute method invocations very quickly if there is only one superclass. When multiple superclasses are permitted, it becomes difficult to arrange memory for maximum efficiency.

Another reason not to support multiple inheritance is that it adds a new layer of complexity to the language. If a class has several superclasses and two of the superclasses share a method with the same name and arguments, then which method is inherited by the class? Various language designs get around this problem in different ways, but no way is as easy as simply limiting the class to one superclass.

11.5.1 Interfaces for Multiple Inheritance

Although the JVM does not support multiple inheritance of code, it does support multiple inheritance of interfaces. Since interfaces have no implementations, they are not subject to the problems of multiple inheritance. Interfaces can be used to help implement multiple inheritance.

Suppose you want to implement this class hierarchy, which is expressed in a Java-like language that supports multiple inheritance:

```
class Person
{
    String getName() { /* Implementation of getName() */ }
    int getSalary() { /* Implementation of getSalary() */ }
}

class FootballPlayer extends Person
{
    void wearHelmet() { /* Wear a football helmet */ }
    String getTeam() { /* Return the player's football team */ }
}

class BaseballPlayer extends Person
{
    void swingBat() { /* Swing a baseball bat */ }
    String getTeam() { /* Return the player's baseball team */ }
}

class DeionSanders extends BaseballPlayer, FootballPlayer
{
}
```

We start by declaring an interface for each class. The definition of `DeionSanders` inherits multiple interfaces:

```
.interface Person
.method getName()Ljava/lang/String;
.end method
.method abstract getSalary()I
.end method
```

```
.interface FootballPlayer
.implements Person
.method abstract wearHelmet()V
.end method
.method abstract getTeam()Ljava/lang/String;
.end method
.end class

.interface BaseballPlayer
.implements Person
.method abstract swingBat()V
.end method
.method abstract getTeam()Ljava/lang/String;
.end method
.end class

.interface DeionSanders
.implements FootballPlayer
.implements BaseballPlayer
.end class
```

To be useful, these interfaces must be implemented by classes.

11.5.2 Implementing the Interfaces

In order to use these interfaces, classes that implement them must be provided. We will call these classes Person$Impl, FootballPlayer$Impl, BaseballPlayer$Impl, and DeionSanders$Impl. Each class implements the corresponding interface and provides implementations for the methods. The implementations are defined according to the semantics given in the original program.

The class Person$Impl involves no inheritance, so we'll look at it first. Its methods are implemented according to the definitions provided in the original source code:

```
.class Person$Impl
.implements Person
.method public getName()L/java/lang/String;
   ;; Compute name and return it
.end method

.method public getSalary()I
   ;; Compute salary and return it
```

```
.end method
.end class
```

Since FootballPlayer$Impl and BaseballPlayer$Impl have to implement only one interface, they can inherit the definitions of getName and getSalary from Person$Impl. For those methods which are defined just for the class (getTeam and wearHelmet from FootballPlayer, getTeam and swingBat from BaseballPlayer), these methods are implemented in the class according to the definition in the original source:

```
; Implement the FootballPlayer interface
.class FootballPlayer$Impl
.super Person$Impl
.implements FootballPlayer
.method public getTeam()Ljava/lang/String;
    ;; Compute and return the player's football team
.end method

.method public wearHelmet()V
    ;; Wear a football helmet
.end method
.end class

; Implement the BaseballPlayer interface
.class BaseballPlayer$Impl
.super Person$Impl
.implements BaseballPlayer
.method public getTeam()Ljava/lang/String;
    ;; Compute and return the player's baseball team
.end method

.method public swingBat()V
    ;; Swing a baseball bat
.end method
.end class
```

Implementing DeionSanders$Impl is a bit trickier. It defines no methods of its own, but it needs to have both wearHelmet from FootballPlayer$Impl and swingBat from BaseballPlayer$Impl. Unfortunately, DeionSanders$Impl can't inherit from both FootballPlayer$Impl and BaseballPlayer$Impl, because the JVM forbids multiple inheritance of implementation. Fortunately, there are several ways to solve this problem.

One way is to use one class or the other as the superclass. It will inherit the methods from that class, but not from the other. Methods that are not inherited must be rewritten, perhaps by copying the code from the implementation. Suppose we choose `FootballPlayer$Impl` as the base class of `DeionSanders$Impl`:

```
.class DeionSanders$Impl
.super FootballPlayer$Impl

; All the FootballPlayer method implementations are inherited
; The BaseballPlayer-specific methods must be written explicitly

.method swingBat()V
    ;; Copy the code from BaseballPlayer$Impl.swingBat
.end method
.end class
```

Using this definition of `DeionSanders$Impl`, calling `getTeam` on a DeionSanders object returns the team as a football player (the Dallas Cowboys). Depending on the semantics of the original language, this may or may not be the correct answer. In the real world, there are two different answers to the question "What team does Deion Sanders play for?" (As of the time of this writing, the answers are the Dallas Cowboys and the San Francisco Giants.)

Consider the equivalent classes in C++, which supports multiple inheritance:

```
class Person
{
    public:
        virtual char* getName() { /* Implement name */ }
        virtual int getSalary() { /* Implement getSalary */ }
};

class FootballPlayer : public Person
{
    public:
        virtual char* getTeam() { /* Implement getTeam */ }
        virtual void wearHelmet() { /* Implement wearHelmet */ }
};

class BaseballPlayer : public Person
{
    public:
        virtual char* getTeam() { /* Implement getTeam */ }
```

```
        virtual void swingBat() { /* Implement swingBat */ }
    };

    class DeionSanders : public FootballPlayer, BaseballPlayer
    {
    };
```

Any call to `team` through a pointer to a `DeionSanders` object would be ambiguous. The C++ compiler rejects programs with ambiguous calls. The caller of the `getTeam` method must explicitly disambiguate the call by including the name of the class containing the method to invoke:

```
DeionSanders *ds = new DeionSanders();
ds->getTeam();                    // This is an error, since
                                  // it is ambiguous
ds->FootballPlayer::getTeam();    // Returns the Cowboys
ds->BaseballPlayer::getTeam();    // Returns the Giants
```

In Eiffel, the `DeionSanders` class itself would be illegal because of the ambiguity. The ambiguity can be fixed through renaming:

```
class DeionSanders
    inherit
    FootballPlayer rename getTeam as getFootballTeam end
    BaseballPlayer rename getTeam as getBaseballTeam end
end
```

In the Common Lisp Object System, this kind of ambiguity is legal. A call to the `getTeam` method of a `DeionSanders` object would return the football team, since by default the object uses the first method matching the name. By using the Meta Object Protocol, the default way of searching for method implementations can be changed to use whatever search order is desired.

Another way to implement `DeionSanders$Impl` is to use neither class as the base class. Instead, each object possesses private instances of both `FootballPlayer$Impl` and `BaseballPlayer$Impl`, called `super1` and `super2`. Whenever a method is called, the class *defers* the implementation of that method by calling the equivalent method on either the `super1` object or the `super2` object. The class `java/lang/Object` is used as the base class.

```
.class DeionSanders$Impl
.super java/lang/Object
.field private super1 LFootballPlayer$Impl;
.field private super2 LBaseballPlayer$Impl;
```

```
.method wearHelmet ()V
   ; Defer wearHelmet to the FootballPlayer object
   aload_0
   getfield DeionSanders$Impl/super1 LFootballPlayer$Impl;
   invokevirtual FootballPlayer$Impl/wearHelmet ()V
   return
.end method

.method swingBat ()V
   ; Defer swingBat to the BaseballPlayer object
   aload_0
   getfield DeionSanders$Impl/super2 LBaseballPlayer$Impl;
   invokevirtual BaseballPlayer$Impl/swingBat ()V
   return
.end method

.method getTeam()Ljava/lang/String;
   ;; Do you defer this to super1 or super2? See below
.end method

.method getName()Ljava/lang/String;
   ;; Do you defer this to super1 or super2? See below
.end method

.method getSalary()I
   ;; Do you defer this to super1 or super2? See below
.end method

.method <init> ()V
   ;; Initialize the super1 and super2 classes to instances of
   ;; BaseballPlayer$Impl and FootballPlayer$Impl, respectively
.end method
.end class
```

Although this technique solves the asymmetry between Football-
Player$Impl and BaseballPlayer$Impl, it does run into a problem with
getTeam, getName, and getSalary. Both methods must be implemented, since the
FootballPlayer and BaseballPlayer interfaces both require it. It is not obvious
which object these methods should be deferred to. In the real world, the person
Deion Sanders has only a single name but two salaries, one as a baseball player
and one as a football player. He also plays for two different teams.

Again, it is up to the semantics of the underlying language to resolve how these difficulties should be resolved. Different languages resolve these ambiguities differently, and programmers using each language find that the semantics of the language sometimes do and sometimes don't capture their intention. This is one of the reasons multiple inheritance is not included in Java.

11.5.3 Fields

JVM interfaces cannot have fields; they can have only methods. This means that it is not possible to specify fields the same way we specified methods in the interfaces.

One solution is to replace fields with *accessor methods*. Accessor methods are methods that get and set the value of the field. For example, suppose we add a height field to the Person class:

```
float height;          // Height in meters
```

It is not possible to add a height field to the Person interface, since that is not valid in the JVM specification. However, we can add getHeight and setHeight methods to the Person interface. This is similar to the JavaBeans design pattern for properties. By convention, method names beginning with get and set get and set some property of an object.

```
.method abstract getHeight()F
.end method
.method abstract setHeight(F)V
.end method
```

These methods must be implemented in the Person$Impl class. This can be done with a private field height. The method getHeight returns the value of height, and setHeight sets the value of the height field.

```
.field private height F        ; Stores the actual height

.method getHeight()F           ; Get the height
    aload_0
    getfield Person$Impl/height F
    freturn
.end method

.method setHeight(F)V          ; Set the height
    aload_0
    fload_1
```

```
        putfield Person$Impl/height F
        return
    .end method
```

Any access to the `height` field of a `Person` object must be translated into `get-Height` and `setHeight` calls.

11.6   Conclusion

In this chapter we have seen how to compile small languages, like regular expressions, and bits and pieces of larger languages. These and many other languages can be implemented using the Java virtual machine.

There are a variety of reasons to implement other languages in JVM code. Each language has its own flavor. Each programmer has a favorite language. Different programming tasks are better suited to different languages. By implementing compilers for these languages into JVM code, you can gain much of Java's "Write Once, Run Anywhere" capability for any language.

In succeeding chapters, we explore compilers for two languages, Scheme and Prolog. These languages are very different from Java. Scheme is based on the idea of using functions as data. Prolog is based on the idea of using rules to specify program implementations. Certain tasks can be implemented in these languages better than in any other language, including Java. The next chapters discuss in detail how to implement these languages on the Java virtual machine.

For an interesting discussion of extending Java to support other language features, visit `http://wwwipd.ira.uka.de/~pizza`. This site discusses Pizza and GJ, two extended Java languages, which compile into bytecodes.

## CHAPTER 12

Implementing Scheme

SCHEME is a language based on Lisp. Scheme features procedures as first-class entities; that is, procedures are treated just like any other kind of value. They may be passed as arguments to other procedures, stored in variables, or used as return values.

Scheme is weakly typed, which means that it is not necessary for the programmer to specify the type of each variable. This can be an advantage, especially in small programs, since it is often tedious to have to declare each variable. Weak typing allows the programmer to write very general procedures that can take any type of value, instead of having to write separate procedures for each type.

12.1 Scheme Concepts

The fundamental units of Scheme programs are numbers (written like Java numbers), *symbols* (written much like Java variables, except that dashes (-) and some other characters are permitted), and *procedures*. A procedure is a combination of a piece of code and an environment in which the code is to be evaluated.

A Scheme program is called a *form*. Here is an example of a form:

```
(+ 2 3)
```

This form denotes the list containing three entities: the symbol +, the number 2, and the number 3. To run a Scheme program, the Scheme *evaluator* takes the form and a *binding environment*. The binding environment maps symbols to values. Then it applies these rules to the form:

- ◆ A number evaluates to itself.
- ◆ A symbol is evaluated by looking it up in the binding environment. The results of the lookup are the value.

♦ A list is evaluated by evaluating each element of the list. The first element is treated as a procedure. A new binding environment is created, in which the parameters of the procedure are bound to the rest of the list. Then the body of the procedure is evaluated.

For example, in the list (+ 2 3), the symbol + evaluates to a procedure that adds numbers together, and 2 and 3 evaluate to themselves. Then the evaluator calls the procedure, giving it the arguments 2 and 3. The procedure adds 2 and 3 to get 5, which is the final result.

There are a few exceptions to the third rule. Some lists have keywords in the first position; these are evaluated differently from other lists. These lists are called *special forms*.

To create a new procedure in Scheme, a special form called a *lambda expression* is used. Here is an example of a lambda expression:

```
(lambda (x) (* x x))
```

This expression evaluates to a new procedure, in this case, one that squares its parameter by multiplying it by itself. A lambda expression is written with the keyword lambda as the first element. The second element is a list of formal parameters. The third element is called the *body* of the lambda expression.

When the procedure is applied to a list of actual parameters, a new binding environment is created in which the symbols in the list of formal parameters are bound to the elements of the list of actual parameters. The new binding environment includes the one in which the lambda expression was first evaluated.

This example demonstrates the application of a lambda expression:[1]

```
(
    (lambda (x) (* x x))
    5
)
```

This is a list with two elements. The first element is a lambda expression, which evaluates to a procedure, as described. The second element of the list is the number 5, which evaluates to itself.

After evaluating the list elements, the evaluator evaluates the whole form by using the first element as a procedure and the second element as the argument to that procedure. To apply the procedure, a new binding environment is created, binding the symbol x to number 5. The new binding environment also contains the

---

[1] As in Java, the carriage returns are not relevant. All examples are written with lots of carriage returns to make the syntax as clear as possible.

environment in which the lambda expression was created, so any symbol not explicitly defined in the new environment is inherited.

Next, the body of the lambda expression is evaluated with respect to the new binding environment. The symbol * is not defined in the new binding environment, but it is defined in the environment in which the lambda was first evaluated. It evaluates to a procedure that multiplies its arguments together. The symbol x is evaluated, yielding the value 5, since that's the result of looking up the symbol x in the binding environment.

Finally, the evaluator applies the multiplication procedure to the numbers 5 and 5, returning 25. The value of the entire form is 25.

Another special form is the if special form:

```
(if
    (< a b)
    b
    a
)
```

This is an expression that returns the maximum of a and b. The if special form starts by evaluating the second element of the list, called the *test*. In this case, the test is the expression (< a b). The symbol < evaluates to a procedure that compares its arguments. It returns the symbol #t if the first is less than the second, #f otherwise. The symbol #t is interpreted as "true," the symbol #f as "false."

The third and fourth elements of the if special form are called the *true-expression* and the *false-expression*. If the test returns #f, then the value of the if expression is the result of evaluating the false-expression. Otherwise, the value of the if expression is the result of evaluating the true-expression.

Only the true-expression or the false-expression is evaluated, not both. That's why if is a special form rather than a procedure. If it were a procedure, then both the true-expression and the false-expression would be evaluated. If they have side effects, like printing a value, then both sets of side effects would happen, which would be incorrect.

Suppose a is bound to 5 and b is bound to 26. Consider the expression

```
(if (< a b) b a)
```

To evaluate this expression, the evaluator first evaluates the test: a and b evaluate to 5 and 26, respectively, and < evaluates to the less-than comparison procedure. Then the comparison procedure is called with 5 and 26, which returns #t, since 5 < 26. Because the test returned #t, the evaluator evaluates the true-expression, which is the form b. The form b evaluates to 26, making 26 the result of the program.

The `define` special form creates new entries in the binding environment. Here's an example:

```
(define max
    (lambda (a b)
        (if (a < b)
            b
            a
        )
    )
)
```

When evaluated, the `define` special form defines a new symbol called `max` in the binding environment. The value of this symbol is the result of evaluating the form that is the third element of the list. That form is

```
(lambda (a b)
    (if (a < b) b a)
)
```

This code evaluates to a procedure that takes two arguments, returning the value of the first if it is the greater one, the value of the second otherwise. The effect is to create a new function called `max` that returns the greater of its two arguments. After `max` has been defined, the expression

```
(max 5 26)
```

evaluates to 26.

Unlike Java, all the parentheses are important; you can't just add new ones wherever you want. For example, suppose you tried to evaluate

```
((max 5 26))
```

The evaluator would try to evaluate the first element of the list, (max 5 26), which evaluates to 26. Then it would try to apply 26 as a procedure. Since 26 is a number, not a procedure, an error would result.

A symbol may be rebound with the `set!` special form:

```
(set! x 10)
```

This special form rebinds x to 10 in the local binding environment. It should be used only on symbols that already have a binding, either from a `lambda` expression or from a `define`. For example,

```
(define sqr                 ; Define sqr to square its
    (lambda (x)             ; argument
        (* x x)))
```

```
(sqr 10)                    ; This results in 100
(set! sqr                   ; Define sqr to double its
   (lambda (y)              ; argument
      (+ x x)))
(sqr 10)                    ; This results in 20
```

The first time (sqr 10) is evaluated, the evaluator uses the original definition found in the define, which multiplies the argument times itself. The second time (sqr 10) is evaluated, the symbol sqr has been redefined to be the sum of the argument and itself, so it returns a different value.

12.2 Compiling Scheme into Bytecodes

In this section, we describe an implementation of a Scheme evaluator that works by compiling Scheme code into JVM bytecodes, then executing the byte-codes. We use the class Integer to represent numbers and String to represent symbols.

For procedures (the result of evaluating lambda expressions), we start with this base class:

```
class abstract Procedure
{
    Environment env;
    public abstract Object call(Object args[]);
}
```

When a lambda expression is evaluated, the evaluator creates a new subclass of Procedure. The new subclass implements the call method. The call method evaluates the body of the lambda expression and returns the result. The array args holds the arguments to the procedure.

The binding environment env is the environment in which the procedure was compiled. It is used to look up symbols. The definition of Environment is

```
class Environment
{
    private Hashtable cache = new Hashtable();
    private Environment ancestor;

    /** Create the environment given the ancestor */
    public Environment(Environment ancestor)
    {
        this.ancestor = ancestor;
    }
```

```
/** Return the value of sym */
public Object lookup(String sym) throws UnboundSymbolException
{
    Object o = cache.get(sym);
    if(o == null)
        return o;
    if(ancestor == null)
        throw new UnboundSymbolException(sym);
    return ancestor.lookup(sym);
}

/** Bind the symbol to the value */
public void bind(String symbol, Object value)
{
    cache.put(symbol, value);
}
}
```

The hash table cache maps symbols (Strings) to values (Objects). Each environment contains a pointer to the previous environment, called the *ancestor*. The lookup method looks up the symbol in the cache. If it is not found, it attempts to look it up in the ancestor. If it's not found in any environment, then an exception is thrown, indicating that the symbol is not bound.

The evaluator compiles each form into bytecodes that have the same semantics as the form. Each form evaluates to a value. The bytecodes leave the value of that form on the stack.

Numbers compile into instances of the class Integer. To compile the form

```
5
```

the compiler generates this code:

```
new java/lang/Integer                      ; Create an integer
dup
iconst_5                                   ; Push the value
invokespecial java/lang/Integer/<init>(I)V ; Construct the
                                           ; object
```

To compile a symbol, the program looks up the symbol in the current binding environment using the lookup method. The compiler keeps the current binding environment in local variable 1. To compile the form

```
x
```

the compiler generates this code

```
aconst_1                                     ; Push the environment
ldc "x"                                      ; Push the symbol
invokevirtual Environment/lookup
    (Ljava/lang/String;)Ljava/lang/Object;; Call lookup
```

The compiler generates a procedure application whenever it sees a form that is a list that is not one of the special forms like lambda or if. An example of an application is

```
(+ 2 3)
```

To compile an application, the generated code must first evaluate each form in the list. Each form in this list is either a symbol or a number. The three forms compile to three code fragments:

```
; Fragment 1: +
aconst_1                                     ; Push the envionment
ldc "+"                                      ; Push the symbol
invokevirtual Environment/lookup
    (Ljava/lang/String;)Ljava/lang/Object; ; Look up the + symbol


; Fragment 2: 2
new java/lang/Integer                        ; Create the number 2
dup
iconst_2
invokevirtual java/lang/Integer/<init>(I)V


; Fragment 3: 3
new java/lang/Integer                        ; Create the number 3
dup
iconst_3
invokevirtual java/lang/Integer/<init>(I)V
```

This code evaluates all the subforms of the procedure application. The first fragment must evaluate to a procedure. In the default Scheme environment, the + symbol is bound to a procedure that performs addition on its arguments. The default binding environment is explained in section 12.5.

To invoke the procedure, two things must be done. First the arguments must be put into an array, since the procedure accepts only a single array argument. Then the `call` method must be invoked. The resulting code is as follows:

```
;; Fragment 1 goes here


; Ensure that it is a procedure
checkcast Procedure


; There is now a procedure on the stack
; Next, build up its arguments. There are going to be two of them,
; as can be seen by looking at the length of the form
iconst_2                              ; Create a two-element
anewarray java/lang/Object            ; array of Objects


; Store the result of fragment 2 into array element 0
dup                                   ; Dup the array
iconst_0
;; Fragment 2 goes here
aastore                               ; Store the element


; The array is still on the stack, thanks to the dup
; Repeat for the second argument
dup                                   ; Dup the array
iconst_1
;; Fragment 3 goes here
aastore                               ; Store the element


; Now there are two things on the stack: the procedure and an
; array of arguments. Call the procedure
invokevirtual Procedure/call
    ([Ljava/lang/Object;)Ljava/lang/Object;
```

This code begins by evaluating the first element of the list, which should evaluate to a `Procedure`. Then it evaluates each of the other elements, storing the results in an array. Finally, it uses `invokevirtual` to invoke the `call` method on the procedure, using the array as the list of arguments. This leaves the result of the method invocation on the stack.

12.3 Compiling Lambda Expressions

Until now we've assumed the existence of various procedures in the binding environment. To create new procedures, Scheme uses the lambda expression. One such lambda expression is

```
(lambda (x) (* x x))
```

which produces the square of whatever number is fed into it.

To evaluate this expression, the compiler produces a new class. The class is a subclass of `Procedure`, and it implements `call` to evaluate the body of the lambda expression. The body of the lambda expression is the form

```
(* x x)
```

which compiles into the code

```
; Evaluate (* x x)
aconst_1                                 ; Push the environment
ldc "*"                                  ; Push the symbol
invokevirtual Environment/lookup
    (Ljava/lang/String;)Ljava/lang/Object; ; Look up the *
                                         ; symbol

checkcast Procedure                      ; Ensure * evaluates
                                         ; to a Procedure

iconst_2                                 ; Create the array for
anewarray java/lang/Object               ; the arguments

dup                                      ; Dup the array ref
iconst_0                                 ; Store into element 0
aconst_1                                 ; Look up x
ldc "x"
invokevirtual Environment/lookup
    (Ljava/lang/String;)Ljava/lang/Object;
aastore                                  ; Store x into
                                         ; array[0]
```

```
dup                                    ; Dup the array ref
iconst_1                               ; Store into element 1
aconst_1                               ; Look up x again
ldc "x"
invokevirtual Environment/lookup
    (Ljava/lang/String;)Ljava/lang/Object;
aastore                                ; Store x into array[1]

; Call the * procedure on x and x
invokevirtual Procedure/call
    ([Ljava/lang/Object;)Ljava/lang/Object;
```

This code evaluates the body of the lambda expression. It is created by using the patterns described earlier for symbol lookup and procedure calls.

To complete the procedure, a few things must be added to the body. First a new binding environment must be created to bind x to the argument. Then the new binding environment must be put into variable 1, where the code is expecting it. At the end, the result must be returned. The resulting procedure looks like this:

```
; The lambda expression doesn't specify a name, so we'll just
; call it anonymous. Subsequent lambdas will be compiled into
; anonymous2, anonymous3, etc.
.class anonymous1
.super Procedure

; Define the call method
.method public call ([Ljava/lang/Object;)Ljava/lang/Object;

; Create a new binding environment, which uses the env field as
; its ancestor
new Environment
dup
aload_0                              ; Get this.env
getfield Environment/env LEnvironment;
invokespecial Environment/<init>(LEnvironment;)V

; The new binding environment is on the stack
; Now bind x in the new environment to the first argument
dup
ldc "x"                              ; Get symbol x
```

```
aload_1                              ; Get the value of arg[0]
iconst_0
aaload
invokevirtual Environment/bind       ; Do the binding
              (Ljava/lang/String;Ljava/lang/Object;)V

astore_1                             ; Store the new binding
                                     ; environment in var 1

;; Insert the code shown for (* x x)
areturn                              ; Return the result
.end method
```

The class will also require a constructor. The constructor takes a binding environment as its parameter. The superclass constructor is called, which stores the argument into the field env. The constructor is

```
.method public <init>(LEnvironment;)V
aload_0
aload_1
invokespecial Procedure/<init>(LEnvironment;)V
return
.end method
```

The class is now complete. The Scheme evaluator loads this class, perhaps using the ByteArrayClassLoader discussed in chapter 8.

The evaluation of the lambda expression is not quite complete. A lambda expression is supposed to evaluate to a procedure. To complete the evaluation of the lambda expression, the evaluator must generate code to create an instance of the anonymous1 class and place it on the stack. It must also initialize the binding environment of that instance to the environment in which the code was compiled. The code looks like this:

```
new anonymous1              ; Create an instance
dup
aload_1                     ; Push the local environment
invokespecial anonymous1/<init>(LEnvironment;)V
```

When this code is executed, it creates an instance of the anonymous1 class and leaves it on the stack, matching the definition of a lambda expression: the value of the expression is a procedure that evaluates the body of the expression in a new binding environment.

To show how all this works together, this code applies a lambda expression to some arguments:

```
((lambda (x) (* x x)
  5)
```

This is a procedure application, much like those we discussed earlier. The first element is the lambda expression. The evaluator generates the new class anonymous1. To evaluate the whole expression, the evaluator generates and executes this code:

```
new anonymous1              ; Create the lambda object
dup                         ; with the current
                            ; environment
aload_1
invokespecial anonymous1/<init>(LEnvironment;)V

iconst_1                    ; Create the argument array
anewarray java/lang/Object

dup                         ; Dup the array
iconst_0                    ; Store the number 5 in
new java/lang/Integer       ; element 0
dup
iconst_5
invokespecial java/lang/Integer/<init>(I)V
aastore

; Now the procedure and its argument are on the stack
; Call the procedure
invokevirtual Procedure/call
   ([Ljava/lang/Object;)Ljava/lang/Object;
```

This code uses the local variable 1, which holds the binding environment. If this form is evaluated as part of some other form, then local variable 1 is initialized by the containing form. At the topmost level, there is a default binding environment.

This code causes the JVM to create an instance of the anonymous1 object, create an argument array containing the number 5, and invoke the call method of anonymous1. Going back to the definition of the anonymous1 class at the beginning of this section, you can see that this will bind x to 5 and then perform the computation (* x x), which will result in 25. This result is returned as the result of the procedure call, and the net effect of all of this code is to leave the value 25 on the stack. This is the correct answer.

12.4 Example

One interesting use of lambda expressions is to return other lambda expressions. For example, look at this program:

```
(define add
    (lambda (x)
        (lambda (y)
            (+ x y))))
```

This code creates a new procedure called add, which takes one argument named x. When add is called, it binds x to its parameter and returns a new procedure that takes another variable named y. When this procedure is called, it uses both x and y to produce the result. Some uses of add:

```
(define add2 (add 2))    ; Creates add2
(add2 3)                 ; Returns 5
(add2 1000)              ; Returns 1002
```

The procedure add2 has its own copy of the variable x, even if add is called again:

```
(define add99 (add 99))  ; Creates add99
(add99 3)                ; Returns 102
(add2 3)                 ; Still returns 5
(add99 (add2 5))         ; Returns 106
```

Notice how add2 and add99 can be used in conjunction, each with its own definition of x. The binding environments can be pictured as in Figure 12.1. In order to make this picture legible, environment ancestor pointers and empty binding environments have been omitted.

The procedure named anonymous2 computes (lambda (x) (lambda (y) (+ x y))). Its own binding environment is empty, but it contains a pointer back to the default binding environment. There are two instances of the procedure anonymous3, with two different binding environments. The ancestor of each of these binding environments is the empty binding environment for anonymous2 whose ancestor in turn is the top-level binding environment.

The symbol add points to an instance of anonymous2. When you evaluate (add 2), the call method of anonymous2 is invoked. The argument is x. The body evaluates the form (lambda (y) (+ x y)). The call method of anonymous2 begins by binding its first argument to x:

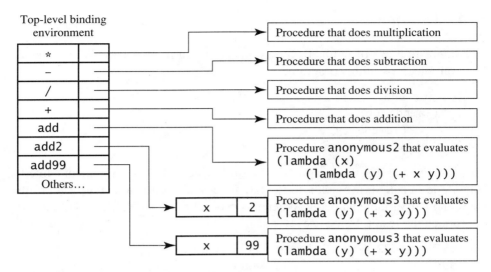

FIGURE 12.1: *Binding environment with add2 and add99*

```
; Evaluate (lambda (y) (+ x y))
.method call([Ljava/lang/Object;)Ljava/lang/Object;
new Environment
dup
aload_0                              ; Get this.env, which is
getfield Environment/env LEnvironment; ; is the default
                                     ; environment
invokespecial Environment/<init>(LEnvironment;)V

; The new binding environment is on the stack
; Now bind x in the new environment to the value of argument 0
dup                              ; Dup the binding environment
ldc "x"                          ; Get symbol x
aload_1                          ; Get the value of arg[0]
iconst_0
aaload
invokevirtual Environment/bind   ; Do the binding
             (Ljava/lang/String;Ljava/lang/Object;)V
astore_1                         ; Store the environment
                                 ; in local 1
```

Next comes the body, which evaluates the form (lambda (y) (+ x y)).
Assume that this lambda has been compiled into a class called anonymous3. The

next thing anonymous2 has to do is create an instance of anonymous3, giving it the current binding environment as its environment. Remember that the current binding environment has a binding for x and points back to the original binding environment for anonymous2.

To create anonymous3, the code is

```
new anonymous3              ; Create the lambda object
dup
aload_1                     ; With the current environment
invokespecial anonymous3/<init>(LEnvironment;)V
areturn
```

This code creates an instance of anonymous3 with the newly created binding environment. This is how add2 and add99 can both exist without interfering with one another. When add is called the first time, with value 2, an environment is created binding x to 2, and it is stored in one instance of the class anonymous3. The second time add is called, with 99, another new environment is created that binds x to 99. This new environment is stored in a different instance of anonymous3. The two objects share the same code, since they have the same class, but they have different binding environments.

12.5   Scheme Library

Unlike in Java, the symbol + in Scheme has no special meaning, Instead of translating into a special instruction such as iadd, it is treated just like any other procedure application. The definition of this procedure can be written in Java like this:

```
class plus extends Procedure
{
    /** Add all my arguments together.
     * They are expected to be Integers.
     */
    Object call(Object args[])
    {
        int sum = 0;
        for(int i = 0; i < args.length; i++)
            sum += ((Integer) args[i]).intValue();
        return new Integer(sum);
    }
}
```

This procedure unwraps each of the arguments and adds them together. At the end they are wrapped up into an `Integer` object, and that result is returned. It is capable of adding any number of arguments together.

Unlike Java, Scheme permits procedures to be called with any number of arguments of any type. This is why the `call` method takes an array of `Objects` as its argument. The form

```
(+ 1 2 3 4 5 6 7 8 9 10)
```

will result in 55.

In the default Scheme binding environment, the symbol + is bound to an instance of the class `plus`. The Scheme specification calls for a large library in the default environment. These procedures perform arithmetic, list manipulation, I/O, and other useful functions.

Although `plus` is written in Java, it meets the requirements of a Scheme procedure: it extends `Procedure` and overrides `call` to do something useful. When a Scheme evaluator begins, it creates a default binding environment that is the ancestor of all future binding environments. That way, no matter where the code executes, it is always possible to find the definition of +.

Creation of the global binding environment looks like this:

```
// The global environment has no ancestor, so the ancestor is null
Environment globalEnv = new Environment(null);
globalEnv.bind("+", new plus());
globalEnv.bind("-", new minus());
// A lot of other really handy procedures are implemented in the
// default binding environment
```

A Scheme evaluator begins with the default binding environment. When a lambda expression is evaluated, its binding environment includes the default binding environment as an ancestor. If that lambda expression causes another lambda expression to be evaluated, as in the example of the `add` symbol shown earlier, the resulting procedure will also include the default binding environment. In this way, common symbols like + are made available to all procedures. We have taken a shortcut here: `plus` and `minus`, unlike lambda expressions, do not use the environment, so we don't initialize the env field.

12.6   Optimizing Scheme

The simple compilation techniques proposed here are woefully inefficient. Fortunately, by taking a less short-sighted view of the compilation process, performance can be greatly improved.

12.6.1 Static Scoping

In the implementation described in section 12.5, each time a variable is referenced, the binding environment has to find the name of the variable in a hash table. If it fails to find it there, it must check the ancestral binding environments. This search can be expensive, since it involves computing the hash value and a `String` comparison. It is especially expensive for symbols in the default binding environment like +, which may require several hash table lookups.

A Scheme compiler can take advantage of the fact that Scheme has *static scoping*. "Static scoping" means that the binding environment is set when a lambda expression is first evaluated instead of when the lambda is applied. Static scoping can be used to replace the expensive search through hash tables with a much cheaper one, since the compiler knows where to find each symbol when the code is compiled.

Earlier we looked at this Scheme program:

```
(define add
    (lambda (x)
        (lambda (y)
            (+ x y)))
(define add2 (add 2))
(define add99 (add 99)))
```

It creates two different anonymous procedures, `anonymous2` and `anonymous3`, corresponding to the outer and inner lambda expressions. The first is the result of evaluating the outer lambda expression (lambda (x) (lambda (y) (+ x y)). It creates a binding environment that binds x, then evaluates the form (lambda (y) (+ x y)). The binding environment points back to the default binding environment for symbols other than x.

The second anonymous procedure is produced by evaluating the first. It creates a binding environment that binds y, then evaluates the form (+ x y). The ancestor of that binding environment is the one in which the inner lambda expression was evaluated.

Consider the evaluation of the form (add2 3). A new binding environment is created that binds y to 3. The binding environments look like Figure 12.2. In this diagram the relevant binding environments ancestors are shown. Ancestor pointers are represented by curved lines. The current computation is the box labeled "Computing (+ x y)." The environment binds y to 3, and the curved line shows the environment's ancestor pointer. The ancestor of that is the environment of `anonymous2`, and the ancestor of that is the default binding environment.

The same situation would hold if `add99` were invoked. The new environment would look identical, except the value of x would be different. In both cases, y is

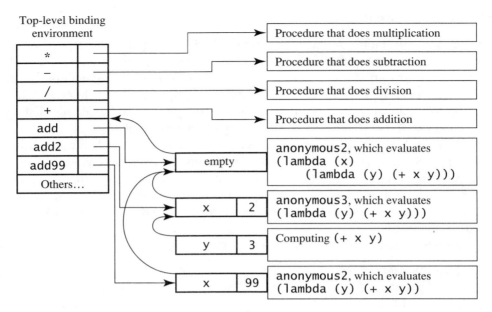

FIGURE 12.2: *While evaluating (add2 3)*

the first element in the current environment. You would have to look back one environment for x, three for +. The symbols x and y are each in the first position, and + is in the fourth position.

This information can be used to create a better kind of binding environment, which looks up bindings by position rather than by name. The environment is implemented like this:

```
public class Environment
{
    /** A list of previous binding environments. The first element
     * is always this. The second is always the immediate ancestor,
     * and so on. The last element is the default binding
     * environment.
     */
    public Environment ancestors[];

    /** The values of the symbols, indexed by position */
    public Object value[];
```

```
/** Values are looked up by position and by environment */
public Object lookup(int position, int ancestor)
{
    return ancestors[ancestor].value[position];
}
}
```

The new definition of lookup uses a list of ancestors instead of a single ancestor pointer. This means that instead of having to recursively call lookup on previous ancestors, it can instead jump directly to the correct ancestor. Also, instead of having to look up the position in a hash table using the name of the symbol, it uses only the position of that symbol in the list. This is a simple array lookup, which is much faster than a hash table lookup.

The new definition of Environment requires a change in the way variables are accessed and the way they are bound. The definition of call in anonymous3 using this definition of Environment looks like this:

```
.method call([Ljava/lang/Object;)Ljava/lang/Object
.var 0 is this Lanonymous3;
.var 1 is args Ljava/lang/Object; from initialize to code
.var 1 is bindings LEnvironment; from code to end

initialize:
; Create a new binding environment
new Environment
dup
aload_0                        ; Get this.env
getfield Environment/env LEnvironment;
invokespecial Environment/<init>(LEnvironment;)V

; args contains the bindings for the current
; environment. Set the value array of the environment to
; the argument array
dup                            ; Dup the array ref
aload_1                        ; Store args in value
putfield Environment/value [Ljava/lang/Object;
astore_1                       ; Location 1 holds the
                               ; new environment
```

```
; Now comes evaluation of the body. Instead of loading variables
; by name, they are loaded by position. From the diagram, these
; positions are
; Symbol     Position        # of ancestors back
; y            0                  0
; x            0                  1
; +            3                  3

; Get +
aload_1                             ; Get the environment
iconst_3                            ; Push position (3)
iconst_3                            ; Push ancestor (3)
invokevirtual Environment/lookup(II)Ljava/lang/Object;

iconst_2                            ; Create the arguments to +
anewarray java/lang/Object         ; Call this array "args"
; Get x and store it args[0]
dup                                 ; Dup the array
iconst_0                            ; Push position 0
aload_1                             ; Get the environment
iconst_0                            ; Push position (0)
iconst_1                            ; Push ancestor (1)
invokevirtual Environment/lookup(II)Ljava/lang/Object;
aastore                             ; Store x in args[0]

; Get y and store it in args[1]
dup                                 ; Dup the array
iconst_1                            ; Push position 1
aload_1                             ; Get the environment
iconst_0                            ; Push position (0)
iconst_0                            ; Push ancestor (0)
invokevirtual Environment/lookup(II)Ljava/lang/Object;
aastore                             ; Store y in args[1]

; Now invoke + on x and y and return the result
invokevirtual Procedure/call
   ([Ljava/lang/Object;)Ljava/lang/Object
end:
areturn
```

This way of doing things has turned a hash table lookup into an array reference, which is much faster.

12.6.2 Using Local Variables

The compiled code can be sped up even further by passing variables the way Java does: as local variables. That way, they never need to be put into the environment at all. This saves both the array lookup when the variables are evaluated and the need to create an array for the arguments to the procedure calls.

This is a little more complicated that it sounds, for several reasons. First, it means that each `call` statement is different. In the previous examples, each instruction to invoke `call` was identical. The arguments are passed as an array of `Object`s. Second, it makes defining procedures like + more difficult. As described earlier, Scheme allows methods to take an arbitrary number of arguments, which means that the same definition of + can be used for both (+ 2 3) and (+ 1 2 3 4 5 6). In the Java virtual machine, the number of arguments passed must be the same as the number of parameters the method expects to receive.

These problems can be solved by redefining `Procedure`:

```
class Procedure
{
    public Object call()
        { return call(new Object[0]); }
    public Object call(Object a)
        { return call(new Object[1] { a }); }
    public Object call(Object a, Object b)
        { return call(new Object[2] { a, b }); }
    public Object call(Object a, Object b, Object c)
        { return call(new Object[3] { a, b, c }); }
    public Object call(Object[] args)
    {
        throw new RuntimeException("Wrong number of arguments");
    }
}
```

When a lambda expression is evaluated, it produces a new class that subclasses `Procedure` and overrides the `call` method with the appropriate number of arguments. A procedure like +, which takes an arbitrary number of arguments, overrides the last definition of `call`, which takes an array of arguments, just as before.

In the body of a procedure that takes three or fewer arguments, when a symbol is evaluated that is an argument to the current procedure, the procedure uses the `aload` instruction to push the argument instead of making a call to `lookup`. The binding environment is used for all other lookups. A new binding environment has to be created only if there is a lambda expression anywhere within the body. This can be determined by examining the code.

For example, let's examine the code for this expression:

```
(lambda (x) (* x x))
```

This code causes a new procedure to be compiled; let's call it anonymous4. The definition of this procedure is

```
.class anonymous4
.super Procedure
; Override the definition of call which takes 1 argument
.method call(Ljava/lang/Object;)Ljava/lang/Object;

; There is no need to create a new environment, since there
; are no lambdas in the body.

; Compute and return the value of (* x x). First evaluate *, x,
; and x

aload_0                                    ; Evaluation of * involves
getfield anonymous4/env LEnvironment;; a lookup call
ldc "*"
invokevirtual Environment/lookup
    (Ljava/lang/String;)Ljava/lang/Object;
checkcast Procedure                        ; Make sure it's a
                                           ; Procedure

aload_1                                     ; Push x. It is stored in
                                           ; the argument (variable 1)

aload_1                                     ; Push x again

; Call * with 2 arguments
invokevirtual Procedure/call
    (Ljava/lang/Object;Ljava/lang/Object;)Ljava/lang/Object;

areturn
.end method
```

This procedure calls the multiplication procedure with two arguments. The definition of the multiplication procedure must be prepared to handle any number of arguments.

Procedures that take more than three arguments override the last definition of call, as if it took an arbitrary number of parameters. These procedures have to pay the higher price of getting their arguments using lookup instead of from local variables. Since procedures that take more than three arguments are uncommon, this is a price which will not be paid very often.

12.6.3 Inlining

Another nice effect of static scoping is that not only will you find the variables in the same locations each time, you will also find the same values, as long as they have not been redefined.

Suppose this is your program:

```
(define pi 3.14)
(define area
    (lambda (r)
        (* pi (square r))))
```

It defines area as a method that computes the area of a circle with radius r. It would be nice to be able to inline the value of pi and square so that area really executes

```
(* 3.14 (* r r))
```

This code substitutes 3.14 for pi and expands the call to square. This is more efficient, since it substitutes a constant value for a symbol lookup, and it eliminates the overhead of the call to square. However, it can cause problems. Suppose somebody came along and decided that the value of pi was insufficiently precise:

```
(set! pi 3.14159)
```

This code redefines pi. If the value of pi were inlined into area, then the definition of area would now be incorrect. The easiest way to handle the problem is to force the user to explicitly recompile the program whenever set! is used.

12.6.4 Tail Recursion

Inlining is not always possible. For example, consider a definition like this:

```
(define factorial (lambda (x value-so-far)
    (if (< x 1)
        value-so-far
        (factorial (- x 1) (* x value-so-far)))
    ))
```

This is a recursive definition of `factorial`. If the compiler tried to inline `factorial`, it would find that the expanded definition contained another use of `factorial`. The compiler could go on forever like that.

There is a way to avoid the overhead of having to call `factorial` over and over again. The compiler can notice that the last thing the definition does is to call `factorial` again. The compiler can replace the recursive call with a loop. Compiled into bytecodes, this becomes

```
;; The code to handle the binding of x goes here
loop:
    ;; Code to evaluate (< x 1) not shown
    ifeq success         ; Loop until x < 1

    ; If the test fails:

    ;; Code to compute (* x value-so-far) and bind it to value-
    ;; so-far not shown
    ;; Code to compute (- x 1) and bind it to x not shown
    goto loop            ; Loop again
success:
    ;; Code to get the value of value-so-far from the environment
    ;; not shown
    areturn
```

This code has the same effect, but it doesn't require a new stack frame to be created for each multiplication. It thus executes much more quickly.

12.6.5 Using Type Information

Although Scheme is a language with very weak typing, it is still sometimes possible to prove things about the type of an expression during compilation. For example, the form

```
5
```

will certainly result in an integer. Under some circumstances, it may be possible to avoid the effort of wrapping the number in an `Integer` wrapper and use it directly as a JVM `int` value.

A compiler can recognize that the default binding of the + symbol means adding numbers together. Consider this form:

```
(+ 2 3)
```

In earlier discussions, this form produced rather ungainly code that looked up the symbol +, created two new `Integer` objects, stored them in an array, and called the procedure. The procedure unwrapped the objects, then created yet another object to hold the result.

A sufficiently intelligent optimizing compiler that practices inlining can recognize that only integer values are used in this form and generate this code instead:

```
iconst_2        ; Push 2
iconst_3        ; Push 3
iadd
```

An even better optimizing compiler might recognize that this entire form will evaluate to 5 and optimize the entire thing to

```
iconst_5
```

However, this simple-sounding optimization is not so simple to implement. One complication is in method arguments. In previous examples we used the class `Object` to represent every argument. Doing this depended on the fact that numbers were wrapped up in `Integer` objects. If this is no longer true, how are method arguments defined?

Another complication occurs with Scheme lists, which are heterogeneous. That is, a list may contain entities of any type. A JVM array can't hold both `int`s and `Object`s.

The simplest answer is that the optimization shown is used only in limited circumstances. Whenever an `int` value is passed to a method that is expecting any object, it must be wrapped up in an `Integer` object.

More sophisticated optimizers can recognize when a method applies only to `int` values. For example, consider this expression:

```
(lambda (x) (* x x))
```

The optimizer can infer that x must be a number because the * operation is applied. This means that instead of defining the `call` method to take two `Object`s, it can instead take two `int`s.

Further complicating matters is the fact that in real Scheme, there are other types of numbers besides integers. The full Scheme specification calls for floating-point numbers, fractions, and arbitrary-length whole numbers. There exist other solutions that an optimizer can use to handle these types as well, using overloaded method definitions, but they are not discussed here.

## CHAPTER 13

Implementing Prolog

THE name Prolog stands for "predicate logic." The language is designed to look a lot like logic, with axioms and rules. It may look a little odd if you've never seen it before, but it's a complete language, just like Java. In theory, any program written in Java can be reproduced in Prolog.

Prolog is a rule-based language. You define your rules, then you ask a question. The Prolog system uses the rules to find out the answers to your questions.

Prolog is often used in natural language processing, planning, and computer vision applications. Languages like Prolog are becoming increasingly popular in the field of knowledge representation and particularly for agent-oriented programming.

13.1   Introduction to Prolog

Here is an example of a Prolog program:

```
inside(baltimore, maryland).
inside(maryland, united_states).
inside(california, united_states).
inside(san_francisco, california).
```

These are *rules* that tell Prolog that Maryland is inside the United States, that Baltimore is inside Maryland, and so on.

Some terminology: the word before the parentheses is called the *predicate,* and the list inside the parentheses is called the *arguments.* In the first rule, the word `inside` is the predicate, and `baltimore` and `maryland` are the arguments. Order is significant: `inside(baltimore, maryland)` means that Baltimore is inside Maryland, but `inside(maryland, baltimore)` means that Maryland is inside Baltimore. Since the latter fact would not be true in the real world, it is not included in the program.

13.1.1 Asking Questions

You can use these rules to ask a number of questions. For example, you can ask:

```
?- inside(baltimore, maryland).
```

The ?- is the prompt from the Prolog system when you ask a question. The Prolog system will respond

```
Yes
```

You can also use placeholders called *variables,* which are written beginning with an upper-case letter. Words written beginning with lower-case letters are called *constants.* If a position inside a predicate is a variable, then it is called *free;* if it is a constant, then it is called *bound.* For example,

```
?- inside(X, united_states).
```

This query asks for the `inside` predicate with the first position free and the second position bound. Prolog responds:

```
Yes, X=maryland
Yes, X=california
```

Prolog looks through its program, looking for any rules that match the question. For positions that are free, Prolog substitutes the corresponding constant in the rule for the variable in the question. This process is called *unification.*

After unification, if the rule and the question match exactly, then Prolog responds that it has found an answer to the question. It also prints out a list of substitutions that had to be made to make the rule and the question match.

Prolog found two different answers to this question, Maryland and California. It tried to match against all four rules it knows. For the first rule,

```
inside(baltimore, maryland).
```

Prolog was able to match X with `baltimore`, but the substituted question `inside(baltimore, united_states)` did not match the rule `inside(baltimore, maryland)`. Prolog gave up on this rule and tried again. This is called *backtracking.*

Prolog backtracked to the next rule:

```
inside(maryland, united_states).
```

After substituting `maryland` for X, Prolog found that the rule exactly matches the question. This is a valid answer to the question, so Prolog printed `Yes`, followed by the substitution X=maryland, which was necessary to make the question succeed.

Prolog then backtracked again to see if there were any more answers. It did not find an answer with the rule `inside(san_francisco, california)`, but it found another answer with `inside(california, united_states)`. After that, there were no more rules to check, so Prolog stopped.

13.1.2 Binding Patterns

You may ask your question with any combination of variables and constants. The pattern of bound and unbound arguments is called the *binding pattern*. Using the same program, you could also ask,

```
?- inside(san_francisco, X).
```

Prolog responds,

```
Yes, x = california
```

You could even ask with all variables in both positions:

```
?- inside(X, Y).
```

Prolog responds,

```
Yes, X=maryland, Y=united_states
Yes, X=baltimore, Y=maryland
Yes, X=california, Y=united_states
Yes, X=san_francisco, Y=california
```

13.1.3 Implications

If you ask,

```
?- inside(baltimore, united_states).
```

Prolog responds,

```
No
```

Clearly, something a bit smarter is required here, since Baltimore is certainly within the United States. Prolog should be able to figure this out somehow, since Baltimore is inside Maryland and Maryland is within the United States. It would be good to have a rule that states this.

This kind of rule is called an *implication*. The following rules specify `within`, an implication that expresses the definition in the previous paragraph:

```
within(X, Y) :- inside(X, Y).
within(X, Y) :- inside(X, Z), within(Z, Y).
```

The first rule says that X is within Y if X is inside Y. The second rule says X is within Y if there is some Z such that Z is found inside X and Z is within Y.

The part before the `:-` is called the *head* of the rule; the part after the `:-` is called the *body*. Prolog matches the query with the head of the rule. If it matches, then it makes the same variable substitutions in the body as in the head. Then it treats the body as a series of questions. If it can answer those questions, then it has found an answer to the original question.

Let's try these rules out on

```
?- within(baltimore, united_states).
```

Prolog looks up its rules for `within`. It tries the first rule, substituting `baltimore` for X and `united_states` for Y. This succeeds so far, so Prolog tries to fulfill the body of the rule. It substitutes for X and Y, and then Prolog asks,

```
?- inside(baltimore, united_states).
```

As shown earlier, there is no rule that lets Prolog conclude that `baltimore` is inside the `united_states`. So this rule fails.

Prolog backtracks and tries the other rule for `within`. Again, X unifies with `baltimore` and Y unifies with `united_states`. Since this matches the head of the rule, Prolog substitutes these bindings into the body. There is no binding yet for Z.

Now Prolog has to see if it can satisfy the body of the rule. So Prolog asks itself,

```
?- inside(baltimore, Z).
```

Using the rules for `inside`, it discovers that this is true if Z is `maryland`. Then it goes to the second part of the rule, `within(Z, Y)`.

Now Prolog knows that Z is `maryland` and Y is `united_states`, so it sets out to see if `within(maryland, united_states)` is true. It goes back to the first rule for `within` and asks itself,

```
inside(maryland, united_states).
```

Prolog finds that this is true, which means that `within(maryland, united_states)` is also true, which means that `within(baltimore, united_states)` is true as well. So Prolog prints

```
Yes
```

Prolog then backtracks again, trying to find additional ways to prove that Baltimore is within the United States. It finds no more answers.

13.1.4   Binding Patterns and Implications

You can use `within` using variables as well as constants. If you ask,

```
within(san_francisco, X).
```

Prolog reports,

```
Yes, X=california
Yes, X=united_states
```

13.1.5 Facts as Rules

The rule

```
inside(baltimore, maryland).
```

also has a head and a body. The head is `inside(baltimore, maryland)` and the body is empty. An empty body always succeeds. This fact is equivalent to

```
inside(baltimore, maryland) :- true.
```

where `true` is a predicate that always succeeds. A rule that always succeeds is called a *fact*. The Prolog language does not make any distinction between facts and other rules, except for the syntactic sugar that lets you omit `:- true` from facts. This does not change the language; it only makes it a little easier to read and write.

Some facts may have variables in the head. For example, the fact

```
inside(good, X).
```

means that there is some good in everybody.

13.1.6 More About Unification

When the same variable is used multiple times, two terms unify only when there is a consistent substitution. That is, you must be able to use the same value each time the variable is found.

```
foo(b, X, b)
foo(Y, a, Y)
```

These unify when `X=a` and `Y=b`.

By contrast, this unification cannot succeed:

```
foo(b, X, c)
foo(Y, a, Y)
```

There is no consistent way to substitute for `Y` in the second term, since in one case it must match `b` and in the other it must match `c`.

Two variables always unify with each other. This means that whenever you find a substitution for one, you must substitute it exactly with the other. For example:

```
bar(X, a)
bar(Y, Y)
```

To unify these terms, variables X and Y must unify, since they appear in corresponding places. Y and a also unify, for the same reason. Since X and Y are unified and Y and a are unified, X and a must also unify. This means that to unify these two expressions, you must substitute a for X and also substitute a for Y.

Another thing about unification: within a single expression, variable names are meaningful only to the point where they match each other. Between expressions, you can replace one variable name with another, as long as you do it consistently. Suppose you want to unify

```
baz(X, Y)
baz(Z, X)
```

These terms unify when the first X unifies with Z and the second X unifies with Y. The two Xs are different, since they appear in different expressions. For this reason, many Prolog implementations internally replace all variable names with meaningless ones beginning with underscores, like this:

```
baz(_0, _1)
baz(_2, _3)
```

This is equivalent to the two expressions shown earlier for baz. Within an expression, the same variable name must be used in each case. So the two expressions shown earlier for foo are equivalent to

```
foo(b, _4, c)
foo(_5, a, _5)
```

The point is that variable names are meaningless except within a single expression. They may be substituted for other variable names whenever you find it convenient.

13.2   Implementation Basics

To implement Prolog we need to start with some basic items. First, all constants are represented by Strings. Variables are represented by instances of the class Var. Each variable has a name and a binding:

```
public class Var
{
    String name;
    Object binding;
}
```

The value of binding is the value the variable is bound to. It may be a constant or another variable. If the binding field is set to null, then the variable is considered unbound.

Next, we need something to represent terms like `inside(baltimore, mary-land)`. This kind of term is called a *structure*. Structures are implemented as instances of the class `Structure`:

```
public class Structure
{
    public Object predicate;
    public Object arg[];
}
```

13.3 Unification

The key to a Prolog implementation is unification. Two things unify if there is a substitution of the variables so that they are equal. For example, consider the question

```
?- inside(baltimore, X).
```

What Prolog does is to look at all its rules and see whether there is a way to substitute for X such that X is identical to one of its rules. Prolog was given this rule:

```
inside(baltimore, maryland).
```

It's easy to see that if X is `maryland`, then the two become identical. Thus Prolog reports,

```
Yes, X=maryland
```

13.3.1 Unification Algorithm

The code to handle unification is kept in a class called `Prolog`. This method implements unification:

```
public static boolean unify(Object x, Object y)
{
    x = deref(x);
    y = deref(y);

    if(x.equals(y))
        return true;
    if(x instanceof Var) {
        setBinding((Var) x, y);
        return true;
    }
```

```
    if(y instanceof Var) {
        setBinding((Var) y, x);
        return true;
    }


    return false;
}
```

The unification algorithm begins by *dereferencing* x and y. Dereferencing is the process of substituting a variable's binding for the variable itself. This ensures that the variable is used consistently in all cases.

Dereferencing is performed by the method deref, which checks to see whether its argument is a bound variable; if so, it returns the current binding of that variable. The variable may be bound to another variable, so deref repeats the procedure until the variable is completely dereferenced. Constants and unbound variables dereference to themselves. Here is the code for deref:

```
public static Object deref(Object x)
{
    while(x instanceof Var && ((Var) x).binding != null)
        x = ((Var) x).binding;
    return x;
}
```

After dereferencing both values, unify checks to see whether they are equal. If they are equal, then they unify without doing any additional work and unify returns true.

If x is a variable, then it can be unified with y by setting the binding of x to y; the reverse is true for y. The binding is done using setBinding, which is discussed in the next section. Then unify returns true.

If x and y are not equal and neither x nor y is a variable, then they do not unify. In that case, unify returns false.

13.3.2 Managing Bindings

The method setBinding sets the binding of a variable to a value. The code for setBinding is

```
public static void setBinding(Var var, Object val)
{
    var.binding = val;
    trail.push(var);
}
```

Setting var's `binding` field to `val` binds var to val.

This Prolog implementation makes use of a stack called the `trail` to keep track of variable bindings. Whenever Prolog binds a variable to a value, it pushes the variable onto the trail. The trail is represented using the `Stack` class in `java.util`:

```
static Stack trail = new Stack();
```

During backtracking, any variables bound during the code being backtracked over must become unbound. This allows later code to establish new bindings for these variables. This is done by a method called `undoBindings`:

```
static void undoBindings(Object token)
{
    Object var;
    while((var = trail.pop()) != token)
        if(var instanceof Var)
            ((Var) v).binding = null;
}
```

The method `undoBindings` searches for a *token* that marks some point in the stack. It unbinds all variables until it finds the token.

The token is used within the code implementing a rule. The code pushes a new token onto the stack when it begins code that it will backtrack over. All bindings on the stack below the token should not be touched; all bindings above the token are unbound. To obtain a token and push it onto the stack, the rule uses `markTrail`:

```
static Object markTrail()
{
    Object token = new Object();
    trail.push(token);
    return token;
}
```

The caller must remember the token for later use with `undoBindings`.

`undoBindings` repeatedly pops the stack looking for the token. Until it finds it, it unbinds all the Vars it finds on the stack by setting its binding to `null`.

13.4 Rules as Programs

With the preliminaries out of the way, we can turn to compiling Prolog rules into bytecodes. We will turn each predicate into a class. The class has a method which, when you call it, has the semantics of the rules for the predicate.

13.4.1 `inside`

Think of `inside` as a method that takes two arguments, X and Y. It returns `true` when the arguments unify with one of the four definitions of `inside` shown in section 13. If either X or Y is a variable, then it is bound to a value such that one of the facts holds true. The definition of `inside`, written in pseudo-Java, is

```
boolean inside(Object X, Object Y)
{
    if(unify(X, "baltimore") && unify(Y, "maryland"))
        yield true;
    if(unify(X, "maryland") && unify(Y, "united_states"))
        yield true;
    if(unify(X, "california") && unify(Y, "united_states"))
        yield true;
    if(unify(X, "san_francisco") && unify(Y, "california"))
        yield true;
    yield false;
}
```

Instead of returning true or false, the code instead performs a `yield`. The pseudo-instruction `yield` is like `return`, except that it remembers where it was when it returned. Each time you call `inside`, it picks up after the previous `yield`. Section 13.5 discusses how to implement `yield` using JVM instructions.

Consider the query

```
?- inside(X, united_states).
```

It can be implemented using the `inside` method:

```
Var X = new Var();
while(inside(X, "united_states"))
    System.out.println("X = " + deref(X));
```

When run, this code prints

```
X = maryland
X = california
```

The `inside` method is silent about its failures and yields `true` only on its successes until no more successes are possible. It fails to match `inside(baltimore, maryland)`, but it finds a way to match `inside(maryland, united_states)`, so it yields `true` with X set to `maryland`. The other two facts are checked similarly. After it has found that X = `california` is a successful substitution, `inside` does not find any more ways to unify the request with the rules it knows. Therefore, it yields `false`, which will terminate the loop.

It is necessary to call `deref` on X since we are interested in what X is bound to, not the variable X itself. Thus if X is bound to the string `maryland`, `deref(X)` will be `maryland`. In more complicated rules it is common to have one variable bound to another, and sometimes `deref` has to follow many links to get to the final value.

13.4.2 `within`

There are two different definitions for `within`:

```
within(X, Y) :- inside(X, Y).
within(X, Y) :- inside(X, Z), within(Z, Y).
```

One way to look at `within` is as a function that takes two arguments, X and Y, and returns `true` if it was able to find bindings that satisfy either rule. This is an outline of these rules written in a pseudo-Java style:

```
boolean within(X, Y)
{
    while(inside(X, Y))
        yield true;
    while(inside(X, Z))
        while(within(Z, Y))
            yield true;
    yield false;
}
```

The `yield` instruction is used here to mean that the program signals that it has found a binding but that there may be more. The method returns its value, but when you call `within` again it picks up right after the most recent `yield`. This is much like the `yield` used in Sather iterators, as discussed in section 11.3.1.

13.4.3 `yield` and Backtracking

Defining `yield` this way implements backtracking. To compile `within(X, Y)`, the program first tries all the ways it can to find `inside(X, Y)`, which is the first definition of `within`. When that fails, it starts looking at the second definition of `within`, which first tries to find a Z such that `inside(Z, Y)` is true. Once it has found a value for Z, it tries to see if `within(Z, Y)` is true.

The question

```
?- within(X, united_states).
```

can be answered by this method:

```
test()
{
    Var X = new Var();
    while(within(X, "united_states"))
         System.out.println("X = " + deref(X));
}
```

This code calls `within` to find out what's inside the United States.

First, `within` tries to find out what is immediately inside `united_states` by calling `inside(X, "united_states")`. The first thing `inside` finds is `maryland`, so it binds `X` to `maryland`.

The method `inside` yields `true` to `within`, which yields `true`. Although the method has `yielded`, it is still on the call stack, since it has not yet reached the end of the code. `X` is still bound to `maryland`. The call stack and variable bindings look like this:

Bindings

X	maryland
Y	united_states

Call stack

inside(X, "united_states")
within(X, "united_states")
➘ test

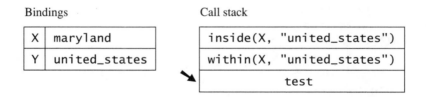

The symbol ➘ indicates that the code is currently executing the method `test`, even though there are still two other calls on the stack. The program prints

```
X = maryland
```

Now `test` loops back and calls `within` again. The program picks up where it left off right after the `yield` in `within`. The variable `X` is made unbound so that the code can find new bindings for `X`. (The pseudocode shown does not show how variables become unbound. This will be discussed in greater detail in section 13.5.)

Next `within` loops back to call `inside` again, which continues after its first yield. The second test within `inside` fails, but the third test successfully binds `X` to `california`. Now `inside` and `within` yield again, and `test` prints

```
X = california
```

Going back into `within`, the program finds that `inside` has no more bindings for X, so it returns control to `within`. The binding of X to `california` is unbound. The Java stack now looks like this:

Bindings   Call stack

X	unbound
Y	united_states

within(X, "united_states")
test

Now `within` has another rule to try: `inside(X, Z), within(Z, Y)`. First `within` calls `inside(X, Z)`. Z is a new variable, created just for the current code.

The method `inside` finds the first answer to this by binding X to `baltimore` and Z to `maryland`, and it yields `true`. The method `within` takes this binding of Z and recursively asks `within(Z, Y)`. The call stack now looks like this:

Bindings   Call stack

X	baltimore
Y	united_states
Z	maryland

within(Z, Y)
within(X, "united_states")
test

The new `within` asks itself by its first rule if `inside(maryland, united_states)` is true. This is true, so `inside` yields `true` to the second call of `within`, which yields `true` to the first call of `within`, which yields `true` to the code shown. Now there is another binding for X, and the program prints

    X = baltimore

Now the program returns to its original call of `within`, which loops back to see if it can prove `within(maryland, united_states)` again. It discovers that it cannot, and eventually it prints

    X = san_francisco

Finally, the program is out of paths to follow, and it stops.

13.5   Implementing Rules

Now that we have some idea of how within should work, we discuss a way to
implement it in JVM code. Because the JVM does not have a yield operation, we
have to implement one ourselves. This is a simplified form of the technique used
to compile Sather iterators in section 11.3.1.

The key to implementing yield is to create an object for each method. This
object remembers the state of processing when the method was last called. The
object has a single method, call, which contains the code for the method. Every
time the code calls for a yield, the call method does a return. Before it
returns, it sets a variable called state$, which indicates where in the body of
the method it left off. The call method begins with a tableswitch, which is used
to jump to the location right after the last return, as indicated by the state$ field.

The object must remember not only the last instruction the program was in
but also what all of the variable bindings were. For this reason, everything that
appeared in the pseudocode as a local variable is made a field of the class.

13.5.1   Implementing within

With these ideas in mind, here's how to implement within in Oolong:

```
.class within
.field state$ I              ; Remembers the state
.field inside_1 Linside;    ; The inside for the first loop
.field inside_2 Linside;    ; The inside for the second loop
.field within_2 Lwithin;    ; The within used in the second loop
.field Z LVar;               ; The variable Z
.field stackTag Ljava/lang/Object;     ; The token
```

This code declares the fields that will be needed to implement within. The variable state$ keeps track of the current location being executed within the code.

The fields inside_1, inside_2, and within_2 are used to implement the subgoals used in the rules. The fields are used to implement backtracking. While evaluating the first rule for within, the code creates an instance of inside and keeps
it in inside_1. For the second rule, inside_2 and within_2 are used.

When within calls within recursively, each instance of within keeps its own
copy of the within_2 field. This keeps the system from becoming confused while
evaluating recursive rules.

The field Z is also used in evaluating the second rule. It holds the intermediate
results of finding Z.

The field `stackTag` holds the token used for backtracking. Before each rule, the stack undoes all the bindings on the trail from the previous rule down to the current `stackTag`. Then it pushes a new token and remembers it in the `stackTag`.

This is the beginning of the `call` method:

```
.method call(Ljava/lang/Object;Ljava/lang/Object;)Z
.var 0 is this Lwithin;
.var 1 is X Ljava/lang/Object;
.var 2 is Y Ljava/lang/Object;
aload_0
getfield within/state$ I      ; Get the state from this
tableswitch 0                 ; Jump to the appropriate state:
    state0                    ; The beginning
    state1                    ; After the first yield
    state2                    ; After the second yield
    default: fail             ; All other cases
```

The first thing the method does is to resume from its last location by checking the `state$` field. There are four possible states: `state0` (the initial state), `state1` (right after the first `yield`), `state2` (right after the second `yield`), and `fail`, the state that indicates that there are no more matches. The system always begins with `state$` set to 0, so the code always begins at the next line (`state0`).

```
    rule1:
    state0:
        aload_0                 ; Undo bindings from prior calls
        getfield within/stackTag Ljava/lang/Object;
        invokestatic Prolog/undoBindings (Ljava/lang/Object;)V

        aload_0                 ; Mark the trail
        invokestatic Prolog/marktrail ()Ljava/lang/Object;
        putfield stackTag Ljava/lang/Object;

        aload_0                 ; Create a new inside object
        new inside              ; Store it in inside_1
        dup
        invokespecial inside/<init>()V
        putfield within/inside_1 Linside;

    loop0:                      ; Loop while inside yields true
```

```
    aload_0                  ; Call inside(X, Y)
    getfield within/inside_1 Linside;
    aload_1
    aload_2
    invokevirtual inside/call
        (Ljava/lang/Object;Ljava/lang/Object;)Z

    ifeq rule2               ; Go to the next rule
                             ; if inside returns false

    aload_0                  ; Remember that the new state is 1
    iconst_1
    putfield within/state$ I

    iconst_1                 ; Yield true
    ireturn
state1:                      ; Pick up here when called again
    goto loop0               ; See whether there are any more
                             ; bindings for inside(X, Y)
```

The above code implements the pseudocode

```
while(inside(X, Y))
    yield true;
```

First, the code undoes any bindings from previous calls by calling undoBindings. Initially the stackTag is null, so no changes are made to the trail. Then the code pushes a new tag onto the trail with markTrail, and stores the resulting tag in stackTag.

Next, the code creates an instance of inside and stores it in inside_1. This allows the code to pick up using the same inside after the yield, which ensures that inside backtracks correctly. The method inside has its own state and may yield true more than once with different bindings. The code must ensure that all bindings are retrieved before going on to the second rule.

After initializing inside_1, the code goes into its while loop, beginning at loop0 and ending at the goto. On each pass through the loop, the field inside_1 is fetched and its call method invoked. The arguments are the X and Y passed to within.

When inside fails, within moves to the code at rule2, which implements the second rule. If inside succeeds, then within must yield true. It performs the `yield` by returning the constant 1. Before it can do that, it must set up `state$` so that it picks up right after the `return` next time this method is called. This is done by storing 1 in `state$`.

The label `state1` occurs right after the `ireturn`. This causes the system to loop back to find any more results from `inside`.

13.5.2 Implementing Conjunctions

Here is the code for `rule2`:

```
rule2:
    aload_0             ; Undo bindings down to the stack tag.
    getfield within/stackTag Ljava/lang/Object;
    invokestatic Prolog/undoBindings(Ljava/lang/Object;)V

    aload_0             ; Mark the trail
    invokestatic Prolog/markTrail()Ljava/lang/Object;
    putfield stackTag Ljava/lang/Object;

    aload_0             ; Create a new inside object
    new inside          ; Store it in inside_2
    dup
    invokespecial inside/<init>()V
    putfield within/inside_2 Linside;

    aload_0             ; Create a new variable for Z
    new Var             ; Store it in Z
    dup
    invokespecial Var/<init>()V
    putfield within/Z LVar;

loop2:                  ; While (inside(X, Z))
    aload_0
    getfield within/inside_2 Linside;
    aload_1             ; Call inside(X, z)
    aload_0
    getfield within/Z LVar;
```

```
        invokevirtual inside/call
           (Ljava/lang/Object;Ljava/lang/Object;)Z
        ifeq endloop2      ; Terminate the outer loop when
                           ; inside fails

        aload_0            ; Create a new within object
        new within         ; Store it in within_2
        dup
        invokespecial within/<init>()V
        putfield within/within_2 Lwithin;

loop3:                     ; While(inside(Z, Y))
        aload_0
        getfield within/within_2 Linside;
        aload_1            ; Call inside(Z,Y)
        aload_0
        getfield within/Z LVar;
        invokevirtual within/call
           (Ljava/lang/Object;Ljava/lang/Object;)Z
        ifeq endloop3      ; Terminate the inner loop if
                           ; within fails

        aload_0            ; Remember that the new state is 2
        iconst_2
        putfield within/state$ I

        iconst_1           ; Yield true
        ireturn
state2:                    ; Go here when
        goto loop3
endloop3:
        goto loop2
endloop2:
```

This code is somewhat long, but it's constructed along the same lines as the code for rule1. The difference is that this time there are two subgoals that must be satisfied instead of one. This is called a *conjunction*.

The two subgoals share the intermediate variable Z. When this rule begins, it creates a new Variable and stores it in Z. That way the value of Z is remembered after control yields back to the calling method.

Where `rule1` had one loop, `rule2` has two loops, which are called `loop2` and `loop3`; `loop3` is nested with `loop2`. Loop `loop2` loops over the results from `inside(X, Z)`, and `loop3` loops over the results of `within(Z, Y)`. Before beginning `loop3`, a new instance of `within` is created. This resets `within` to handle a new binding of Z. (If we tried to use the old instance of `within`, its state would be incorrect.)

There is a new state associated with this code, `state2`, which occurs right after the `ireturn` instruction. This allows the code to return to the inner loop after `true` is yielded.

Here is the final bit of code for `call`:

```
fail:              ; No more rules to try, so fail.
    iconst_0       ; Return false, since there are
    ireturn        ; no more bindings
.end method
```

This state is done when there are no more rules to apply. When the code from `rule2` is done, it goes to `endloop2`. The labels `endloop2` and `fail` refer to the same instruction, since the two labels occur right next to each other with no intervening code. The code here returns `false`. The caller should stop calling this object, since there are no more answers to be found.

13.5.3 Constructing `within`

Since instances of `within` are created, a constructor is required. A trivial one will do:

```
.method <init>()V
aload_0
invokespecial java/lang/Object()V
return
.end method
```

13.6   Compiling Facts

The code in section 13.5 used the class `inside` without defining it. Here again are the rules for `inside`:

```
inside(maryland, united_states).
inside(baltimore, maryland).
inside(california, united_states).
inside(san_francisco, california).
```

One difference between the definitions for `inside` and those for `within` is that the rules for `inside` have constants instead of variables in the head. Another is that the body is empty. The Prolog compiler first transforms the rules so that the heads contain only variables; this also takes care of the empty body. After the transformation,

```
inside(X, Y) :- =(X, maryland), =(Y, united_states).
inside(X, Y) :- =(X, baltimore), =(Y, maryland).
inside(X, Y) :- =(X, california), =(Y, united_states).
inside(X, Y) :- =(X, san_francisco), =(Y, california).
```

This code makes use of the special predicate =. The predicate = returns `true` if the two arguments can be made to unify, `false` otherwise. Unlike other predicates, = returns `true` at most once. This means that it is unnecessary to backtrack on a call to =.

The predicate = is implemented as a call to `unify`. Here is pseudocode for `inside`:

```
boolean inside(Object X, Object Y)
{
    stackTag = Prolog.markTrail();
    if(unify(X, "maryland") && unify(Y, "united_states"))
        yield true;
    Prolog.undoBindings(stackTag);
    stackTag = Prolog.markTrail();
    if(unify(X, "baltimore") && unify(Y, "maryland"))
        yield true;
    Prolog.undoBindings(stackTag);
    stackTag = Prolog.markTrail();
    if(unify(X, "california") && unify(Y, "united_states"))
        yield true;
    Prolog.undoBindings(stackTag);
    stackTag = Prolog.markTrail();
    if(unify(X, "san_francisco") && unify(Y, "california"))
        yield true;
    yield false;
}
```

This code is similar to actual Java code, except for the `yield` statements; `yield` is handled the same way it is handled in `within` (section 13.5).

```
.class public inside
.field state$ I                        ; Keep track of state
.field stackTag Ljava/lang/Object;     ; Stack token
```

```
.method call(Ljava/lang/Object;Ljava/lang/Object;)Z
    aload_0
    getfield inside/state$ I
    tableswitch 0
    state0
    state1
    state2
    state3
    default: fail

state0:
    aload_0                  ; Mark the trail
    invokestatic Prolog/markTrail()Ljava/lang/Object;
    putfield inside/stackTag Ljava/lang/Object;

    aload_1                  ; Try to unify X and maryland
    ldc "maryland"
    invokestatic Prolog/unify
        (Ljava/lang/Object;Ljava/lang/Object;)Z
    ifeq state1              ; If they don't unify,
                             ; go to next state
    aload_2                  ; Unify Y and united_states
    ldc "united_states"
    invokestatic Prolog/unify
        (Ljava/lang/Object;Ljava/lang/Object;)Z
    ifeq state1              ; If they don't unify,
                             ; go to next state
        ; We have successfully matched the arguments against
        ; maryland and united_states. Go to next state and
        ; return true
    aload_0                  ; Remember that the new state is 1
    iconst_1
    putfield inside/state$ I

    iconst_1                 ; Yield true
    ireturn

state1:
    aload_0              ; Undo bindings from the last rule
    getfield inside/stackTag Ljava/lang/Object;
    invokestatic Prolog/undoBindings(Ljava/lang/Object;)V
```

```
;; The rest of states 1, 2, and 3 have been omitted. They
;; follow the same pattern used for state0:
;;      Undo bindings
;;      Mark the stack
;;      Try to unify the arguments with the rule head
;;      If that succeeds, set the state variable and return true

fail:
    iconst_0            ; Fail
    ireturn
.end method
```

This code is much like the code for within. One difference is that instead of creating inside and within objects and calling call, this code uses unify, defined in the class Prolog (it was discussed in section 13.3.1). The method unify returns true if it can match the arguments to the method with the particulars of that rule.

Because only unify is being used, there is no need to loop. If it succeeds, it will succeed only once. There is no reason to try again. This makes the body a bit simpler, because there is no need to jump into the middle of a loop. When yielding, the code sets the state$ variable to the beginning of the next rule.

13.7   Case Study

An implementation of a Prolog compiler much like the one described in this chapter is provided with this book in the package COM.sootNsmoke.prolog. The compiler is contained in the class COM.sootNsmoke.prolog.PrologCompiler. It has a main that expects its arguments to be files containing Prolog assertions, like the ones shown in section 13.1. If you place the code from section 0 into a file within.P, you can compile it with

```
java COM.sootNsmoke.prolog.PrologCompiler within.P
```

This produces two class files: within_2.class and inside_2.class. The class names include the number of arguments. For example, inside becomes inside_2 and within becomes within_2. This is because real Prolog allows you to write rules with the same name but different numbers of arguments. Rules composed this way have different heads; they answer different questions (compare with the Java method overloading).

There are several differences between the code shown in this chapter and the code produced by the compiler. The differences were introduced to make the discussion in this chapter simpler.

The stack trail is contained within the class `Prolog`. Each compiled rule requires an instance of this class. Usually, all rule instances share the same instance of `Prolog`. This eliminates the need for static variables in `Prolog`. (Static variables tend to make threading difficult, as well as other software engineering difficulties, so I try to avoid them.)

An additional data type is supported: cons cells. Cons cells are familiar to Lisp and Scheme programmers as the basic data type for building up data structures. They are most commonly used in Prolog for building up lists. There is a special Prolog syntax for lists:

```
[alpha, bravo, charlie]
```

This is really a set of three cons cells. The head of the first cell is `alpha`, and the tail is the list `[bravo, charlie]`.

You can also write a list with the head of the list separated from the tail of the list by a vertical bar (|). The list above is equivalent to

```
[alpha | [bravo, charlie]]
```

or

```
[alpha | [bravo | [charlie]]]
```

Lists may contain variables. For example, if you had the rule

```
list([alpha, bravo, charlie]).
```

and you ask,

```
?- list([X | Y]).
```

you get

```
X = alpha, Y = [bravo, charlie].
```

To make asking questions easier, a trivial Prolog interpreter is provided as the `main` of `Prolog`. It accepts only a single term. When it starts, it prints the prompt

```
?-
```

You may type in your question at the prompt, like `list([X | Y])`. It prints the list of answers, then gives another prompt. You may use any rules that have previously been compiled.

14

W HEN writing any program, the first challenge is to get it to ~~rectly~~. The next challenge is often to get the program to ru~~.~~ ~~virtual~~ machine programs can be made faster in a number of ways.

14.1 Fast Virtual Machines

The best way to speed up a sluggish JVM program is to get a faster JVM implementation. This gives you a performance boost without risking the correctness of your program.

JVMs are available from a variety of sources and run on many different kinds of computers. Even on the same computer, the performance of one JVM implementation can be 20 times faster than that of another. Performance differences between JVM implementations stem from a variety of sources.

The most important performance improvement in JVM implementations is the just-in-time code generator, or JIT. Non-JIT JVMs interpret each bytecode in the class as it is running. These JVMs are easy to write, but they are often slow, since the computer must interpret each bytecode as well as perform the operation the bytecode calls for. A JIT works by translating JVM bytecodes into native machine code for the platform. The native code runs faster because no CPU cycles need to be spent on the JVM interpreter itself.

Most compilers for languages other than Java translate the program into native code during compilation. These system-dependent binary programs are distributed in native code format. This means that each binary program is limited to the target platform it was compiled for. A JIT translates programs into native code after the classes are loaded. Native code is not generated until it is needed (thus the name just-in-time). This means that the program can be optimized for precisely the conditions on the computer when the program is run. If the computer is modified (for

355

is added), the next time the program is run the JIT can auto-
program to take advantage of the additional memory.

piler can make many optimizations to the instructions as it is com-
m. It can take advantage of the processor it is running on by using
uctions specific to that processor. It can order the instructions to take maximum advantage of the pipelining the processor provides. (Pipelining enables one
processor to run several sequential instructions simultaneously, using different
parts of the chip.)

A JIT can even make optimizations as the program is running. This is the key
idea of the HotSpot™ JVM. HotSpot can identify which parts of the program are
used most and spend special effort optimizing that code. This allows the system to
make optimizations on the fly, something ordinary optimizers cannot do. HotSpot
can even regenerate native code when new classes are loaded if these classes upset
the assumptions that had been made during previous optimizations (for example,
by introducing a subclass of a class that previously had no subclasses, which
might make it impossible to inline certain methods). See section 14.3 for more
about inlining.

As these and other optimizations are incorporated in JVM implementations,
JVM programs run faster and faster. It is possible that in the future, Java programs
will even run faster than the corresponding C++ programs, because the compiler
is capable of seeing optimizations at runtime that a C++ programmer or compiler
cannot at compile time.

14.1.1 Garbage Collection Performance

One big difference in performance between JVM implementations depends on the
garbage collector. The simplest garbage-collecting systems require all threads in
the system to wait while all of the still-reachable objects are found. Smarter
schemes allow better performance.

In the simplest garbage-collection schemes, the garbage collector starts with
each reference in the local variable array and operand stack. It marks each object
referenced in the local variable array or operand stack as *live*. (This applies to all
the operand stacks and local variables on the Java stack, not just the currently
active one.) Then the garbage collector checks each field within each live object.
If this field points to another object, this object is also marked live.

This process is repeated until there are no more fields to check. Any objects
that are not marked live are considered *garbage*. These objects are no longer
accessible; if they were accessible, then there would have been some path that
marked them as live. The memory for garbage objects can be reclaimed.

If the threads were allowed to continue during the marking process, one
thread might move the last reference to a still-reachable object from a storage

location that hasn't been checked yet to one that has, making a still reachable object appear unreachable. That object would be reclaimed, since the garbage collector never saw a reference to it, making further references to the object return incorrect results or even crashing the system.

Figure 14.1 shows the results of a garbage collection operation. Any object that can be referenced from the stack or the variable pool is considered live. Objects that can be reached from other live objects, like object 3, are also live. Objects that aren't live are garbage, and may be collected; these are shown in gray. Garbage objects may still hold references to other objects, live or garbage, but they're still garbage.

This garbage collection technique is very effective and easy to implement, but it can drastically reduce performance: sometimes the system shuts down for long periods while garbage collection occurs. The system may try to do garbage collection

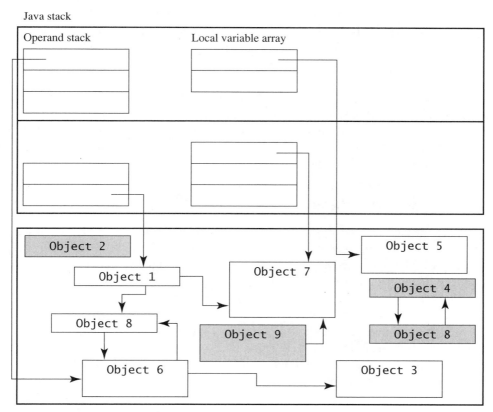

FIGURE 14.1: *Live and dead objects*

when the CPU isn't otherwise occupied, but the longer garbage collection takes the more likely it is that something will require the CPU's attention.

More sophisticated garbage collection techniques, such as *generational garbage collection,* work with subsets of the heap, allowing the garbage collection to run quickly. Generational garbage collection takes advantage of the assumption that an object that has been alive for a long time probably has a long lifespan and will continue to live for some time. Recently allocated objects are more likely to be temporary, which means they can be reclaimed soon.

Objects are grouped into *generations* based on when they were created. The newer generations are checked more frequently, since they are more likely to contain garbage, while older generations are checked less often.

Because the garbage collector looks at only a portion of the heap, it is easier to take advantage of short lulls in system load, and the system may be able to perform garbage collection without affecting performance at all.

As time goes on, it may be necessary to move the objects in memory. There may be plenty of space left, which comes from reclaiming small objects, but this space is fragmented. In Figure 14-1 it would be hard to find a place to put a large new object, since the objects are scattered all over memory. If all the objects were packed together more tightly there would be plenty of space. This is called *compaction*.

In compaction, objects are copied from one memory location to another. If the objects to be copied are large, this may take a lot of time. Different JVM implementations have different policies for when compaction occurs and which objects are to be moved. Better implementations try to pack long-lived objects together so that they don't have to be moved very often.

14.1.2 Implementing References

The Java virtual machine specification leaves the virtual machine implementor a lot of room for choosing techniques that perform quickly. Usually, these techniques involve a tradeoff. The implementor may be forced to choose between speed and memory. Many techniques make some programs slower and others faster.

For example, the JVM implementor may decide to represent references with a pointer to an object in memory. Another implementor may choose to use a pointer-to-a-pointer, also called a *handle*. Figure 14.2 shows the difference between the two techniques.

If references are implemented as pointers, the objects can be hard to move in memory when compaction is done, since compaction entails updating all the pointers. This is done either by maintaining a list of all pointers to be updated or by sweeping through the whole memory and updating all pointers. Either way, it can be expensive, especially if there are many references.

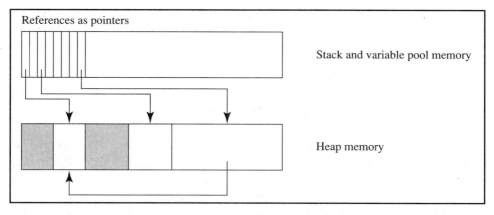

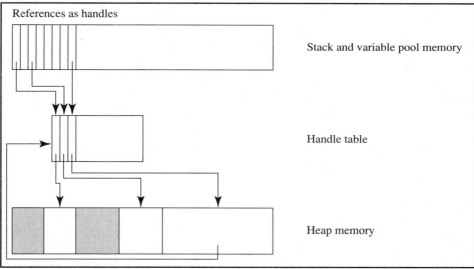

FIGURE 14.2: *Two ways to implement references*

If references are implemented as handles, moving an object is easy: the object can be moved, and only the handle needs to be updated. Since the handles are all the same size, it isn't necessary to compact the handle table. However, every time you want to use a reference, it must be dereferenced twice, once to find the location in the handle table and once to find the object itself.

Performance can be improved by temporarily preventing the object from moving. Then you can use the pointer directly, instead of the handle. This is known as *pinning the handle*. This improves performance, since only one pointer link needs to be followed, instead of two. However, pinning can cause problems as well. If a handle remains locked for too long, then memory gradually becomes full of immovable objects. Effective compaction is impossible, and the memory becomes badly fragmented.

14.2   Bytecode Optimization Techniques

Besides getting a faster JVM implementation, it is also possible for one compiler to generate bytecodes that run more efficiently on the same JVM. Redundant operations can be eliminated. Slow operations can be replaced with fast ones.

One reason for implementing bytecode optimization is that you can take advantage of the semantics of the original language. For example, some of the techniques discussed in this section produce incorrect results in a multithreaded environment. If you are writing a compiler for a language that does not support multithreading, then you can perform optimizations not available to languages that must properly support threads.

Similarly, the Java language makes it difficult to perform inlining operations between classes, due to the binary compatibility requirements in *The Java Language Specification*. A compiler for a language other than Java does not have to respect these binary compatibility requirements.

Many of the techniques discussed in this section are based on assembly language optimization techniques.

14.2.1   Warning

The optimizations described in this section can also be performed automatically by the JVM implementation itself. Generally, the more effort you go through to perform these optimizations yourself, the harder it will be for the JVM's optimizer to perform additional optimizations.

Professor Donald Knuth said, "Premature optimization is the root of all evil." Think carefully before spending a lot of time optimizing your programs at the bytecode level. Your work may actually make performance worse instead of better.

14.2.2   Constant Propagation

Constant propagation involves replacing variables with constants, if the optimizer proves that the variable does not change. For example, consider this snippet of JVM code:

```
.method static subtract32([I)V
.var 0 is array [I
.var 1 is n I
.var 2 is i I
   bipush 32           ; Push the constant 32
   istore_1            ; Store it in n
   iconst_0            ; Initialize i to 0
   istore_2
loop:
   aload_0
   aload_0             ; Push the array
   iload_2             ; Push i
   iaload              ; Push array[i]
   iload_1             ; Push n
   isub                ; Compute array[i]-n
   iload_2             ; Store the result in array[i]
   iastore

   iinc 2 1            ; Increment i
   aload_0             ; Loop if i <= array.length
   arraylength
   if_icmple loop
```

This code subtracts the value of n (variable 1) from each element of the array. If you examine the code, you will discover that the value of n never changes; it is always 32. Therefore, you can replace the instruction

```
iload_1           ; Push n
```

with the more efficient

```
bipush 32         ; Push 32
```

The bipush instruction is more efficient that the iload instruction because iload requires fetching a value from memory, which is usually much slower than the CPU itself. Loading a constant can be performed without fetching anything from memory, since the value is part of the instruction itself.

Constant propagation is made difficult in many systems by *pointer shadowing*. Pointer shadowing occurs when two different pointers refer to the same space in memory. Pointer shadowing makes it hard to predict what parts of the program will cause which memory to change. If the optimizer knows that a piece of memory will not change, it can eliminate code that cannot affect the outcome of the computation.

In the JVM instruction set, there is no way to "shadow" a local variable. That is, there is no way to have multiple pointers to the same local variable. This makes it easier to detect whether or not a particular local variable will change during the course of a loop. In the constant propagation example code, it is obvious that there is no way to change the value of n because only the currently executing method has access to it.

A similar optimization can be performed with fields. This optimization is more difficult than that for local variables because it is possible to have multiple references to the same object. By carefully examining local variables, it is sometimes possible to prove that there is only one reference to an object. For example, if the object is created within the body of the method and there are no instructions that store into the field, then you can treat the field as a constant.

14.2.3 Strength Reduction

In *strength reduction,* an expensive operation is replaced by an operation that does the same job but is less costly to run. This is a more general form of constant propagation. To do this, you have to know which operations are likely to be more expensive than others. This differs from JVM implementation to JVM implementation.

For this reason, strength reduction is best performed by the JVM implementation itself. Some JIT compilers perform strength reduction when compiling the Java bytecodes into native instructions. Generally, the JIT can do a better job than you can of making these decisions, since the JIT is optimized for the particular computer it runs on. The JIT developer knows exactly how fast any given instruction can run.

One operation that is typically slow is multiplication. For example,

```
x * 32
```

is equivalent to

```
x << 5
```

Generally, performing the left shift operation (<<) is faster than doing a multiply (*) for the same reason people find multiplying by 1,000 easier than multiplying by 317.

Even if the value isn't exactly a power of 2, it may be faster to rephrase multiplication in terms of shifts and addition. This way,

```
x * 34
```

is equivalent to

```
x << 5 + x << 1
```

Sometimes you can compute the results of an operation even before it is executed and replace the code with a simple push of the results. Consider this Java code:

```
int seconds_in_a_day = 60*60*24;
```

A naïve compiler might compile this to

```
bipush 60
bipush 60
imul
bipush 24
imul
```

A better compiler would generate

```
ldc 86400
```

This single instruction is likely to execute significantly faster than the five instructions. Although the difference may seem trivial, when it is executed a million times the differences add up.

14.2.4 Loop Unrolling

In some loops, the time it takes to execute the body of the loop may not be all that much larger than the loop tests. Consider, for example, this code to count the number of 1 bits in the int m:

```
for(int i = 0; i < 32; i++)
    n += m >> i & 1;
```

A naïve Java compiler might generate this code:

```
loop:
iload_1             ; Compare i to 32
bipush 32
if_icmpge break     ; Break when i >= 32
iload_3             ; Push n
iload_2             ; Push m
iload_1             ; Push i
ishr                ; Compute m >> i
iconst_1
iand                ; Compute m >> i & 1
iadd                ; Add that value to n
iinc 1 1            ; Increment i
goto loop           ; Loop again
```

This code will increment i 32 times and test if i is less than 32 the same number of times. It's obvious that the test will fail the first 31 times and succeed the last time. You can eliminate the tests by "unrolling" the loop, like this:

```
iload_2      ; Push m
iconst_0     ; Push 0
ishr         ; Compute m >> 0
iconst_1     ; Push 1
iand         ; Compute m >> 0 & 1 (the first bit)
iload_3      ; Push n
iadd         ; Add the result to n

iload_2      ; Push m
iconst_1     ; Push 1
ishr         ; Compute m >> 1
iconst_1     ; Push 1
iload_3      ; Add n
iand         ; Compute m >> 1 & 1 (the second bit)

;; Repeat this pattern 29 more times

iload_2      ; Push m
bipush 31    ; Push 31
ishr         ; Compute m >> 31 (the leftmost bit)
iconst_1     ; Push 1
iload_3      ; Push n
iadd         ; Add the last bit to n
```

Although this greatly expands the size of the resulting code, the total number of instructions executed is reduced. It also allowed us to completely eliminate local variable 1, which had been used as the loop counter. This results in a speedup of 200% to 400%, depending on the virtual machine implementation used.

14.2.5   Peephole Optimization

Compilers often generate code that has redundant instructions. A peephole optimizer looks at the resulting bytecodes to eliminate some of the redundant instructions. This involves looking at the bytecodes a few instructions at a time, rather than doing wholesale reorganization of the code. The name "peephole optimization" comes from the tiny "window" used to view the code.

A peephole optimizer is frequently applied as the last stage of a compiler before code is written to disk. Sometimes it is applied earlier, before other optimizations are done, and then applied again afterwards.

For example, consider this statement:

```
if(a == b)                  // This is if #1
    foo();                  //      True case of if #1
else
                            //      False case of if #1
    if(a == c)              //      This is if #2
        bar();              //          True case of if #2
    else
        baz();              //          False case of if #2
```

A Java compiler might generate this code:

```
        iload_1
        iload_2
        if_icmpeq label1                 ; This is if #1
            iload_1                      ;      False case of if #1
            iload_3
            if_icmpeq label2             ;      This is if #2
                invokestatic cls/baz()V ;      False case of if #2
                goto label3             ;      Skip true case of if #2
label2:
                invokestatic cls/bar()V ;      True case of if #2
label3:
            goto label4                 ;      Skip true case of if #1
label1:
            invokestatic cls/foo()V     ;      True case of if #1
label4:
```

The line

```
goto label3
```

just goes to another goto, which goes to label4. It would be more efficient to replace this line directly with

```
goto label4
```

Another common set of code produced by Java compilers occurs when assignments are used as statements. Since an assignment is an expression, it should leave a value on the stack; that value is the value assigned. However, when the expression is used as a statement, that value must be removed, since statements leave no values on the stack.

For example, the Java code

```
x = y = z;
```

might compile to

```
.var 0 is x I
.var 1 is y I
.var 2 is z I
iload_2          ; Push z
dup              ; Duplicate the value, so that the
                 ; result is the value assigned
istore_1         ; Store it in y. This leaves the
                 ; result of y=z on the stack.
dup              ; Repeat the pattern: duplicate the value
istore_0         ; Store it in x
pop              ; Remove the value
```

The first dup is appropriate, since we want to leave the value of z on top of the stack to be assigned to x. However, when the pattern is naively repeated, the second dup is unnecessary. A peephole optimizer might replace it with

```
iload_0          ; Push z
dup              ; Copy it for the second assignment
istore_1         ; Store it in y
istore_2         ; Store it in x
```

This eliminates both the dup and the pop, but the resulting code has the same effect.

A peephole optimizer yields some of the same results as strength reduction. If a peephole optimizer sees this code

```
bipush  60
bipush  60
imul
bipush  24
imul
```

it can recognize that it is equivalent to

```
sipush  3600
bipush  24
imul
```

which can be further reduced to

```
ldc 86400
```

Table 14.1 lists some other rules for a peephole optimizer. The variables x and y stand for any field or local variable. For the operations aload and astore, you may perform the same operations on the corresponding float and int instructions.

TABLE 14.1: *Poophole optimization rules*

Replace	With	Reason
Dup swap	dup	The result of a dup is two of the same element; swapping produces an identical result.
swap swap		A double swap accomplishes nothing.
iinc 1 1 iinc 1 1	iinc 1 2	Since it takes just as long to increment by 2 as to increment by 1 (on most systems), you might as well do the increment just once.
nop		A nop instruction has no effect, so you might as well eliminate it.
getfield x getfield x	getfield x dup	Two getfield instructions one immediately after the other leave no opportunity for the field value to change, so you can replace the second one with a dup. *Exception:* If the field is marked volatile, then its value may be changed by some other thread, and this optimization would be in error.
aload x aload x	aload x dup	Some systems have special fast operations for duplicating the top element of the stack.
astore x aload x	dup astore x	Some systems have special fast operations for duplicating the top element of the stack.
aload x astore x		These instructions cancel each other out.
astore x astore x	astore x pop	Storing into the same variable twice is unnecessary; only the second store needs to be performed.
aload x pop		These instructions cancel each other out.
aload x aload y areturn	aload y areturn	Since the value of x is left on the top of the stack at the time of the return, there is no reason to push it. This optimization applies to any instruction except a method invocation, branch instruction, or storing into a field.

It may not be correct to apply peephole optimization techniques when the peephole includes an instruction that is the destination of a goto. For example, in this code

```
        iinc 1 1                ; Increment variable i
loop:   iinc 1 1                ; Increment i again
        ;; Use variable i
        goto loop
```

it would be an error to combine the first two lines into

```
        iinc 1 2                ; Increment i 2
```

because the destination loop would suddenly disappear, and the resulting code might be meaningless.

Exercise 14.1

Consider this Java code:

```
i = i + i
```

Give the Oolong code that a simple Java compiler would generate. Then optimize the code by hand.   ▲

14.3   Inlining

An important optimization technique is inlining. In inlining, an invoke instruction is replaced by the code that is called. This saves the overhead of having to push the arguments onto the stack, create a new stack frame, and handle the result.

For example, you may want to inline the methods width and height in area:

```
class Rectangle
{
    float x1, y1, x2, y2;

    final float width()
    {
        return x2 - x1;
    }

    final float height()
    {
```

```
        return y2 - y1;
    }

    float area()
    {
        return width() * height();
    }
}
```

The unoptimized version of area is

```
.method area()F
aload_0
invokevirtual Rectangle/width ()F
aload_0
invokevirtual Rectangle/height ()F
fmul
freturn
.end method
```

It may take even more time to perform the method invocation than it does to perform the subtraction. The overhead of the method invocation can be eliminated by including the code for width and height in the definition for area:

```
.method area()F
aload_0
getfield Rectangle/x2 F
aload_0
getfield Rectangle/x1 F
fsub

aload_0
getfield Rectangle/y2 F
aload_0
getfield Rectangle/y1 F
fsub

fmul
freturn
.end method
```

Note that this can be done *only* if the methods are marked `final` or if the entire class is `final`. Otherwise, somebody might redefine the methods in a subclass:

```
/** A rectangle that can be angled, defined by 3 points:
 *                 (x1, y1) ------------- (x2,y1)
 *                    /             /
 *                 (x3, y3) ------------- (x3+x2-x1, y3+y2-y1)
 */
class Parallelogram extends Rectangle
{
    float x3, y3;

    float width()
    {
        return Math.sqrt((x1-x3)*(x1-x3) + (y1-y3)*(y1-y3));
    }
    float height()
    {
        return Math.sqrt((x2-x1)*(x2-x1) + (y1-y2)*(y1-y2));
    }
}
```

Methods that are `static` are also good candidates for inlining, since they cannot be overridden in subclasses.

Sometimes the optimizer can prove the exact runtime type of an object. For example, if the object was just created with a `new` instruction, then the optimizer knows exactly what type of object is on top of the stack. The optimizer can treat this object as if it were a member of a final class, since it can be sure that the methods won't be overridden.

A JVM implementation may be able to inline methods that are not final if it has reason to believe that the nonfinal methods are never actually overridden. This may occur if there are no subclasses of the class with the method. If new subclasses are introduced later, the JVM may have to undo some of its optimizations.

14.3.1   Inlining Fields

Inlining can also be done with `final` fields, replacing a reference to the field with its value. This is basically identical to constant propagation (section 14.2.2).

This example shows a field that can be inlined:

```
class Teapot
{
```

```
    /** Brewing time is 3 minutes, or 180,000 milliseconds */
    public final static long TIME_TO_BREW = 180000;

    void makeTea()
    {
        // Make tea, then let it steep
        Thread.sleep(TIME_TO_BREW);
    }
}
```

The value TIME_TO_BREW can be substituted into the method makeTea:

```
.method makeTea()V
;; Make tea, then let it steep
ldc2_w 180000
invokestatic java/lang/Thread/sleep(J)V
return
.end method
```

The ldc instruction replaces the much slower instruction

```
getstatic Teapot/TIME_TO_BREW J
```

Since the TIME_TO_BREW is final, it can't change while the program is running. However, this can be done only within the same class.

Consider the class TeaParty:

```
class TeaParty
{
    void chat()
    {
        // Chat while the tea brews
        Thread.sleep(Teapot.TIME_TO_BREW);
    }
}
```

It is tempting to optimize chat in the same way makeTea is optimized. The Java language forbids this optimization between classes. This injunction applies to both fields and methods. Suppose somebody who liked stronger tea came along and changed the definition of Teapot so that TIME_TO_BREW was set to 200000. This would require recompiling TeaParty, but since nothing in Teapot references TeaParty, the compiler may not know it has to recompile.

14.3.2 Separate Compilation

The ability of a Java program to respond correctly even when other classes change is called *binary compatibility*. *The Java Language Specification* devotes all of chapter 13 to binary compatibility between `class` files.

While the compiler may not perform this optimization, the same sort of optimization may be performed by the JVM implementation itself. Once the classes are loaded into the JVM, they may not change. This allows the JVM implementation to make optimizations that a Java compiler may not make.

Most other languages do not have this restriction. They may require that all related classes be recompiled when any one class is changed. The C and C++ languages are examples.

Other languages are silent on the issue, which means that a compiler designer may choose when compilation must be done. The decision affects users of your compiler who may find themselves either compiling more frequently than they would like or encountering mysterious errors and saying to themselves, "I thought I changed that!" It also affects users of the resulting programs, who might appreciate the performance improvements of your optimizing compiler.

CHAPTER **15**

Security and the Virtual Machine

THE first popular use of Java was to permit web surfers to download applets into their web browsers. This greatly extended the capabilities of web browsers, but some people were concerned that the capabilities had been extended too far, allowing malicious applet writers to wreak havoc on the computer of anybody using the applets. They pointed out that Java is a full-featured language, which would allow applet writers to do just about anything. It is extremely difficult to prove things about computer programs written in conventional languages, and it is usually easy to hide malicious code in an innocent-looking program.

The Java platform provides a solution to these security fears. The platform contains checks designed to prevent unfriendly behavior by limiting the capabilities of applets, placing potentially harmful operations off-limits. To ensure that these checks cannot be circumvented, the Java virtual machine contains a verification algorithm that eliminates the possibility of behavior that could be used to bypass the security checks.

This chapter examines the relationship between the Java platform's security architecture and the verification algorithm, and it shows how the verification algorithm helps ensure the promises of the Java platform's security policy.

15.1   Java Platform and Need for Security

The JVM instruction set has very little ability to interface with your computer system. There are no instructions to read files, connect to sockets, or use system resources other than memory and the CPU. While that's a very safe way to live, it's not a very interesting one, since people who use Java programs want to do things like save their work, print it out, get information over the network, and so on. These capabilities are exposed to programs running on the JVM through a set of application programming interfaces, collectively called the Java platform.

To enable the platform, the JVM is extended though use of native methods, methods written in the native language of the computer instead of in bytecodes. Because they are implemented in native code, native methods have the ability to do just about anything on your computer. Therefore, access to native methods must be controlled, and the controls must not be able to be bypassed.

The verification process allows the JVM to make certain promises about code that is executed. Chapter 6 discusses the verification algorithm. In the rest of this chapter, we see how the algorithm prevents applets from bypassing the security constraints of the system.

15.2 Security Promises of the JVM

Here are some of the promises the Java virtual machine makes about programs that have passed the verification algorithm:

- ◆ Every object is constructed exactly once before it is used.
- ◆ Every object is an instance of exactly one class, which does not change through the life of the object.
- ◆ If a field or method is marked `private`, then the only code that ever accesses it is found within the class itself.
- ◆ Fields and methods marked `protected` are used only by code that participates in the implementation of the class.
- ◆ Every local variable is initialized before it is used.
- ◆ Every field is initialized before it is used.
- ◆ It is impossible to underflow or overflow the stack.
- ◆ It is impossible to read or write past the end of an array or before the beginning of the array.
- ◆ It is impossible to change the length of an array once it has been created.
- ◆ Final methods cannot be overridden, and final classes cannot be subclassed.
- ◆ Attempts to use a `null` reference as the receiver of a method invocation or source of a field cause a `NullPointerException` to be thrown.

The Java platform security architecture depends on all these promises and many more. The verification algorithm, which enforces these promises, was outlined in chapter 6. A more complete description is available in *The Java Virtual Machine Specification,* chapter 4. You can check the algorithms out for yourself. Part of the strength of the Java platform security architecture lies in the fact that many independent reviewers have checked the algorithms.

15.3   Security Architecture and Security Policy

The Java platform builds a *security architecture* on top of the protections promised by the JVM. A security architecture is a way of organizing the software that makes up the Java platform so that potentially harmful operations are isolated from unprivileged code but available to privileged code. Most code is unprivileged; only carefully selected pieces of code are privileged to perform potentially dangerous operations. The security architecture is responsible for making sure that unprivileged code does not masquerade as privileged code.

The core of the Java platform security architecture under Java platforms 1.0 and 1.1 is the SecurityManager class.[1] This class decides which pieces of code can perform certain operations and which cannot. Collectively, these decisions are called the *security policy*. The security policy is enforced by the Java platform classes, which check the SecurityManager before proceeding with any operations under the control of the SecurityManager.

Only one instance of the SecurityManager can be installed, and once it is installed it cannot be removed. It is called the *security manager*. By default, there is no security manager, and all operations are permitted. The class java.lang.System is responsible for ensuring that there is only one security manager. It provides the static methods getSecurityManager and setSecurityManager to get and set the security manager.

The SecurityManager class has a set of methods that are called by the Java platform code before proceeding with certain potentially harmful operations. These methods throw a SecurityException if the operation is forbidden. If no exception is thrown, then the caller may assume that the operation is permitted, and it can proceed with the operation. Table 15.1 describes the operations that are checked by the SecurityManager in the Java 1.02 platform.

The security manager uses a variety of factors to determine whether an operation is permitted or not. These factors include the source of the code attempting the operation and the preferences of the user (discussed further in sections 15.3.2

---

[1]   On the Java 2 platform, the core of the security architecture is shifted to a class called AccessController, which falls outside the scope of this book. See http//java.sun.com for more information.

TABLE 15.1: *Security checks*

Method	Operation checked	Called by
checkAccept (String host, int port)	Accepting a socket connection from host on port	ServerSocket.accept
checkAccess (Thread g)	Modifying the thread g	Thread.stop Thread.suspend Thread.resume Thread.setPriority Thread.setName Thread.setDaemon
checkAccess (ThreadGroup g)	Modifying the thread group g	ThreadGroup.<init> ThreadGroup.setDaemon ThreadGroup.setMaxPriority ThreadGroup.stop ThreadGroup.resume ThreadGroup.destroy
checkConnect (String host, int port)	Opening a socket to host on port	Socket.connect
checkCreateClassLoader()	Creating a class loader	ClassLoader.<init>
checkDelete(String file)	Deleting a file	File.delete
checkExec(String cmd)	Creating a subprocess	Runtime.exec
checkExit(int status)	Exiting the JVM	Runtime.exit
checkLink(String lib)	Loading a library	Runtime.load Runtime.loadLibrary
checkListen(int port)	Listening at a port	Socket.listen
checkPackageAccess (String package)	Attempting to access package	ClassLoader.loadClass
checkPackageDefinition (String package)	Defining a class in package	ClassLoader.loadClass
checkPropertiesAccess()	Reading or writing properties	System.getProperties System.setProperties
checkPropertyAccess (String property)	Reading the property named property	System.getProperty
checkRead (FileDescriptor fd)	Reading from the file descriptor fd	FileInputStream.<init>
checkRead(String file)	Reading from the file named file	FileInputStream.<init>

TABLE 15.1: *Security checks* (continued)

Method	Operation checked	Called by
checkSetFactory()	Setting a socket factory	ServerSocket SetSocketFactory
checkWrite (FileDescriptor fd)	Writing to a file descriptor	FileOutputStream.<init>
checkWrite(String f)	Writing to a file named file	FileOutputStream.<init>

and 15.3.3). First we present an example of how the security architecture and the security policy interact.

15.3.1 Example

The security architecture demands that before a file is opened for reading, the security manager will be checked to see whether the code requesting the file is allowed to open the file. This is a sensible policy, since the ability to read files gives a program access to potentially important and confidential information.

The most important ways to read files are through the FileInputStream or FileReader classes in the java.io package. These classes include native methods that are implemented in a machine-dependent way to interact with the computer's file system. Before these methods can be used, an instance of FileInputStream or FileReader must be constructed. Following the security architecture, all the publicly accessible constructors of FileInputStream and FileReader begin with a call to the checkRead method of SecurityManager:

```
/** Open the file named filename */
public FileInputStream(String filename) throws
    FileNotFoundException
{
    SecurityManager security = System.getSecurityManager();
    // If a security manager is present, check it.
    if (security != null)
        security.checkRead(name);
    // Open the file named filename; code omitted
}
```

The system's security manager is found by calling System.getSecurityManager(). There may not be a security manager installed, in which case the FileInputStream is free to open the file. If the security manager has not been established, then any code may set it. Secure systems, like web browsers, install a security manager before any applets are loaded.

If a security manager is present, then its checkRead method determines whether or not the code that called the constructor is allowed to read the file. How it decides this is a matter of the security policy of the particular system. If it decides that the read is not allowed, then a SecurityException is thrown.

This is where the JVM's promises become important. If an exception is thrown from checkRead, it will not be caught in the body of the constructor, causing the constructor to terminate abnormally. Since the constructor did not complete normally, the FileInputStream object is not constructed. If the code attempts to use the object before it has been constructed, then the verification algorithm rejects the program.

If the checkRead method returns normally, then the FileInputStream constructor also returns normally. Now that the FileInputStream object is constructed, all the public methods of FileInputStream, including read, may be invoked on it. The methods don't need to check for permission again, since the existence of the object implies that permission was granted.

15.3.2   Basic Applet Security Policy

For the writers of web browsers, security is of tremendous concern, since a malicious or mistaken applet could cause problems for many, many web surfers. For this reason, the Java applet security policy is very restrictive. The security manager discriminates between two kinds of classes: system classes (loaded by the JVM automatically) and applets (loaded by a custom class loader from over the network). The web browser implements its own security manager, which subclasses SecurityManager. Let's call it the AppletSecurityManager.

The AppletSecurityManager can ascertain the source of the applet by looking at the applet's class loader. Each class maintains a permanent association with its class loader. Anybody can find out which class loader loaded the class by invoking getClassLoader, a method of Class. Since Class is final, the verification algorithm ensures that the method getClassLoader cannot be overridden, so it is not possible for a class to lie about its class loader. The class loader can track information about the source of the applet.

The security manager needs to know which class is invoking the operation. For example, suppose an applet called NastyApplet tries to create a FileInputStream so that it can read the system's password file. In order to do that, it must call the constructor for FileInputStream, or the verification algorithm will reject the applet before it gets a chance to run. As shown in section 15.3.1, the constructor for `FileInputStream` calls `checkRead` in the security manager. The Java stack now looks like this:

Method	Class	Class loader
checkread	AppletSecurityManager	none
<init>	FileInputStream	none
attack	NastyApplet	AppletClassLoader
run	NastyApplet	AppletClassLoader

The `SecurityManager` provides the method `currentClassLoader`, which looks down the execution stack for the first method that comes from a class that was loaded by a class loader. Since `AppletSecurityManager` and `FileInput-Stream` are part of the browser itself, they are loaded without any class loader. The `SecurityManager` looks down the stack until it finds the `run` method from `NastyApplet`, which was loaded by `AppletClassLoader`.

The policy of the web browser is that no applet may try to read a file. The web browser's security policy is implemented by the class `AppletSecurityManager`. Part of the definition of `AppletSecurityManager` is

```
class AppletSecurityManager extends SecurityManager
{
    public void checkRead(String name) throws SecurityException
    {
        ClassLoader loader = currentClassLoader();
        if(loader instanceof AppletClassLoader)
            throw new SecurityException("file.read");
    }
}
```

Since the class loader is an `AppletClassLoader`, a security exception is thrown. It is not caught in the constructor for `FileInputStream`, so that method does not terminate normally. The `FileInputStream` is therefore invalid and may not be used to read any files. Security has been preserved.

15.3.3 More Sophisticated Policies

The security policy of the basic class loader, while effective at preventing security problems, is too tight for much work to get done, since it's not possible for an applet to save work or read previously written files.

A more sophisticated policy might allow applets to read and write files in a certain *sandbox* area: all files beginning with a certain absolute path would be permitted, all others denied. In some browsers, the system properties `acl.read` and `acl.read.default` control the sandbox area. If the user had configured `acl.read` as /sandbox, then a word processing applet would be permitted to read /sandbox/ Letter.doc but the NastyApplet would not be allowed to read /etc/passwd.

Even this seemingly safe idea has some potential problems. The NastyApplet might try to fool the system by opening /sandbox/../etc/passwd, which names the password file on some systems. This is easily prevented by checking for relative references like "..", but it gives some idea of the sort of thing security developers must consider. This sort of potential security problem is beyond the domain of the JVM itself.

Another kind of security policy allows some code more trust than others. An applet programmer may cryptographically sign the bytecodes that make up the applet. The cryptographic signature makes it possible to determine whether the applet has been altered after it has been signed, since the signature is made from the original bytecodes that have been encrypted with the programmer's private key. Use of the programmer's public key allows the applet user to ascertain the source of the signature. Since the programmer's private key should be truly private, the signature uniquely identifies that programmer as the source of the code.

To make these more sophisticated security policies possible, the standard Java platform version 1.1 and later contain code in the `java.security` package to provide the code necessary for doing encryption, decryption, and signature verification. The classes in this package were designed to prevent applets from interfering with them, and they depend on the promises of the JVM to ensure that the cryptographic routines are not tampered with.

15.4   Some Potential Attacks

JVM security is often discussed in terms of the Java language. The Java compiler rejects programs that attempt some kinds of attacks, such as reading private variables or casting an object reference to an invalid type. However, some attackers may try to bypass the compiler errors by writing in Oolong instead of Java or by writing bytecodes directly. In this section, we show how the Java virtual machine thwarts some potential attacks on system security.

15.4.1   Implementation Details

Examples in this section frequently involve private methods and fields of standard classes. Private methods and fields are not necessarily consistent from JVM implementation to JVM implementation; the `private` keyword denotes parts of the code that are implementation dependent.

Security must not depend on the fact that the attacker does not know the implementation details of the system. An attacker may guess what private methods are being used, since the attacker can easily obtain a copy of the same virtual machine implementation the victim is using. If the attack is through an applet, then the attacker can reasonably assume that the victim is using one of the popular Java-supporting web browsers and may use attacks using private implementation details of these browsers.

Fortunately, the JVM provides a strong base for making the implementation secure, even if the attacker knows how the system was implemented. This section shows how some potential attacks are thwarted, either by the verification algorithm or by the runtime system, which depends on the verifier.

15.4.2 Protecting the Security Manager

The system has exactly one security manager, which is kept by the `java.lang.System` class. It is retrieved with `getSecurityManager`, a static method in `java.lang.System`.

Initially, there is no security manager, and `getSecurityManager` returns `null`. The security manager can be set with `setSecurityManager`:

```
AppletSecurityManager asm = new AppletSecurityManager();
System.setSecurityManager(asm);
```

The first time `setSecurityManager` is called, it sets the security manager. After that, all calls to `setSecurityManager` will throw a `SecurityException` without setting the manager. This prevents anybody else, such as a malicious applet, from altering the security manager. It is the job of the browser to set the security manager before loading any applets.

Each JVM implementation can implement the `System` class differently. In subsequent sections, we assume that it stores the security manager in a private field called `security`:

```
package java.lang;
public final class System
{
    private static SecurityManager security;

    public static SecurityManager getSecurityManager()
    {
        return security;
    }
```

```
public static setSecurityManager(SecurityManager sm)
{
    if(security == null)
        throw new SecurityException
            ("SecurityManager already set");
    security = sm;
}
}
```

The integrity of the `security` field is critical, since an applet that could set that field could control the security policy of the system. This makes `security` a likely target for attack.

15.4.3 Bypassing Java Security

The most straightforward attack would be to try to set the `security` field. The attacker's applet might be written in Java:

```
public class NastyApplet extends Applet
{
    void attack()
    {
        System.security = null;
        // The security manager is null, so everything is
        // permitted
        // Put code to wreak havoc here
    }
}
```

When this class is compiled, the Java compiler will notice that the `security` field is private to the `System` class and refuse to compile the file. This would not stop a determined attacker, who would proceed to rewrite the applet in Oolong:

```
.class public NastyApplet
.super java/applet/Applet

.method attack()V
aconst_null                  ; Install null as the
                             ; security manager
putstatic java/lang/System/security Ljava/lang/SecurityManager;
;; Wreak havoc
.end method
```

This is a valid Oolong program. Once you have downloaded the applet into your web browser, the attacker's applet will try to use the `attack` method to cause trouble.

The JVM prevents this attack from succeeding by running the verification algorithm on the class when it is loaded. All the information needed about what fields are accessed is present in the code. That is, it isn't necessary to run the applet to find out which fields it may try to access. The verification algorithm finds that the `security` field is `private`, so this code cannot access it. The verification algorithm causes the system to refuse to load this class, thwarting the attack before the applet starts to run.

The following method is perfectly safe because the potentially dangerous code can never actually be executed:

```
.method attack()V
return
; Just kidding. There's no way to execute the next line, since
; the method always returns before it gets here
aconst_null              ; Install null as the
                         ; security manager
putstatic java/lang/System/security Ljava/lang/SecurityManager;
return
.end method
```

The verification algorithm rejects this applet just because of the presence of this security-violating instruction, even though the dangerous code is unreachable.

There is no way to bypass the verification step, since it occurs automatically when the `resolveClass` method is invoked in the `ClassLoader` that loads the class. The class is unusable until it has been resolved. When it is resolved, the verification algorithm catches the attack and refuses to load the class. If it is never loaded, then it can never be executed, so the attack is avoided.

15.4.4 Using Unconstructed Objects

Some classes depend on their constructors to control who may create instances. For example, the `setSecurityManager` method in `java.lang.System` is public, which permits anybody to set the security manager.

An applet might try to install its own security manager:

```
class WimpySecurityManager extends SecurityManager
{
    // Override the methods so that they don't do anything
}
```

```
class MaliciousApplet extends Applet
{
   SecurityManager mySecurityManager = new
      WimpySecurityManager();
   System.setSecurityManager(mySecurityManager);
   // Now I can do anything I want!
}
```

This attack won't work, even though setSecurityManager is public. The reason is that you're not allowed to create your own SecurityManager once a security manager has been installed. The SecurityManager's constructor has code to check if there already is a security manager installed:

```
public class SecurityManager
{
   protected SecurityManager()
   {
      if (System.getSecurityManager() != null)
         throw new SecurityException(
            "security manager already installed.");
      // Continue constructing the security manager
   }
}
```

The verification algorithm requires that each constructor call a superclass constructor. Since this is the only constructor for SecurityManager, the WimpySecurityManager must call it. In the example, the Java compiler creates a default constructor for WimpySecurityManager, which calls the constructor for SecurityManager. That constructor finds that a SecurityManager has already been created and throws a SecurityException. Since the system won't permit use of an unconstructed object, the attacker can never install the WimpySecurityManager as the security manager of the system.

Suppose, however, that the attacker wrote a constructor for WimpySecurity-Manager that didn't call the constructor:

```
.class WimpySecurityManager
.super java/lang/SecurityManager

.method public <init>()V
return                  ; Don't call the superclass constructor!
.end method
```

The JVM verification algorithm rejects `WimpySecurityManager`, since one of the things the verification algorithm checks is that each constructor calls a superclass constructor somewhere in the body of the constructor.

The attacker might try to fool the verification algorithm by hiding the call:

```
.method public <init>()V
goto end                     ; Skip over the superclass constructor
aload_0
invokespecial java/lang/SecurityManager/<init> ()V
end:
return
.end method
```

The verification algorithm discovers that the superclass `<init>` method is not always called, and it rejects this class. Another attempt might involve hiding the call behind an `if` instruction:

```
.method public <init>(I)V
.limit locals 2
iload_1
ifeq end             ; Skip the superclass constructor if
aload_0              ; the argument is nonzero
invokespecial java/lang/SecurityManager/<init> ()V
end:
return
.end method
```

This constructor calls the superclass constructor if the argument is nonzero; otherwise, it skips it. However, any path through the method must call the superclass constructor, or the verification algorithm rejects it. The verification algorithm does not have to run the code to determine whether the constructor will be called. All the verification algorithm has to do is to prove that there is a way through the method that does not involve the superclass constructor call, to provide sufficient grounds to reject the entire class.

This must be true of all constructors. Even if you provide a valid constructor as well as an invalid one, the verification algorithm still rejects the class. The goal is that the verification algorithm must be able to prove that the superclass constructor is called no matter which constructor is called and no matter which arguments are provided.

15.4.5 Invalid Casts

An attacker would gain a lot of information if the JVM permitted invalid casts, especially with `reference` types. An attacker may assume, often correctly, that a `reference` is represented internally by a pointer into memory. The attacker may be able to guess how the object is stored. If the system could be fooled into thinking that the object had a different class, it might permit a program to read or write fields on an object where access would otherwise be denied.

For example, a web browser might keep a copy of the user's private key for signing messages. The `Message` class is public to permit programs to sign messages, but the private key should not be revealed, even to those programs allowed to do the signing.

```
public class Message
{
    private PrivateKey private_key;

    /** Sign the data, but don't reveal the key
    public byte[] sign(byte[] data);
}
```

An attacker might try to get the private key by creating a class like `Message` but with different permissions:

```
public class SneakyMessage
{
    public PrivateKey private_key;
}
```

This class is likely to have the same layout in memory as `Message`. If the attacker could cast a `Message` into a `SneakyMessage`, then the value of `private_key` would appear to be public.

Fortunately, this can't happen. This attack, written in Java, might look like this:

```
void attack(Message m)
{
    SneakyMessage hack = (SneakyMessage) m;
    // Read the private_key field from hack
}
```

The Java compiler rejects this class, pointing out that the cast from `Message` to `SneakyMessage` will never succeed. The attacker might try to bypass the compiler like this:

```
.class SneakyApplet
.super java/applet/Applet

.method attack(LMessage;)V
aload_1                 ; Variable 1 contains a Message
                        ; Try to get the private key out
getfield SneakyMessage/private_key Ljava/security/PrivateKey;
;; Use the private key
.end method
```

The verification algorithm rejects this code, even though the `private_key` in SneakyMessage is public, since it knows that a SneakyMessage is not a Message and vice versa. Since variable 1 contains a Message, not a SneakyMessage, the `getfield` instruction is invalid.

Some people are surprised that the verification algorithm makes this determination, since it is not always possible to prove that variable 1 contains a Message. This is possible because it is not the verification algorithm's job to prove that variable 1 contains a nonsneaky Message before rejecting this class. Rather, the verification algorithm tries to prove that variable 1 does contain a SneakyMessage in order to accept the `getfield` instruction. This is not true, since variable 1 is initialized to a Message and the variable is never altered, so the verification algorithm rejects the code.

It is easy to create code leading up to the `getfield` where it is impossible to be sure what the top of the stack is without actually running the code:

```
.method attack(LMessage;LSneakyMessage;I)
iload_3                 ; Push the number
ifeq attack             ; If it is 0, then try the attack
    aload_2             ; Push the sneaky message
    goto continue       ; Continue with the attack
attack:
    aload_1             ; Push the message, which we try to
continue:               ; treat as a sneaky message
getfield SneakyMessage/private_key Ljava/security/PrivateKey;
```

At the last instruction, the value on top of the stack may or may not be SneakyMessage, depending on the value of the third argument to the method. The verification algorithm will unify two stack pictures at `continue`: One with a SneakMessage and one with a Message. The unification is Object. This makes the `getfield` instruction invalid, so the class is rejected.

15.4.6   Changing the Class of a Reference

The checkcast instruction changes the verification algorithm's perception of the class of an object. The attack method could be rewritten using checkcast:

```
.method attack(LMessage;)V
aload_1                    ; Variable 1 contains a Message
checkcast SneakyMessage    ; Ask the verifier to believe it is
                           ; a SneakyMessage
                           ; Try to get the private key out
getfield SneakyMessage/private_key Ljava/security/PrivateKey;
;; Use the private key
.end method
```

The verification algorithm approves this code, and the applet gets a chance to run. However, the attack is still ineffective, because the checkcast instruction checks the actual type of the value on top of the stack when the program is running. Since the value on top of the stack is really a Message, and a Message is not a SneakyMessage, the checkcast instruction throws an exception. The exception transfers control away from the getfield instruction, so the information is not compromised.

The checkcast instruction does not affect the underlying object. It only changes the verification algorithm's perception of the object as the class is being loaded. The verification algorithm attempts to prove that the program is safe. The checkcast instruction tells the verification algorithm, "You cannot prove that this is safe, but if you check it out as the program runs, you will find that the cast will succeed."

As the program runs, each time checkcast is encountered the JVM checks to ensure that the class of the argument is really a SneakyMessage. If it fails, the JVM throws a ClassCastException. Because no Message can be a SneakyMessage, this code always causes the exception to be thrown.

There is one way for the code to get past the checkcast at runtime. If the Message is null, then the checkcast allows the program to proceed. However, this doesn't help the attacker, since any attempt to read fields from a null reference will be met with a NullPointerException.

15.4.7   Reading Uninitialized Fields

When an object is first created, it may be assigned a place in memory where something important used to be. For example, the web browser may have the user's password to some web site stored in a Connection object. The Connection

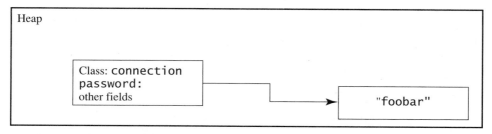

FIGURE 15.1: *A Connection object points to your password*

object and the password string live somewhere in the system's memory, as in Figure 15.1.

Later, the garbage collector may move the Connection object. Things don't really move in a computer's memory; instead, they are copied to a new location and the old location is forgotten. Suppose a user creates a new object that is assigned to the memory space that the Connection object used to occupy. An attacker might hope that the memory looks like Figure 15.2. The first field in MyObject, field1, happens to fall in the same place as the password field of the Connection used to. Before field1 is initialized, it appears to contain a reference to the value that used to be the password field of the Connection object. Although it is unlikely that this would happen, it is not impossible, and the applet code could use this information in a malicious fashion.

Fortunately, the virtual machine prevents this attack by requiring that all fields be initialized before they are read. If the field does not have an explicit initializer, it is implicitly initialized to 0 for numeric fields or null for reference fields. This

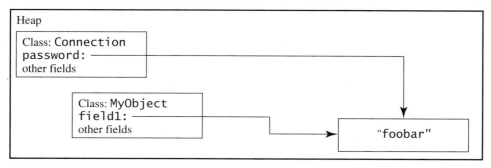

FIGURE 15.2: *Connection moved, and a new object in the same memory*

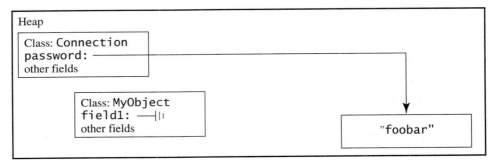

FIGURE 15.3: *field1 is initialized immediately*

happens immediately after the object is created, before it can be used. Therefore, in reality the picture looks like Figure 15.3. Even though the new object occupies the same memory space as the Connection used to, it is unable to access the values that used to be there because field1 is initialized to null before the code has a chance to read the old value.

15.4.8 Array Bounds Checks

Another kind of memory-based attack is to try to read past the ends of an array. To extend an earlier example, suppose that the user created an array of ten bytes that just happened to be placed next to an important place in memory (Figure 15.4). The first ten elements of the array are safe to be read and written. The location that would hold the eleventh byte, however, is the beginning of the password string. If

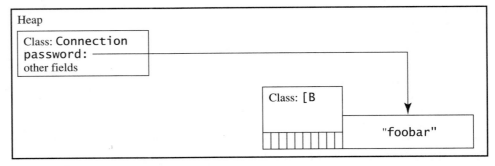

FIGURE 15.4: *Password object in memory immediately after an array*

an applet were to read beyond the end of the array, the password would be revealed.

The only way to read those bytes is to use the `baload` instruction:

```
bipush 10
newarray byte        ; Create an array of ten bytes
bipush 10            ; Try to read the eleventh byte
baload
```

Both the size of the array and the array element to be accessed are determined by operands on the operand stack, not by instruction arguments. This means that there is no way for the virtual machine to be certain what these values will be without running the program.

Therefore, this sort of error cannot be caught by the verification algorithm. Instead, this attack is stopped by the `baload` instruction. Each time the instruction is executed, the length of the array is checked to ensure that the element does not fall out of bounds. If it does, an `ArrayIndexOutOfBoundsException` is thrown.

The bounds check operation is part of the `baload` instruction and all the other array load instructions. The virtual machine does not depend on the program to check array bounds before accessing elements. This removes some responsibility from the programmer, while still ensuring that array bounds are respected.

15.4.9 Catching Exceptions

An attacker might try to catch exceptions that are intended to prevent harmful things from happening to the system. The attack would try to ignore the exceptions.

For example, it was shown earlier that the `SecurityManager` initializer does not permit a second `SecurityManager` to be created once one has been installed. If the initializer detects the existence of another security manager, it throws a `SecurityException`, which prevents the new `SecurityManager` from being used.

Suppose that the attacker catches the exception from the `SecurityManager` constructor within the constructor of `WimpySecurityManager`:

```
.class WimpySecurityManager

.method <init>()V
.catch java/lang/SecurityException from begin to end using
handler
begin:
    aload_0          ; Call the superclass constructor
    invokevirtual java/lang/SecurityManager/<init>()V
```

```
end:
    return                    ; If I'm allowed to invoke the
                              ; constructor, then something is wrong
handler:                      ; Since a SecurityException is thrown,
                              ; control continues here
    return                    ; See if I can return with the object
                              ; only partially constructed
.end method
```

The JVM refuses to load this code because it fails to pass the verification algorithm. One of the verification algorithm's goals in tracing through a constructor is that every `return` is on a path through a call to a superclass constructor. Because all the lines between `begin` and `end` are covered by an exception handler, any of them might throw an exception.

This means that there is a path through the method that does not invoke the constructor. The verification algorithm judges the method to be invalid, which means that the entire class is invalid. This class is rejected, and the system is safe.

15.4.10   Hidden Code

An attacker might try to hide bytecodes inside other bytecodes. Consider an innocuous-looking piece of Oolong code like this:

```
sipush -19712
ineg
```

This code could actually contain a potential attack hidden in the bytecodes. When assembled, the above code produces the following bytecodes:

Location	Value	Meaning
0050	11	sipush
0051	b3	0xb300=-19712
0052	00	
0053	74	ineg

An attacker could generate a class file in which the next bytes were

Location	Value	Meaning
0054	a7	goto
0055	ff	0xfffd=-3
0056	fd	

The `goto` points to location 51, which is in the middle of the `sipush` instruction. It is not possible to write this code in Oolong, since the Oolong assembler will permit a label only between instructions, not in the middle of an instruction.

The attacker hopes that when the code reaches the instruction at location 54, it will attempt to go back three bytes to the byte at 51. If we interpret the bytes at location 51 as bytecodes, we get

```
0051    b3      putstatic
0052    00              0x0074=116
0054    74
```

This is an interpretation of the bytes' attempts to read the field contained in the constant 116.

The attacker might make the constant 116 a Fieldref to a private field like security in java.lang.System, hoping to wipe out the security manager for the system. The attacker hopes that the JVM will not attempt to verify the bytecodes interpreted in this fashion. The attacker hopes that the system will assume that it has checked the code statically, and won't try to check whether or not the field is private at runtime.

There is nothing wrong with the bytes at locations 51 through 53, as long as they are interpreted properly. The problem is the code at 54, which tries to jump into the middle of an instruction. The JVM discovers that the code is attempting to branch into the middle of an instruction, and it will reject the class.

Of course, not all code like this is necessarily harmful. This code may just come from an overly clever programmer who attempted to shrink the code by reinterpreting it this way, and the code may be perfectly safe to execute. However, the verification algorithm never promised that it would accept all safe programs. It only promises to reject all that do not meet certain criteria, which includes all unsafe programs. Because this program does not follow the rules, it is rejected.

15.5   Conclusion

We have seen how the Java platform security architecture is based on the promises made by the Java virtual machine. Both simple and complex security policies can be implemented, depending on the degree of sophistication required and the time and effort the policy implementor wants to exert to ensure that the policy is consistent with good practice. It is critical that the implementor understand the guarantees made by the JVM to understand how the security measures might be circumvented.

CHAPTER **16**

Threads and Synchronization

THE Java platform supports multitasking through *threads*. Each thread is a separate flow of control, executing concurrently with all other threads. If the computer has several CPUs available, separate threads may execute literally at the same time. If not, the JVM implementation can let each thread run for a while, then interrupt it to let a different thread run.

The features that make up the Java platform thread model are divided between the JVM itself and the class `java.lang.Thread`. This class is found on all Java platforms. It contains methods for spawning new threads, controlling thread priority, and stopping and starting thread execution.

The JVM's support for threads lies in its ability to provide synchronization. Synchronization allows two threads to communicate with each other so that resources can be shared safely between threads. Think of synchronization as a traffic light. There is a common resource (the intersection) and two simultaneous threads (lanes of cars) that want to use the intersection. It is critical that only one thread proceed. If both were allowed to proceed, disaster would ensue. If neither one were allowed to go, nobody would get anywhere.

To maximize traffic flow, many traffic lights use sensors to detect when a car wants to use the intersection. Otherwise, on lightly traveled roads, drivers would find themselves staring at a red light with nobody in sight. However, it is not enough to have the traffic light change to green immediately for anybody who trips the sensor. If two cars arrive at exactly the same time, which one gets the green light? In the traffic light, a computer decides which one came first and gives that car the first green light. If they appear to have come at the same time, it doesn't matter which one goes first, but it is crucial that only one goes first.

Synchronization works best when there is a single controlling authority in charge of access. At many intersections, it is unwise to let drivers control access to the intersection by cooperation between them. If two drivers arrive at the same time, there is often much waving of hands and honking of horns while each driver tries to signal to the other to go first. And when a driver does decide to go, the driver must move carefully, to ensure that the other driver hasn't made the decision to go simultaneously. Instead, the drivers agree to let the traffic light control the intersection.

In the JVM, different threads agree to let the JVM itself synchronize between threads. Threads request locks, and the JVM provides the lock to exactly one thread at a time. Requesting a lock is like tripping the sensor for the traffic light: it is a request to proceed, but the JVM ensures that one thread doesn't proceed while another possesses the lock. In the JVM, locks are called *monitor*s.

As in the traffic light, only code that chooses to observe the synchronization restrictions actually pays any attention to the locks. It is up to the programmer to use the synchronization instructions and methods in all code that accesses a shared resource.

If the computer you are using has only a single processor, then it is the job of the JVM to switch back and forth between threads, which means that monitor requests can never occur quite simultaneously. However, if the computer has multiple processors, then two lock requests may occur literally at the same time. It is the responsibility of the JVM implementor to ensure that only one thread obtains control of a monitor at a time.

16.1   Threads

In the JVM, a thread is represented by an instance of the class `Thread`. The thread is initialized with an object that implements the interface `Runnable`. `Runnable` has the single method `run`. The `run` method defines the thread's task. Figures 16.1 and 16.2 show the `Runnable` and `Thread` classes.

When the `start` method is called on the thread, a new flow of control begins, running concurrently with all other threads. (This is called *spawning* a new thread.) A new Java stack is created for the new flow of control. The new thread shares the heap and class area with the other threads. The first element on the new

```
package java.lang;
public interface Runnable
{
    public abstract void run();
}
```

FIGURE 16.1: *The interface Runnable*

```
package java.lang;
public class Thread implements Runnable
{
    /** Constructors for Thread.
     * Runnable r defaults to this.
     * String name defaults to "Thread-n", where n is a counter.
     * ThreadGroup group defaults to null. When group is null, the new
     * thread is put in the same group as the current thread.
     */
    public Thread();
    public Thread(Runnable r);
    public Thread(ThreadGroup group, Runnable r);
    public Thread(String name);
    public Thread(ThreadGroup, String name);
    public Thread(Runnable r, String name);
    public Thread(ThreadGroup group, Runnable r, String name);

    /** Causes this thread to begin execution.
     * The Java virtual machine calls the run method of this thread. */
    public synchronized void start();

    /** Executes the run method of the Runnable, if there is one.
     * Otherwise, do nothing */
    public void run();

    /** Forces the thread to stop executing */
    public synchronized void stop();

    /** Set the thread's priority */
    public final void setPriority(int);

    /** Get the thread's priority */
    public final int getPriority();

    /** Cause the current thread to yield control */
    public static void yield();

    /** Cause the current thread to sleep for m milliseconds
     * and n nanoseconds */
    public static void sleep(long m, int n);
    public static void sleep(long m);

    /* Other fields and methods omitted. */
}
```

FIGURE 16.2: *Part of Thread*

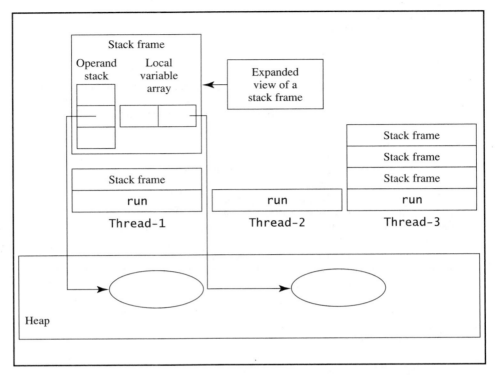

FIGURE 16.3: *JVM with multiple threads*

stack is a call to the run method of the Runnable object. The new thread proceeds until the run method terminates.

Figure 16.3 depicts a JVM with three threads running. For each thread, the first method on the Java stack is the run method. Each frame in each Java stack still has its own operand stack and its own local variable array.

16.1.1 Example: Multithreaded Web Server

Following is part of an implementation of a simple multithreaded web server. It consists of two classes: WebServer, which runs the server itself, and WebServerConnection, which handles an individual request in a separate thread.

```
import java.io.*;
import java.net.*;
```

```java
/**
 * This represents a connection between a web browser and the
 * web server. The run method reads the browser's request, then
 * provides the requested page
 */
class WebServerConnection implements Runnable
{
    Socket connection;

    public WebServerConnection(Socket connection)
    {
        this.connection = connection;
    }

    /**
     * This method handles a single request from a web browser.
     * Because it is a separate thread, it can execute
       simultaneously with other requests
     */
    public void run()
    {
        // Read the request from connection.getInputStream()
        // Write the results to connection.getOutputStream()
        // Close the socket
        // Returning terminates this thread
    }
}

/** This class runs the web server. It sets up a ServerSocket
 * on port 80 to listen for requests. When a web browser
 * connects to that port, a new WebServerConnection is spawned
 * in a separate thread so that the server may continue to
 * listen for new connections
 */
public class WebServer
{
    public static void main(String args[])
    {
        try {
```

```
            // Listen on port 80
            ServerSocket sock = new ServerSocket(80);
            while(true)
            {

                // Wait for a connection
                Socket connection = sock.accept();

                // Spawn a new connection to handle the socket
                Runnable connect =
                    new WebServerConnection(connection);
                Thread t = new Thread(connect);

                // Set it going
                t.start();
            }
        }
        catch(Exception e) {
            // Handle errors
        }
    }
}
```

The main in WebServer listens for connections from web browsers. When it receives one, it creates a WebServerConnection, which is a Runnable object. It places the connection in a new thread. The call to t.start starts the new thread and returns immediately. This allows the server to go back and listen for new requests while the WebServerConnection handles the request.

Now there are two things happening at once. The original thread running WebServer.main continues by looping back to accept another socket connection. The newly spawned thread executes the method WebServerConnection.run to service the connection. If a new request comes in while the first is being handled, the server spawns yet another thread, and then all three continue simultaneously. The new thread continues until it reaches the end of its run method or when an exception causes it to leave run. When that happens, the new thread is terminated.

Since Thread implements Runnable, it is common to subclass Thread instead of implementing Runnable. An equivalent way to implement WebServerConnection is

```
class WebServerConnection extends Thread
```

This allows the programmer to condense the Thread creation and Runnable creation into the single call:

```
Thread connect = new WebServerConnection(connection);
```

which creates the new `WebServerConnection`, using itself as the `Runnable`. The new combination `Thread` and `Runnable` is then started with

```
connect.start();
```

16.1.2 Exceptions and Threads

Although the declaration of `run` in `Runnable` specifies that it does not throw any exceptions, it is still possible for `run` to raise uncaught exceptions. Because `run` does not declare any exceptions, a Java compiler prohibits any implementation of `run` from throwing certain kinds of exceptions. This is actually a feature of the Java language, not the JVM itself. The JVM does not require you to declare which exceptions are thrown. If you write in Oolong, your program may throw an exception from `run`. Even in Java, certain classes of exceptions are permitted, specifically those that are subclasses of `Error` or `RuntimeException`.

Since `run` is at the bottom of the execution stack, there is no method further down the execution stack to handle the exception. The `run` method terminates, but no exception handler is invoked.

The `ThreadGroup` containing the thread is notified about the death of the thread by an invocation of the `uncaughtException` method, which usually prints a stack dump to the console. The stack dump is familiar to most Java programmers, who at one time or another have tried to call a method on `null`, which causes a `NullPointerException` that is not handled. The stack dump you see comes from `uncaughtException`.

Typically, threads use the default thread group. You can create new thread groups that have different error handling for uncaught exceptions. Thread groups fall outside the scope this book. For more information, look at the documentation for `java.lang.Thread` and `java.lang.ThreadGroup`.

You might expect that the thread invoking `start` would get a chance to handle the exception. Recall that the original thread has continued to execute after it invoked `start`, which returns almost immediately, without waiting for the run method to complete. It is probably doing something totally unrelated by the time the child thread throws the exception and is unprepared to handle an exception.

16.2   Sharing State Between Threads

Each thread has its own Java stack. The Java stack is a sequence of stack frames. Each stack frame represents a method call, with its own program counter, local variable array, and operand stack. The local variable array and operand stack are not shared between threads, so there is no need to synchronize on them.

ll threads share the same heap. Threads may attempt to use the same object e same time. If only one thread can be allowed to work with an object, as the M example discussed earlier shows, then it may be necessary to lock the ject. The JVM provides instructions to enable threads to lock objects (discussed section 16.3).

Even if the object is not locked, the JVM still provides some protection for the fields of the object. Reading and writing fields (with `getfield`/`putfield` or `getstatic`/`putstatic`) are atomic operations; that is, they are indivisible and cannot be interrupted by switching between threads. It is impossible to read a field in one thread while another thread writes to it, and vice versa. It is also impossible for two threads to write to a field at the same time. (This is not true for `long` or `double` values; see section 16.2.2).

16.2.1 Need for Synchronization

To see the sort of havoc that could be caused by the simultaneous read and write of a value, suppose that there is an object with an `int` field that should contain either +1 or −1. There are two threads, one of which reads the field with `get-field`, the other of which writes to the field with `putfield`. In Figure 16.4, each square represents one byte of the 32-bit `int` value, which originally contains +1. One thread wants to change it to −1 at the same time another thread wants to read the value. At the point the reader reads the thread, the writer is only half done with its work: only the left two bytes have been written. The value is nonsensical: it is interpreted as −65,535, which is neither 1 nor −1, even though no thread intended to write such a nonsensical value.

The JVM specification forbids this from happening. Once a thread begins to write, it must complete the operation before anybody else is allowed to read, even if the object has not explicitly been locked. What happens is shown in Figure 16.5.

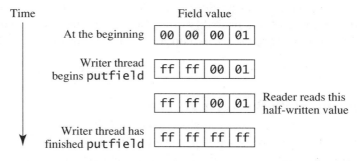

FIGURE 16.4: *Perils of improper synchronization*

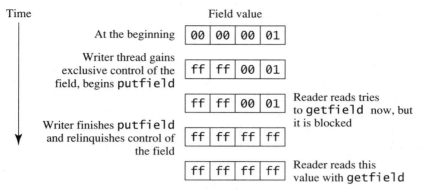

FIGURE 16.5: *Synchronization preserves integrity*

Because the reader is blocked from reading the field while the writer is setting the field value, the reader never sees the nonsense value that occurs halfway through writing. Instead, it sees only the final value.

If both the reader and the writer happen at precisely the same time, or if two writers try to set a field at precisely the same time, the JVM is responsible for picking one or the other and letting it proceed while blocking the other. It does not matter which one is picked to proceed, only that exactly one proceeds at a time.

For example, suppose both read and write occur at the same time and the reader thread is picked to go first (Figure 16.6). The writer has been blocked from proceeding until the reader has finished getting the value of the field. This means that the reader reads the value of the field before it is set. Immediately after that,

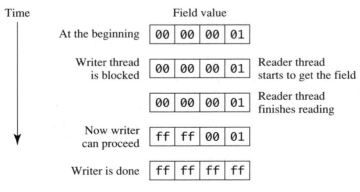

FIGURE 16.6: *Reader goes first*

the value changes. The JVM could just as easily choose the writer thread to proceed instead of the reader thread, in which case the reader would read the new value of the field.

One thread may require that the field not change its value until it has performed some more complex operation. For example, the value of this field may be linked to the value of another field, and both of them must be set at the same time without any intervening read operations. The thread must communicate to the other threads that it wishes exclusive access to the object. For this reason, the JVM provides monitors and object locks, as discussed in section 16.3.

16.2.2   Exception: `long`s and `double`s

There is an exception to this rule: `long` and `double` fields may be read and written as two separate atomic operations. Many systems provide hardware support for atomic reads and writes of 32-bit values, but not for the 64-bit values required by `long` or `double` values. This can lead to the sort of error shown in Figure 16.4.

If you write a program in which objects containing double-word values are shared between threads, it is critical that you use locks to ensure that this sort of half-written value doesn't occur.

16.3   Monitors and Object Locks

Each object has a *monitor* associated with it. The JVM guarantees that a monitor may be owned by at most one thread. This provides JVM programmers with the ability to implement many different kinds of synchronization control.

The JVM has two instructions for operating on monitors: `monitorenter` and `monitorexit`. When a thread issues the `monitorenter` instruction, it acquires the monitor of the object on top of the stack. If some other thread owns the monitor for that object, the thread requesting the object will block until the monitor is released. The monitor is released when the `monitorexit` instruction is performed on the same object.

Because only one thread may own a monitor at a time, programs may use the monitor to synchronize between threads. One use of this synchronization is for locks. If the threads agree that they must acquire the monitor on some object before performing an operation, then that object acts like a lock: only one thread may perform that operation at a time.

For example, suppose that you have a number of threads running. Each thread writes diagnostic messages to the console. A thread should be able to write an entire message to the console before another thread begins to write its message. If two threads tried to write messages to the console at the same time, the console would be unreadable.

The solution is to use monitors to control access to the System.out object so that only one thread may use it at a time:

```
getfield java/lang/System/out
    Ljava/io/PrintStream;                ; Push System.out
monitorenter                             ; Lock it

; Only one thread at a time can be in this code, since the
; monitorenter will block until no other thread is using the
; System.out object.
; This is called the critical section

;; Insert code here which dumps a message to System.out

getfield java/lang/System/out
    Ljava/io/PrintStream;                ; Push System.out
monitorexit                              ; Release it
```

Because of the monitorenter instruction, at most one thread may be in the critical section at a time. The critical section prints out the entire message before executing the monitorexit instruction, ensuring that messages do not overlap.

If several threads are waiting for the monitor at the same time, only one gets it. The others continue to wait. Different virtual machine implementations have different techniques for choosing which thread will get control of the monitor next. Generally, implementations will try to distribute control of the monitor fairly among the threads.

It is important to note that this is purely an advisory lock. Programs that use monitorenter obtain the lock before using the object. The JVM doesn't enforce that restriction; it must be written explicitly by the programmer. The part the JVM plays is to ensure that only one thread owns the monitor at a time.

A thread can keep a monitor lock as long as it wants. It may even exit the method containing the monitorenter instruction. This is a simple implementation of semaphores using the monitor instructions:

```
.class sem

; P: gain control of semaphore
.method p()V
aload_0
monitorenter              ; Leave method without exiting monitor
```

```
return
.end method

; V: release semaphore
.method V()V
aload_0
monitorexit                    ; Now release the monitor
return
.end method
```

This use of the monitor instructions is strongly discouraged, since it is very easy for the programmer using methods like these to forget to release a monitor that is held. This can easily lead to deadlock, in which two threads wait forever for the other one to surrender a monitor. Instead, it is better to have a `monitorexit` for each `monitorenter` instruction within a single method. This is the approach used by Java compilers (see section 16.3.1 for more details on how it does this).

A thread may obtain the monitor more than once. In order to release the monitor, it must use `monitorexit` exactly as many times as it calls `monitorenter` on the object. For example:

```
.class MyClass
.method foo(Ljava/lang/Object;)V
    aload_1                     ; Push the object to lock
    monitorenter                ; Lock it. The lock count is 1

    aload_0                     ; Call bar with the lock object
    aload_1
    invokevirtual MyClass/bar (Ljava/lang/Object;)V

    aload_1                     ; Release the lock. Now the lock
    monitorexit                 ; count is 0, and others may get it
.end method

; This method is called from foo
.method bar(Ljava/lang/Object;)V
    aload_1                     ; Lock the object again. The lock
    monitorenter                ; count is now 2

    ;; Do some stuff

    aload_1                     ; Release the object. The lock count
    monitorexit                 ; is 1
```

```
    return
.end method
```

Once a thread has the monitor, additional locks on the monitor will happen almost instantaneously. There is no need for the thread to compete for ownership of the monitor.

Each `monitorenter` increases the lock count by 1, and each `monitorexit` decreases it by 1. Only when the lock count reaches 0 may other threads have the chance to get it. The race for the monitor happens immediately after the lock count reaches 0. For example:

```
aload_0                    ; Lock the object
monitorenter

aload_0                    ; Push the lock object twice
dup
monitorexit                ; Lock it once, then try to get
monitorenter               ; it again immediately
```

Even though the `monitorenter` occurs immediately after the `monitorexit`, there is no guarantee that the same thread will get the lock again immediately. It has to wait its turn with all the other threads waiting for the monitor on this object.

16.3.1 Synchronization in Java

In Java, `monitorenter` and `monitorexit` instructions are generated in pairs by a `synchronized` statement. A `synchronized` statement looks like this:

```
synchronized(obj)
{
    // In here, the current thread has exclusive access to obj
}
```

When this is compiled, the `synchronized` block is surrounded by `monitorenter` and `monitorexit` instructions. To ensure that the monitor is always released, an exception handler is used to catch all exceptions. The code compiles to

```
.catch all from begin to end using handler
    aload_1                ; Push the Object
    monitorenter           ; Lock it

begin:
    ;; The body of the synchronized statement goes here
end:
```

```
    aload_1                                 ; Release the lock
    monitorexit
    return

; If any exceptions occur during the synchronized statement,
; this exception handler will be executed. It ensures that
; the lock is released
handler:
    aload_1                                 ; Release the lock
    monitorexit
    return
```

16.3.2 Synchronized Methods

We said before that the monitorenter and monitorexit instructions are advisory locks. There is no way to require that a monitorenter be executed before using an object. It is up to the programmer using an object to know whether an object should be locked before use. Any thread failing to obtain a lock before using an object may corrupt the data in that object. Consider, for example, a shared log file:

```
.class LogFile

.field static theLog LLogFile;            ; The main log file

.method printMessage(Ljava/lang/String;)V
;; Print the message
.end method
```

To log a message, it is expected that the thread lock the log object before use:

```
getstatic Logfile/theLog LLlogFile;       ; Get the log file
monitorenter                              ; Lock it

getstatic Logfile/theLog LLlogFile;       ; Get the log file
ldc "Some log string"
invokevirtual LogFile/printMessage
    (Ljava/lang/String;)V                 ; Print a message

getstatic Logfile/theLog LLlogFile;       ; Release the lock
monitorexit
```

If the monitorenter or monitorexit instructions are forgotten, or if the program has a way to execute one without executing the other, there will be problems. A `monitorenter` without a `monitorexit` will cause the log to be held indefinitely. If the program issues a `monitorexit` without having already obtained the lock, the JVM will cause an `IllegalMonitorStateException` to be thrown.

For this reason, the JVM provides a way to force a program to acquire the monitor on an object before invoking a method on the object. By declaring a method `synchronized`, any thread attempting to use that method obtains a lock on the object first. To ensure that the log must be locked before the `printMessage` method can be called, declare it like this:

```
.method synchronized printMessage(Ljava/lang/String;)V
```

When this method is invoked, the JVM automatically acquires the monitor for the object on which the method is invoked. If the monitor is currently owned by some other thread, then the current thread blocks until the monitor becomes free.

When the method ends, whether normally through a `return` instruction or abnormally because of an exception being thrown, the monitor is released automatically. This guarantees that the thread cannot accidentally keep control of the monitor after leaving the method.

Only one thread at a time may use the `LogFile`, even without explicit `monitorenter` instructions. Users of `synchronized` methods are relieved of the responsibility of explicitly obtaining the locks themselves.

It is important to note that the lock lasts only as long as the call to `printMessage`. If it were necessary to print two messages in a row without any intervening messages, it would be necessary to lock the object in the calling code:

```
aload_1              ; Push the log
monitorenter         ; And lock it
;; Invoke printMessage for the first message
;; Invoke printMessage for the second message
aload_1              ; Release the log
monitorexit
```

A lock on the log is obtained three times by this thread: once by the `monitorenter` instruction and twice by the two calls to `printMessage`. During the interval between calls to `printMessage`, the current thread still has the lock, and nobody else can call `printMessage` since the call is `synchronized`. Both the `monitorenter` and `synchronized` method calls obtain the same lock.

That means that while in `printMessage`, the current thread has the same lock twice. This does not present a problem, since a thread can reobtain a lock it already has without waiting. The lock count increases to 2. When the call to `printMessage` ends, the lock count drops to 1, which means that the thread continues to hold the monitor.

A `synchronized` method can call another `synchronized` method on the same object. It can even call itself, recursively. Since it already has the lock on the object, it increases the lock count. Each time the method returns, the lock count decreases. When the topmost call returns, the lock count drops to 0, and other threads can try to obtain the lock.

You can `synchronize` static methods, too. In that case, the object that is locked is the `Class` object corresponding to the class. For example, suppose you need a class `Counter`, which maintains a one-up counter to be used by several threads. It's necessary to synchronize access to the counter value. A possible definition of the class:

```
.class Counter
.field static private next I  ; The next value of the counter

; A method to increment and return the counter
.method synchronized static getNextCounter ()I
.limit stack 2
getstatic Counter/next I      ; Get the field
istore_0                      ; Store it in a local value
iload_0                       ; Increment the value
iconst_1
iadd
putstatic Counter/next I      ; Store the increment value
iload_0                       ; Return the original value
ireturn
.end method
```

Within the body of `getNextCounter`, the thread obtains a lock on the object returned by `Class.forName("Counter")` (or `Counter.class`, in the notation of Java 1.1). This object is unique within the JVM; that is, any thread requesting `Counter.class` receives a reference to the same object. This means that all threads attempting to synchronize on the class are trying to synchronize on the same object.

16.4   Scheduling

On most computers, the CPU can execute only one thread at a time. Even on large multiprocessor computers, there are usually more threads than there are CPUs. Therefore, some threads must be suspended while other threads execute. In order to be fair, the system lets each thread run for some amount of time, then interrupts it and lets some other thread run. The plan for deciding which thread to execute and how long to let it run is called *scheduling*.

The JVM makes few promises about how scheduling occurs. Fairness is not guaranteed. This allows virtual machine implementers flexibility in porting the JVM to other operating systems. Some implementations have a separate native operating system level thread for each Java thread, and the scheduling behavior is consistent with the operating system's thread scheduler. This technique is usually used on Windows implementations and on Solaris 2.6.

Another common implementation uses "green threads," a threading library that doesn't depend on the native OS threads. Green threads are found in some older versions of Java, particularly on Unix-based systems. Green threads depend on the programmer to do most of the scheduling.

Ordinarily, a thread yields control of the CPU only when doing an activity involving operating system control, such as I/O or sleeping. If your application depends on fair division of CPU time among threads, it may help to include calls to `Thread.yield`, which permits the thread scheduler to give control to a different thread.

A portable JVM program cannot make any assumptions about thread scheduling. It may be interrupted at any point in its processing. It may also permit one thread to go forever without sharing the CPU.

You can make hints to the thread scheduler about priority with the `Thread.setPriority` method. This `method` takes an `int` between `MIN_PRIORITY` and `MAX_PRIORITY`. The JVM specification makes no guarantees about the meaning of priority levels, but in general higher values are more likely to get control of locks and are more likely to be scheduled for the CPU.

For example, to create a low-priority thread that uses spare CPU cycles to compute pi:

```
Thread pi = new PiThread();
pi.setPriority(Thread.MIN_PRIORITY);
pi.start();
```

You should not assume that a high-priority thread will always take precedence over a low-priority thread. The priority is only a hint to the scheduler, not a requirement. A high-priority thread may be put to sleep for a while to give a low-priority thread a chance to run.

Because low-priority threads may run even if higher-priority threads exist, it is not possible to write mutual exclusion code using thread priorities. The reasoning goes like this: if I have exactly one thread that has the highest priority, and I ask it to do all the work that may not be interrupted, then that work will always be done before any other thread is scheduled.

Unfortunately, this reasoning is incorrect. No matter what the priority distributions are, it is still possible for a low-priority thread to run instead of a high-priority thread. Instead, you should use the synchronization primitives through `synchronized` methods and monitor locks; the virtual machine guarantees that these will be effective.

16.4.1   Surrendering Control of the CPU

A thread may be interrupted at any time by the thread scheduler to allow another thread to run. In addition, a thread may voluntarily give up control of the CPU. It may do this while it's waiting for input from some device or just to be cooperative with the other threads.

One way to surrender control is to `sleep`, which causes the thread to stop for a certain number of milliseconds (or milliseconds and nanoseconds, if two arguments are provided, though few JVM implementations can actually deliver control at that fine-grained a level). When the specified period has passed, the thread again competes with the other threads for control of the CPU. It does not necessarily regain control immediately after sleeping, especially if there are other CPU-hungry threads running.

For example, a mail client may want to have a thread that polls the mail server for email every five minutes.

```
.class PollThread
.implements Runnable

.method public run()V
loop:
    invokestatic PollThread/check_mail()V
    ldc2_w 300000            ; Sleep for 5 minutes =
                             ; 300,000 milliseconds
                             ; before checking again
begin:
    invokestatic java/lang/Thread/sleep(J)V
end:
    goto loop
.end method
```

The `yield` method is similar to `sleep`, except no argument is required. Instead, the current thread goes back into the pool of threads waiting to execute. If there are no other threads running, the current thread continues immediately. If other threads are running, the JVM schedules the thread to run again. If the program is running on a system that doesn't divide time well between threads, you might throw in occasional `yield` calls:

```
;; Do a bunch of stuff

; Give other threads a chance to run
invokestatic java/lang/Thread/yield()V


;; Do some more stuff
```

This call helps the threads to share better.

16.4.2 Waiting for Another Thread

Another method similar to sleep is `join`. When you `join` to a thread, you wait until that thread finishes. For example, suppose you're writing a chess-playing program and you want to spawn off a number of threads to help make a decision. This will help take advantage of multiple CPUs. When all of the threads have completed, you make your move:

```
// Consider all possible boards one move away from this position
Board boards[] = current_board.nextMoves();

// Spawn off a thread for each board
Thread threads = new Thread[boards.length];
for(int i = 0; i < boards.length; i++)
{
    // Create a thread to consider this board
    threads[i] = new ChessThread(board[i]);
    thread[i].start();
}

// Now, wait for all threads to complete
try {
    for(int i = 0; i < threads.length; i++)
        threads[i].join();
}
catch(InterruptedException e) {
    // We've been interrupted
}
```

This code waits for the first thread to terminate, then waits for the second thread, and so on. Some threads may wait a long time to return. Like `sleep`, `join` may take an argument that specifies how long to sleep. The program can set a time limit on the total time it will wait:

```
int limit = 300000;              // Wait up to 5 minutes
try {
    for(int i = 0; i < threads.length && limit > 0; i++)
    {
        long begin = System.currentTimeMillis();
        threads[i].join(limit);
        long end = System.currentTimeMillis();
        limit -= end - begin;          // Subtract time waited
    }
}
catch(InterruptedException e) {
    // We've been interrupted
}
```

The variable `limit` is set to the maximum waiting time. Each time it attempts to join with a thread (that is, wait for that thread to terminate), it calculates the beginning time and ending time of the waiting period. It subtracts that difference from the limit so that the next time the allowed wait time will be shorter. Eventually, either all the threads join, or the total time expires.

16.5   Conclusion

The core of synchronization is the monitor, which allows an object to be owned by exactly one thread. When one thread owns the monitor on an object, all other threads wishing to take control of the monitor must wait until the owning thread relinquishes control.

The `monitorenter` and `monitorexit` instructions and the `synchronized` method keyword are just the beginning. The class `java.lang.Thread` provides many other ways to take advantage of monitors. Many features of thread control have not been discussed fully here, because they are well documented at the Java level. Have a look at the documentation for `java.lang.Thread` and `java.lang.ThreadGroup` for these features. For an introduction to the topic, try *The Java Programming Language,* by Ken Arnold and James Gosling, which has a good introduction to threads in Java. Then read *Concurrent Programming in Java,* by Doug Lea. It contains many good examples of how to use threads to take advantage of concurrency in your programs.

Tables

A.1 Instructions by Opcode

Mnemonic	Hex	Dec	Mnemonic	Hex	Dec
nop	00	0	iload_1	1b	27
aconst_null	01	1	iload_2	1c	28
iconst_m1	02	2	iload_3	1d	29
iconst_0	03	3	lload_0	1e	30
iconst_1	04	4	lload_1	1f	31
iconst_2	05	5	lload_2	20	32
iconst_3	06	6	lload_3	21	33
iconst_4	07	7	fload_0	22	34
iconst_5	08	8	fload_1	23	35
lconst_0	09	9	fload_2	24	36
lconst_1	0a	10	fload_3	25	37
fconst_0	0b	11	dload_0	26	38
fconst_1	0c	12	dload_1	27	39
fconst_2	0d	13	dload_2	28	40
dconst_0	0e	14	dload_3	29	41
dconst_1	0f	15	aload_0	2a	42
bipush	10	16	aload_1	2b	43
sipush	11	17	aload_2	2c	44
ldc	12	18	aload_3	2d	45
ldc_w	13	19	iaload	2e	46
ldc2_w	14	20	laload	2f	47
iload	15	21	faload	30	48
lload	16	22	daload	31	49
fload	17	23	aaload	32	50
dload	18	24	baload	33	51
aload	19	25	caload	34	52
iload_0	1a	26	saload	35	53

Mnemonic	Hex	Dec	Mnemonic	Hex	Dec
istore	36	54	dup_x2	5b	91
lstore	37	55	dup2	5c	92
fstore	38	56	dup2_x1	5d	93
dstore	39	57	dup2_x2	5e	94
astore	3a	58	swap	5f	95
istore_0	3b	59	iadd	60	96
istore_1	3c	60	ladd	61	97
istore_2	3d	61	fadd	62	98
istore_3	3e	62	dadd	63	99
lstore_0	3f	63	isub	64	100
lstore_1	40	64	lsub	65	101
lstore_2	41	65	fsub	66	102
lstore_3	42	66	dsub	67	103
fstore_0	43	67	imul	68	104
fstore_1	44	68	lmul	69	105
fstore_2	45	69	fmul	6a	106
fstore_3	46	70	dmul	6b	107
dstore_0	47	71	idiv	6c	108
dstore_1	48	72	ldiv	6d	109
dstore_2	49	73	fdiv	6e	110
dstore_3	4a	74	ddiv	6f	111
astore_0	4b	75	irem	70	112
astore_1	4c	76	lrem	71	113
astore_2	4d	77	frem	72	114
astore_3	4e	78	drem	73	115
iastore	4f	79	ineg	74	116
lastore	50	80	lneg	75	117
fastore	51	81	fneg	76	118
dastore	52	82	dneg	77	119
aastore	53	83	ishl	78	120
bastore	54	84	lshl	79	121
castore	55	85	ishr	7a	122
sastore	56	86	lshr	7b	123
pop	57	87	iushr	7c	124
pop2	58	88	lushr	7d	125
dup	59	89	iand	7e	126
dup_x1	5a	90	land	7f	127

Mnemonic	Hex	Dec
ior	80	128
lor	81	129
ixor	82	130
lxor	83	131
iinc	84	132
i2l	85	133
i2f	86	134
i2d	87	135
l2i	88	136
l2f	89	137
l2d	8a	138
f2i	8b	139
f2l	8c	140
f2d	8d	141
d2i	8e	142
d2l	8f	143
d2f	90	144
i2b	91	145
i2c	92	146
i2s	93	147
lcmp	94	148
fcmpl	95	149
fcmpg	96	150
dcmpl	97	151
dcmpg	98	152
ifeq	99	153
ifne	9a	154
iflt	9b	155
ifge	9c	156
ifgt	9d	157
ifle	9e	158
if_icmpeq	9f	159
if_icmpne	a0	160
if_icmplt	a1	161
if_icmpge	a2	162
if_icmpgt	a3	163
if_icmple	a4	164

Mnemonic	Hex	Dec
if_acmpeq	a5	165
if_acmpne	a6	166
goto	a7	167
jsr	a8	168
ret	a9	169
tableswitch	aa	170
lookupswitch	ab	171
ireturn	ac	172
lreturn	ad	173
freturn	ae	174
dreturn	af	175
areturn	b0	176
return	b1	177
getstatic	b2	178
putstatic	b3	179
getfield	b4	180
putfield	b5	181
invokevirtual	b6	182
invokespecial	b7	183
invokestatic	b8	184
invokeinterface	b9	185
unused	ba	186
new	bb	187
newarray	bc	188
anewarray	bd	189
arraylength	be	190
athrow	bf	191
checkcast	c0	192
instanceof	c1	193
monitorenter	c2	194
monitorexit	c3	195
wide	c4	196
multianewarray	c5	197
ifnull	c6	198
ifnonnull	c7	199
goto_w	c8	200
jsr_w	c9	201

A.2   Instructions Alphabetically

Mnemonic	Hex	Dec	Mnemonic	Hex	Dec
aaload	32	50	dload_0	26	38
aastore	53	83	dload_1	27	39
aconst_null	01	1	dload_2	28	40
aload	19	25	dload_3	29	41
aload_0	2a	42	dmul	6b	107
aload_1	2b	43	dneg	77	119
aload_2	2c	44	drem	73	115
aload_3	2d	45	dreturn	af	175
anewarray	bd	189	dstore	39	57
areturn	b0	176	dstore_0	47	71
arraylength	be	190	dstore_1	48	72
astore	3a	58	dstore_2	49	73
astore_0	4b	75	dstore_3	4a	74
astore_1	4c	76	dsub	67	103
astore_2	4d	77	dup	59	89
astore_3	4e	78	dup_x1	5a	90
athrow	bf	191	dup_x2	5b	91
baload	33	51	dup2	5c	92
bastore	54	84	dup2_x1	5d	93
bipush	10	16	dup2_x2	5e	94
caload	34	52	f2d	8d	141
castore	55	85	f2i	8b	139
checkcast	c0	192	f2l	8c	140
d2f	90	144	fadd	62	98
d2i	8e	142	faload	30	48
d2l	8f	143	fastore	51	81
dadd	63	99	fcmpg	96	150
daload	31	49	fcmpl	95	149
dastore	52	82	fconst_0	0b	11
dcmpg	98	152	fconst_1	0c	12
dcmpl	97	151	fconst_2	0d	13
dconst_0	0e	14	fdiv	6e	110
dconst_1	0f	15	fload	17	23
ddiv	6f	111	fload_0	22	34
dload	18	24	fload_1	23	35

Mnemonic	Hex	Dec
fload_2	24	36
fload_3	25	37
fmul	6a	106
fneg	76	118
frem	72	114
freturn	ae	174
fstore	38	56
fstore_0	43	67
fstore_1	44	68
fstore_2	45	69
fstore_3	46	70
fsub	66	102
getfield	b4	180
getstatic	b2	178
goto	a7	167
goto_w	c8	200
i2b	91	145
i2c	92	146
i2d	87	135
i2f	86	134
i2l	85	133
i2s	93	147
iadd	60	96
iaload	2e	46
iand	7e	126
iastore	4f	79
iconst_0	03	3
iconst_1	04	4
iconst_2	05	5
iconst_3	06	6
iconst_4	07	7
iconst_5	08	8
iconst_m1	02	2
idiv	6c	108
if_acmpeq	a5	165
if_acmpne	a6	166
if_icmpeq	9f	159

Mnemonic	Hex	Dec
if_icmpge	a2	162
if_icmpgt	a3	163
if_icmple	a4	164
if_icmplt	a1	161
if_icmpne	a0	160
ifeq	99	153
ifge	9c	156
ifgt	9d	157
ifle	9e	158
iflt	9b	155
ifne	9a	154
ifnonnull	c7	199
ifnull	c6	198
iinc	84	132
iload	15	21
iload_0	1a	26
iload_1	1b	27
iload_2	1c	28
iload_3	1d	29
imul	68	104
ineg	74	116
instanceof	c1	193
invokeinterface	b9	185
invokespecial	b7	183
invokestatic	b8	184
invokevirtual	b6	182
ior	80	128
irem	70	112
ireturn	ac	172
ishl	78	120
ishr	7a	122
istore	36	54
istore_0	3b	59
istore_1	3c	60
istore_2	3d	61
istore_3	3e	62
isub	64	100

Mnemonic	Hex	Dec
iushr	7c	124
ixor	82	130
jsr	a8	168
jsr_w	c9	201
l2d	8a	138
l2f	89	137
l2i	88	136
ladd	61	97
laload	2f	47
land	7f	127
lastore	50	80
lcmp	94	148
lconst_0	09	9
lconst_1	0a	10
ldc	12	18
ldc_w	13	19
ldc2_w	14	20
ldiv	6d	109
lload	16	22
lload_0	1e	30
lload_1	1f	31
lload_2	20	32
lload_3	21	33
lmul	69	105
lneg	75	117
lookupswitch	ab	171
lor	81	129
lrem	71	113
lreturn	ad	173

Mnemonic	Hex	Dec
lshl	79	121
lshr	7b	123
lstore	37	55
lstore_0	3f	63
lstore_1	40	64
lstore_2	41	65
lstore_3	42	66
lsub	65	101
lushr	7d	125
lxor	83	131
monitorenter	c2	194
monitorexit	c3	195
multianewarray	c5	197
new	bb	187
newarray	bc	188
nop	00	0
pop	57	87
pop2	58	88
putfield	b5	181
putstatic	b3	179
ret	a9	169
return	b1	177
saload	35	53
sastore	56	86
sipush	11	17
swap	5f	95
tableswitch	aa	170
wide	c4	196

A.3   Instructions by Category

This section contains a listing of the instructions and what they do, grouped by category. Here is a key to the descriptions:

a	The top slot of the stack. May be an int, float, or reference.
b	The second stack slot. May be an int, float, or reference.
c	The third stack slot. May be an int, float, or reference.
d	The fourth stack slot. May be an int, float, or reference.
ab	The long or double on top of the stack, made up of slots a and b.
cd	The long or double second on the stack, made up of slots c and d.

A.3.1   Arithmetic

Mnemonic	Arguments	Description
dadd		Add double (ab+cd)
dcmpg		Compare double
dcmpl		Compare double
ddiv		Divide double (ab/cd)
dmul		Multiply double (ab*cd)
dneg		Negate double (-ab)
drem		Remainder double (ab%cd)
dsub		Subtract double (ab-cd)
fadd		Add float (a+b)
fcmpg		Compare float
fcmpl		Compare float
fdiv		Divide float (a/b)
fmul		Multiply float (a*b)
fneg		Negate float (-a)
frem		Remainder float (a%b)
fsub		Subtract float (a-b)
i2b		Convert int to byte
i2c		Convert int to char
i2s		Convert int to short

Mnemonic	Arguments	Description
iadd		Add int (a+b)
iand		Bitwise and ints (a & b)
idiv		Divide ints (a/b)
imul		Multiply ints (a*b)
ineg		Negate int (-a)
ior		Bitwise or ints (a | b)
irem		Remainder int (a%b)
ishl		Shift int left (a << b)
ishr		Shift int right (a >> c)
isub		Subtract int (a-b)
iushr		Unsigned shift int right (a >>> c)
ixor		Bitwise xor ints (a ∧ b)
ladd		Add long (ab+cd)
land		Bitwise and longs (ab & cd)
lcmp		Compare longs
ldiv		Divide long (ab/cd)
lmul		Multiply long (ab*cd)
lneg		Negate long (-ab)
lor		Bitwise or longs (ab | cd)
lrem		Remainder longs (ab%cd)
lshl		Shift long left (bc << 9)
lshr		Shift long right (bc >> 9)
lsub		Subtract long (ab-cd)
lushr		Unsigned shift long right (bc >>> 9)
lxor		Bitwise x or longs (ab ∧ cd)

A.3.2   Array

Mnemonic	Arguments	Description
aaload		Push array element a from array b
aastore		Store a in array element b of array c
anewarray	class	Create array of class, length a
arraylength		Length of array a
athrow		Throw exception a

Mnemonic	Arguments	Description
baload		Push array element a from array b
bastore		Store a in array element b of array c
caload		Push array element a from array b
castore		Store a in array element
daload		Push array element a from array b
dastore		Store ab in array element
faload		Push array element a from array b
fastore		Store a in array element b of array c
iaload		Push array element a from array b
iastore		Store a in array element
laload		Push array element a from array b
lastore		Store ab in array element c of array d
multianewarray	class n	Create multidimensional array with first n dimensions initialized to lengths a, b, c. . .
newarray	type	Create array of type, length a
saload		Push array element a from array b
sastore		Store a in array element b of array c

A.3.3   Constant

Mnemonic	Arguments	Description
aconst_null		Push null reference
bipush	n	Push int between −128 and 127
dconst_0		Push 0 (double)
dconst_1		Push 1 (double)
fconst_0		Push 0 (float)
fconst_1		Push 1 (float)
fconst_2		Push 2 (float)
iconst_0		Push 0 (int)
iconst_1		Push 1 (int)
iconst_2		Push 2 (int)
iconst_3		Push 3 (int)
iconst_4		Push 4 (int)
iconst_5		Push 5 (int)

Mnemonic	Arguments	Description
iconst_m1		Push −1(int)
lconst_0		Push 0 (long)
lconst_1		Push 1 (long)
ldc	x	Push x (a constant int, float, or String)
ldc_w	x	Push x (a constant int, float, or String)
ldc2_w	x	Push x (a constant long or double)
sipush	n	Push int between −32,768 and 32767

A.3.4   Control

Mnemonic	Arguments	Description
areturn		Return reference from method
dreturn		Return double from method
freturn		Return float from method
goto	label	Branch always
goto_w	label	Branch always to label
if_acmpeq	label	Branch if a == b
if_acmpne	label	Branch if a != b
if_icmpeq	label	Branch if a > b
if_icmpge	label	Branch if a >= b
if_icmpgt	label	Branch if a > b
if_icmple	label	Branch if a <= b
if_icmplt	label	Branch if a < b
if_icmpne	label	Branch if a != b
ifeq	label	Branch if a == 0
ifge	label	Branch if a >= 0
ifgt	label	Branch if a > 0
ifle	label	Branch if a <= 0
iflt	label	Branch if a < 0
ifne	label	Branch if a != 0
ifnonnull	label	Branch if a is not null
ifnull	label	Branch if a is null

Mnemonic	Arguments	Description
ireturn		Return int from method
jsr	label	Branch to label; push return location
jsr_w	label	Jump to label
lookupswitch	tag1: label1 tag2: label2... default: labeln	Branch to label1 on tag1, label2 on tag2,..., labeln otherwise
lreturn		Return long from method
nop		Do nothing
ret	n	Branch to location in variable n
return		Return from method
tableswitch	n label1 label2 . . . default: labeln	Branch to label1 on n, label2 on n+1,..., labeln otherwise

A.3.5 Data Type Conversion

Mnemonic	Arguments	Description
d2f		Convert double ab to float
d2i		Convert double ab to int
d2l		Convert double ab to long
f2d		Convert float a to double
f2i		Convert float a to int
f2l		Convert float a to long
i2d		Convert int a to double
i2f		Convert int a to float
i2l		Convert int a to long
l2d		Convert long ab to double
l2f		Convert long ab to float
l2i		Convert long ab to int

A.3.6   Object

Mnemonic	Arguments	Description
checkcast	class	Throw exception if a is not an instance of class
getfield	class/field desc	Push object field from object a
getstatic	class/field desc	Push static field
instanceof	class	Push 1 if a is class, 0 otherwise
invokeinterface	class/method desc n	Invoke method through interface with n argument words
invokespecial	class/method desc	Invoke method directly
invokestatic	class/method desc	Invoke static method
invokevirtual	class/method desc	Invoke method virtually
new	class	Create new object of class
putfield	class/field desc	Store a in object field
putstatic	class/field desc	Store a in static field

A.3.7   Stack Manipulation

Mnemonic	Arguments	Description
dup		Duplicate a
dup_x1		Duplicate a, insert under b
dup_x2		Duplicate a, insert under c
dup2		Duplicate ab
dup2_x1		Duplicate ab, insert under c
dup2_x2		Duplicate ab, insert under d
pop		Remove a
pop2		Remove ab
swap		Swap a and b

A.3.8   Synchronization

Mnemonic	Arguments	Description
monitorenter		Gain control of monitor of a
monitorexit		Release monitor of a

A.3.9 Variable

Mnemonic	Arguments	Description
aload	n	Push local variable n
aload_0		Push local variable 0
aload_1		Push local variable 1
aload_2		Push local variable 2
aload_3		Push local variable 3
astore	n	Store a in local variable n
astore_0		Store a in local variable 0
astore_1		Store a in local variable 1
astore_2		Store a in local variable 2
astore_3		Store a in local variable 3
dload	n	Push local variables n and n+1
dload_0		Push local variables 0 and 1
dload_1		Push local variables 1 and 2
dload_2		Push local variables 2 and 3
dload_3		Push local variables 3 and 4
dstore	n	Store ab in local variables n and n+1
dstore_0		Store ab in local variables 0 and 1
dstore_1		Store ab in local variables 1 and 2
dstore_2		Store ab in local variables 2 and 3
dstore_3		Store ab in local variables 3 and 4
fload	n	Push local variable n
fload_0		Push local variable 0
fload_1		Push local variable 1
fload_2		Push local variable 2
fload_3		Push local variable 3
fstore	n	Store a in local variable n
fstore_0		Store a in local variable 0
fstore_1		Store a in local variable 1
fstore_2		Store a in local variable 2
fstore_3		Store a in local variable 3
iinc	n increment	Increment local variable
iload	n	Push local variable n
iload_0		Push local variable 0
iload_1		Push local variable 1
iload_2		Push local variable 2

Mnemonic	Arguments	Description
iload_3		Push local variable 3
istore	n	Store a in local variable n
istore_0		Store a in local variable 0
istore_1		Store a in local variable 1
istore_2		Store a in local variable 2
istore_3		Store a in local variable 3
lload	n	Push local variables n and n+1
lload_0		Push local variables 0 and 1
lload_1		Push local variables 1 and 2
lload_2		Push local variables 2 and 3
lload_3		Push local variables 3 and 4
lstore	n	Store ab in local variables n and n+1
lstore_0		Store ab in local variables 0 and 1
lstore_1		Store ab in local variables 1 and 2
lstore_2		Store ab in local variables 2 and 3
lstore_3		Store ab in local variables 3 and 4
wide	instruction arguments	Like instruction, except using wider range of values

Oolong Reference

OOLONG is an assembly language for the Java virtual machine, based on the Jasmin language by Jon Meyer. It is designed to allow you to write programs at the bytecode level without having to mess about with individual bytes.

Sections B.1 and B.2 document the Oolong assembler and the Gnoloo disassembler. They are used to create and edit class files using the Oolong language. Section B.3 describes the DumpClass program, which is used to print a byte-by-byte deconstruction of a class file.

These programs are written in Java, using the Java 1.0.2 platform. They should be compatible with any current Java platform.

The Synopsis heading of each section, which describes the usage of the programs, assumes that you have a program called java which implements a Java virtual machine. This is the name of the JVM implementation which comes with Sun's Java Development Kit. Different JVM implementations use different names.

Section B.4 provides a reference to the Oolong syntax. Section B.5 is an alphabetical listing of all Oolong instructions.

B.1   Using the Oolong Assembler

Name
    COM.sootNsmoke.oolong.Oolong   Assemble an Oolong source file.

Abbreviated name
    Oolong

Synopsis
    java COM.sootNsmoke.oolong.Oolong [-g] [-n] [-d directory]
        file1.j …
    java Oolong [-g] [-n] [-d directory] *file1.j* …

Description

Oolong reads the file *file1.j*, which is expected to contain a number of class descriptions in the Oolong language, as described in section B.4. The compiled classes are placed in separate files. The name of the file is the name of the class (with any package name removed) with the extension .class.

For example, suppose *file1.j* contains this class declaration:

```
.class foo/bar
```

The resulting file will be called bar.class.

The main executable class is called COM.sootNsmoke.oolong.Oolong. The class Oolong, in the default package, is also provided, which has a main method that calls the main in COM.sootNsmoke.oolong.Oolong. This class is a convenience if you don't want to type the longer name when compiling.

Options

-g	Use .line and .var directives to generate debugging information.
-n	Generate debugging information, but use automatically generated line numbers. The automatically generated line numbers correspond to the lines of the source code.
-d directory	Place generated .class files into directory.

B.2   Gnoloo

Name
COM.sootNsmoke.oolong.Gnoloo   Disassemble a class file into Oolong.

Abbreviated name
Gnoloo

Synopsis
```
java COM.sootNsmoke.oolong.Gnoloo [-d directory] file1.class …
java Gnoloo [-d directory] [-] file1.class …
```

Description

Gnoloo generates an Oolong source file, as described in section B.4, which corresponds to the source file. The source file should be a .class file, like that produced from a Java compiler or the Oolong assembler. If the input is not a `.class` file or is an improperly formatted class file, then disassembly is not possible.

By default, Gnoloo creates a file called *file1.j* for the input class *file1.class*. This file is in the Oolong language, suitable for use with the Oolong assembler.

If the argument - is given, then the output will go to the standard output device (as given by `System.out`).

Note that the input is the name of a `class` file, *not* the name of a Java class.

The main executable class is called `COM.sootNsmoke.oolong.Oolong`. The class `Oolong`, in the default package, is also provided, which has a `main` method that calls the `main` in `COM.sootNsmoke.oolong.Oolong`. This class is a convenience if you don't want to type the longer name when compiling.

Options

-d `directory`   Place generated `.j` files into `directory`.

-                        Write output to `System.out` instead of to the source file.

B.3   DumpClass

Name
COM.sootNsmoke.oolong.DumpClass   Print a detailed description of a class file.

Abbreviated name
DumpClass

Synopsis
java COM.sootNsmoke.oolong.DumpClass *file1.class* …
java DumpClass *file1.class* …

Description
DumpClass writes a complete description of the input `class` file, detailing what each byte means. DumpClass can be used to examine the internal structure of a `class` file. Some uses include

◆ Examining broken `class` files that cannot be disassembled

◆ Looking for verification errors

◆ Learning more about how the `class` file format works

The format of the output is divided into three columns: location, hex dump, and interpretation. The location gives the offset into the file in hexadecimal. The hex dump shows the bytes at that location. The interpretation column says what those bytes mean.

B.4   Oolong Language

An Oolong program is a set of *directives*. A directive is marked by a period (.) at the beginning of the line, followed by a keyword. Most directives take up exactly one line; the .method directive spans multiple lines and is terminated with the .end method.

B.4.1   Comments

Format
```
; any text
```

Description
An Oolong comment is written with a semicolon (;), and it lasts until the end of the line. Comments may appear by themselves on a line or in the middle of a directive or instruction.

Examples
```
; This is a comment

.field count I            ; Declare the field count as int

new Foo                   ; Create a new instance of the Foo class

invokevirtual Foo/bar     ; Invoke the bar method on class Foo
              (I)V        ; which takes an int and returns void
```

B.4.2   .source

Format
```
.source filename
```

Description
Causes the assembler to generate a SourceFile attribute to the class file. This allows a debugger to locate the original source code when debugging the class file.

The *filename* should be just the file name; it should not contain any directory information.

Examples

Suppose you translate a file called `Hello.java` into an Oolong class `Hello.j`. Add the following line to `Hello.j`:

```
.source Hello.java
```

B.4.3 .class

Format

```
.class [public] [super] [abstract] [interface] [final] classname
```

Description

Declares the name of the class being created. The name includes the package name, separated by slashes (/). All directives following the .class declaration apply to this class.

The meanings of the keywords are:

Keyword	Meaning
public	This class may be used from anywhere. If it's not given, only other classes with the same package name may refer to it.
final	This class may not be subclassed; that is, no class may use this as a superclass.
super	In the method bodies for this class, the invokespecial instruction has a special meaning when it's used on methods of superclasses.
interface	This class may be used as an interface. The abstract keyword should also be specified. All of the method bodies should be marked abstract.
abstract	Creating instances of this class is not allowed. This keyword should be given if any of the methods are marked abstract.

Examples

```
.class Foo              ; Declare Foo in the default
                        ; package with default protection.
                        ; The ACC_SUPER bit is not set.
```

```
.class public super Moe/Bar    ; Declare Bar in the package Moe
                               ; to be public and with the
                               ; ACC_SUPER bit set.

.class super COM/sootNsmoke/oolong/Oolong
                               ; Declare the class Oolong in the
                               ; package COM/sootNsmoke/oolong
                               ; with the ACC_SUPER bit set

.class public super abstract java/io/Socket
                                   ; Declare the abstract class Socket

.class public interface java/util/Enumeration
                               ; Declare the interface Enumeration
                               ; in the java/util package
```

B.4.4   .interface

Format
```
.interface classname
```

Description
Declares an interface class. The .interface directive is an abbreviation for

```
.class public abstract interface
```

Example
```
.interface java/util/Enumeration   ; Declare the interface
                                   ; Enumeration in the
                                   ; java/util package.
```

B.4.5   .end class

Format
```
.end class
```

Description
Optional; marks the end of the class declaration.

Example
```
.class public super Foo
```

```
;; A set of field and method declarations of the class Foo.

.end class      ; End the declaration of class Foo
```

B.4.6 .super

Format
```
.super classname
```

Description
Declares the superclass of a class. If this declaration is not present, the superclass java/lang/Object is assumed. There may be at most one .super directive per class.

Examples
```
.super java/lang/Object  ; Explicitly declare Object to be
                         ; the superclass
                         ; Declare this class to be a
                         ; subclass of COM.sootNsmoke.
                         ; instseq.instruction
.super COM/sootNsmoke/instseq/Instruction
```

B.4.7 .implements

Format
```
.implements interface-classname
```

Description
Declares the name of an interface that the class implements. The name *interface-classname* should name a class with the interface parameter set. This class should provide implementations for all methods declared in *interface-classname*.

Examples
```
.implements java/util/Enumeration ; This class should define
                                  ; hasMoreElements()Z and
                                  ; nextElement()Ljava/lang/
                                  ; Object;
```

B.4.8 .field

Format

```
.field [public] [private] [protected] [static] [final]
       [volatile] [transient] fieldname descriptor
```

Description

Adds a new field to the class file. The *descriptor* gives the type of the field.

In the class file the bits corresponding to the keywords will be set. The meanings of the keywords follow.

Keyword	Meaning
public	This field may be accessed from code in any class.
private	This field may only be accessed from code within this class.
protected	This field may be accessed from code within the same package as this class, or from any subclass of this class.
static	This field is a class-wide property.
final	Once initialized, this field's value may not be set again.
volatile	This field's value may be set in different threads; its value should not be cached.
transient	This field's value should not be saved when the object is saved.

Examples

A static boolean field:

```
.field static isEmpty Z
```

A field that holds an array of arrays of ints:

```
.field public matrix [[I
```

A static transient field that holds an array of Strings:

```
.field static transient cachedValues [Ljava/lang/String;
```

B.4.9 .method

Format

```
.method [public] [private] [protected] [static] [final]
        [synchronized] [native] [abstract] methodname descriptor
```

Description

Adds a new method to the class file. The *descriptor* describes the arguments and return types of the method. For each of the optional keywords in front of the method name, the corresponding bit is set in the access_flags of the method.

Following the method description is a collection of instructions that form the implementation of the method (these instructions are described in section B.5). These instructions are compiled into a Code attribute that is added to the method.

If the method is marked native or abstract, then the list of instructions should be empty and no Code attribute is generated.

The method is terminated with the .end method directive, as described in section B.4.16.

The meanings of the keywords follow.

Keyword	Meaning
public	This method is available to all other classes.
private	This method may be accessed only from within this class.
protected	This method may be accessed from any class in the same package or any class that is a subclass of this class.
static	This method is a class method.
final	This method may not be overridden in subclasses.
synchronized	The JVM will obtain a lock on this object before invoking the method. If this method is static then the JVM will obtain a lock on the Class object corresponding to this class.
native	This method is implemented in native code; no implementation is provided.
abstract	This method has no implementation.

Examples

A static method that takes an array of Strings as an argument, returning void:

```
.method public static main([Ljava/lang/String;)V
return
.end method
```

An abstract method that takes no arguments and returns an Object:

```
.method public nextElement()Ljava/lang/Object;
; No method body, since this is an abstract method
.end method
```

A constructor that takes two arguments, a String and a boolean:

```
.method public <init>(Ljava/lang/String;Z)V
;; Body of the method goes here
.end method
```

A synchronized method:

```
.method synchronized write(Ljava/lang/String;)V
;; In here, the thread has a lock on the object in variable 0
.end method
```

B.4.10 .limit locals

Format
```
.limit locals limit
```

Description
Sets the limit on local variables. If not given, the assembler will try to compute it.

Examples
```
.method add(II)I
.limit locals 5        ; Use up to 5 local variables
                       ; Variable 0 is this
                       ; Variables 1 and 2 are the arguments
                       ; Variables 3 and 4 may be used for any
                       ; purpose
```

B.4.11 .limit stack

Format
```
.limit stack limit
```

Description
Sets the limit on the amount of stack that may be used in the execution of the method. If not given, the assembler will try to compute it.

Examples
```
.method public static main([Ljava/lang/String;)V
.limit stack 2             ; This method uses at most
                           ; 2 stack entries
                           ; Stack height is initially 0
```

```
getstatic java/lang/System/out Ljava/io/PrintStream;
                        ; Stack height is now 1
ldc "Hello, world"      ; Stack height is now 2
invokevirtual java/io/PrintStream/println(Ljava/lang/String;)V
                        ; Stack height is now 0
return
.end method
```

B.4.12 .line

Format

```
.line number
```

Description

Instructs the assembler to generate an entry in the LineNumberTable attribute for the method. The instruction after the .line directive is marked as the first instruction corresponding to the line numbered *number* in the original source code. This information is used by debuggers to match bytecodes to the original source if the Oolong program is generated as an intermediate result from some other language.

Example

If you have the Java program in Hello.java:

```
class Hello                                      // Line 1
{                                                // Line 2
    public static void main(String a[])          // Line 3
    {                                            // Line 4
        System.out.println("Hello, world");      // Line 5
        return;                                  // Line 6
    }                                            // Line 7
}                                                // Line 8
```

If this were translated into Oolong, but you want to use the resulting class file to debug the original source, the .line directives would look like this:

```
.source Hello.java

.method static main([Ljava/lang/String;)V
.line 5
getstatic java/lang/System/out Ljava/io/PrintStream;
aload "Hello, world"
invokevirtual java/io/PrintStream/println (Ljava/lang/String;)V
```

```
.line 6
return
.end method
```

B.4.13 .var

Format
```
.var number is name type [from begin to end]
```

Description
For debugging purposes, assigns the *name* to the local variable numbered *number*. That variable is expected to have a value that conforms to the type specified by *type*.

If *begin* and *end* are given, then the name applies to that local variable only in that range. Otherwise, it applies to the entire method.

Example
In this example, the class Foo has a field called temperatures, which is an array of floats. In the find_temp method, variable 0 is called this through the entire range of the method. Variable 1 is passed in as an argument. Variable 1 is an int called i from range1 to range2. After i is used as an index into the temperatures array, it is no longer necessary. Variable 1 is now used to store temp, which is a float value.

```
.class Foo

.field temperatures [F

.method find_temp(I)F
.var 0 is this LFoo;
.var 1 is i I from range1 to range2
.var 1 is temp F from range2 to range3

range1:
    aload_0                      ; Get this, which should be a Foo
                                 ; Get the temperatures field
    getfield Foo/temperatures [F
    ; Here, variable 1 should be an int. The debugger will know
    ; it by the name i
    iload_1                      ; push i
```

```
    faload                          ; Get a temperature
    fstore_1                        ; Store the temperature in 1

range2:
    ; Variable 1 no longer contains i. Now it contains
    ; temp, which is a float
    fload_1                         ; Retrieve temp
    freturn                         ; Return it

range3:
.end method
```

B.4.14 `.throws`

Format
`.throws` *classname*

Description
Adds *classname* to the `Exceptions` attribute for the method, letting a Java compiler know that the method may throw the exception named *classname*.

Several `.throws` directives may appear in each method. The effect is cumulative; the method may throw any of the listed exceptions.

Examples
```
.throws java/lang/Throwable            ; May throw anything

.throws java/io/SecurityException      ; This method may throw a
.throws java/lang/InterruptedException ; SecurityException or an
                                       ; InterruptedException
```

B.4.15 `.catch`

Format
`.catch` *classname* `from` *label1* `to` *label2* `using` *label3*

Description
Designates *label3* as an exception handler for the class *classname* in the range of instructions from *label1* to *label2*. Includes the instruction after *label1* but does not include the instruction after *label2*.

If *classname* is all, then all exceptions will be caught. This corresponds to a catch_type entry of 0 in the method's exception_table.

Examples

```
.catch java/lang/NullPointerException from begin to end using
   handler
;; Code here is not in the exception handler

begin:
;; If a NullPointerException is thrown from here to end, then
;; control will pass to handler

end:
;; This is outside the exception range again

handler:
;; If a NullPointerException is thrown from begin to end, then
;; control passes here. The top of the stack will contain
;; the caught exception
```

The .catch all is used for something that absolutely must be done. For example, in this piece of code, the OutputStream in variable 1 must be closed, even if an exception is thrown:

```
.var 1 is out java/io/OutputStream
.catch all from try_begin to try_end using finally
try_begin:
;; Write some stuff to out

; If the write was successful, then close out
aload_1
invokevirtual java/io/OutputStream/close ()V
return
try_end:

finally:
; Even if the write was unsuccessful,
; make sure that the stream is closed
aload_1
invokevirtual java/io/OutputStream/close ()V
return
```

B.4.16 .end method

Format
```
.end method
```

Description
Marks the end of a method. There should be one .end method directive for each .method directive.

Examples
```
.method public toString()Ljava/lang/String;
;; Body of the toString method
.end method
```

B.5   Instructions

An Oolong instruction corresponds to a single bytecode instruction in the class file. Each instruction is written as a single mnemonic. Depending on the instruction, the mnemonic may be followed by one or more arguments to the instruction.

The following table summarizes all of the available Oolong instructions. The rest of the section provides notes on the arguments.

Mnemonic	Arguments	Description
aaload		Push array element
aastore		Store a in array element
aconst_null		Push null reference
aload	n	Push local variable n
aload_0		Push local variable 0
aload_1		Push local variable 1
aload_2		Push local variable 2
aload_3		Push local variable 3
anewarray	class	Create array of class, length a
areturn		Return reference from method
arraylength		Length of array a
astore	n	Store a in local variable n
astore_0		Store a in local variable 0
astore_1		Store a in local variable 1

Mnemonic	Arguments	Description
astore_2		Store a in local variable 2
astore_3		Store a in local variable 3
athrow		Throw exception
baload		Push array element
bastore		Store a in array element
bipush	n	Push int between −128 and 127
caload		Push array element
castore		Store a in array element
checkcast	class	Throw exception if a is not class
d2f		Convert double to float
d2i		Convert double to int
d2l		Convert double to long
dadd		Add doubles (ab+cd)
daload		Push array element
dastore		Store a in array element
dcmpg		Compare doubles
dcmpl		Compare doubles
dconst_0		Push 0 (double)
dconst_1		Push 1 (double)
ddiv		Divide doubles (ab/cd)
dload	n	Push local variable n
dload_0		Push local variable 0
dload_1		Push local variable 1
dload_2		Push local variable 2
dload_3		Push local variable 3
dmul		Multiply doubles (ab*cd)
dneg		Negate double (-ab)
drem		Remainder doubles (ab%cd)
dreturn		Return double from method
dstore	n	Store ab in local variable n
dstore_0		Store a in local variable 0
dstore_1		Store a in local variable 1
dstore_2		Store a in local variable 2
dstore_3		Store a in local variable 3
dsub		Subtract doubles (ab-cd)
dup		Duplicate a

Mnemonic	Arguments	Description
dup_x1		Duplicate b
dup_x2		Duplicate c
dup2		Duplicate ab
dup2_x1		Duplicate bc
dup2_x2		Duplicate cd
f2d		Convert float to double
f2i		Convert float to int
f2l		Convert float to long
fadd		Add floats (a+b)
faload		Push array element
fastore		Store a in array element
fcmpg		Compare floats
fcmpl		Compare floats
fconst_0		Push 0 (float)
fconst_1		Push 1 (float)
fconst_2		Push 2 (float)
fdiv		Divide floats (a/b)
fload	n	Push local variable n
fload_0		Push local variable 0
fload_1		Push local variable 1
fload_2		Push local variable 2
fload_3		Push local variable 3
fmul		Multiply floats (a*b)
fneg		Negate float (-a)
frem		Remainder floats (a%b)
freturn		Return float from method
fstore	n	Store a in local variable n
fstore_0		Store a in local variable 0
fstore_1		Store a in local variable 1
fstore_2		Store a in local variable 2
fstore_3		Store a in local variable 3
fsub		Subtract floats (a-b)
getfield	class/field desc	Push object field
getstatic	class/field desc	Push static field
goto	label	Branch always
goto_w	label	Branch always to label

Mnemonic	Arguments	Description
i2b		Convert int to byte
i2c		Convert int to char
i2d		Convert int to double
i2f		Convert int to float
i2l		Convert int to long
i2s		Convert int to short
iadd		Add ints (a+b)
iaload		Push array element
iand		Bitwise and ints (a & b)
iastore		Store a into array element
iconst_0		Push 0 (int)
iconst_1		Push 1 (int)
iconst_2		Push 2 (int)
iconst_3		Push 3 (int)
iconst_4		Push 4 (int)
iconst_5		Push 5 (int)
iconst_m1		Push −1(int)
idiv		Divide ints (a/b)
if_acmpeq	label	Branch if a == b
if_acmpne	label	Branch if a != b
if_icmpeq	label	Branch if a > b
if_icmpge	label	Branch if a >= b
if_icmpgt	label	Branch if a > b
if_icmple	label	Branch if a <= b
if_icmplt	label	Branch if a < b
if_icmpne	label	Branch if a != b
ifeq	label	Branch if a == 0
ifge	label	Branch if a >= 0
ifgt	label	Branch if a > 0
ifle	label	Branch if a <= 0
iflt	label	Branch if a < 0
ifne	label	Branch if a != 0
ifnonnull	label	Branch if a is not null
ifnull	label	Branch if a is null
iinc	n increment	Increment local variable
iload	n	Push local variable n

Mnemonic	Arguments	Description
`iload_0`		Push local variable 0
`iload_1`		Push local variable 1
`iload_2`		Push local variable 2
`iload_3`		Push local variable 3
`imul`		Multiply `int`s (a*b)
`ineg`		Negate `int` (-a)
`instanceof`	class	Push 1 if a is class, 0 otherwise
`invokeinterface`	class/method desc n	Invoke method through interface with n argument words
`invokespecial`	class/method desc	Invoke method directly
`invokestatic`	class/method desc	Invoke `static` method
`invokevirtual`	class/method desc	Invoke method virtually
`ior`		Bitwise or `int`s (a | b)
`irem`		Remainder `int`s (a%b)
`ireturn`		Return `int` from method
`ishl`		Shift `int` left (a << b)
`ishr`		Shift `int` right (a >> c)
`istore`	n	Store a in local variable n
`istore_0`		Store a in local variable 0
`istore_1`		Store a in local variable 1
`istore_2`		Store a in local variable 2
`istore_3`		Store a in local variable 3
`isub`		Subtract `int`s (a-b)
`iushr`		Unsigned shift `int` right (a >>> c)
`ixor`		Boolean xor `int`s (a ^ b)
`jsr`	label	Branch to label; push return location
`jsr_w`	label	Jump to label
`l2d`		Convert `long` to `double`
`l2f`		Convert `long` to `float`
`l2i`		Convert `long` to `int`
`ladd`		Add `long`s (ab+cd)
`laload`		Push array element
`land`		Boolean and `long`s (ab & cd)

Mnemonic	Arguments	Description
lastore		Store a in array element
lcmp		Compare longs
lconst_0		Push 0 (long)
lconst_1		Push 1 (long) ldc
ldc_w	x	Push x (a constant int, float, or String)
ldc2_w	x	Push x (a constant long or double)
ldiv		Divide longs (ab/cd)
lload	n	Push local variable n
lload_0		Push local variable 0
lload_1		Push local variable 1
lload_2		Push local variable 2
lload_3		Push local variable 3
lmul		Multiply longs (ab*cd)
lneg		Negate long (-ab)
lookupswitch	tag1: label1 tag2: label2 ... default: labeln	Branch to label1 on tag1, label2 on tag2, ..., labeln otherwise
lor		Boolean or longs (ab | cd)
lrem		Remainder longs (ab%cd)
lreturn		Return long from method
lshl		Shift long left (bc << 9)
lshr		Shift long right (bc >> 9)
lstore	n	Store ab in local variable n
lstore_0		Store a in local variable 0
lstore_1		Store a in local variable 1
lstore_2		Store a in local variable 2
lstore_3		Store a in local variable 3
lsub		Subtract longs (ab-cd)
lushr		Unsigned shift long right (bc >>> a)
lxor		Boolean xor longs (ab ^ cd)
monitorenter		Gain control of monitor of a
monitorexit		Release monitor of a
multianewarray	class n	Create multidimensional array with first n dimensions initialized to lengths a,b,c...
new	class	Create new object of class
newarray	type	Create array of type, length a
nop		Do nothing

Mnemonic	Arguments	Description
pop		Remove a
pop2		Remove ab
putfield	class/field desc	Store a in object field
putstatic	class/field desc	Store a in static field
ret	n	Branch to location in variable n
return		Return from method
saload		Push array element
sastore		Store a in array element
sipush	n	Push int between −32,768 and 32767
swap		Swap a and b
tableswitch	n label1 label2 ... default: label*n*	Branch to label1 on n, label2 on n+1, ..., label*n* otherwise
wide	instruction arguments	Like instruction, except using wider range of values

B.5.1 Instructions with No Arguments

Most instructions require no arguments; the instruction is written with just the mnemonic. For example:

```
aload_0        ; Push the reference in variable 0

freturn        ; Return a float value

ladd           ; Add two longs

monitorenter   ; Acquire the monitor
```

B.5.2 Integers

Integer values are specified as in Java. They may be either numerical constants or single-character literals. For example,

```
bipush 65      ; Push the int 65
bipush 0x41    ; Ditto
bipush 'A'     ; Same
```

B.5.3   Labels

A label indicates a particular instruction. When an instruction has a label as its argument, the destination is the next instruction after the label. For example,

```
goto label              ; Jump to the nop instruction
;; This code is skipped
label:
    nop
    aload_0
    arraylength
    ifeq label          ; Jump again to the nop instruction
```

The instruction identified by `label` is the `nop` instruction.

B.5.4   Classes

Some instructions, such as `new`, require classes as arguments. These arguments are written as the fully qualified class name, using slashes (/) as the separators between package components. For example,

```
new java/lang/String      ; Create a String
```

B.5.5   Fields and Methods

The general format of a field access or method invocation instruction is

```
mnemonic classname/entity desc
```

where *classname* is the name of the class, *entity* is the name of the field or method, and *descriptor* is the field or method descriptor. For example, to access a method:

```
invokevirtual java/io/PrintStream/println (Ljava/lang/String;)V
```

In this case, *classname* is java/io/PrintStream, *entity* is println, and *desc* is (Ljava/lang/String;)V.

For a field:

```
getstatic java/lang/Math/PI D
```

Here, *classname* is java/lang/Math, *entity* is PI, and *desc* is D.

B.5.6   `invokeinterface`

In the case of the `invokeinterface` instruction, there is an additional argument: the number of stack elements used in the call, including the object itself. This information is redundant, since it can be determined from the descriptor, but it is required by the JVM. For example,

```
invokeinterface Interface/method (JJ[Ljava/lang/String;)D 6
```

invokes a method through the interface called `Interface`, which requires three arguments, two `long`s and an array of `String`s. The number in this case is 6: one for the `Interface` object, two for each of the `long`s, and one more for the `String` array. The `double` returned is not included.

B.5.7 `multianewarray`

The `multianewarray` instruction is used to create a multidimensional array, with the first *n* dimensions initialized.

The first argument of a `multianewarray` call is the type descriptor of the type that is to be created. It must be an array type; that is, the descriptor must begin with one or more left brackets (`[`). The second element describes how much of the array should be initialized. For example,

```
bipush 30
bipush 90
sipush 1000
multianewarray [[[[[I 3
```

creates a five-dimensional array of `int`s. The first three dimensions are initialized to 30, 90, and 1000 elements. This is equivalent to the Java expression

```
new int[30][90][1000][][]
```

which is an array 30 elements long. Each element of the array is 90 elements long. Each element of *that* array is 1000 elements long. Each of those $30 \times 90 \times 1000 = 2,700,000$ elements is initially `null`, but it can hold a two-dimensional array of `int`s.

B.5.8 `ldc`, `ldc_w`, and `ldc2_w`

These three instructions are used to push a constant value onto the stack. These values are represented as in Java. In Oolong, `ldc` and `ldc_w` generate identical code. The JVM distinguishes between these two instructions depending on which element of the constant pool holds the value of the constant. If the value is 256 or less, the `ldc` is used; otherwise, `ldc_w` is used. Since the Oolong assembler manages the constant pool, it decides whether to use an `ldc` or `ldc_w` opcode.

The `ldc2_w` instruction is used for `double` and `long` values, that is, values that take up two stack entries. For example,

```
ldc "Some string"                   ; Push a String
ldc 3.14                            ; Push a floating-point constant
ldc_w 3.14                         ; The same
ldc2_w 3.1415925358979323D         ; Push a double constant
```

B.5.9   newarray

The newarray instruction is used to create a single-dimensional array of one of the base types. The argument specifies the basic type to create. It may be specified either as the Java type name (`int`), the Java type descriptor (`I`), or the bytecode internal number for the type (10). This table summarizes the possible values; all values in the same row are equivalent.

Java name	Descriptor	Value
boolean	Z	4
char	C	5
float	F	6
double	D	7
byte	B	8
short	S	9
int	I	10
long	J	11

For example,

```
sipush 10
newarray J          ; Create a ten-element array of longs
```

B.5.10 tableswitch

The `tableswitch` instruction takes a base value, specified as an integer, followed by a set of labels. If the value is equal to the base value, control transfers to the first label. If it is one greater than the base, it goes to the second label, and so on.

The `default` case is required; it specifies where to go if the value is lower than the base or if it is greater than the number of provided labels allowed. For example,

```
tableswitch 'A'
    caseA
    caseB
```

```
        caseC
        default: invalidLetter

    caseA:                  ; Handle a letter A

    caseB:                  ; Handle a letter B

    caseC:                  ; Handle a letter C

    invalidLetter:          ; Throw an exception
```

B.5.11 `lookupswitch`

The `lookupswitch` instruction is much like `tableswitch` (section B.5.10), except
that instead of a single value, explicit combinations of cases and labels are provided. The cases are `int` constants. As with `tableswitch`, the default case is
required. For example,

```
    lookupswitch
        'A': caseA
        'B': caseB
        'C': caseC
        default: invalidLetter
```

This could also be written as

```
    lookupswitch
        65: caseA
        66: caseB
        67: caseC
        default: invalidLetter
```

or as

```
    lookupswitch
        0x41: caseA
        0x42: caseB
        0x43: caseC
        default: invalidLetter
```

Answers to Selected Exercises

Exercise 2.3

```
.class Refrigerator
.field temperature F
.field numberOfEggs I
.field leftoverPizzas [LPizza;
```

Exercise 2.4

```
.class BinaryTree
.field left LBinaryTree;
.field right LBinaryTree;
.field data Ljava/lang/Object;
```

Exercise 2.5

```
.method printTable(Ljava/io/OutputStream;[[Ljava/lang/String;)V
.method protected addInts
    (Ljava/lang/Integer;Ljava/lang/Integer;)Ljava/lang/Integer
.method native static shutdown()V
```

Exercise 2.6

```
.method public computeSum(FFF)F
fload_1        ; Push the first argument
fload_2        ; Push the second argument
fadd           ; Add them
fload_3        ; Push the third argument
fadd           ; Add that to the result so far
freturn        ; Return the result
.end method
```

Exercise 2.7

```
.method static computeSum(FF)F
fload_0      ; First argument is argument 0 now
fload_1      ; Second argument is argument 1 now
fadd         ; Sum them
freturn      ; Return the result
.end method
```

Exercise 2.8

The class must implement all the methods of MarathonRunner and JavaProgrammer. To successfully implement JavaProgrammer, the class must provide implementations for all the methods of Amiable and Clever.

```
.class MarathonRunningJavaProgrammer
.super Person
.implements MarathonRunner
.implements JavaProgrammer

; implement run from marathonRunner
.method public run(F)V
;; Implementation omitted
.end method

; Implement solvePuzzles from Clever (via JavaProgrammer)
.method public solvePuzzles()V
;; Implementation omitted
.end method

; Implement smile and shakeHands from Amiable (via JavaProgramer)
.method public shakeHands (LAmiable;)V
;; Implementation omitted
.end method

.method public smile ()V
;; Implementation omitted
.end method
```

Exercise 3.1

Original:	**More efficient:**
sipush 9	bipush 9

Original:	**More efficient:**
bipush 4	iconst_4
ldc 1.0	fconst_1
ldc -901	sipush -901
ldc 123456	ldc 123456

The last one is a trick question. For a number that big, an ldc is pretty much the most compact this will get.

Exercise 3.2

Each instruction uses up exactly one stack slot. That's because all the values loaded are ints, even the ones with bipush, sipush, and ldc. Therefore, the answer is 5.

Exercise 3.3

```
.method public static icalc(IIII)I
.var 0 is a
.var 1 is b
.var 2 is c
.var 3 is x
iload_0      ; Push a
iload_3      ; Push x
iload_3      ; Push x again
imul         ; Calculate x^2
imul         ; Calculate ax^2

iload_1      ; Push b
iload_3      ; Push x
imul         ; Push bx

iload_2      ; Push c

iadd         ; Compute bx+c
iadd         ; Compute ax^2+bx+c

ireturn
.end method
```

The result of calling this method with a=1, b=-2, c=-35, and x=7 is 0. The maximum stack height written this way is 3. By rearranging the equation, the maximum stack height can be reduced to 2.

Exercise 3.4

This is more than just a matter of substituting D's for I's; you also have to change the variable numbers because each value takes two slots. The answer:

```
.method public static Dcalc(DDDD)D
.var 0 is a
.var 2 is b
.var 4 is c
.var 6 is x
dload_0       ; Push a
dload 6       ; Push x
dload 6       ; Push x again
dmul          ; Calculate x^2
dmul          ; Calculate ax^2

dload_2       ; Push b
dload 6       ; Push x
dmul          ; Push bx

dload 4       ; Push c

dadd          ; Compute bx+c
dadd          ; Compute ax^2+bx+c

dreturn
.end method
```

The maximum stack height written this way is 6.

Exercise 3.5

```
.method public static icalc2(IIII)I
iload_0       ; Push a
iload_3       ; Push x
imul          ; Calculate ax

iload_1       ; Push b
iadd          ; Calculate ax+b

iload_3       ; Push x
imul          ; Compute ax^2+bx
```

```
iload_2        ; Push c
iadd           ; Compute bx+c

ireturn
.end method
```

This way of calculating reduces the max stack to 2. It also reduces the number of instructions: 2 multiplies instead of 3, and you also save a push of x.

Exercise 3.6

```
.method static public count(I)I
; Variable 0 contains the number to be counted; call it i
; Variable 1 contains the count of bits so far; call it counter
iconst_0
istore_1        ; Initialize counter to 0

; Begin
iload_0         ; Compute i & 1
iconst_1
iand

iload_1         ; Add i&1 to counter
iadd
istore_1

iload_0         ; Shift i right 1
iconst_1
ishr
istore_0

;; Repeat from begin to here 31 more times

iload_1         ; Return the counter
ireturn
.end method
```

The important section of code begins at the Begin comment. It looks at the rightmost bit of i by doing the bitwise and with 1. The result will be 0 if the rightmost bit is 0 and 1 if the rightmost bit is 1. This number is added to the counter.

To prepare for the next counting, the value of i is shifted right by 1, then stored back in variable 0. This means that the next-to-rightmost bit is now the rightmost bit. By repeating the code 32 times, you count all the bits.

Exercise 3.7

For the right barrel shift by 1:

```
.method public static bshr(I)I
iload_0      ; Get the rightmost bit
iconst_1
iand

bipush 31    ; Move it 31 places to the left
ishl         ; This leaves us with the former rightmost bit
             ; followed by 31 zeros.

iload_0      ; Shift the original number right 1
iconst_1
iushr        ; There is a zero in the leftmost bit

ior          ; Use or to set the leftmost bit to the same
             ; as the former rightmost bit.

ireturn
.end method
```

The left shift is similar.

Exercise 3.8

The test is fairly easy. Use a shift to move the xth bit to be the rightmost bit. Then use a mask of 1 to make sure only that bit is set (if any bits are set):

```
.method public static test(II)Z
; Variable 0 is set
; Variable 1 is x
iload_0      ; Push set
iload_1      ; Push x
ishr         ; Shift set x bytes to the right

iconst_1     ; Select just the rightmost bit
iand

ireturn
.end method
```

The set is somewhat harder. Making a mask that sets only the xth bit to v is easy, but the JVM has no operation that says, "Set all the nonzero bits to look like this mask." One way is to force that bit in set to be 0, then use ior to set the bit to match the mask. Here's how:

```
.method public static set(IIZ)I
; Variable 0 is set
; Variable 1 is x
; Variable 2 is v

iconst_1      ; Begin the mask by making a number with all
iload_1       ; zeros except the x-th bit, which is 1
ishl

iconst_m1     ; Invert the mask so it has all 1's except for the
ixor          ; x-th bit, which is 0

iload_0       ; Compute set & mask, which sets only the x-th
iand          ; bit to 0

iload_2       ; Make a number containing just the x-th
iload_1       ; bit set to v; all 0s otherwise.
ishl

ior           ; Use ior to set that bit in set

ireturn       ; Return the new set
.end method
```

Exercise 3.9

The .limit locals should be 9 because of the iload_9. Variables 0, 1, and 4 through 8 are not used, but space must be allocated for them anyway.

To compute the stack limit, annotate each instruction with the height of the stack after the instruction is executed:

```
aload_3      ; 1
iload 9      ; 2
swap         ; 2 <- Note no change
dup          ; 3
astore_2     ; 2
sipush 99    ; 3
bipush 101   ; 4
```

```
imul        ; 3
imul        ; 2
```

Therefore, the `.limit` stack should be 4. The stack height at the end of this code
fragment is 2.

Exercise 4.1

```
.class Dinosaur
.field name Ljava/lang/String;
.field carnivorous Z

.method <init>(Ljava/lang/String;Z)V
aload_0                                            ; Invoke the
                                                   ; superclass
invokespecial java/lang/Object/<init>()V           ; constructor
aload_0                                            ; Push this
aload_1                                            ; Push the name
putfield Dinosaur/name Ljava/lang/String;          ; Store the name
aload_0                                            ; Push this
iload_2                                            ; Push the boolean
putfield Dinosaur/carnivorous Z                    ; Store in
                                                   ; carnivorous

return
.end method
```

Exercise 4.2

```
new Dinosaur             ; Create a dinosaur
dup                      ; Dup it
ldc "Veclociraptor"      ; Push the name
iconst_1                 ; Yes, it's carnivorous
                         ; Invoke the constructor
invokespecial Dinosaur/<init>(Ljava/lang/String;Z)V
```

Exercise 4.3

```
.class CarnivorousDinosaur
.super Dinosaur

.method <init>(Ljava/lang/String;)V
aload_0                  ; Push this
aload_1                  ; Push the name
```

```
    iconst_1                        ; Carnivorous is true
                                    ; Invoke the superclass constructor
    invokespecial Dinosaur/<init>(Ljava/lang/String;Z)V
    return
    .end method
```

To create a Velociraptor:

```
    new CarnivorousDinosaur
    dup
    ldc "Velociraptor"
    invokespecial CarnivorousDinosaur/<init>(Ljava/lang/String;)V
```

Exercise 4.4

```
    .class RightTriangle
    .field a F
    .field b F

    .method hypotenuse()F
    ; Variable 0 contains a RightTriangle object (this)
    aload_0                                      ; Push this
    aload_0                                      ; Get the field a
    getfield RightTriangle/a F
    aload_0                                      ; Get the field b
    getfield RightTriangle/b F
    invokevirtual RightTriangle/sumOfSquares(FF)F ; Compute a^2+b^2
    f2d                                          ; Convert to
                                                 ; double
    invokestatic java/lang/Math/sqrt(D)D         ; Compute square
                                                 ; root
    d2f                                          ; Back to float
    freturn
    .end method
```

Exercise 4.5

```
    .field color Ljava/lang/String;

    .method setColor(Ljava/lang/String;)V
    aload_0                              ; Get this
    aload_1                              ; Get the color
    putfield Dinosaur/color Ljava/lang/String; ; Store the color
```

```
    return
    .end method

    .method setColor(Ljava/awt/Color;)V
    aload_0                                      ; Get this
    aload_1                                      ; Get the color
                                                 ; Call toString
    invokevirtual java/awt/Color/toString()Ljava/lang/String;
    putfield Dinosaur/color Ljava/lang/String; ; Store the color
    return
    .end method
```

Exercise 4.6

```
    aload_0                                            ; Push a
                                                       ; Dinosaur
    getstatic java/awt/Color/green Ljava/awt/Color;    ; Push the
                                                       ; color
    invokevirtual Dinosaur/setColor(Ljava/awt/Color;)V ; Set the
                                                       ; color

    aload_0                                            ; Push a
                                                       ; Dinosaur
    ldc "green"
    invokevirtual Dinosaur/setColor(Ljava/lang/String;)V
```

Exercise 5.1

```
    .method static isUpper(C)Z
    iload_0
    bipush 'A'          ; Is it < 'A'?
    if_icmplt fail      ; Go to fail if it is

    iload_0
    bipush 'Z'          ; Is it > 'Z'?
    if_icmpgt fail      ; Go to fail if it is

    iconst_1            ; If we get here,
    ireturn            ; A <= arg <= Z, so
                        ; return true
    fail:
    iconst_0            ; Return false
```

```
    ireturn
    .end method
```

Exercise 5.2

```
    .method public static main([Ljava/lang/String;)V
    ; Call variable 0 args
    ; Call variable i i
    iconst_0
    istore_1        ; Initialize i to 0

    loop:
    iload_1
    aload_0         ; See if i >= the length of args
    arraylength
    if_icmpge done  ; Break the loop if it is

    getstatic java/lang/System/out Ljava/io/PrintStream;
    aload_0
    iload_1         ; Print a[i]
    aaload
    invokevirtual java/io/PrintStream/println (Ljava/lang/String;)V

    iinc 1 1        ; Increment i

    goto loop       ; Loop again

    done:
    return
    .end method
```

Exercise 5.3

Here's the loop:

```
    .method static printFromAtoB(II)V

    loop:
    getstatic java/lang/System/out Ljava/io/PrintStream;
    iload_0         ; Push and print a
    invokevirtual java/io/PrintStream/println (I)V

    iinc 0 1        ; Increment a
```

```
iload_0          ; Push a
iload_1          ; Push b
if_icmpgt done   ; a>b? goto done
goto loop        ; Otherwise loop again

done:
return
.end method
```

If a > b, then the loop will print out a, then stop, because it will continue only until the lower number (kept in a) is greater than b.

A better solution would be to swap a and b if a > b before the loop begins. There are a number of ways to do this, but the most straightforward is

```
iload_0
iload_1
if_icmple loop   ; Start the loop if a <= b
iload_0          ; Swap a and b using
iload_1          ; the stack
istore_0
istore_1
```

Exercise 5.4

```
.method static isUpper(C)Z
iload_0
tableswitch 'A'
success success success success success success
success success success success success success
success success success success success success
success success success success success success
success success
default: fail

success:
iconst_1
ireturn

fail:
iconst_0
ireturn
.end method
```

Exercise 5.5

```
.method static isUpper(C)Z
iload_0
lookupswitch
'A': success 'B': success 'C': success 'D': success
'E': success 'F': success 'G': success 'H': success
'I': success 'J': success 'K': success 'L': success
'M': success 'N': success 'O': success 'P': success
'Q': success 'R': success 'S': success 'T': success
'U': success 'V': success 'W': success 'X': success
'Y': success 'Z': success
default: fail
success:
iconst_1
ireturn

fail:
iconst_0
ireturn
.end method
```

Exercise 5.6

The two subclasses are

```
.class OutOfMilkException
.super SnackException

.method <init>()V
aload_0                  ; Push this
ldc "Out of milk"        ; Default message
invokespecial SnackException/<init> (Ljava/lang/String;)V
return
.end method
.end class
.class OutOfCookiesException
.super SnackException

.method <init>()V
aload_0                  ; Push this
ldc "No more cookies"    ; Default message
```

```
invokespecial SnackException/<init> (Ljava/lang/String;)V
return
.end method
.end class
```

To add a specific out-of-milk exception handler, add a .catch directive before any of the others:

```
.catch OutOfMilkException from begin2 to end2 using
    NoMilkHandler
.catch SnackException from begin2 to end2 using handler2
.catch java/lang/Exception from begin1 to end1 using handler1

;; Rest of the method

NoMilkHandler:
    ;; Handle the out-of-milk exception
```

If an OutOfCookiesException or any other non-milk-related SnackException occurs between begin2 and end2, then the ordinary handler at handler2 will take care of it. A milk-related OutOfMilkException can be handled differently at NoMilkHandler. More general Exceptions will still be handled at handler1. Non-Exception exceptions, like Throwable and Error, aren't handled in this method at all and are instead passed up to the calling method.

Exercise 5.7

The Java compiler issues an error message like this:

```
GeneralSpecificExceptionExercise.java:11: catch not reached.
```

The Oolong equivalent to this code is

```
.catch Exception from e1begin to e1end using ExceptionHandler
.catch NullPointerException from e2begin to e2end
        using NullPointerExceptionHandler
```

In this code, no code can reach the NullPointerExceptionHandler because any NullPointerException is handled by the ExceptionHandler, which is more general and comes first.

Code that cannot be reached makes the Java language designers nervous; why would you write code you could never execute? They made it an error to have code that can't be reached, including exception handlers that will never execute.

Exercise 5.8

```
.class ArrayIndexExceptionExercise
.method public static main([Ljava/lang/String;)V
.catch java/lang/ArrayIndexOutOfBoundsException
        from loop to end using done
; Call variable 0 args
; Call variable i i
iconst_0
istore_1    ; Initialize i to 0

loop:
getstatic java/lang/System/out Ljava/io/PrintStream;
aload_0     ; Print a[i]
iload_1     ; If we've gone too far, the exception
aaload      ; will occur
invokevirtual java/io/PrintStream/println (Ljava/lang/String;)V

iinc 1 1    ; Increment i

goto loop   ; loop again
end:

done:       ; When an exception is thrown,
pop         ; just pop it off the stack and
return      ; return
.end method
```

This is not the recommended way to handle arrays, but you can do it this way.

Exercise 6.1

The most specific superclass of java.awt.Dialog and java.awt.Panel is java.awt.Container. If you answered java.awt.Component, you're incorrect: Container is more specific than Component.

Exercise 8.1

This program treats each argument as a class name. It loads the class, then tries to create an instance using the default constructor. Throughout, it prints copious information about what classes are being loaded.

First, it looks in the already loaded classes. This uses the JDK 1.1 specification. If you are using JDK 1.0, adjust accordingly.

If the class is not found, it looks to see if the class is stored in the file system relative to the current directory. Following the `class` file naming convention, it substitutes / for ., which turns the package names into directory names. Then it adds `.class` to the end.

If it cannot find the class in the file system, it looks for system class using `findSystemClass`.

```java
import java.io.*;
import java.util.*;

class DebuggingClassLoader extends ClassLoader
{
    public static void main(String a[])
    {
        try {
            DebuggingClassLoader c = new DebuggingClassLoader();
            for(int i = 0; i < a.length; i++)
            {
                Class cls = c.loadClass(a[i], true);
                System.out.println("Making an instance of "
                    + a[i]);
                cls.newInstance();
            }
        }
        catch(Exception e) {
            e.printStackTrace();
        }
    }

    int level = 0;

    public Class loadClass(String name, boolean resolve)
        throws ClassNotFoundException
    {
        Class c = null;

        indent(level);
        System.out.println("Loading " + name +
                        (resolve ? " and " :
                                " but not " )
                        + "resolving");
            level++;
```

```java
c = findLoadedClass(name);
if(c != null)
{
    indent(level);
    System.out.println("Found already loaded class " + c);
}
else
{
    try {
        // Convert the class name to a file name
        InputStream is = new FileInputStream(
            name.replace('.', '/') + ".class");

        byte[] b = new byte[is.available()];
        is.read(b);
        c = defineClass(b, 0, b.length);
    }
    catch(ClassFormatError e1) {
        indent(level);
        System.out.println(e1.getMessage());
        throw new ClassNotFoundException(name+
                        ":" + e1.getMessage());
    }
    catch(IOException e) {
        indent(level);
        System.out.println(name + " must be a system
            class");
        c = findSystemClass(name);
    }
}
indent(level);
System.out.println("Class " + name + " defined as " + c);
if(resolve)
{
    indent(level);
    System.out.println("Resolving " + c);
    resolveClass(c);
}
level--;
indent(level);
System.out.println("Done with " + name);
```

```
        return c;
    }

    void indent(int level)
    {
        for(int i = 0; i < level; i++)
            System.out.print(" ");
    }
}
```

Exercise 14.1

Assume that variable 1 holds i. A simple Java compiler might generate

```
iload_1          ; Push i
iload_1          ; Push i
iadd             ; Compute i+i
istore_1         ; Store into i
```

This is equivalent to multiplying i by 2. Although multiplication may seem more expensive than addition, it is cheaper in this case because it's multiplication by 2, which can be done by a simple ishl instruction:

```
iload_1          ; Push i
iconst_1         ; Push 1
ishl             ; Compute i << 1 == i * 2 = i+i
istore_1         ; Store into i
```

Further Reading

THIS is just the beginning. If you've gotten this far, then you understand how to read and write JVM code, and you understand how Java and other languages can be translated into bytecodes. Here are some suggestions for further reading.

Java and the JVM

The Java Language Specification, by James Gosling, Bill Joy, and Guy Steele. Addison-Wesley 1996.

> Simply the most comprehensive book on Java out there. It is the reference text that defines what Java programs are and what they mean. Despite its weighty subject, it is a lot of fun to read.

The Java Virtual Machine Specification, by Frank Yellin and Tim Lindholm. Addison-Wesley 1998.

> The bible of Java virtual machine programming.

The Java Programming Language, by Ken Arnold and James Gosling. Addison-Wesley 1997.

> A tutorial introduction to the Java programming language, coauthored by James Gosling, the inventor of Java.

`http://java.sun.com/` (Sun Microsystems, Inc.)

> Current information on Java and related topics, including Java releases, security issues, and online documentation.

`http://java.sun.com/docs/` (Sun Microsystems, Inc.)

> Official Java documentation, including current information about books in the official Java series.

Newsgroup

`comp.lang.java.machine`

> This newsgroup covers a variety of JVM-related topics. Common themes include comparing differences between JVM implementations; interpretation of *The Java Virtual Machine Specification;* benchmarking; the future of the JVM.

Other Languages

`http://grunge.cs.tu-berlin.de/~tolk/vmlanguages.html`

> Maintained by Robert Tolksdorf, this web site is a central clearinghouse for a wide variety of other languages for the JVM. It covers a variety of topics: interpreters, preprocessors for Java-like languages into Java, other languages compiled into Java, and other languages compiled into bytecodes.

`http://www.cygnus.com/~bothner/kawa.html` (Per Bothner, Cygnus)

> Another implementation of a Scheme compiler for the JVM. The compiler takes a different approach to Scheme compilation.

`http://www.appletmagic.com/` (Intermetrics)

> One of the first languages translated into the JVM (besides Java, of course) was Ada. This web site demonstrates an application for using Ada to generate applets.

`http://www.cs.indiana.edu/scheme-repository/home.html`

> The Internet Scheme Repository. Contains the official documents that define Scheme and many useful programs written in Scheme.

Compilers

Structure and Interpretation of Computer Programs, by Harold Abelson, Gerald Jay Sussman, and Julie Sussman. MIT Press 1996.

> An excellent introduction to computer science using the Scheme language. The Scheme-to-JVM compiler in this book is based on the Scheme compiler in *Structure and Interpretation*.

Compilers: Principles, Techniques, and Tools, by Alfred V. Aho, Ravi Sethi and Jeffrey D. Ullman. Addison-Wesley 1985.

A textbook on how to write compilers. Goes into detail on how to write parsers and code generators, including an introduction to the theory of languages. Known affectionately as the "Dragon Book" because of the dragon on its cover.

Index

Java™ Technology from Addison-Wesley

ISBN 0-201-37949-X

ISBN 0-201-37963-5

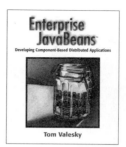

ISBN 0-201-60446-9

ISBN 0-201-43329-X

ISBN 0-201-48543-5

ISBN 0-201-61563-0

ISBN 0-201-30972-6

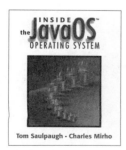

ISBN 0-201-18393-5

ISBN 0-201-32573-X

ISBN 0-201-32582-9

Addison-Wesley Computer and Engineering Publishing Group

How to Interact with Us

1. Visit our Web site

http://www.awl.com/cseng

When you think you've read enough, there's always more content for you at Addison-Wesley's web site. Our web site contains a directory of complete product information including:

- Chapters
- Exclusive author interviews
- Links to authors' pages
- Tables of contents
- Source code

You can also discover what tradeshows and conferences Addison-Wesley will be attending, read what others are saying about our titles, and find out where and when you can meet our authors and have them sign your book.

2. Subscribe to Our Email Mailing Lists

Subscribe to our electronic mailing lists and be the first to know when new books are publishing. Here's how it works: Sign up for our electronic mailing at http://www.awl.com/cseng/mailinglists.html. Just select the subject areas that interest you and you will receive notification via email when we publish a book in that area.

3. Contact Us via Email

cepubprof@awl.com

Ask general questions about our books.
Sign up for our electronic mailing lists.
Submit corrections for our web site.

bexpress@awl.com

Request an Addison-Wesley catalog.
Get answers to questions regarding your order or our products.

innovations@awl.com

Request a current Innovations Newsletter.

webmaster@awl.com

Send comments about our web site.

mikeh@awl.com

Submit a book proposal.
Send errata for an Addison-Wesley book.

cepubpublicity@awl.com

Request a review copy for a member of the media interested in reviewing new Addison-Wesley titles.

We encourage you to patronize the many fine retailers who stock Addison-Wesley titles. Visit our online directory to find stores near you or visit our online store: http://store.awl.com/ or call 800-824-7799.

Addison Wesley Longman
Computer and Engineering Publishing Group
One Jacob Way, Reading, Massachusetts 01867 USA
TEL 781-944-3700 • FAX 781-942-3076

By opening the CDROM package, you are consenting to be bound by and become a party to this Agreement. If you do not agree to all of the terms in this Agreement, return the complete package unopened to the place of purchase for a full refund.

All of the components that make up this CDROM product are distributed under the terms of the GNU General Public License or similar licenses which permit free and unrestricted redistribution. For complete details see http://www.fsf.org/copyleft/gpl.html

WARRANTY:

THIS IS A LIMITED WARRANTY AND IT IS THE ONLY WARRANTY MADE BY ADDISON WESLEY LONGMAN, INC. AND JOSHUA ENGEL. NEITHER ADDISON WESLEY LONGMAN, INC. NOR JOSHUA ENGEL MAKE ANY OTHER EXPRESS WARRANTY OR ANY OTHER WARRANTY OR CONDITION OF NONINFRINGEMENT OF THIRD PARTIES' RIGHTS. THE DURATION OF IMPLIED WARRANTIES INCLUDING WITHOUT LIMITATION, WARRANTIES OF MERCHANTABILITY AND OF FITNESS FOR A PARTICULAR PURPOSE, IS LIMITED TO THE ABOVE LIMITED WARRANTY PERIOD; SOME STATES DO NOT ALLOW LIMITATIONS ON HOW LONG AN IMPLIED WARRANTY LASTS SO THESE LIMITATIONS MAY NOT APPLY TO YOU. NO ADDISON WESLEY LONGMAN, INC. AGENT OR EMPLOYEE IS AUTHORIZED TO MAKE ANY MODIFICATIONS, EXTENSIONS, OR ADDITIONS TO THIS WARRANTY.

If the media is subjected to accident, abuse, or improper use; or if you violate the terms of the Agreement, then this warranty shall immediately be terminated. This warranty shall not apply if the Software is used on or in conjunction with hardware or Software other than the version of hardware and Software with which the Software was designed to be used as described in the Documentation.

THIS WARRANTY GIVES YOU SPECIFIC LEGAL RIGHTS, AND YOU MAY HAVE OTHER LEGAL RIGHTS THAT VARY FROM STATE TO STATE OR BY JURISDICTION.

LIMITATION OF LIABILITY: UNDER NO CIRCUMSTANCES AND UNDER NO LEGAL THEORY, TORT, CONTRACT OR OTHERWISE, SHALL ADDISON WESLEY LONGMAN, INC., JOSHUA ENGEL OR THEIR SUPPLIERS OR RESELLERS BE LIABLE TO YOU OR ANY OTHER PERSON FOR ANY INDIRECT, SPECIAL, INCIDENTAL OR CONSEQUENTIAL DAMAGES OF ANY CHARACTER INCLUDING, WITHOUT LIMITATION, DAMAGES FOR LOSS OF GOODWILL, WORK STOPPAGE, COMPUTER FAILURE OR MALFUNCTION, OR ANY AND ALL OTHER COMMERCIAL DAMAGES OR LOSSES, EVEN IF ADDISON WESLEY LONGMAN, INC., JOSHUA ENGEL OR THEIR SUPPLIERS OR RESELLERS SHALL HAVE BEEN INFORMED OF THE POSSIBILITY OF SUCH DAMAGES, OR FOR ANY CLAIM BY ANY OTHER PARTY. THIS LIMITATION OF LIABILITY SHALL NOT APPLY TO LIABILITY FOR DEATH OR PERSONAL INJURY TO THE EXTENT APPLICABLE LAW PROHIBITS SUCH LIMITATION. FURTHERMORE, SOME STATES DO NOT ALLOW THE EXCLUSION OR LIMITATION OF INCIDENTAL OR CONSEQUENTIAL DAMAGES, SO THIS LIMITATION AND EXCLUSION MAY NOT APPLY TO YOU.

TERMINATION OF LICENSE:

This license will terminate automatically if you fail to comply with the limitations described above. On termination, you must destroy all copies of the Software and Documentation.